GIRL GENIUS

AGATHA HETERODYNE
THE GOLDEN TRILOBITE

A Gaslamp Fantasy
with
ADVENTURE, ROMANCE & MAD SCIENCE

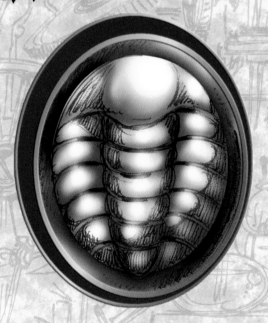

Story by Kaja & Phil Foglio
Pencils by Phil Foglio
Colors by Cheyenne Wright

AIRSHIP
ENTERTAINMENT

OTHER BOOKS FROM AIRSHIP ENTERTAINMENT AND STUDIO FOGLIO

Girl Genius® Graphic Novels

Girl Genius Volume One:
Agatha Heterodyne and the Beetleburg Clank

Girl Genius Volume Two:
Agatha Heterodyne and the Airship City

Girl Genius Volume Three:
Agatha Heterodyne and the Monster Engine

Girl Genius Volume Four:
Agatha Heterodyne and the Circus of Dreams

Girl Genius Volume Five:
Agatha Heterodyne and the Clockwork Princess

Girl Genius Volume Six:
Agatha Heterodyne and the Golden Trilobite

Girl Genius Volume Seven:
Agatha Heterodyne and the Voice of the Castle

Girl Genius Volume Eight:
Agatha Heterodyne and the Chapel of Bones

Other Graphic Novels

What's New with Phil & Dixie Collection

Robert Asprin's MythAdventures®

Buck Godot, zap gun for hire:
• *Three Short Stories*
• *PSmIth*
• *The Gallimaufry*

Girl Genius® is published by:
Airship Entertainment™: a happy part of Studio Foglio, LLC
2400 NW 80th St #129 Seattle WA 98117-4449, USA

Please visit our Web sites at www.airshipbooks.com and www.girlgenius.net

Girl Genius is a registered trademark of Studio Foglio, LLC. Girl Genius, the Girl Genius logos, Studio Foglio and the Studio Foglio logo, Airship Entertainment, Airship Books & Comics & the Airship logo, the Jägermonsters, Mr. Tock, the Heterodyne trilobite badge, the Jägermonsters' monster badge, the Wulfenbach badge, the Spark, Agatha Heterodyne, Trelawney Thorpe, the Heterodyne Boys, Transylvania Polygnostic, the Transylvania Polygnostic University arms, the Secret Cypher Society, Krosp, Castle Wulfenbach, Castle Heterodyne and all the Girl Genius characters are © & ™ 2000-2009 Studio Foglio.

Story by Phil & Kaja Foglio. Pencils by Phil Foglio. Main story colors by Cheyenne Wright. Selected spot illustrations colored by Kaja Foglio and Cheyenne Wright. Logos, Lettering, Artist Bullying & Book Design by Kaja. Fonts mostly by Comicraft– www.comicbookfonts.com.

This material originally appeared from March 2006-February 2007 at www.girlgenius.net.

Second Edition, First Printing: June 2009 • ISBN#: 978-1-890856-42-7 • PRINTED IN THE USA

This book is dedicated to the wonderful online community of webcomics artists, critics and fans. We've never felt so welcome. *Thank you.*

KAJA FOGLIO

Although known primarily in academia for her part in the recording and presenting of the ongoing chronicles of the early life of Agatha Heterodyne, Professor Foglio is also an enthusiast of some of the more esoteric practices of the select Asian subculture known as O-ta-ku. Her knowledge of implausible coeducational harem comedies has been invaluable in reconstructing some of the more nuanced scenarios of the current story. Furthermore, her ability to assemble a traditional box lunch (which changes color, plays orchestral music, and discharges fireworks upon being opened) in under four hours has, on numerous occasions, provided an ideal distraction, allowing her a quick escape, as well as a nourishing meal.

PHIL FOGLIO

As this volume reveals, Professor Foglio is a native of the proud and historic city of Mechanicsburg. He began his career as a street-corner storyteller, embellishing Heterodyne tales for tourists; but quickly became a wanderer when he was unable to resist the inclusion of embarrassing details which made poorly understood historical events *so very* much more interesting. The stories in question resulted in several arrests, a small war, and the infamous Mechanicsburg law barring owls from wearing boots. His latest volume of anecdotes collected from the Jägermonsters, entitled: *Things We've Eaten and the Interesting Ways They Begged For Mercy, Vol. 5* is available from Transylvania Polygnostic University Press. (For which, the Transylvania Polygnostic University Press humbly apologizes.)

CHEYENNE WRIGHT

Professor Wright's mad experiments in color made a major advancement last month, when he purchased a used Alchemy Cannon™ at the semi-annual University "Shop & Swap" party. He now produces color effects by *actually transforming into various elements* specific parts of the canvas upon which he is working. The biggest advantage, he notes, is that it will not fade. The down side is that the cannon requires 16 giga-watts of electricity to color a single page. Plus, the glow from the radioactive elements is keeping him from getting enough sleep. The curious and intrepid can view the results of his latest experiments at www.arcanetimes.com.

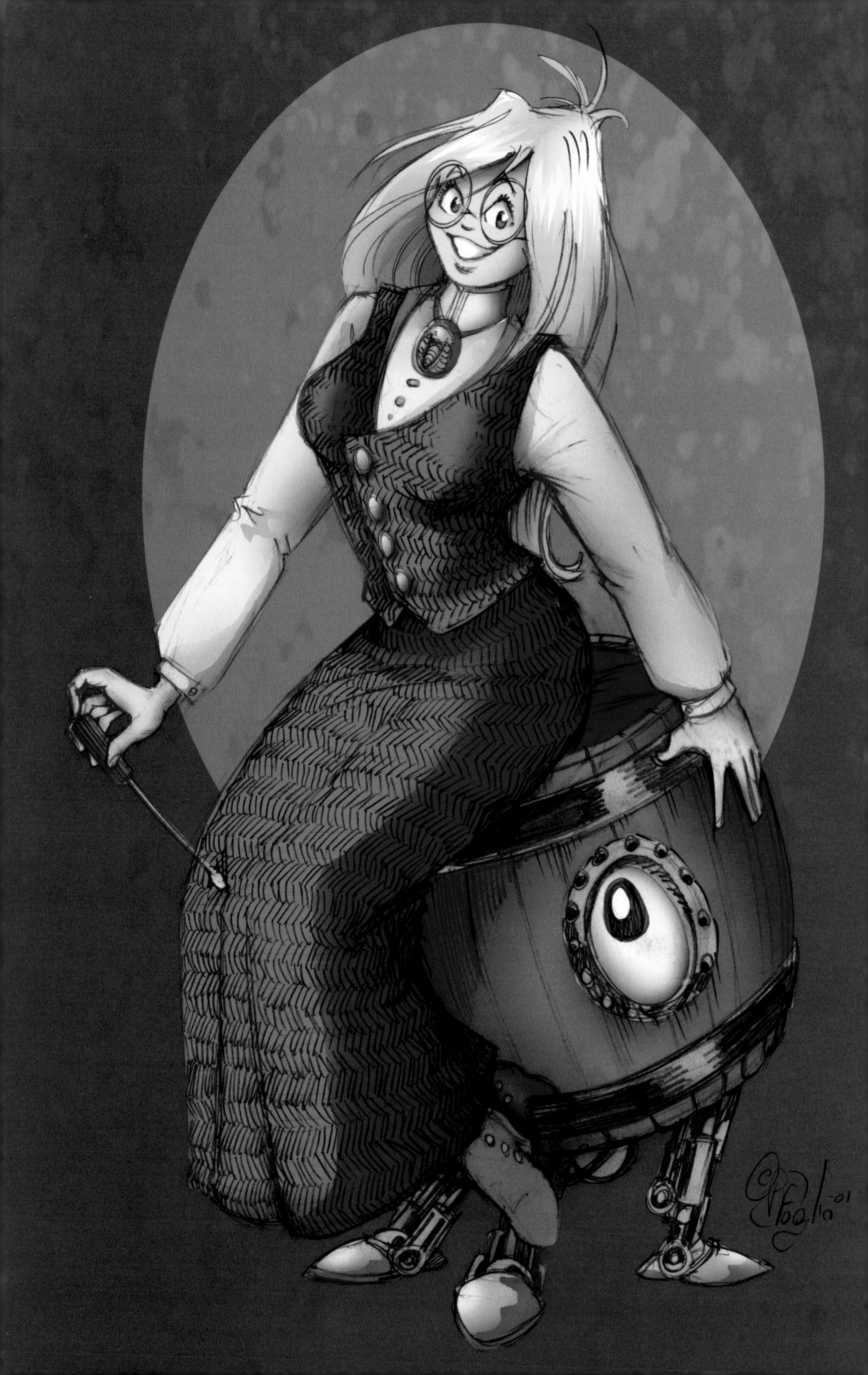

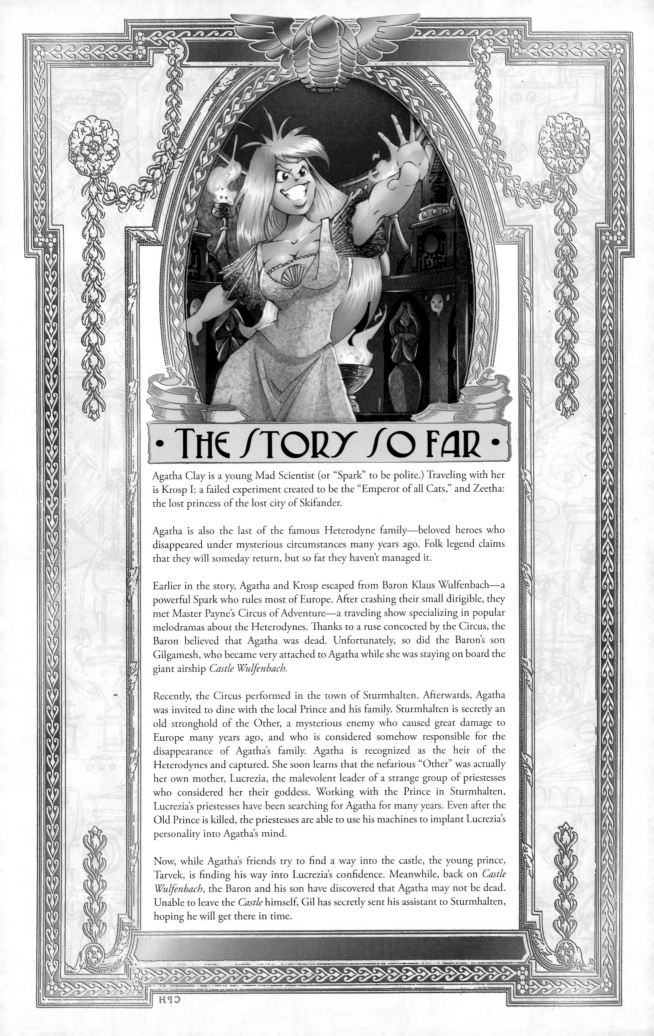

· THE STORY SO FAR ·

Agatha Clay is a young Mad Scientist (or "Spark" to be polite.) Traveling with her is Krosp I: a failed experiment created to be the "Emperor of all Cats," and Zeetha: the lost princess of the lost city of Skifander.

Agatha is also the last of the famous Heterodyne family—beloved heroes who disappeared under mysterious circumstances many years ago. Folk legend claims that they will someday return, but so far they haven't managed it.

Earlier in the story, Agatha and Krosp escaped from Baron Klaus Wulfenbach—a powerful Spark who rules most of Europe. After crashing their small dirigible, they met Master Payne's Circus of Adventure—a traveling show specializing in popular melodramas about the Heterodynes. Thanks to a ruse concocted by the Circus, the Baron believed that Agatha was dead. Unfortunately, so did the Baron's son Gilgamesh, who became very attached to Agatha while she was staying on board the giant airship *Castle Wulfenbach*.

Recently, the Circus performed in the town of Sturmhalten. Afterwards, Agatha was invited to dine with the local Prince and his family. Sturmhalten is secretly an old stronghold of the Other, a mysterious enemy who caused great damage to Europe many years ago, and who is considered somehow responsible for the disappearance of Agatha's family. Agatha is recognized as the heir of the Heterodynes and captured. She soon learns that the nefarious "Other" was actually her own mother, Lucrezia, the malevolent leader of a strange group of priestesses who considered her their goddess. Working with the Prince in Sturmhalten, Lucrezia's priestesses have been searching for Agatha for many years. Even after the Old Prince is killed, the priestesses are able to use his machines to implant Lucrezia's personality into Agatha's mind.

Now, while Agatha's friends try to find a way into the castle, the young prince, Tarvek, is finding his way into Lucrezia's confidence. Meanwhile, back on *Castle Wulfenbach*, the Baron and his son have discovered that Agatha may not be dead. Unable to leave the *Castle* himself, Gil has secretly sent his assistant to Sturmhalten, hoping he will get there in time.

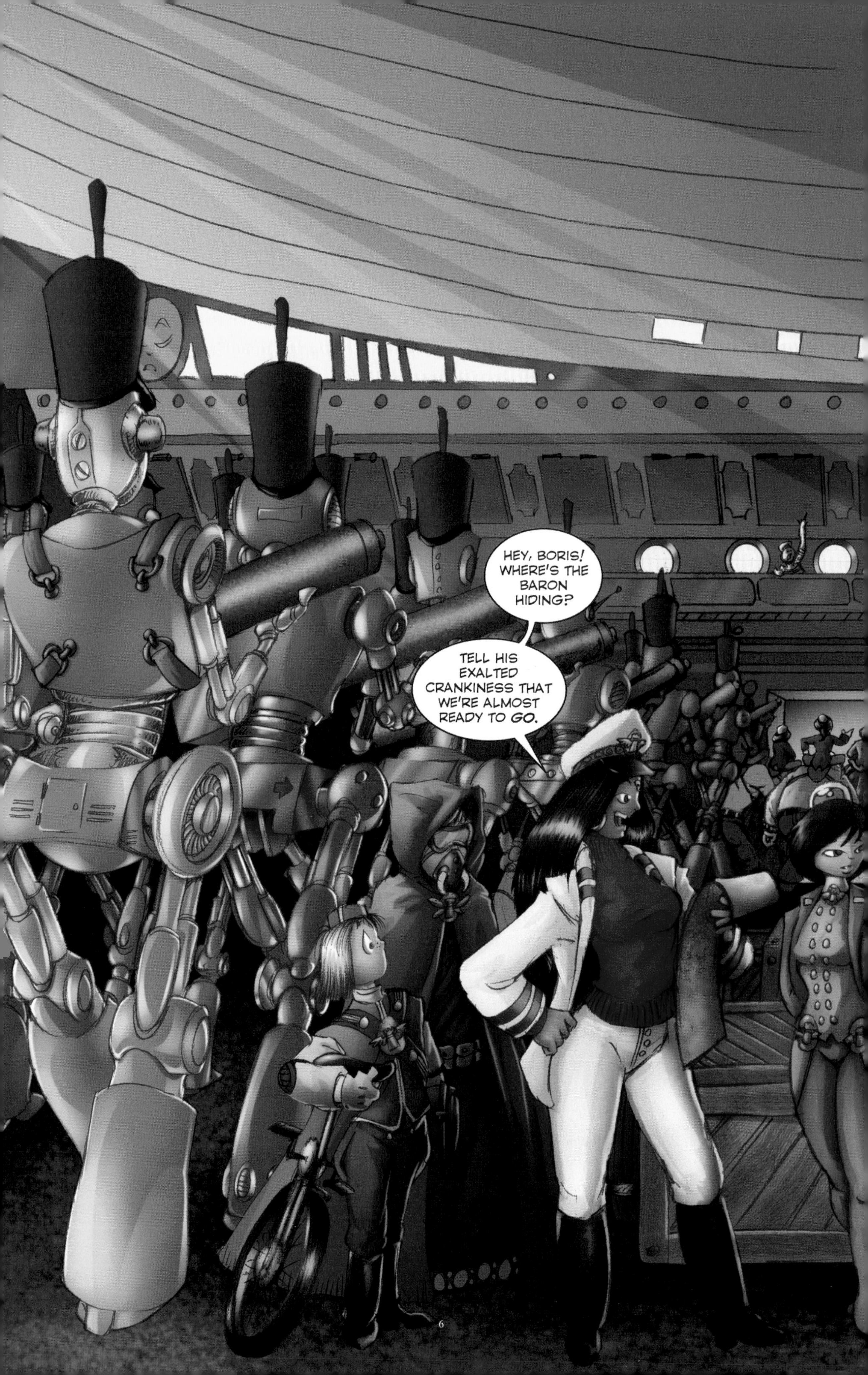
HEY, BORIS! WHERE'S THE BARON HIDING?
TELL HIS EXALTED CRANKINESS THAT WE'RE ALMOST READY TO *GO*.

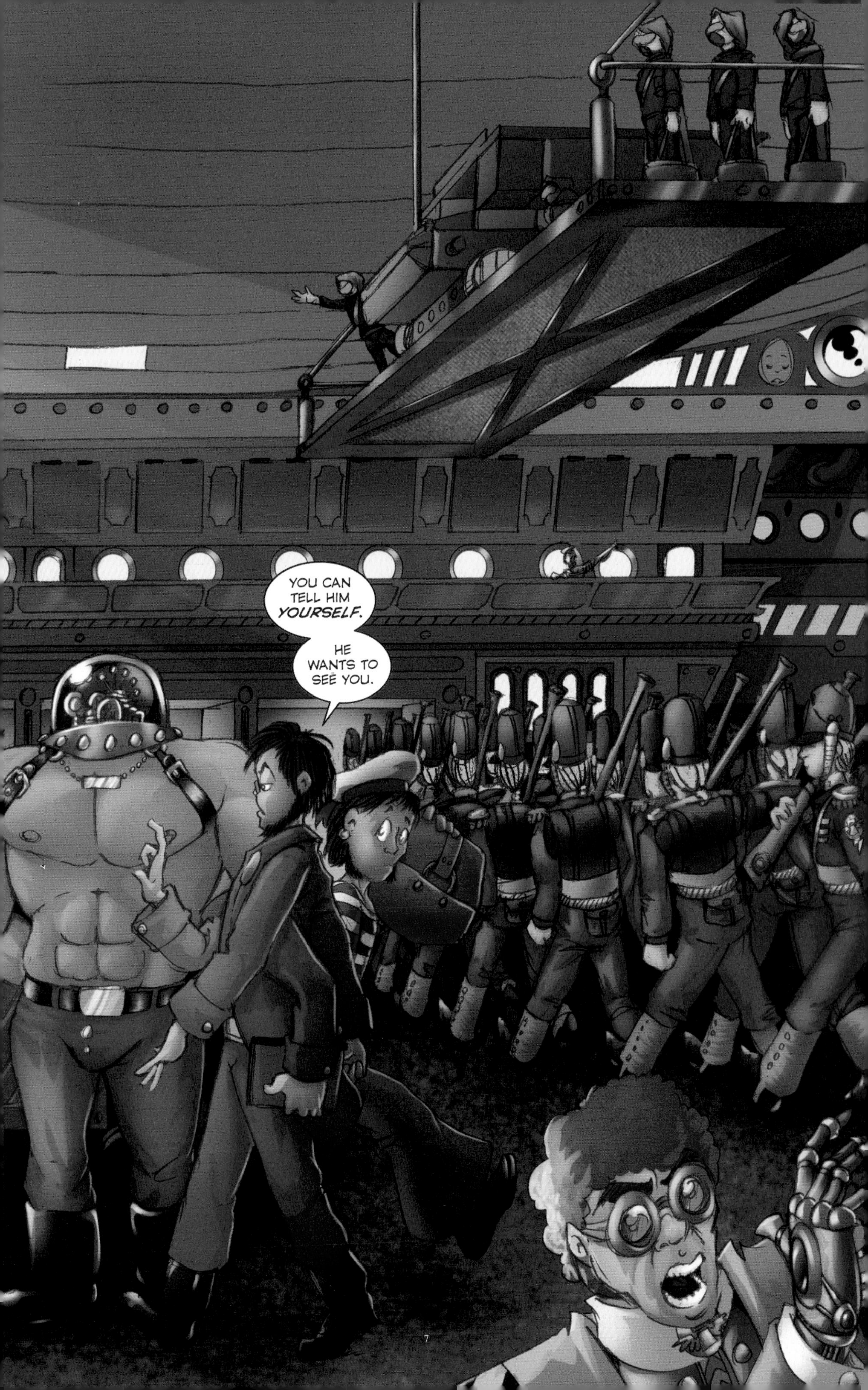
YOU CAN TELL HIM *YOURSELF*.
HE WANTS TO SEE YOU.

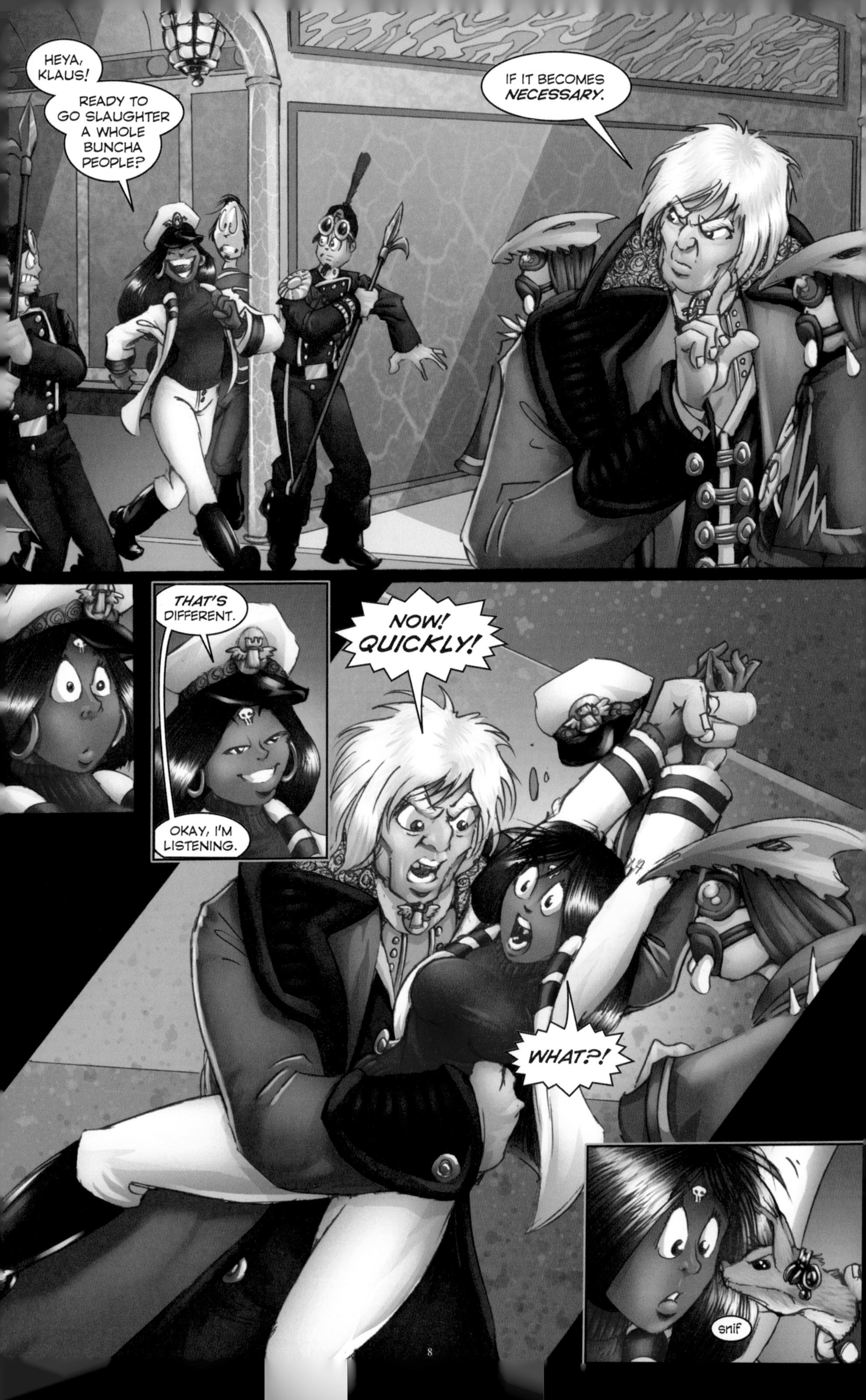
HEYA, KLAUS!
READY TO GO SLAUGHTER A WHOLE BUNCHA PEOPLE?
IF IT BECOMES NECESSARY.
THAT'S DIFFERENT.
OKAY, I'M LISTENING.
NOW! QUICKLY!
WHAT?!
snif

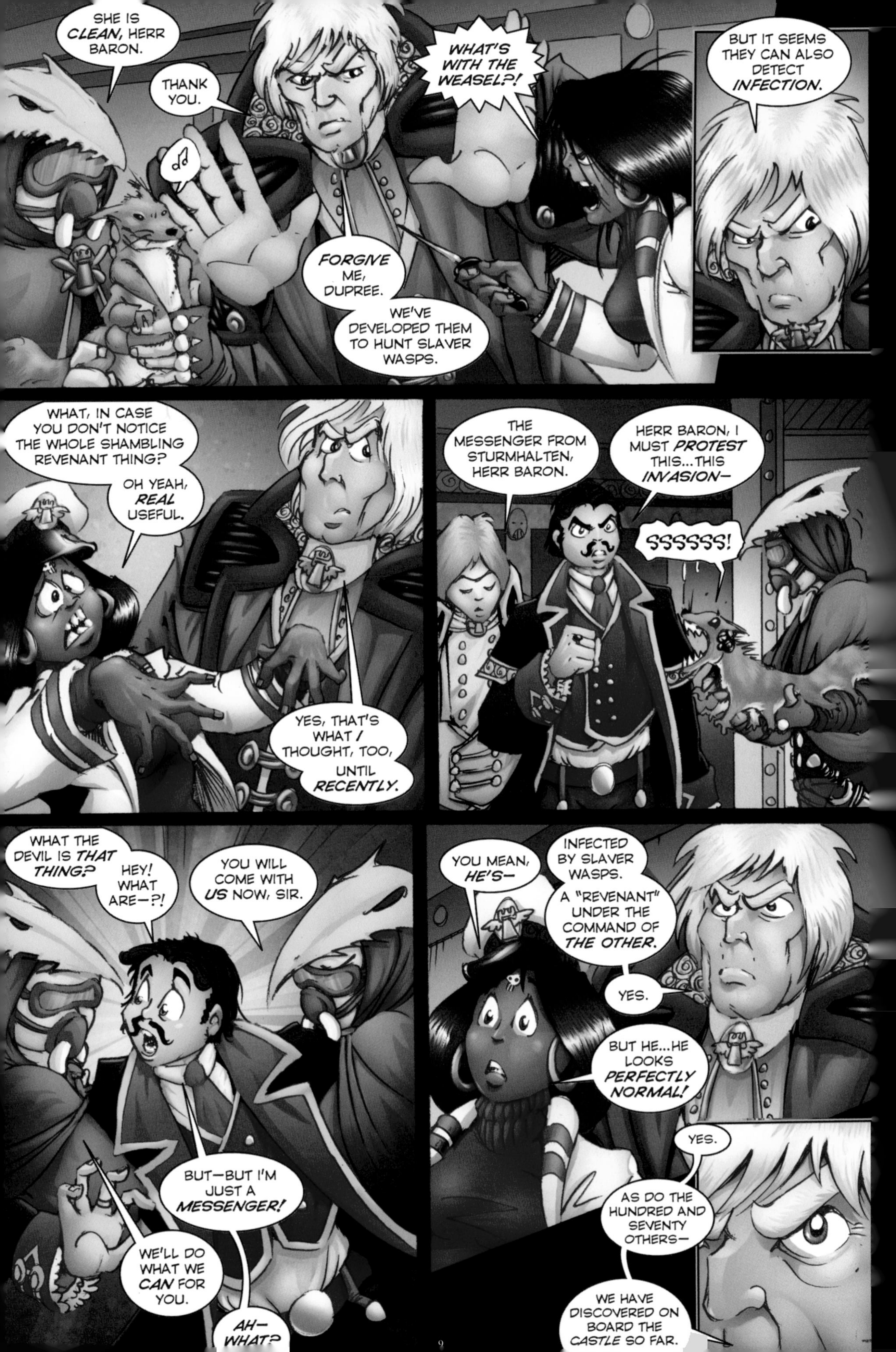
SHE IS CLEAN, HERR BARON.
THANK YOU.
♫
WHAT'S WITH THE WEASEL?!
FORGIVE ME, DUPREE.
WE'VE DEVELOPED THEM TO HUNT SLAVER WASPS.
BUT IT SEEMS THEY CAN ALSO DETECT INFECTION.
WHAT, IN CASE YOU DON'T NOTICE THE WHOLE SHAMBLING REVENANT THING?
OH YEAH, REAL USEFUL.
YES, THAT'S WHAT I THOUGHT, TOO, UNTIL RECENTLY.
THE MESSENGER FROM STURMHALTEN, HERR BARON.
HERR BARON, I MUST PROTEST THIS...THIS INVASION—
SSSSSS!
WHAT THE DEVIL IS THAT THING?
HEY! WHAT ARE—?!
YOU WILL COME WITH US NOW, SIR.
BUT—BUT I'M JUST A MESSENGER!
WE'LL DO WHAT WE CAN FOR YOU.
AH—WHAT?
YOU MEAN, HE'S—
INFECTED BY SLAVER WASPS.
A "REVENANT" UNDER THE COMMAND OF THE OTHER.
YES.
BUT HE...HE LOOKS PERFECTLY NORMAL!
YES.
AS DO THE HUNDRED AND SEVENTY OTHERS—
WE HAVE DISCOVERED ON BOARD THE CASTLE SO FAR.

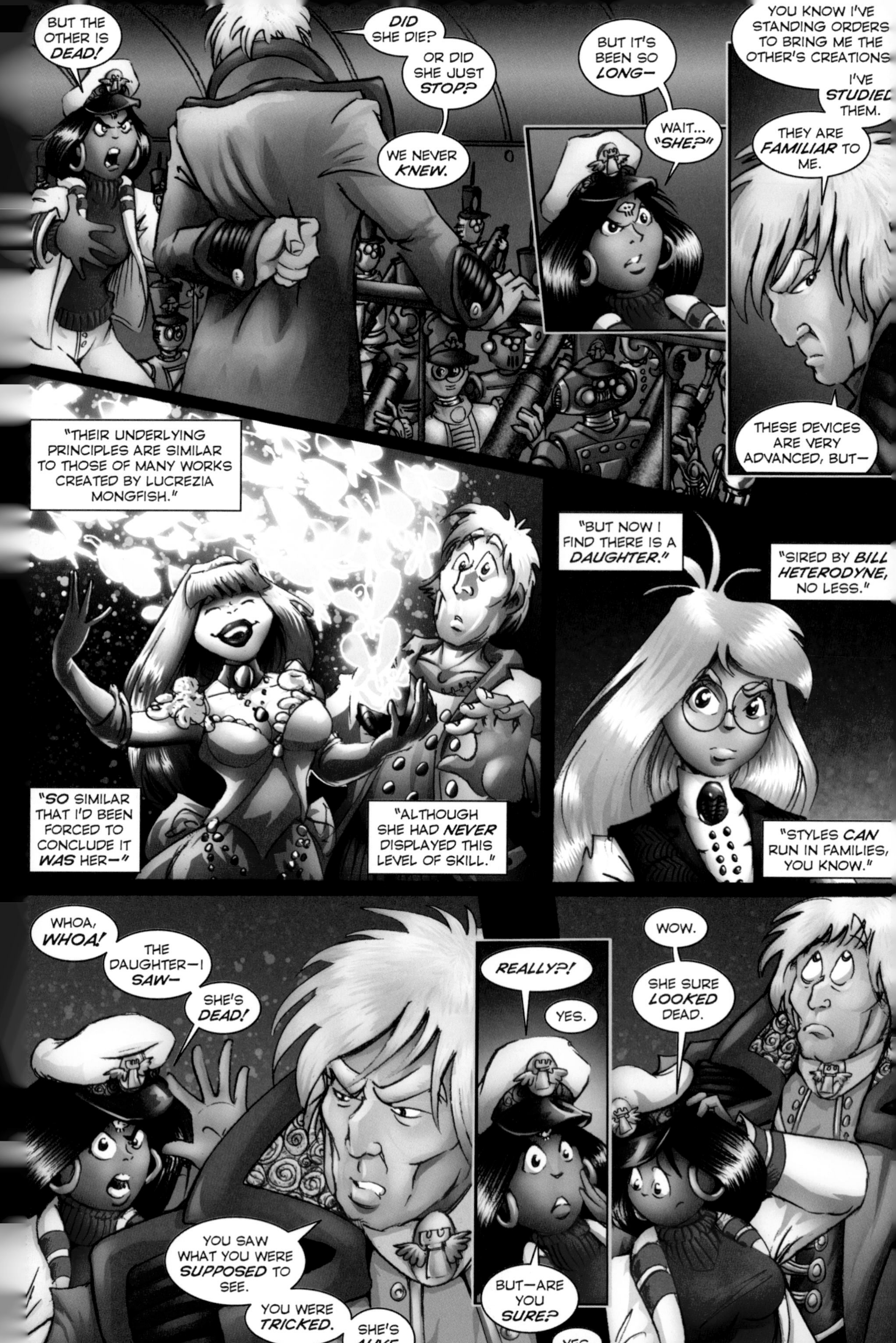
BUT THE OTHER IS *DEAD!*
DID SHE DIE?
OR DID SHE JUST *STOP?*
WE NEVER *KNEW.*
BUT IT'S BEEN SO *LONG—*
WAIT... *"SHE?"*
YOU KNOW I'VE STANDING ORDERS TO BRING ME THE OTHER'S CREATIONS
I'VE *STUDIED* THEM.
THEY ARE *FAMILIAR* TO ME.
THESE DEVICES ARE VERY ADVANCED, BUT—
"THEIR UNDERLYING PRINCIPLES ARE SIMILAR TO THOSE OF MANY WORKS CREATED BY LUCREZIA MONGFISH."
"*SO* SIMILAR THAT I'D BEEN FORCED TO CONCLUDE IT *WAS* HER—"
"ALTHOUGH SHE HAD *NEVER* DISPLAYED THIS LEVEL OF SKILL."
"BUT NOW I FIND THERE IS A *DAUGHTER.*"
"SIRED BY *BILL HETERODYNE,* NO LESS."
"STYLES *CAN* RUN IN FAMILIES, YOU KNOW."
WHOA, *WHOA!*
THE DAUGHTER—I *SAW—*
SHE'S *DEAD!*
YOU SAW WHAT YOU WERE *SUPPOSED* TO SEE.
YOU WERE *TRICKED.*
SHE'S *ALIVE.*
REALLY?!
YES.
BUT—ARE YOU *SURE?*
YES.
WOW.
SHE SURE *LOOKED* DEAD.

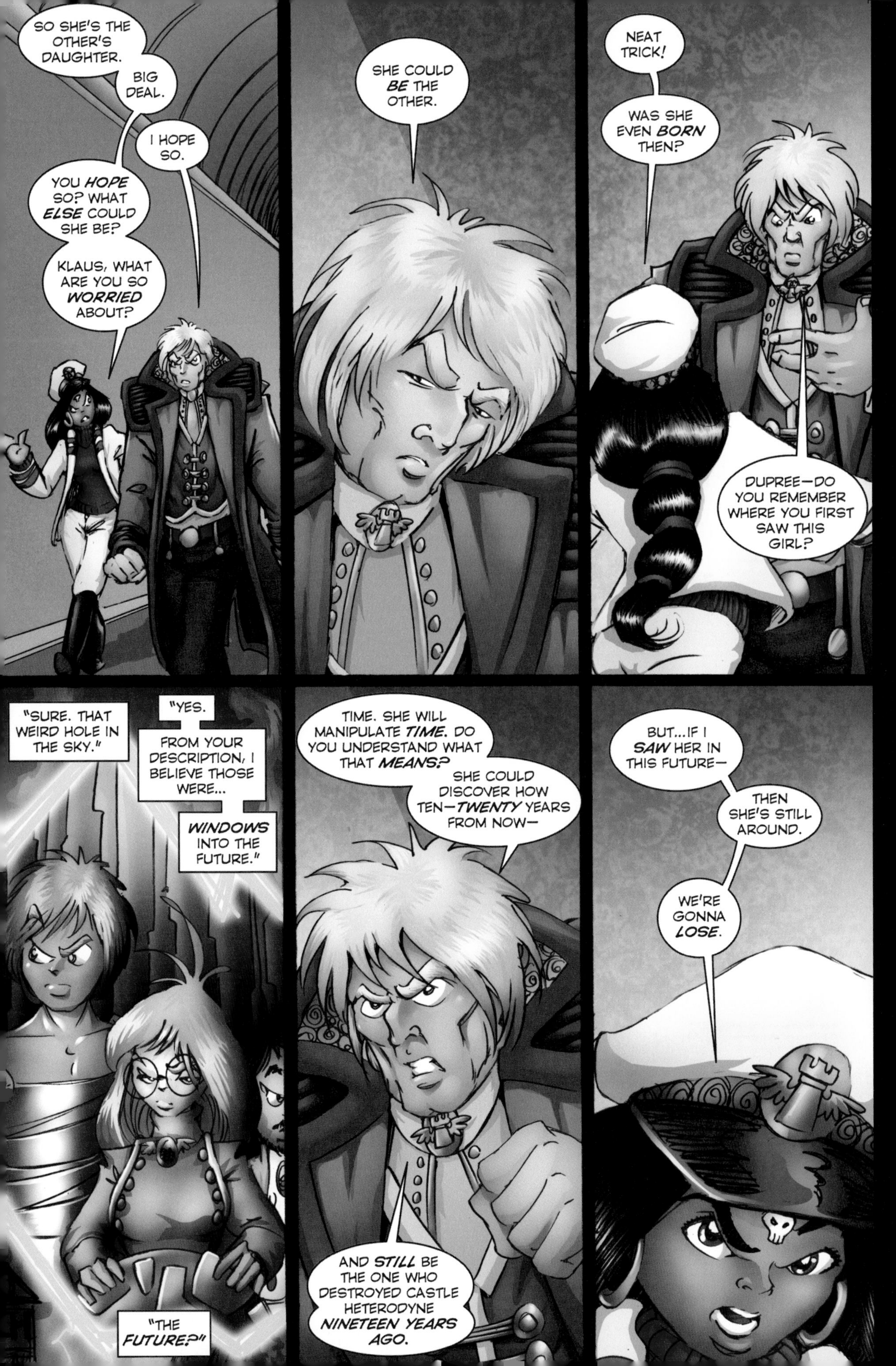

SO SHE'S THE OTHER'S DAUGHTER.
BIG DEAL.
I HOPE SO.
YOU HOPE SO? WHAT ELSE COULD SHE BE?
KLAUS, WHAT ARE YOU SO WORRIED ABOUT?
SHE COULD BE THE OTHER.
NEAT TRICK!
WAS SHE EVEN BORN THEN?
DUPREE—DO YOU REMEMBER WHERE YOU FIRST SAW THIS GIRL?
"SURE. THAT WEIRD HOLE IN THE SKY."
"YES.
FROM YOUR DESCRIPTION, I BELIEVE THOSE WERE...
WINDOWS INTO THE FUTURE."
"THE FUTURE?"
TIME. SHE WILL MANIPULATE TIME. DO YOU UNDERSTAND WHAT THAT MEANS?
SHE COULD DISCOVER HOW TEN—TWENTY YEARS FROM NOW—
AND STILL BE THE ONE WHO DESTROYED CASTLE HETERODYNE NINETEEN YEARS AGO.
BUT...IF I SAW HER IN THIS FUTURE—
THEN SHE'S STILL AROUND.
WE'RE GONNA LOSE.

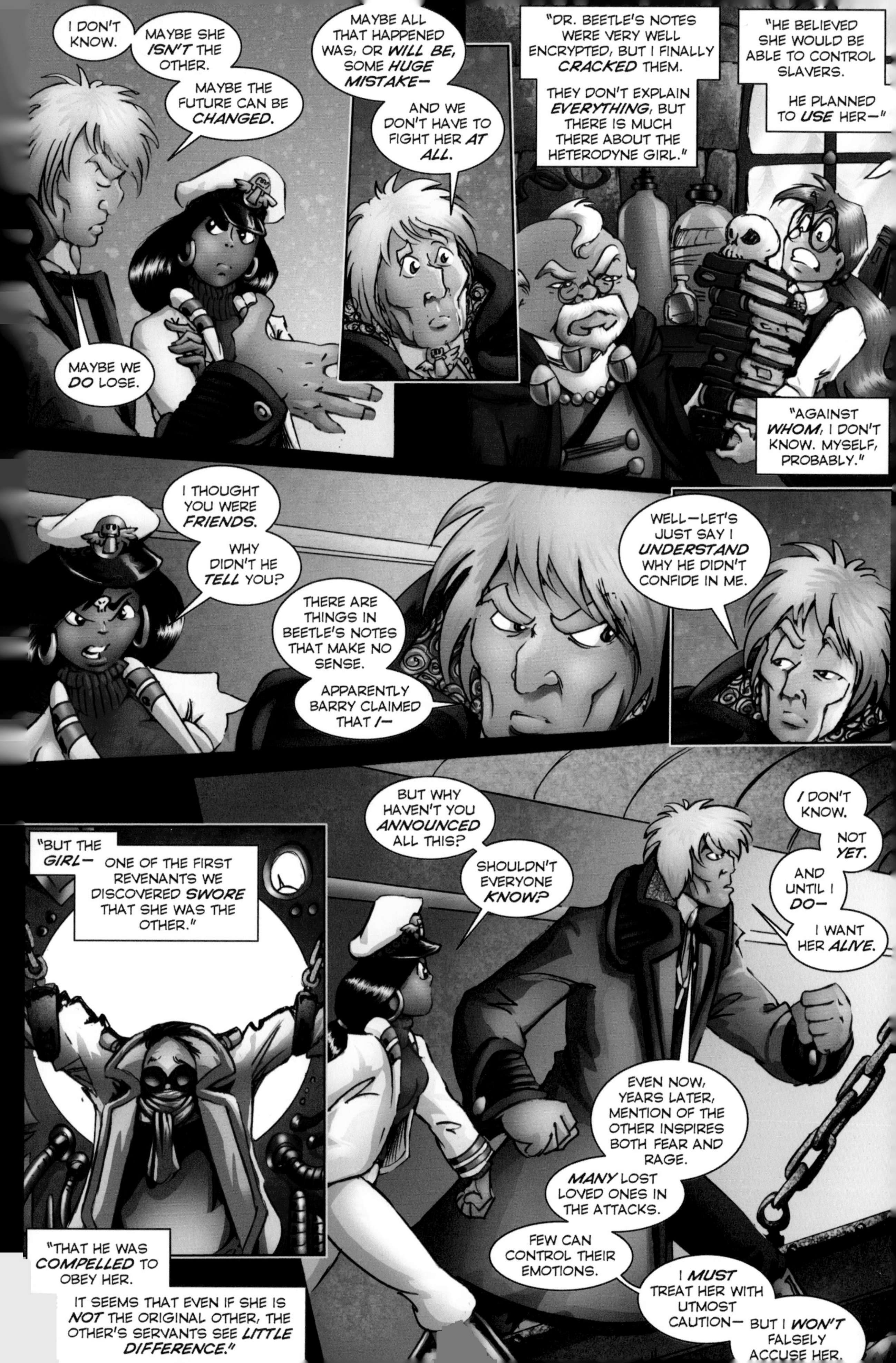
I DON'T KNOW.
MAYBE SHE *ISN'T* THE OTHER.
MAYBE THE FUTURE CAN BE *CHANGED.*
MAYBE WE *DO* LOSE.
MAYBE ALL THAT HAPPENED WAS, OR *WILL BE,* SOME *HUGE MISTAKE—*
AND WE DON'T HAVE TO FIGHT HER *AT ALL.*
"DR. BEETLE'S NOTES WERE VERY WELL ENCRYPTED, BUT I FINALLY *CRACKED* THEM.
THEY DON'T EXPLAIN *EVERYTHING,* BUT THERE IS MUCH THERE ABOUT THE HETERODYNE GIRL."
"HE BELIEVED SHE WOULD BE ABLE TO CONTROL SLAVERS.
HE PLANNED TO *USE* HER—"
"AGAINST *WHOM,* I DON'T KNOW. MYSELF, PROBABLY."
I THOUGHT YOU WERE *FRIENDS.*
WHY DIDN'T HE *TELL* YOU?
THERE ARE THINGS IN BEETLE'S NOTES THAT MAKE NO SENSE.
APPARENTLY BARRY CLAIMED THAT *I—*
WELL—LET'S JUST SAY I *UNDERSTAND* WHY HE DIDN'T CONFIDE IN ME.
"BUT THE *GIRL—*
ONE OF THE FIRST REVENANTS WE DISCOVERED *SWORE* THAT SHE WAS THE OTHER."
"THAT HE WAS *COMPELLED* TO OBEY HER.
IT SEEMS THAT EVEN IF SHE IS *NOT* THE ORIGINAL OTHER, THE OTHER'S SERVANTS SEE *LITTLE DIFFERENCE.*"
BUT WHY HAVEN'T YOU *ANNOUNCED* ALL THIS?
SHOULDN'T EVERYONE *KNOW?*
I DON'T KNOW.
NOT *YET.*
AND UNTIL I *DO—*
I WANT HER *ALIVE.*
EVEN NOW, YEARS LATER, MENTION OF THE OTHER INSPIRES BOTH FEAR AND RAGE.
MANY LOST LOVED ONES IN THE ATTACKS.
FEW CAN CONTROL THEIR EMOTIONS.
I *MUST* TREAT HER WITH UTMOST CAUTION—
BUT I *WON'T* FALSELY ACCUSE HER.

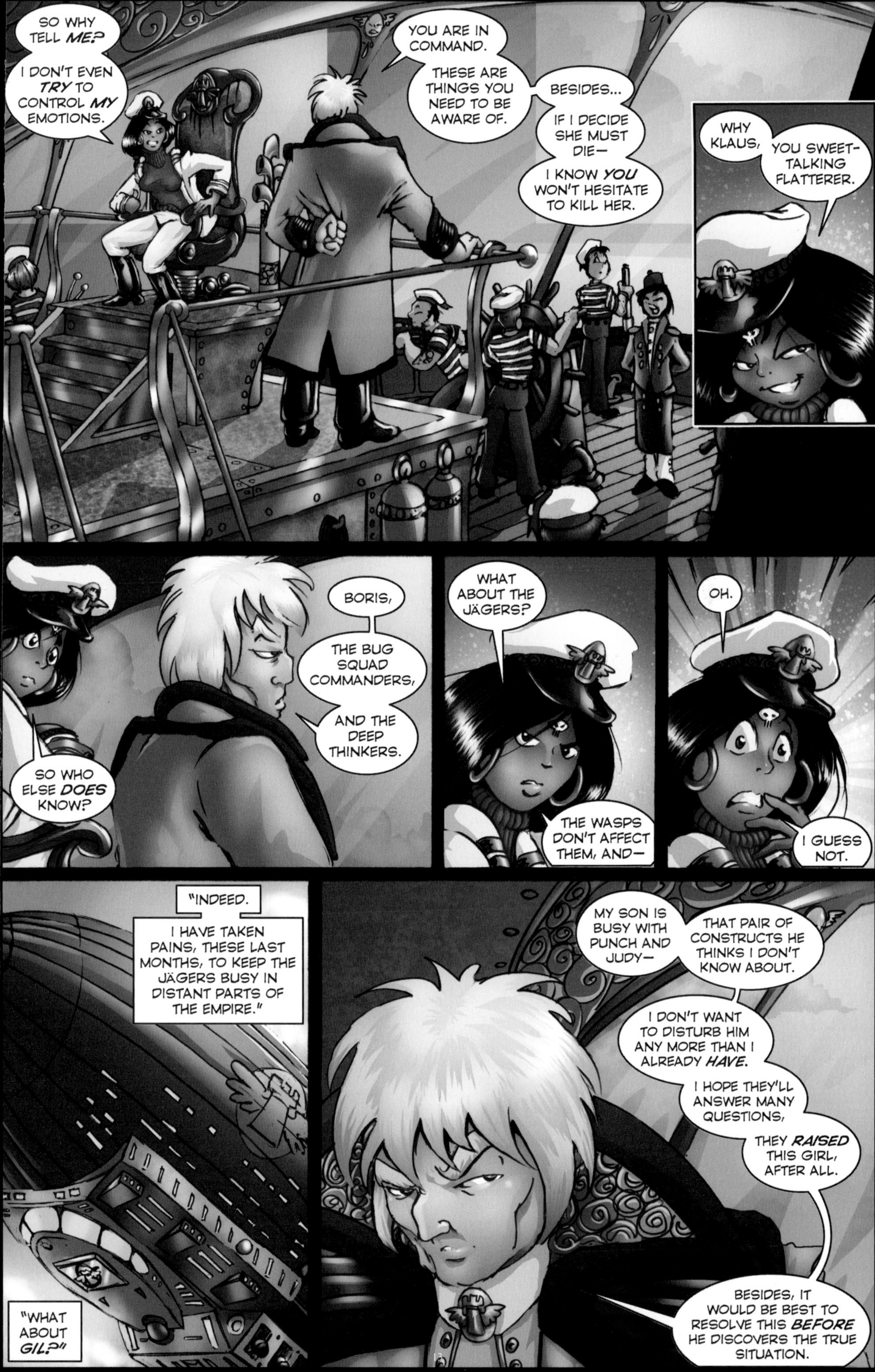

SO WHY TELL *ME?*
I DON'T EVEN *TRY* TO CONTROL *MY* EMOTIONS.
YOU ARE IN COMMAND.
THESE ARE THINGS YOU NEED TO BE AWARE OF.
BESIDES...
IF I DECIDE SHE MUST DIE—
I KNOW *YOU* WON'T HESITATE TO KILL HER.
WHY KLAUS,
YOU SWEET-TALKING FLATTERER.
SO WHO ELSE *DOES* KNOW?
BORIS,
THE BUG SQUAD COMMANDERS,
AND THE DEEP THINKERS.
WHAT ABOUT THE JÄGERS?
THE WASPS DON'T AFFECT THEM, AND—
OH.
I GUESS NOT.
"INDEED.
I HAVE TAKEN PAINS, THESE LAST MONTHS, TO KEEP THE JÄGERS BUSY IN DISTANT PARTS OF THE EMPIRE."
"WHAT ABOUT *GIL?*"
MY SON IS BUSY WITH PUNCH AND JUDY—
THAT PAIR OF CONSTRUCTS HE THINKS I DON'T KNOW ABOUT.
I DON'T WANT TO DISTURB HIM ANY MORE THAN I ALREADY *HAVE.*
I HOPE THEY'LL ANSWER MANY QUESTIONS,
THEY *RAISED* THIS GIRL, AFTER ALL.
BESIDES, IT WOULD BE BEST TO RESOLVE THIS *BEFORE* HE DISCOVERS THE TRUE SITUATION.

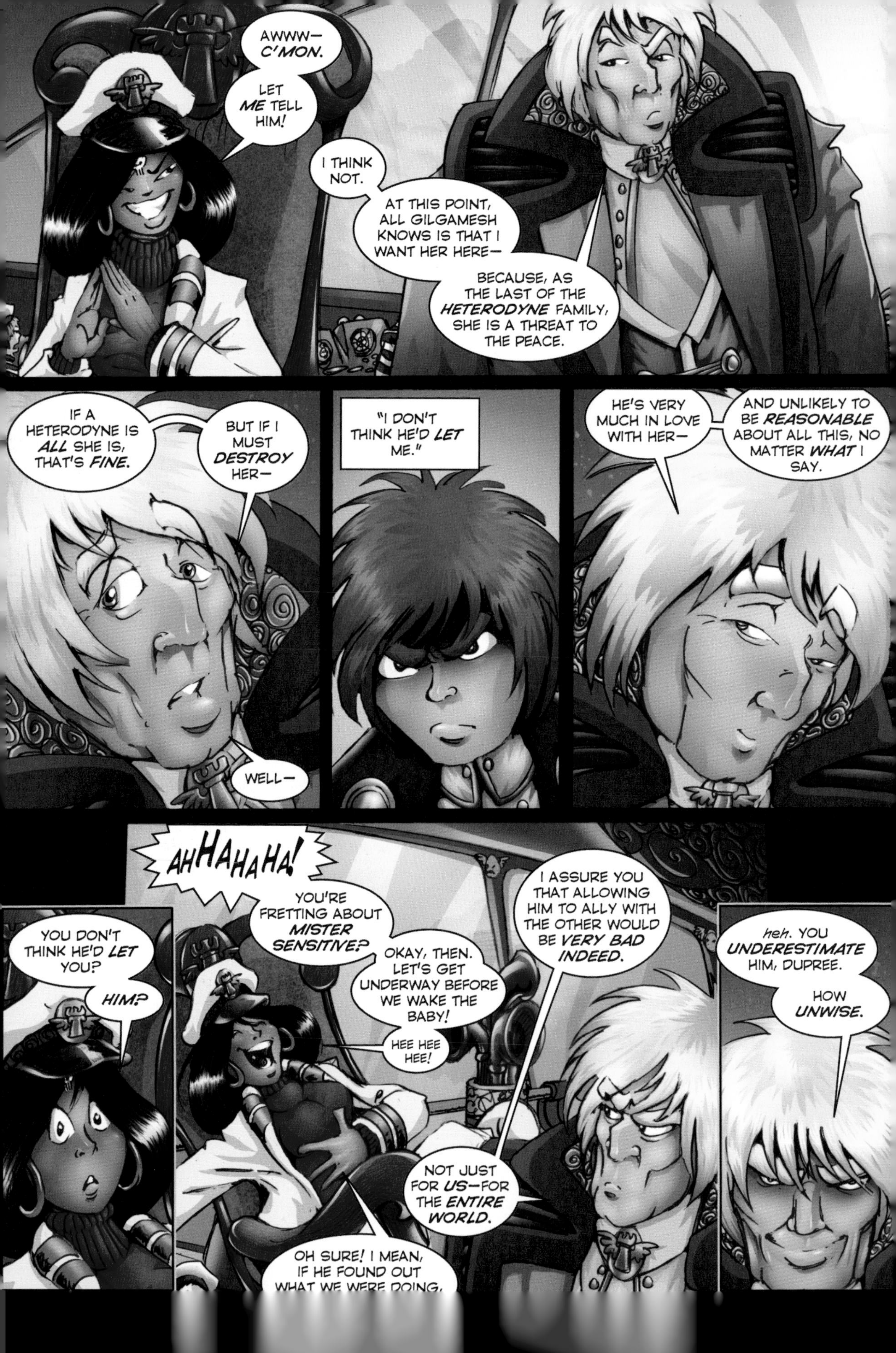
AWWW— C'MON.
LET ME TELL HIM!
I THINK NOT.
AT THIS POINT, ALL GILGAMESH KNOWS IS THAT I WANT HER HERE—
BECAUSE, AS THE LAST OF THE HETERODYNE FAMILY, SHE IS A THREAT TO THE PEACE.
IF A HETERODYNE IS ALL SHE IS, THAT'S FINE.
BUT IF I MUST DESTROY HER—
WELL—
"I DON'T THINK HE'D LET ME."
HE'S VERY MUCH IN LOVE WITH HER—
AND UNLIKELY TO BE REASONABLE ABOUT ALL THIS, NO MATTER WHAT I SAY.
AHHAHAHA!
YOU DON'T THINK HE'D LET YOU?
HIM?
YOU'RE FRETTING ABOUT MISTER SENSITIVE?
OKAY, THEN. LET'S GET UNDERWAY BEFORE WE WAKE THE BABY!
HEE HEE HEE!
OH SURE! I MEAN, IF HE FOUND OUT WHAT WE WERE DOING,
I ASSURE YOU THAT ALLOWING HIM TO ALLY WITH THE OTHER WOULD BE VERY BAD INDEED.
NOT JUST FOR US—FOR THE ENTIRE WORLD.
heh. YOU UNDERESTIMATE HIM, DUPREE.
HOW UNWISE.

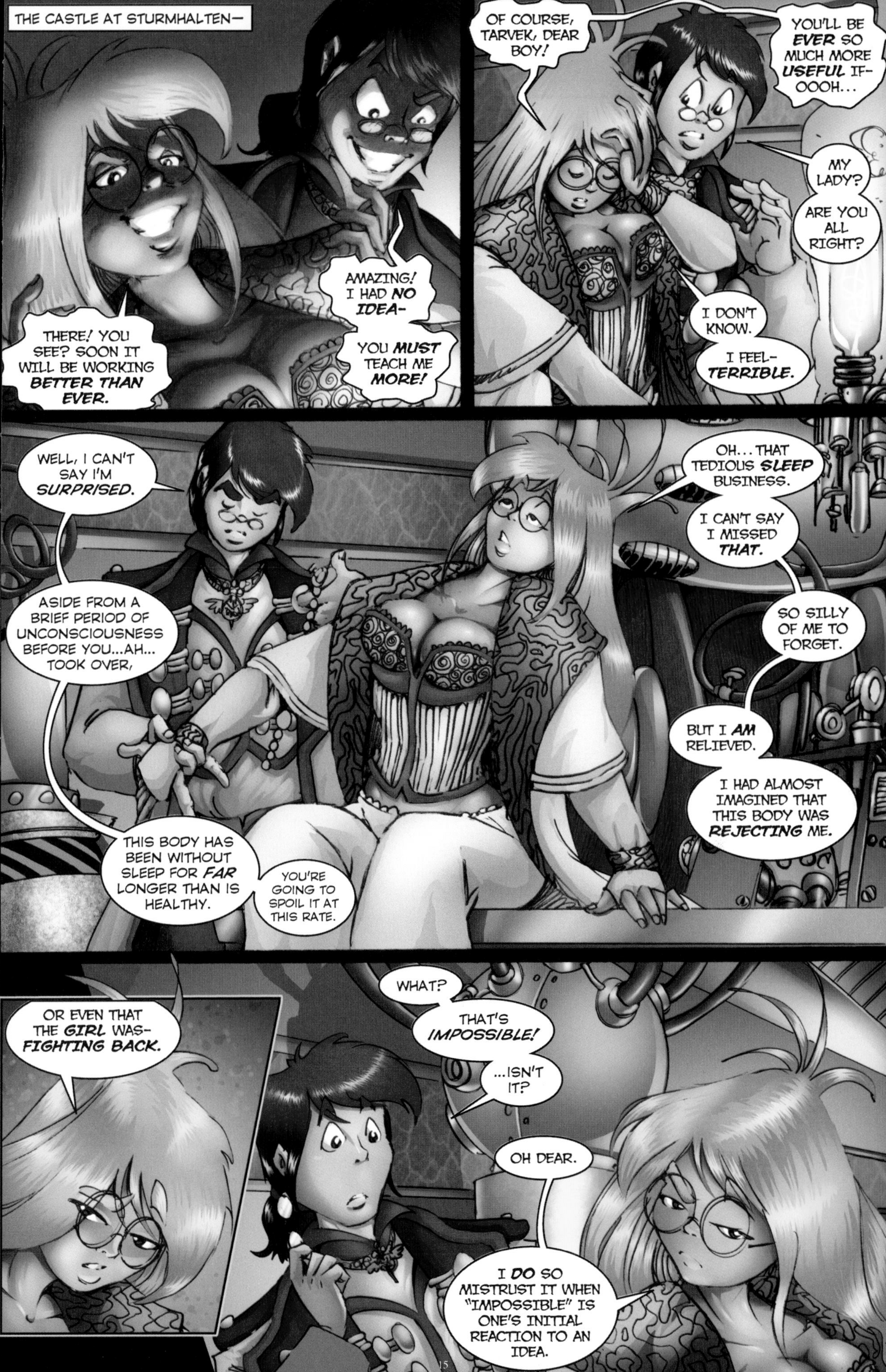
THE CASTLE AT STURMHALTEN—
THERE! YOU SEE? SOON IT WILL BE WORKING BETTER THAN EVER.
AMAZING! I HAD NO IDEA-
YOU MUST TEACH ME MORE!
OF COURSE, TARVEK, DEAR BOY!
YOU'LL BE EVER SO MUCH MORE USEFUL IF— OOOH...
MY LADY?
ARE YOU ALL RIGHT?
I DON'T KNOW.
I FEEL— TERRIBLE.
WELL, I CAN'T SAY I'M SURPRISED.
ASIDE FROM A BRIEF PERIOD OF UNCONSCIOUSNESS BEFORE YOU...AH... TOOK OVER,
THIS BODY HAS BEEN WITHOUT SLEEP FOR FAR LONGER THAN IS HEALTHY.
YOU'RE GOING TO SPOIL IT AT THIS RATE.
OH... THAT TEDIOUS SLEEP BUSINESS.
I CAN'T SAY I MISSED THAT.
SO SILLY OF ME TO FORGET.
BUT I AM RELIEVED.
I HAD ALMOST IMAGINED THAT THIS BODY WAS REJECTING ME.
OR EVEN THAT THE GIRL WAS— FIGHTING BACK.
WHAT?
THAT'S IMPOSSIBLE!
...ISN'T IT?
OH DEAR.
I DO SO MISTRUST IT WHEN "IMPOSSIBLE" IS ONE'S INITIAL REACTION TO AN IDEA.

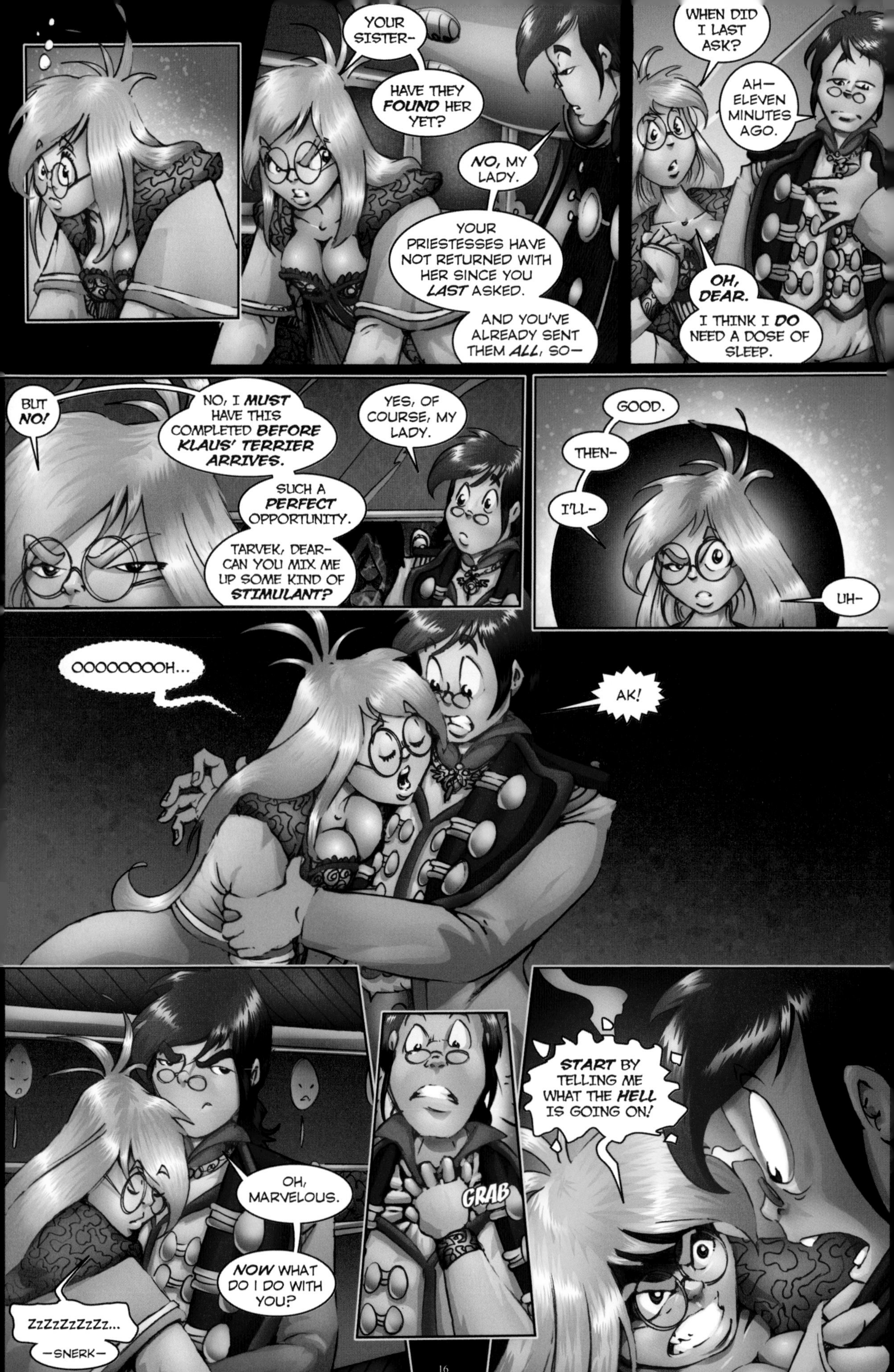
YOUR SISTER-
HAVE THEY FOUND HER YET?
NO, MY LADY.
YOUR PRIESTESSES HAVE NOT RETURNED WITH HER SINCE YOU LAST ASKED.
AND YOU'VE ALREADY SENT THEM ALL, SO—
WHEN DID I LAST ASK?
AH— ELEVEN MINUTES AGO.
OH, DEAR.
I THINK I DO NEED A DOSE OF SLEEP.
BUT NO!
NO, I MUST HAVE THIS COMPLETED BEFORE KLAUS' TERRIER ARRIVES.
SUCH A PERFECT OPPORTUNITY.
TARVEK, DEAR- CAN YOU MIX ME UP SOME KIND OF STIMULANT?
YES, OF COURSE, MY LADY.
GOOD.
THEN-
I'LL-
UH-
OOOOOOOOH...
AK!
OH, MARVELOUS.
NOW WHAT DO I DO WITH YOU?
ZzZzZzZzZz...
—SNERK—
GRAB
START BY TELLING ME WHAT THE HELL IS GOING ON!

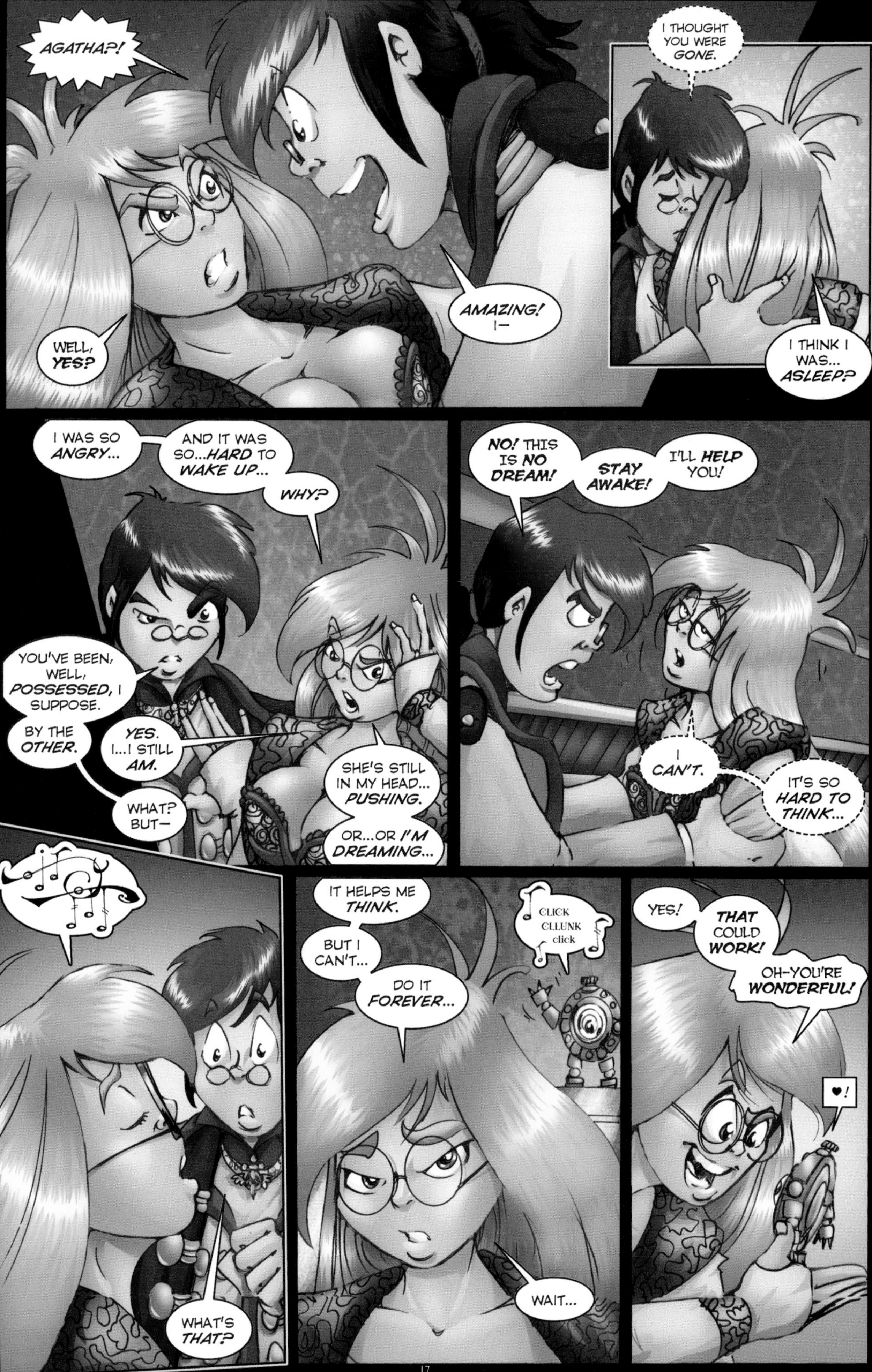
AGATHA?!
WELL, YES?
AMAZING! I—
I THOUGHT YOU WERE GONE.
I THINK I WAS... ASLEEP?
I WAS SO ANGRY...
AND IT WAS SO...HARD TO WAKE UP...
WHY?
YOU'VE BEEN, WELL, POSSESSED, I SUPPOSE.
BY THE OTHER.
YES. I...I STILL AM.
SHE'S STILL IN MY HEAD... PUSHING.
WHAT? BUT—
OR...OR I'M DREAMING...
NO! THIS IS NO DREAM!
STAY AWAKE!
I'LL HELP YOU!
I CAN'T.
IT'S SO HARD TO THINK...
WHAT'S THAT?
IT HELPS ME THINK.
BUT I CAN'T...
DO IT FOREVER...
CLICK CLUNK click
WAIT...
YES!
THAT COULD WORK!
OH-YOU'RE WONDERFUL!
♥!

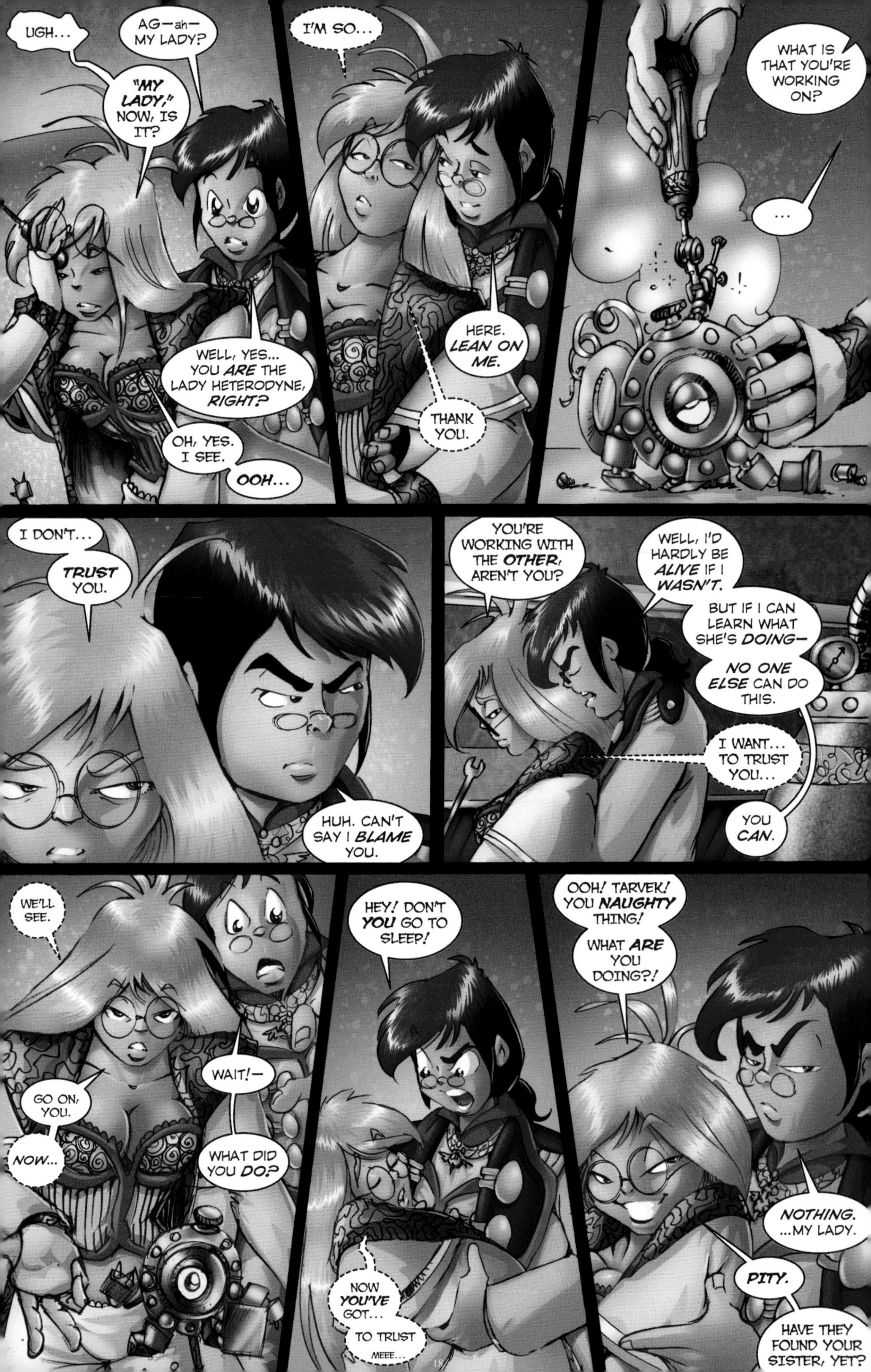

UGH...
AG—ah— MY LADY?
"MY LADY," NOW, IS IT?
WELL, YES... YOU ARE THE LADY HETERODYNE, RIGHT?
OH, YES. I SEE.
OOH...
I'M SO...
HERE. LEAN ON ME.
THANK YOU.
WHAT IS THAT YOU'RE WORKING ON?
...
I DON'T...
TRUST YOU.
HUH. CAN'T SAY I BLAME YOU.
YOU'RE WORKING WITH THE OTHER, AREN'T YOU?
WELL, I'D HARDLY BE ALIVE IF I WASN'T.
BUT IF I CAN LEARN WHAT SHE'S DOING—
NO ONE ELSE CAN DO THIS.
I WANT... TO TRUST YOU...
YOU CAN.
WE'LL SEE.
GO ON, YOU.
NOW...
WAIT!—
WHAT DID YOU DO?
HEY! DON'T YOU GO TO SLEEP!
NOW YOU'VE GOT...
TO TRUST MEEE...
OOH! TARVEK! YOU NAUGHTY THING!
WHAT ARE YOU DOING?!
NOTHING. ...MY LADY.
PITY.
HAVE THEY FOUND YOUR SISTER, YET?

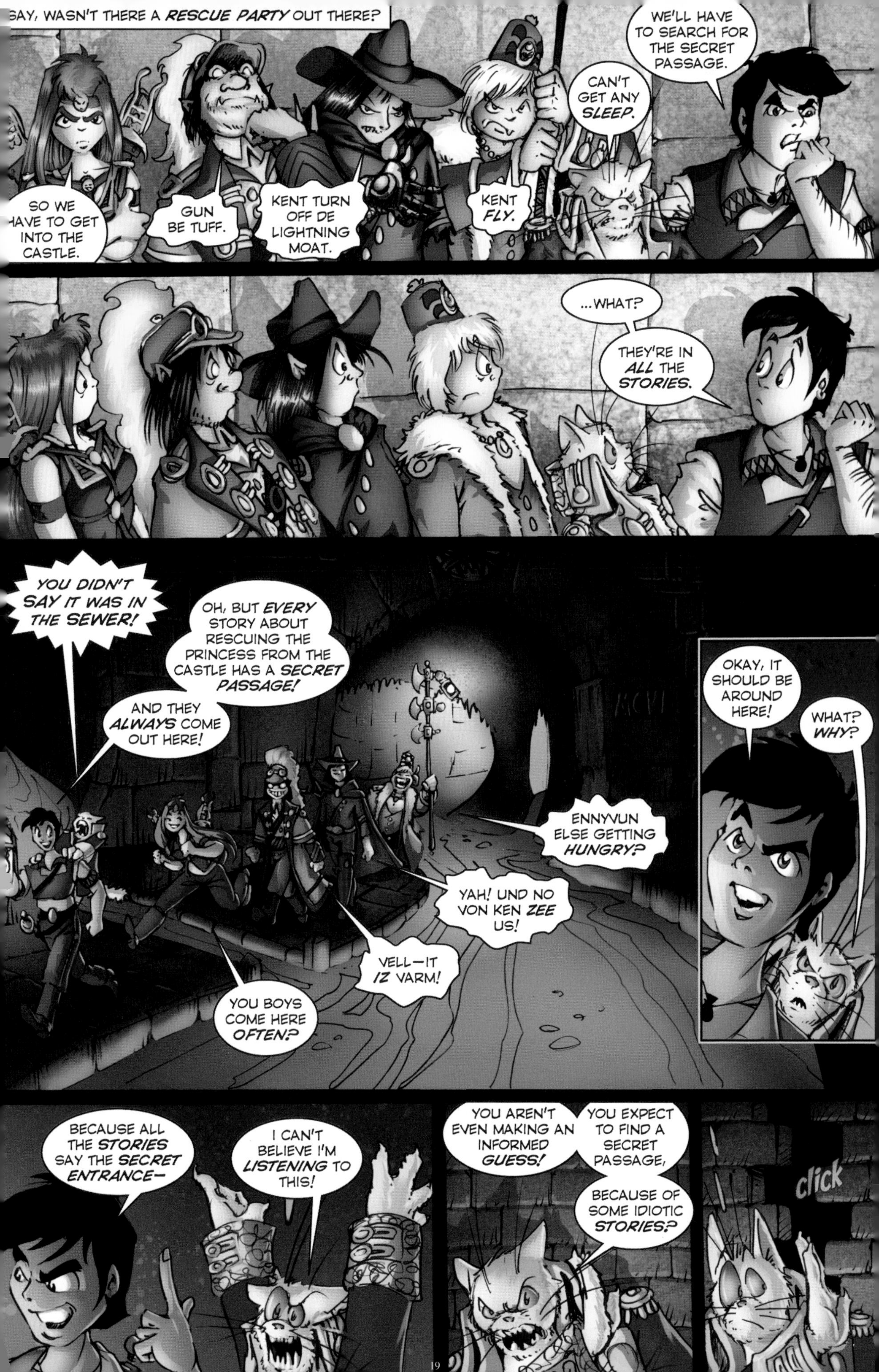
SAY, WASN'T THERE A RESCUE PARTY OUT THERE?
SO WE HAVE TO GET INTO THE CASTLE.
GUN BE TUFF.
KENT TURN OFF DE LIGHTNING MOAT.
KENT FLY.
CAN'T GET ANY SLEEP.
WE'LL HAVE TO SEARCH FOR THE SECRET PASSAGE.
...WHAT?
THEY'RE IN ALL THE STORIES.
YOU DIDN'T SAY IT WAS IN THE SEWER!
OH, BUT EVERY STORY ABOUT RESCUING THE PRINCESS FROM THE CASTLE HAS A SECRET PASSAGE!
AND THEY ALWAYS COME OUT HERE!
ENNYVUN ELSE GETTING HUNGRY?
YAH! UND NO VON KEN ZEE US!
VELL—IT IZ VARM!
YOU BOYS COME HERE OFTEN?
OKAY, IT SHOULD BE AROUND HERE!
WHAT? WHY?
BECAUSE ALL THE STORIES SAY THE SECRET ENTRANCE—
I CAN'T BELIEVE I'M LISTENING TO THIS!
YOU AREN'T EVEN MAKING AN INFORMED GUESS!
YOU EXPECT TO FIND A SECRET PASSAGE,
BECAUSE OF SOME IDIOTIC STORIES?
click

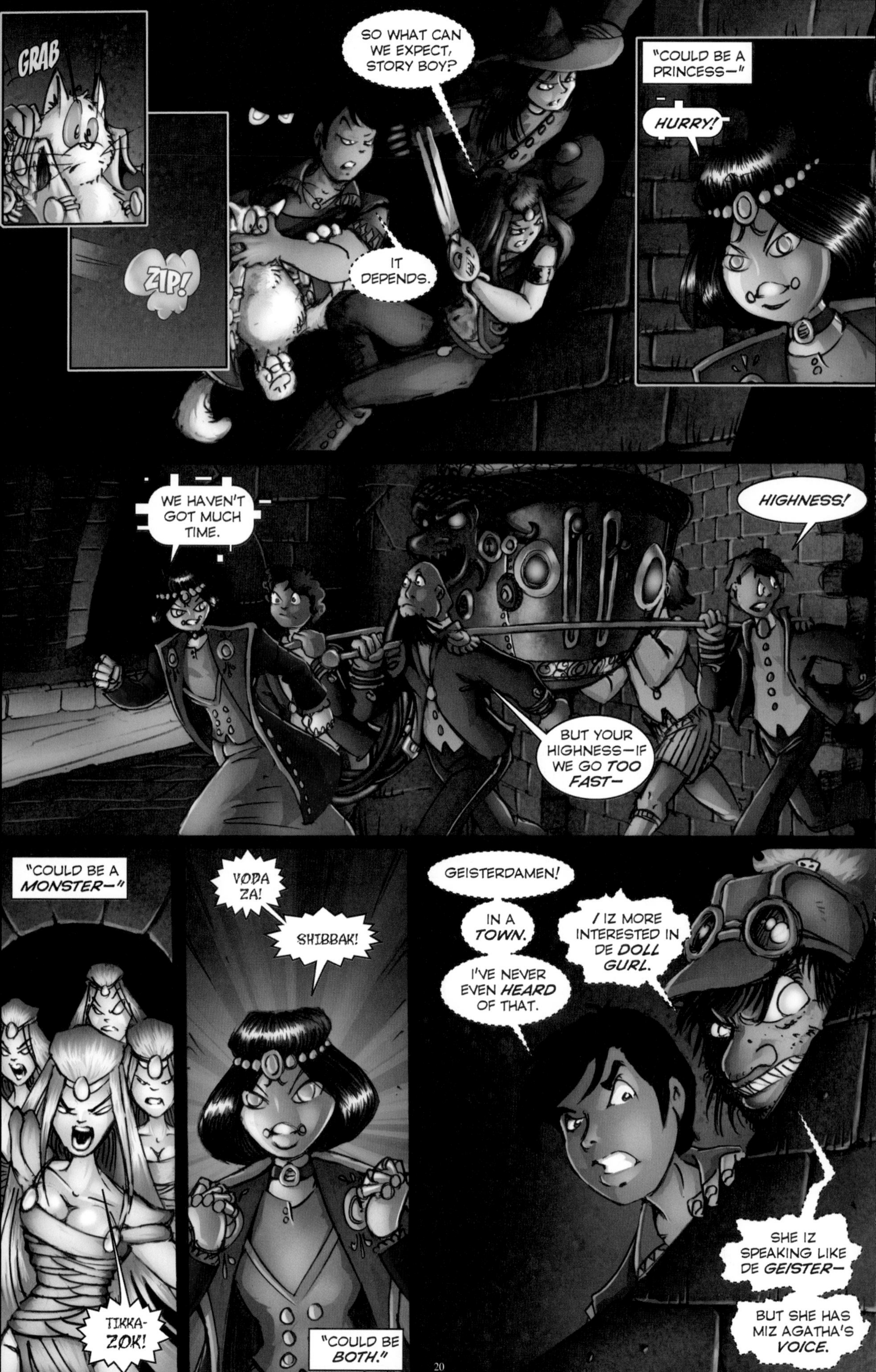
GRAB
ZIP!
SO WHAT CAN WE EXPECT, STORY BOY?
IT DEPENDS.
"COULD BE A PRINCESS—"
HURRY!
WE HAVEN'T GOT MUCH TIME.
HIGHNESS!
BUT YOUR HIGHNESS—IF WE GO TOO FAST—
"COULD BE A MONSTER—"
TIKKA-ZØK!
VØDA ZA!
SHIBBAK!
"COULD BE BOTH."
GEISTERDAMEN!
IN A TOWN.
I'VE NEVER EVEN HEARD OF THAT.
I IZ MORE INTERESTED IN DE DOLL GURL.
SHE IZ SPEAKING LIKE DE GEISTER—
BUT SHE HAS MIZ AGATHA'S VOICE.

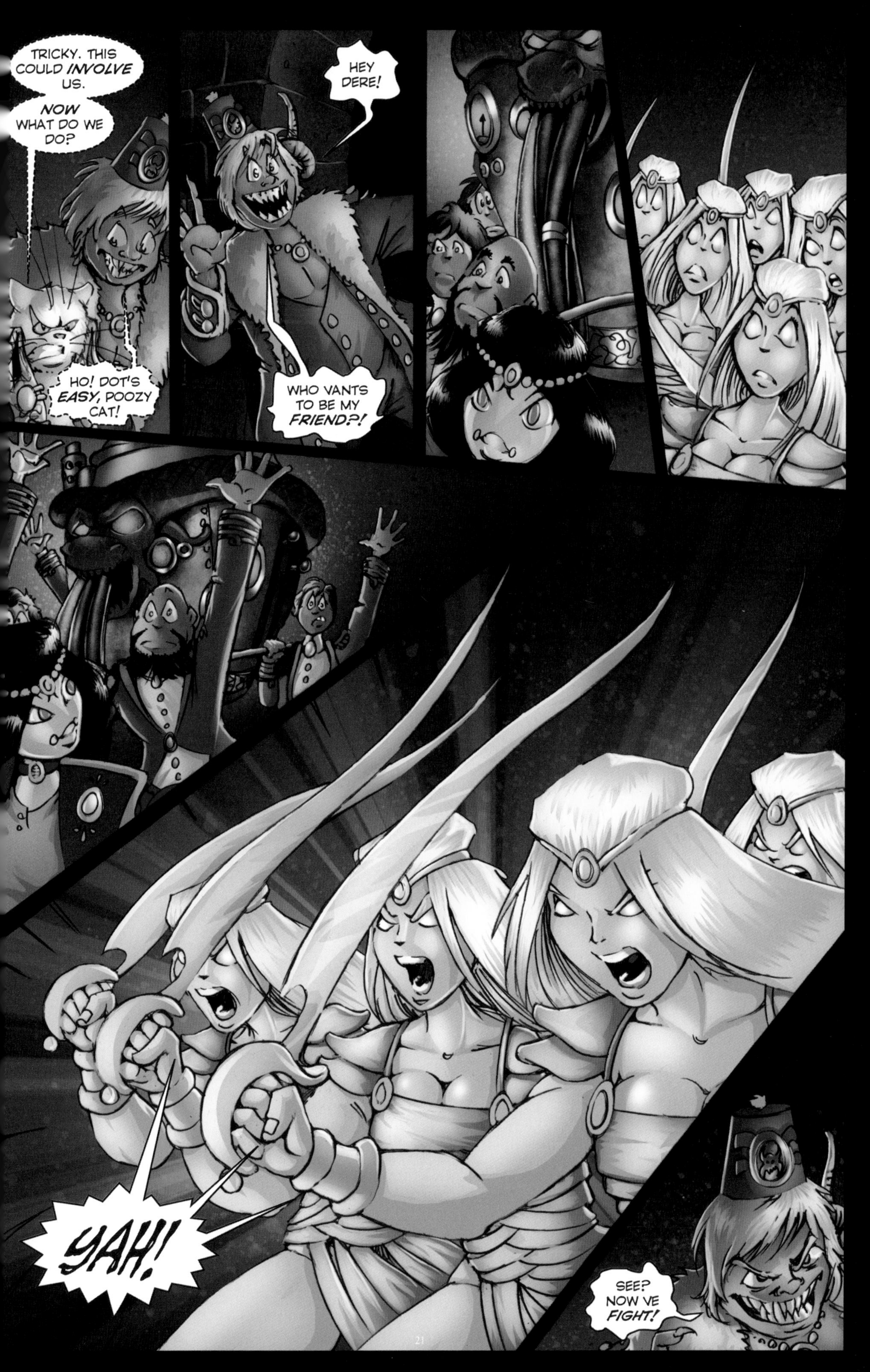
TRICKY. THIS COULD *INVOLVE* US.
NOW WHAT DO WE DO?
HO! DOT'S *EASY,* POOZY CAT!
HEY DERE!
WHO VANTS TO BE MY *FRIEND?!*
YAH!
SEE? NOW VE *FIGHT!*

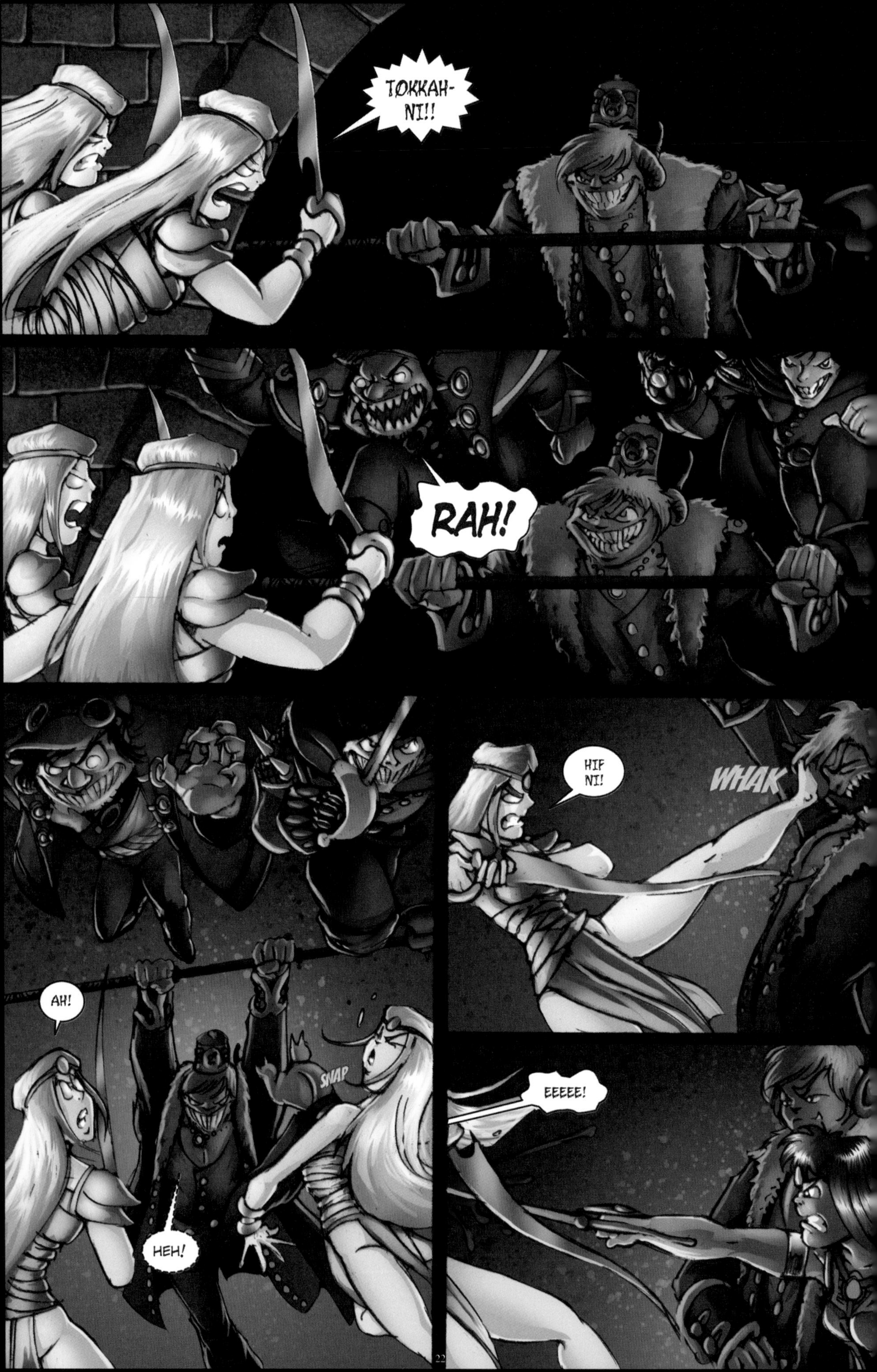
TØKKAH-
NI!!
RAH!
AH!
SNAP
HEH!
HIF
NI!
WHAK
EEEEE!

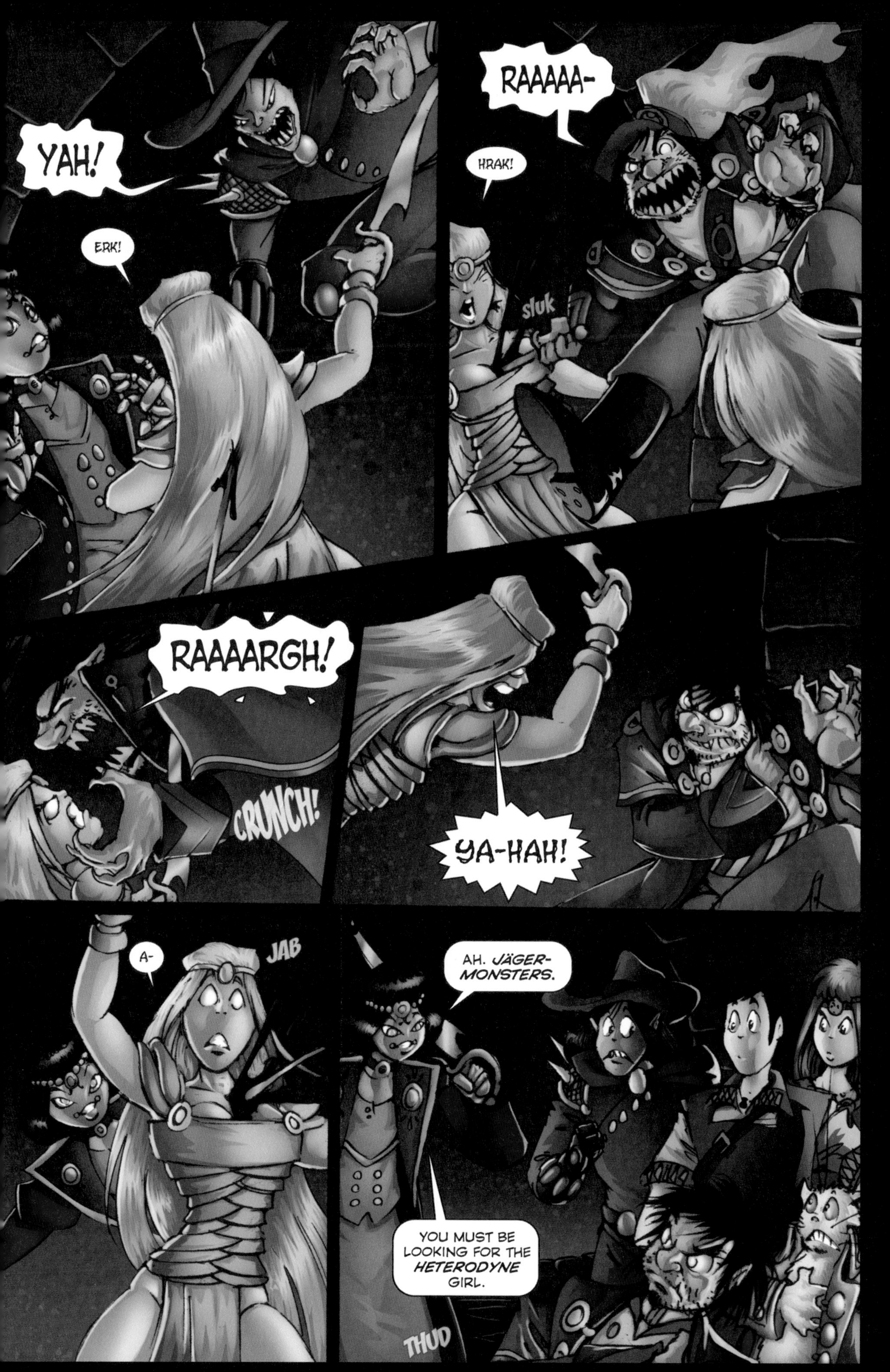
YAH!
ERK!
RAAAAA-
HRAK!
SLUK
RAAAARGH!
CRUNCH!
YA-HAH!
A-
JAB
AH. *JÄGER-MONSTERS.*
YOU MUST BE LOOKING FOR THE *HETERODYNE* GIRL.
THUD

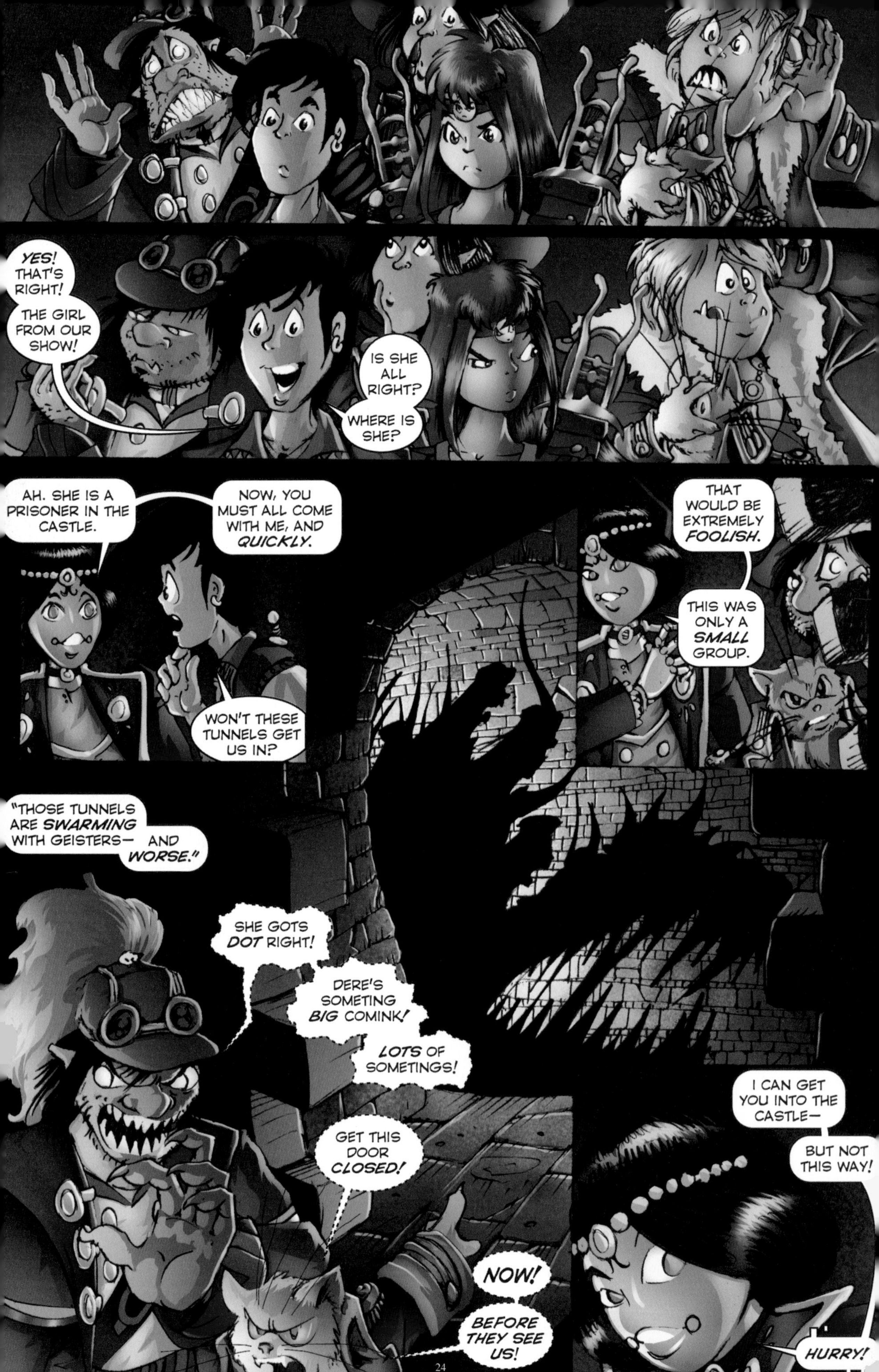

YES! THAT'S RIGHT!
THE GIRL FROM OUR SHOW!
IS SHE ALL RIGHT?
WHERE IS SHE?
AH. SHE IS A PRISONER IN THE CASTLE.
NOW, YOU MUST ALL COME WITH ME, AND QUICKLY.
WON'T THESE TUNNELS GET US IN?
THAT WOULD BE EXTREMELY FOOLISH.
THIS WAS ONLY A SMALL GROUP.
"THOSE TUNNELS ARE SWARMING WITH GEISTERS— AND WORSE."
SHE GOTS DOT RIGHT!
DERE'S SOMETING BIG COMINK!
LOTS OF SOMETINGS!
GET THIS DOOR CLOSED!
NOW!
BEFORE THEY SEE US!
I CAN GET YOU INTO THE CASTLE—
BUT NOT THIS WAY!
HURRY!

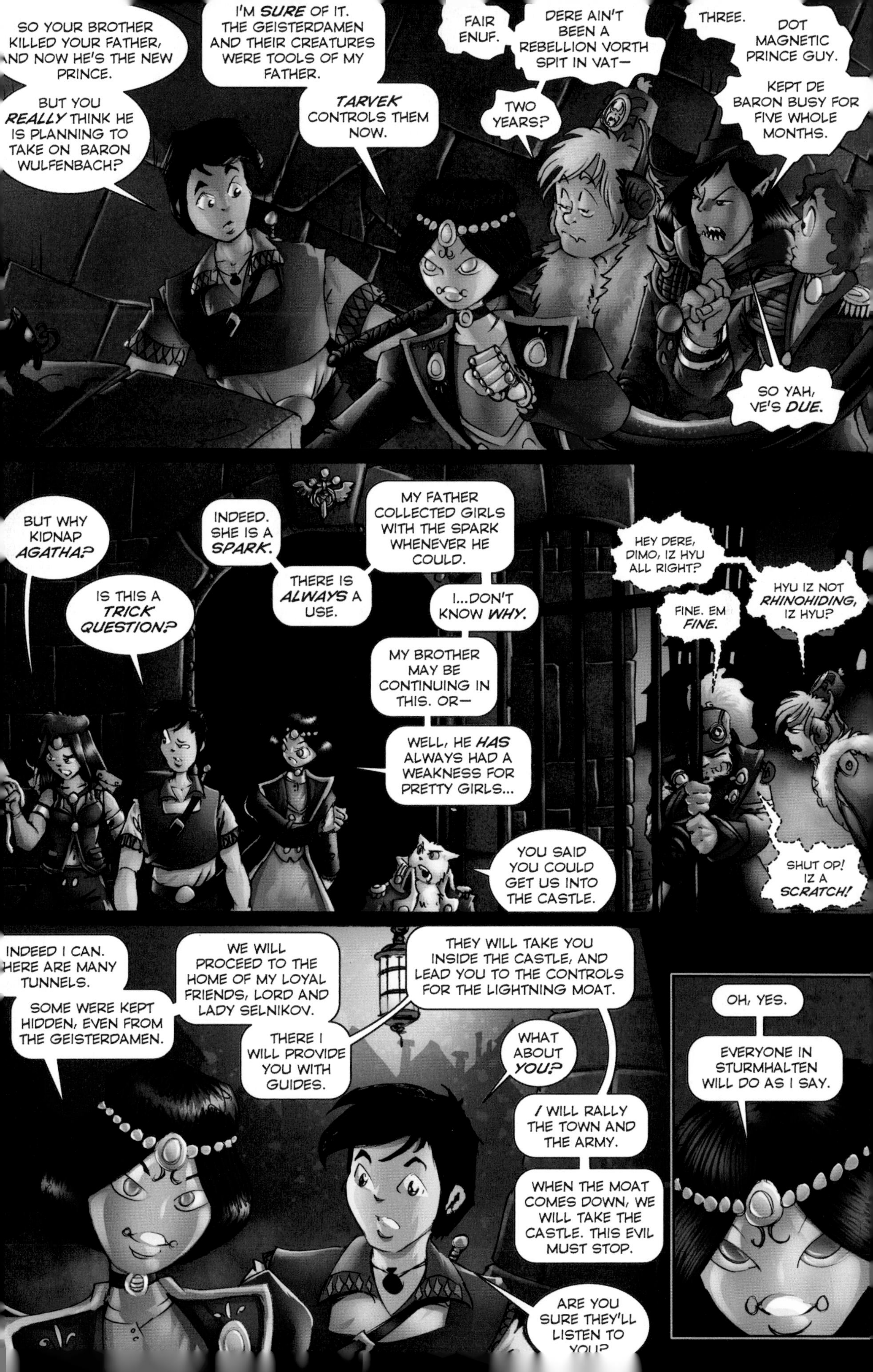
SO YOUR BROTHER KILLED YOUR FATHER, AND NOW HE'S THE NEW PRINCE.
BUT YOU REALLY THINK HE IS PLANNING TO TAKE ON BARON WULFENBACH?
I'M SURE OF IT. THE GEISTERDAMEN AND THEIR CREATURES WERE TOOLS OF MY FATHER.
TARVEK CONTROLS THEM NOW.
FAIR ENUF.
DERE AIN'T BEEN A REBELLION VORTH SPIT IN VAT—
TWO YEARS?
THREE.
DOT MAGNETIC PRINCE GUY.
KEPT DE BARON BUSY FOR FIVE WHOLE MONTHS.
SO YAH, VE'S DUE.
BUT WHY KIDNAP AGATHA?
IS THIS A TRICK QUESTION?
INDEED. SHE IS A SPARK.
THERE IS ALWAYS A USE.
MY FATHER COLLECTED GIRLS WITH THE SPARK WHENEVER HE COULD.
I...DON'T KNOW WHY.
MY BROTHER MAY BE CONTINUING IN THIS. OR—
WELL, HE HAS ALWAYS HAD A WEAKNESS FOR PRETTY GIRLS...
HEY DERE, DIMO, IZ HYU ALL RIGHT?
HYU IZ NOT RHINOHIDING, IZ HYU?
FINE. EM FINE.
SHUT OP! IZ A SCRATCH!
YOU SAID YOU COULD GET US INTO THE CASTLE.
INDEED I CAN. HERE ARE MANY TUNNELS.
SOME WERE KEPT HIDDEN, EVEN FROM THE GEISTERDAMEN.
WE WILL PROCEED TO THE HOME OF MY LOYAL FRIENDS, LORD AND LADY SELNIKOV.
THERE I WILL PROVIDE YOU WITH GUIDES.
THEY WILL TAKE YOU INSIDE THE CASTLE, AND LEAD YOU TO THE CONTROLS FOR THE LIGHTNING MOAT.
WHAT ABOUT YOU?
I WILL RALLY THE TOWN AND THE ARMY.
WHEN THE MOAT COMES DOWN, WE WILL TAKE THE CASTLE. THIS EVIL MUST STOP.
ARE YOU SURE THEY'LL LISTEN TO YOU?
OH, YES.
EVERYONE IN STURMHALTEN WILL DO AS I SAY.

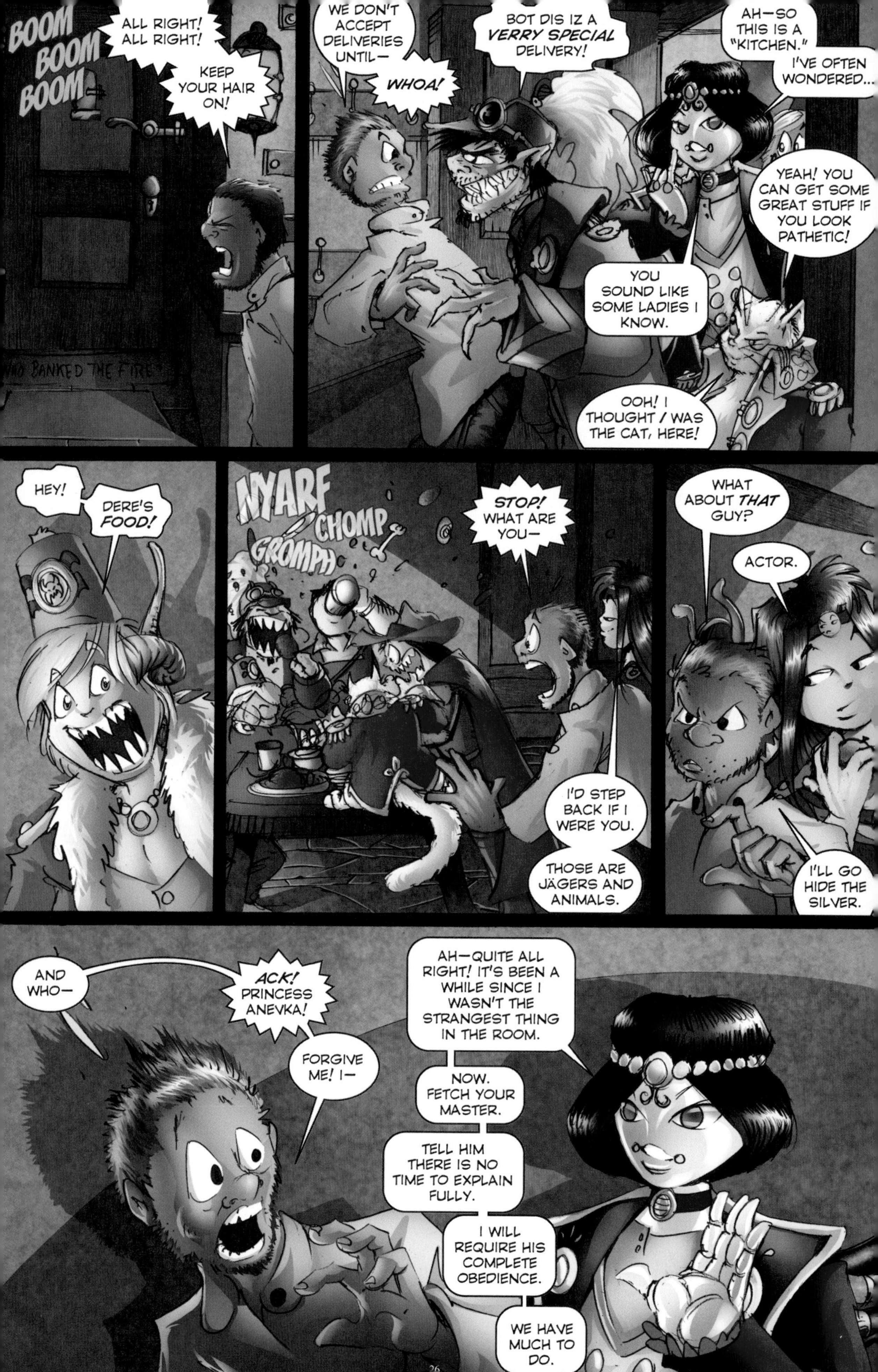
BOOM BOOM BOOM
ALL RIGHT! ALL RIGHT!
KEEP YOUR HAIR ON!
WHO BANKED THE FIRE
WE DON'T ACCEPT DELIVERIES UNTIL—
WHOA!
BOT DIS IZ A VERRY SPECIAL DELIVERY!
AH—SO THIS IS A "KITCHEN."
I'VE OFTEN WONDERED...
YEAH! YOU CAN GET SOME GREAT STUFF IF YOU LOOK PATHETIC!
YOU SOUND LIKE SOME LADIES I KNOW.
OOH! I THOUGHT I WAS THE CAT, HERE!
HEY!
DERE'S FOOD!
NYARF
CHOMP
GROMPH
STOP! WHAT ARE YOU—
I'D STEP BACK IF I WERE YOU.
THOSE ARE JÄGERS AND ANIMALS.
WHAT ABOUT THAT GUY?
ACTOR.
I'LL GO HIDE THE SILVER.
AND WHO—
ACK! PRINCESS ANEVKA!
FORGIVE ME! I—
AH—QUITE ALL RIGHT! IT'S BEEN A WHILE SINCE I WASN'T THE STRANGEST THING IN THE ROOM.
NOW. FETCH YOUR MASTER.
TELL HIM THERE IS NO TIME TO EXPLAIN FULLY.
I WILL REQUIRE HIS COMPLETE OBEDIENCE.
WE HAVE MUCH TO DO.

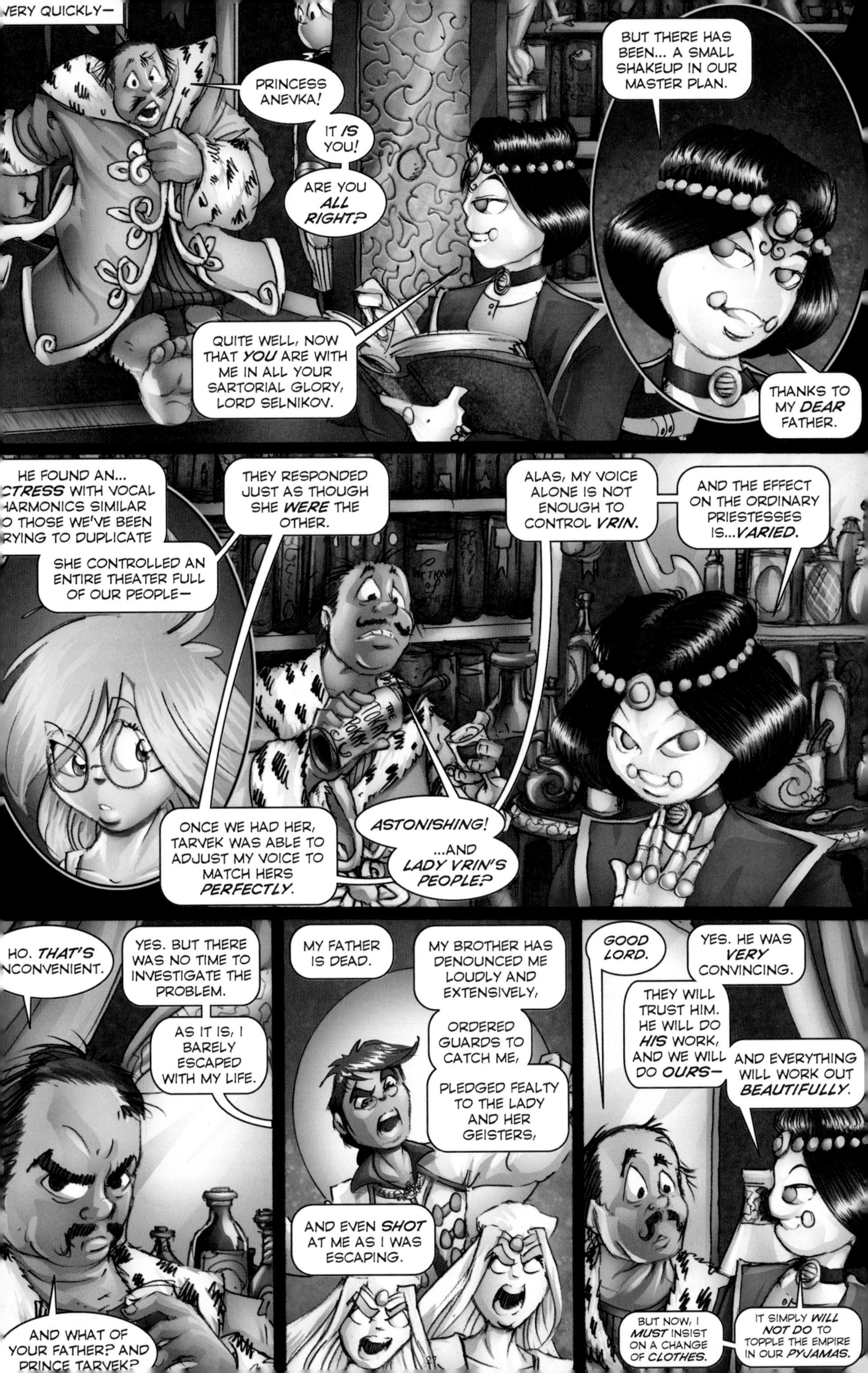

VERY QUICKLY—
PRINCESS ANEVKA!
IT *IS* YOU!
ARE YOU *ALL RIGHT?*
QUITE WELL, NOW THAT *YOU* ARE WITH ME IN ALL YOUR SARTORIAL GLORY, LORD SELNIKOV.
BUT THERE HAS BEEN... A SMALL SHAKEUP IN OUR MASTER PLAN.
THANKS TO MY *DEAR* FATHER.
HE FOUND AN... CTRESS WITH VOCAL HARMONICS SIMILAR O THOSE WE'VE BEEN RYING TO DUPLICATE
SHE CONTROLLED AN ENTIRE THEATER FULL OF OUR PEOPLE—
THEY RESPONDED JUST AS THOUGH SHE *WERE* THE OTHER.
ONCE WE HAD HER, TARVEK WAS ABLE TO ADJUST MY VOICE TO MATCH HERS *PERFECTLY*.
ASTONISHING!
...AND *LADY VRIN'S PEOPLE?*
ALAS, MY VOICE ALONE IS NOT ENOUGH TO CONTROL *VRIN*.
AND THE EFFECT ON THE ORDINARY PRIESTESSES IS...*VARIED*.
HO. *THAT'S* NCONVENIENT.
YES. BUT THERE WAS NO TIME TO INVESTIGATE THE PROBLEM.
AS IT IS, I BARELY ESCAPED WITH MY LIFE.
AND WHAT OF YOUR FATHER? AND PRINCE TARVEK?
MY FATHER IS DEAD.
MY BROTHER HAS DENOUNCED ME LOUDLY AND EXTENSIVELY,
ORDERED GUARDS TO CATCH ME,
PLEDGED FEALTY TO THE LADY AND HER GEISTERS,
AND EVEN *SHOT* AT ME AS I WAS ESCAPING.
GOOD LORD.
YES. HE WAS *VERY* CONVINCING.
THEY WILL TRUST HIM. HE WILL DO *HIS* WORK, AND WE WILL DO *OURS*—
AND EVERYTHING WILL WORK OUT *BEAUTIFULLY*.
BUT NOW, I *MUST* INSIST ON A CHANGE OF *CLOTHES*.
IT SIMPLY *WILL NOT DO* TO TOPPLE THE EMPIRE IN OUR *PYJAMAS*.

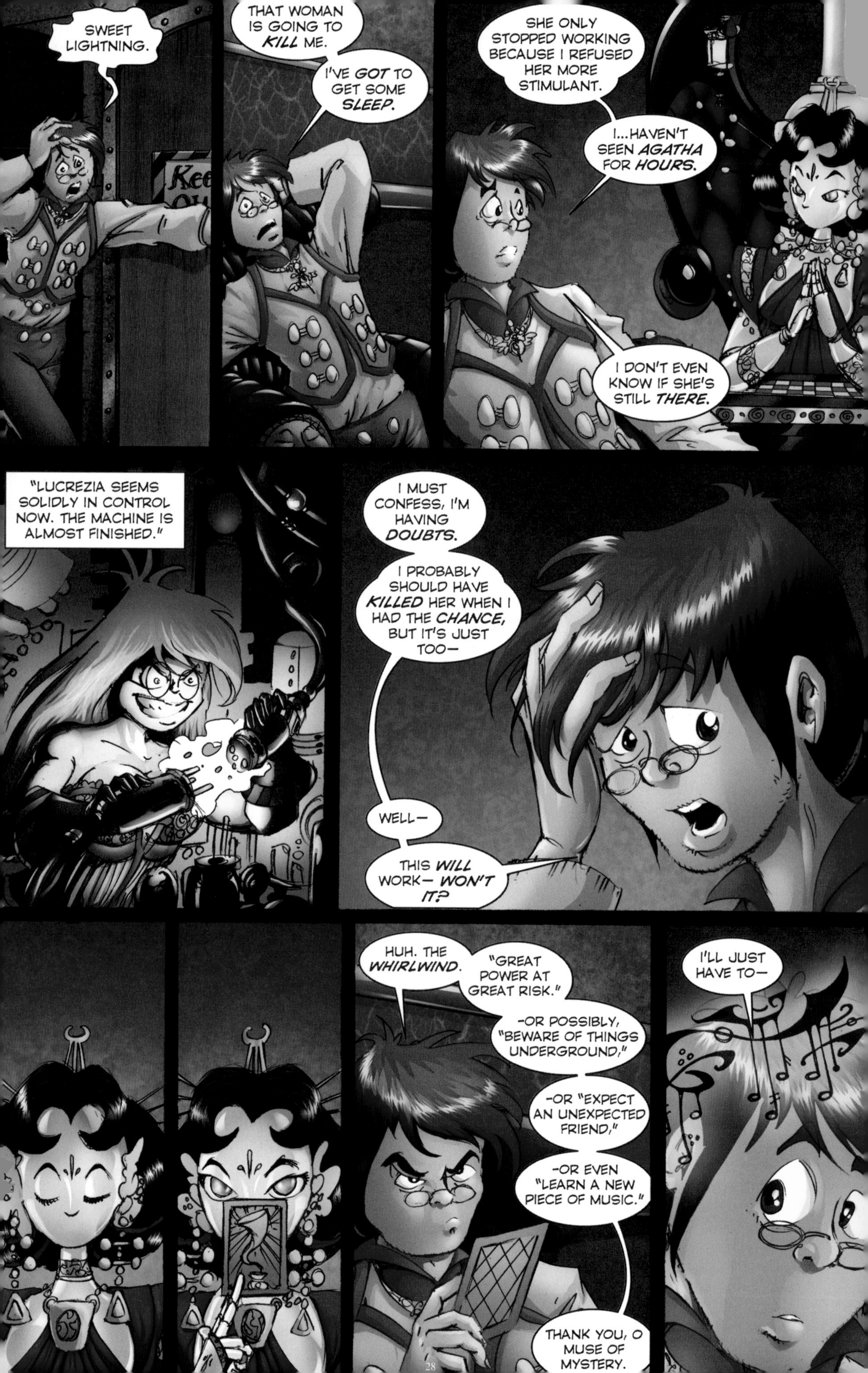
SWEET LIGHTNING.
KEEP OUT
THAT WOMAN IS GOING TO KILL ME.
I'VE GOT TO GET SOME SLEEP.
SHE ONLY STOPPED WORKING BECAUSE I REFUSED HER MORE STIMULANT.
I...HAVEN'T SEEN AGATHA FOR HOURS.
I DON'T EVEN KNOW IF SHE'S STILL THERE.
"LUCREZIA SEEMS SOLIDLY IN CONTROL NOW. THE MACHINE IS ALMOST FINISHED."
I MUST CONFESS, I'M HAVING DOUBTS.
I PROBABLY SHOULD HAVE KILLED HER WHEN I HAD THE CHANCE, BUT IT'S JUST TOO—
WELL—
THIS WILL WORK— WON'T IT?
HUH. THE WHIRLWIND.
"GREAT POWER AT GREAT RISK."
-OR POSSIBLY, "BEWARE OF THINGS UNDERGROUND,"
-OR "EXPECT AN UNEXPECTED FRIEND,"
-OR EVEN "LEARN A NEW PIECE OF MUSIC."
THANK YOU, O MUSE OF MYSTERY.
I'LL JUST HAVE TO—

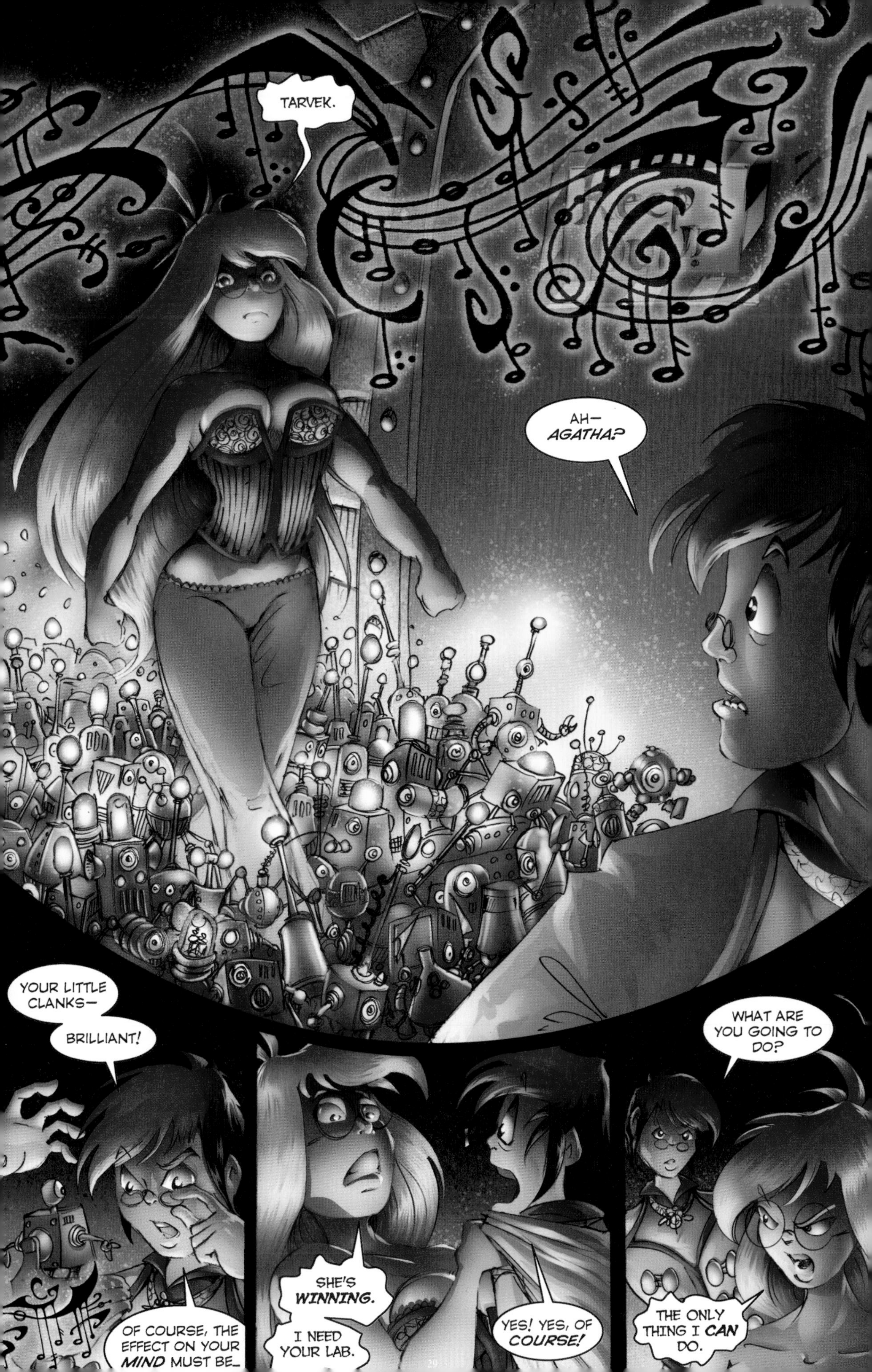
TARVEK.
AH—
AGATHA?
YOUR LITTLE CLANKS—
BRILLIANT!
OF COURSE, THE EFFECT ON YOUR MIND MUST BE—
SHE'S WINNING.
I NEED YOUR LAB.
YES! YES, OF COURSE!
WHAT ARE YOU GOING TO DO?
THE ONLY THING I CAN DO.

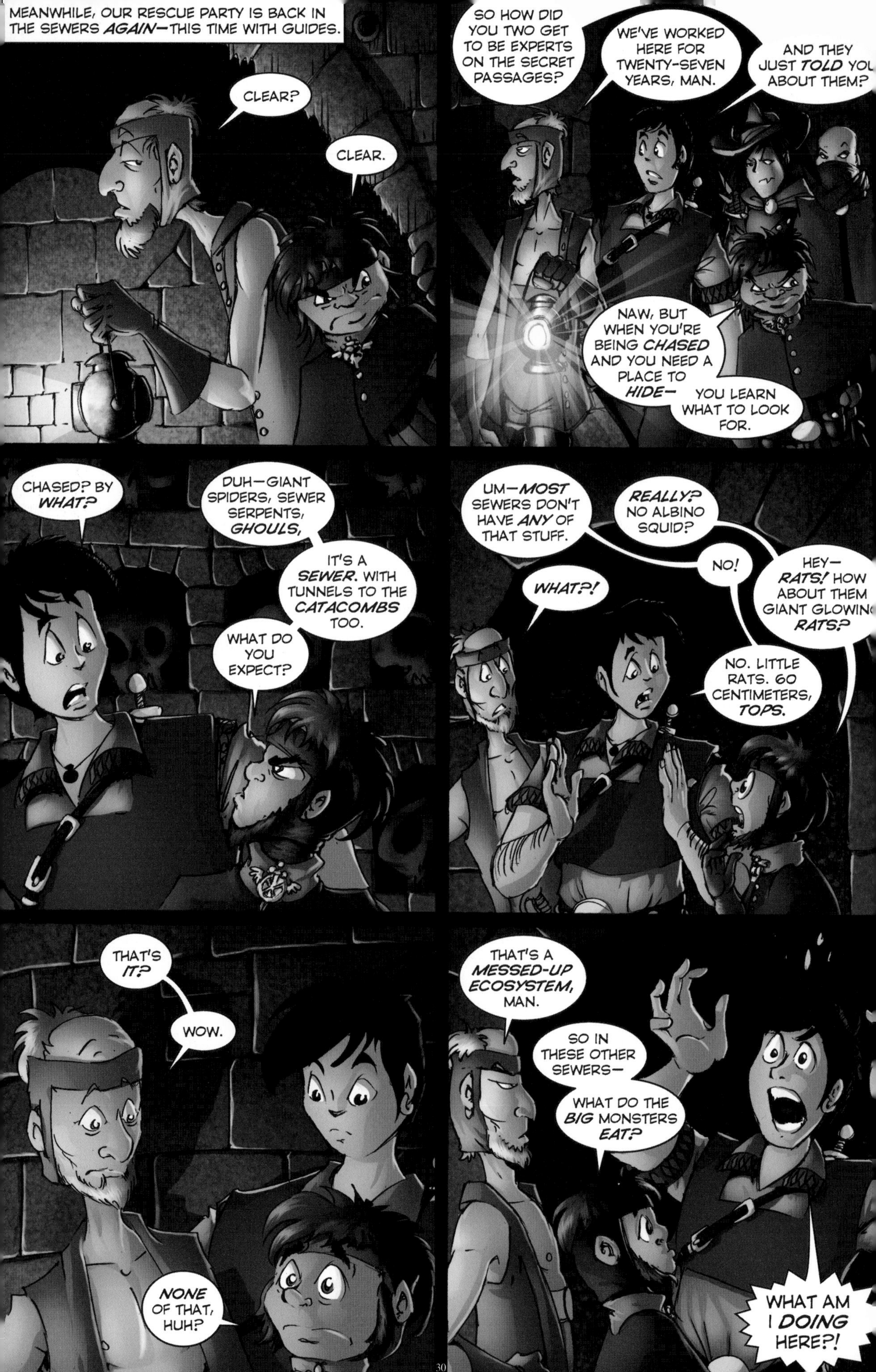
MEANWHILE, OUR RESCUE PARTY IS BACK IN THE SEWERS AGAIN—THIS TIME WITH GUIDES.
CLEAR?
CLEAR.
SO HOW DID YOU TWO GET TO BE EXPERTS ON THE SECRET PASSAGES?
WE'VE WORKED HERE FOR TWENTY-SEVEN YEARS, MAN.
AND THEY JUST TOLD YOU ABOUT THEM?
NAW, BUT WHEN YOU'RE BEING CHASED AND YOU NEED A PLACE TO HIDE—
YOU LEARN WHAT TO LOOK FOR.
CHASED? BY WHAT?
DUH—GIANT SPIDERS, SEWER SERPENTS, GHOULS,
IT'S A SEWER. WITH TUNNELS TO THE CATACOMBS TOO.
WHAT DO YOU EXPECT?
UM—MOST SEWERS DON'T HAVE ANY OF THAT STUFF.
REALLY? NO ALBINO SQUID?
NO!
WHAT?!
HEY— RATS! HOW ABOUT THEM GIANT GLOWING RATS?
NO. LITTLE RATS. 60 CENTIMETERS, TOPS.
THAT'S IT?
WOW.
NONE OF THAT, HUH?
THAT'S A MESSED-UP ECOSYSTEM, MAN.
SO IN THESE OTHER SEWERS—
WHAT DO THE BIG MONSTERS EAT?
WHAT AM I DOING HERE?!

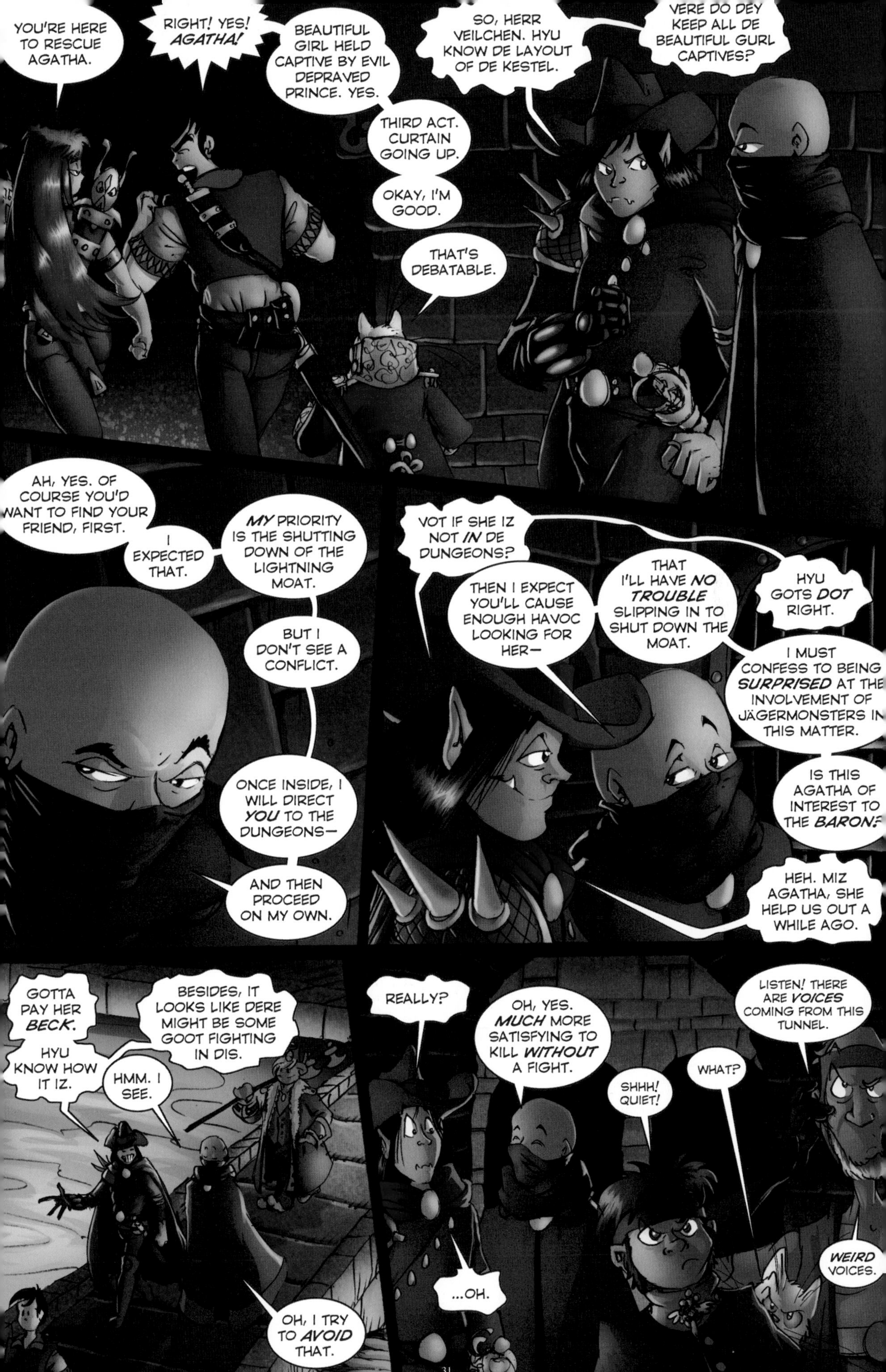
YOU'RE HERE TO RESCUE AGATHA.
RIGHT! YES! *AGATHA!*
BEAUTIFUL GIRL HELD CAPTIVE BY EVIL DEPRAVED PRINCE. YES.
THIRD ACT. CURTAIN GOING UP.
OKAY, I'M GOOD.
THAT'S DEBATABLE.
SO, HERR VEILCHEN. HYU KNOW DE LAYOUT OF DE KESTEL.
VERE DO DEY KEEP ALL DE BEAUTIFUL GURL CAPTIVES?
AH, YES. OF COURSE YOU'D WANT TO FIND YOUR FRIEND, FIRST.
I EXPECTED THAT.
MY PRIORITY IS THE SHUTTING DOWN OF THE LIGHTNING MOAT.
BUT I DON'T SEE A CONFLICT.
ONCE INSIDE, I WILL DIRECT *YOU* TO THE DUNGEONS—
AND THEN PROCEED ON MY OWN.
VOT IF SHE IZ NOT *IN* DE DUNGEONS?
THEN I EXPECT YOU'LL CAUSE ENOUGH HAVOC LOOKING FOR HER—
THAT I'LL HAVE *NO TROUBLE* SLIPPING IN TO SHUT DOWN THE MOAT.
HYU GOTS *DOT* RIGHT.
I MUST CONFESS TO BEING *SURPRISED* AT THE INVOLVEMENT OF JÄGERMONSTERS IN THIS MATTER.
IS THIS AGATHA OF INTEREST TO THE *BARON?*
HEH. MIZ AGATHA, SHE HELP US OUT A WHILE AGO.
GOTTA PAY HER *BECK.*
HYU KNOW HOW IT IZ.
BESIDES, IT LOOKS LIKE DERE MIGHT BE SOME GOOT FIGHTING IN DIS.
HMM. I SEE.
OH, I TRY TO *AVOID* THAT.
REALLY?
OH, YES. *MUCH* MORE SATISFYING TO KILL *WITHOUT* A FIGHT.
...OH.
SHHH! QUIET!
WHAT?
LISTEN! THERE ARE *VOICES* COMING FROM THIS TUNNEL.
WEIRD VOICES.

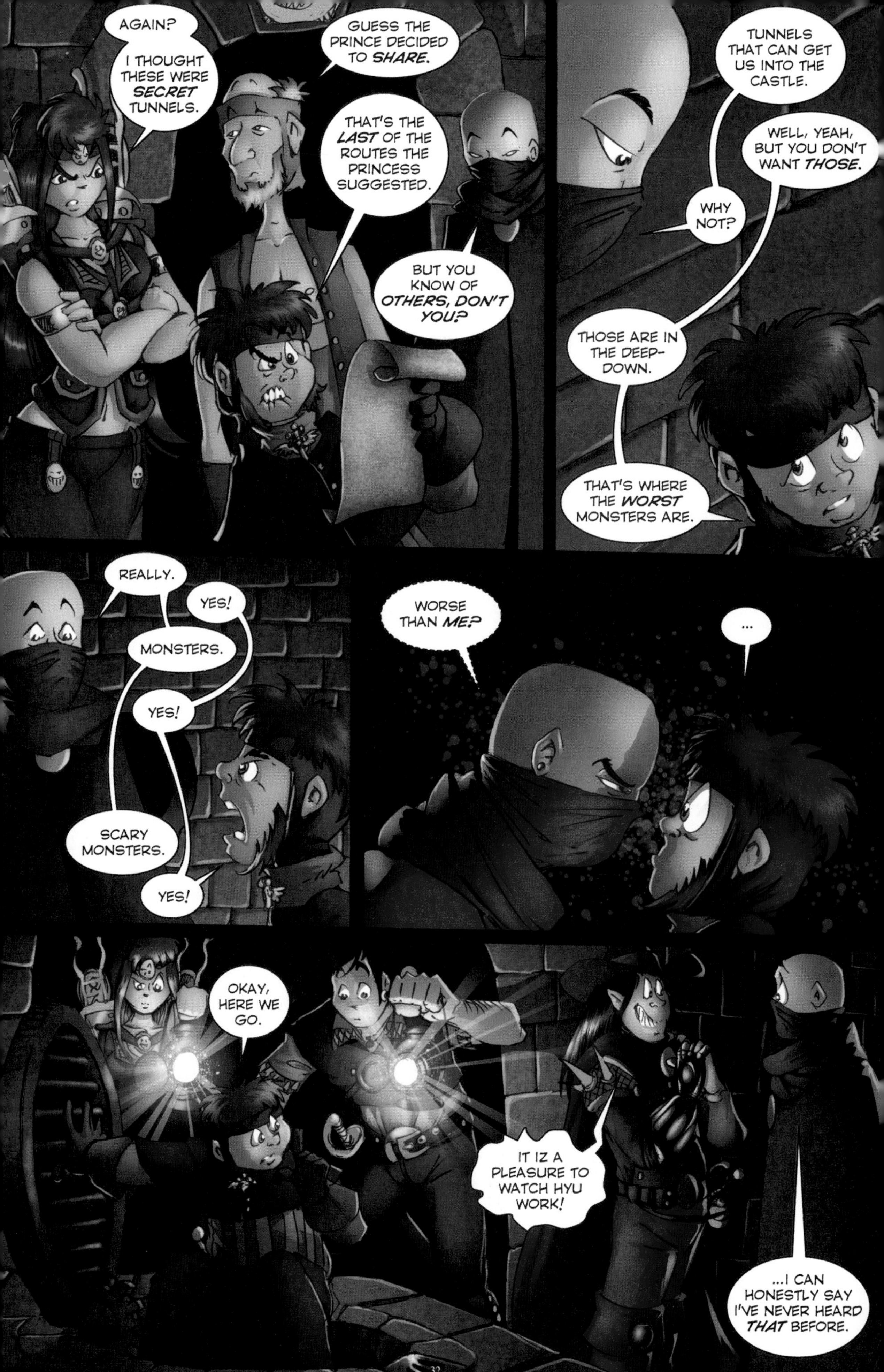
AGAIN?
I THOUGHT THESE WERE SECRET TUNNELS.
GUESS THE PRINCE DECIDED TO SHARE.
THAT'S THE LAST OF THE ROUTES THE PRINCESS SUGGESTED.
BUT YOU KNOW OF OTHERS, DON'T YOU?
TUNNELS THAT CAN GET US INTO THE CASTLE.
WELL, YEAH, BUT YOU DON'T WANT THOSE.
WHY NOT?
THOSE ARE IN THE DEEP-DOWN.
THAT'S WHERE THE WORST MONSTERS ARE.
REALLY.
YES!
MONSTERS.
YES!
SCARY MONSTERS.
YES!
WORSE THAN ME?
...
OKAY, HERE WE GO.
IT IZ A PLEASURE TO WATCH HYU WORK!
...I CAN HONESTLY SAY I'VE NEVER HEARD THAT BEFORE.

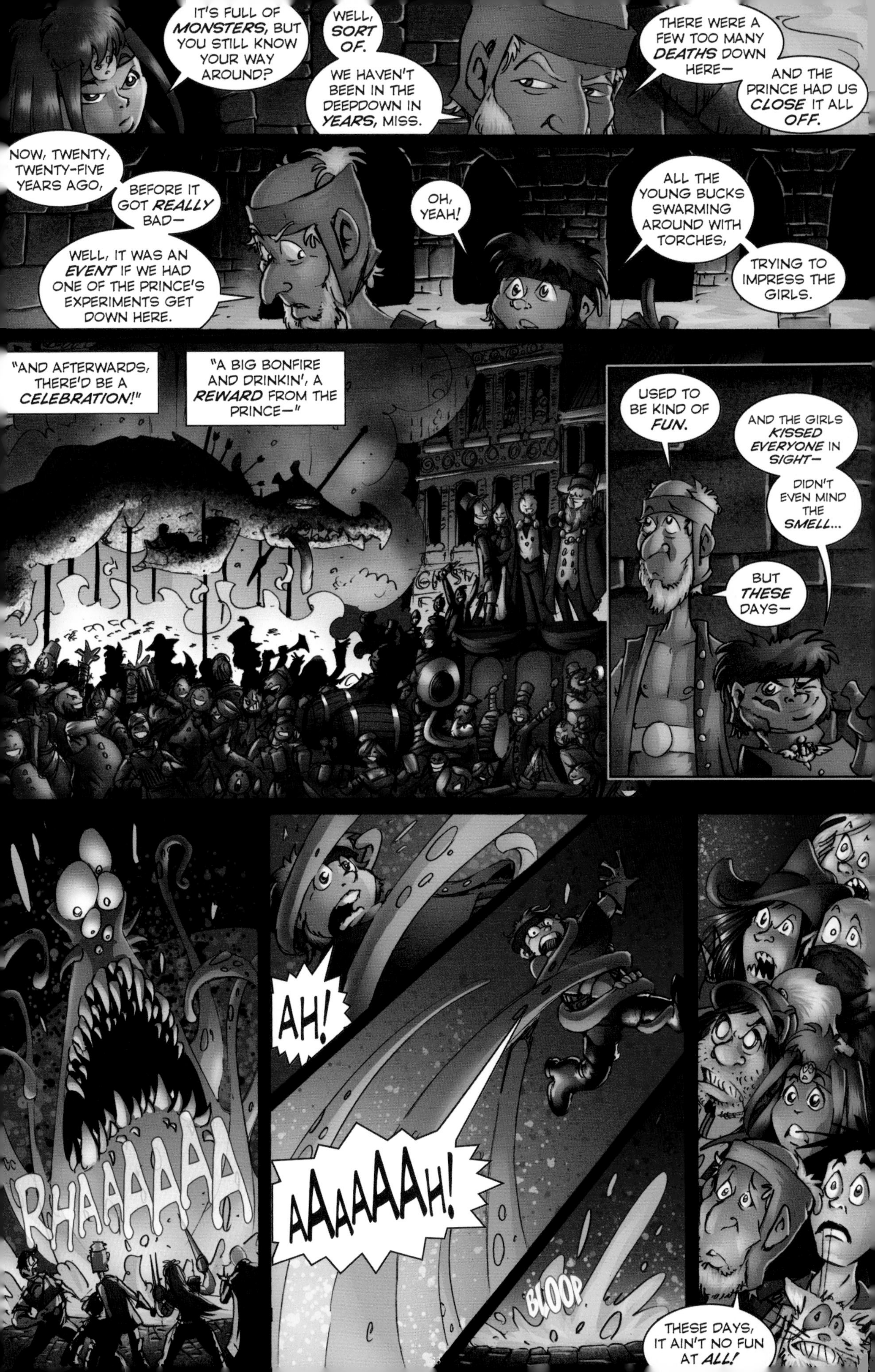
IT'S FULL OF MONSTERS, BUT YOU STILL KNOW YOUR WAY AROUND?
WELL, SORT OF.
WE HAVEN'T BEEN IN THE DEEPDOWN IN YEARS, MISS.
THERE WERE A FEW TOO MANY DEATHS DOWN HERE—
AND THE PRINCE HAD US CLOSE IT ALL OFF.
NOW, TWENTY, TWENTY-FIVE YEARS AGO,
BEFORE IT GOT REALLY BAD—
WELL, IT WAS AN EVENT IF WE HAD ONE OF THE PRINCE'S EXPERIMENTS GET DOWN HERE.
OH, YEAH!
ALL THE YOUNG BUCKS SWARMING AROUND WITH TORCHES,
TRYING TO IMPRESS THE GIRLS.
"AND AFTERWARDS, THERE'D BE A CELEBRATION!"
"A BIG BONFIRE AND DRINKIN', A REWARD FROM THE PRINCE—"
USED TO BE KIND OF FUN.
AND THE GIRLS KISSED EVERYONE IN SIGHT—
DIDN'T EVEN MIND THE SMELL...
BUT THESE DAYS—
RHAAAAAA
AH!
AAAAAAH!
BLOOP
THESE DAYS, IT AIN'T NO FUN AT ALL!

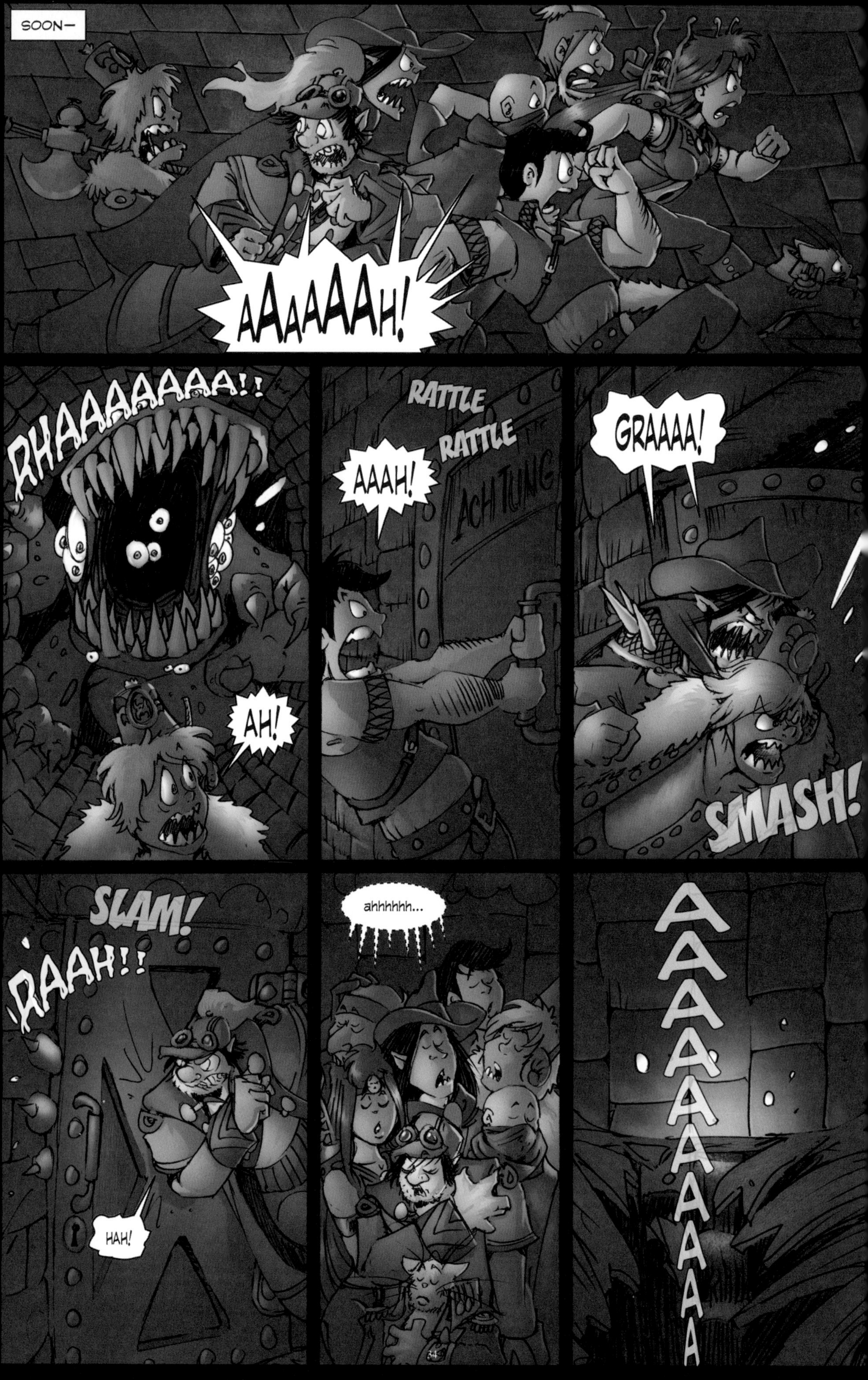
SOON—
AAAAAAH!
RHAAAAAAAA!!
AH!
RATTLE
RATTLE
AAAH!
ACHTUNG
GRAAAA!
SMASH!
SLAM!
RAAH!!
HAH!
ahhhhhh...
AAAAAAAAA

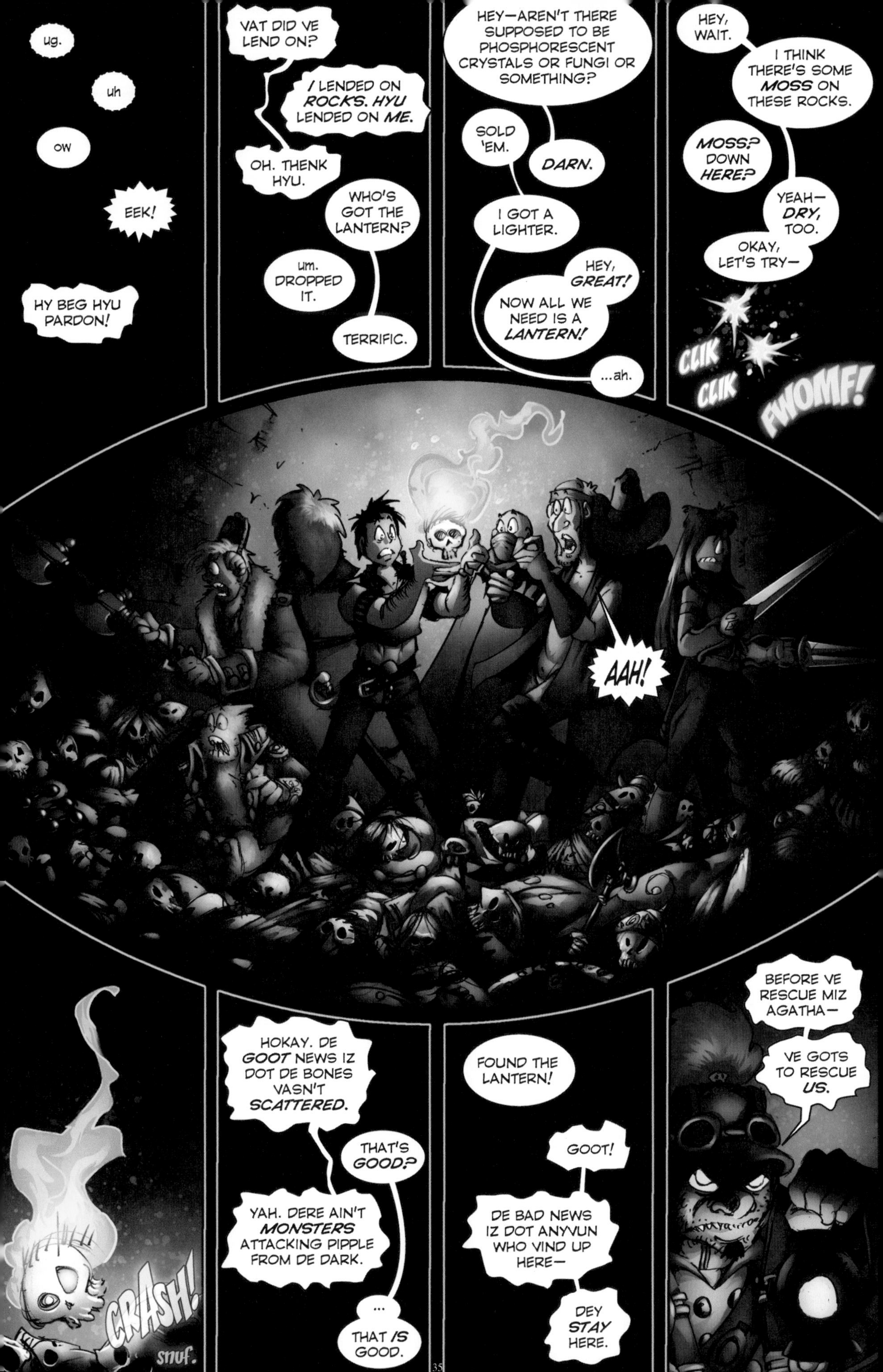
ug.
uh
ow
EEK!
HY BEG HYU PARDON!
VAT DID VE LEND ON?
I LENDED ON ROCKS. HYU LENDED ON ME.
OH. THENK HYU.
WHO'S GOT THE LANTERN?
um. DROPPED IT.
TERRIFIC.
HEY—AREN'T THERE SUPPOSED TO BE PHOSPHORESCENT CRYSTALS OR FUNGI OR SOMETHING?
SOLD 'EM.
DARN.
I GOT A LIGHTER.
HEY, GREAT!
NOW ALL WE NEED IS A LANTERN!
...ah.
HEY, WAIT.
I THINK THERE'S SOME MOSS ON THESE ROCKS.
MOSS? DOWN HERE?
YEAH— DRY, TOO.
OKAY, LET'S TRY—
CLIK
CLIK
FWOMF!
AAH!
CRASH!
snuf.
HOKAY. DE GOOT NEWS IZ DOT DE BONES VASN'T SCATTERED.
THAT'S GOOD?
YAH. DERE AIN'T MONSTERS ATTACKING PIPPLE FROM DE DARK.
...
THAT IS GOOD.
FOUND THE LANTERN!
GOOT!
DE BAD NEWS IZ DOT ANYVUN WHO VIND UP HERE—
DEY STAY HERE.
BEFORE VE RESCUE MIZ AGATHA—
VE GOTS TO RESCUE US.

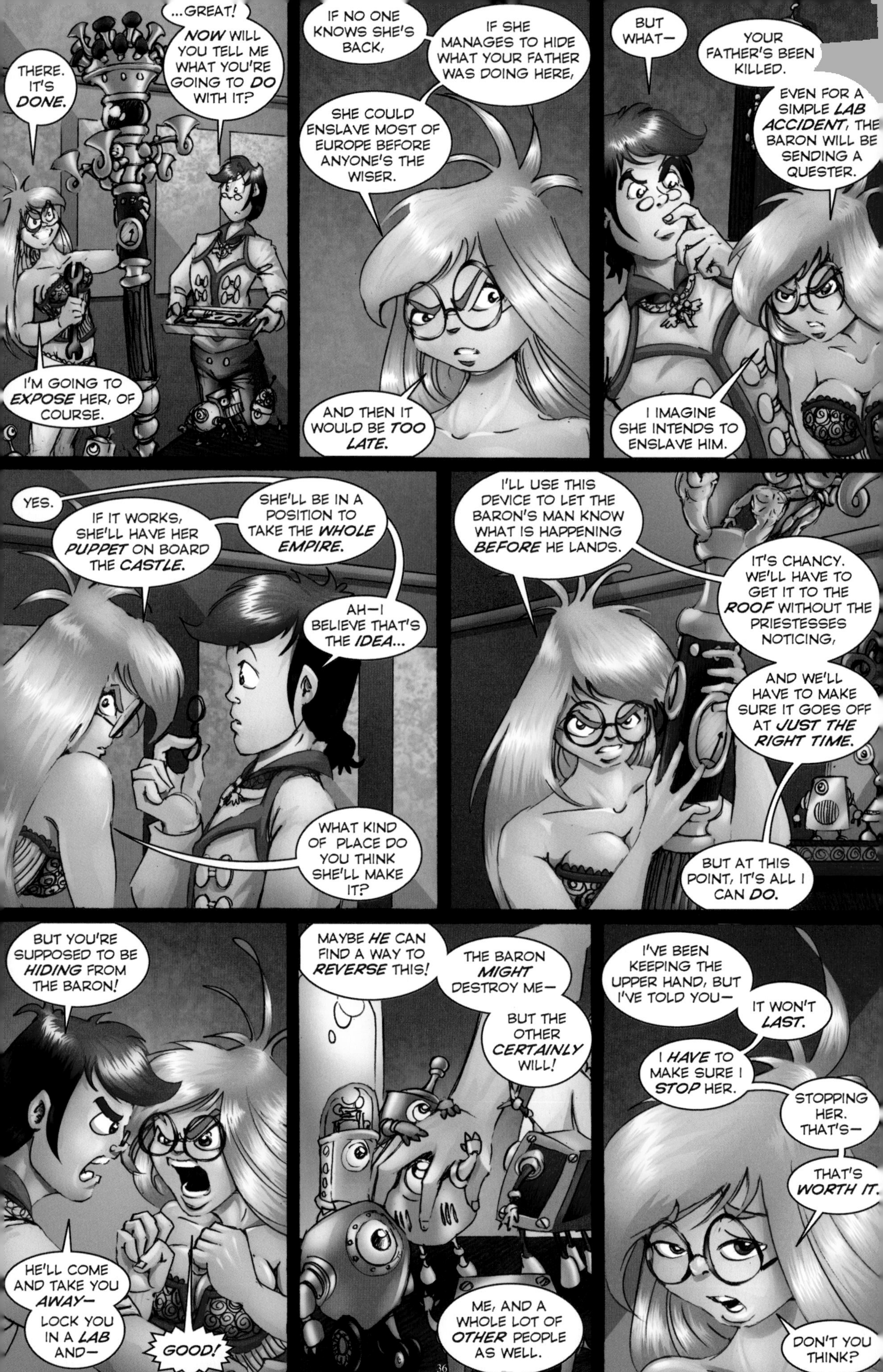
THERE. IT'S DONE.
...GREAT! NOW WILL YOU TELL ME WHAT YOU'RE GOING TO DO WITH IT?
I'M GOING TO EXPOSE HER, OF COURSE.
IF NO ONE KNOWS SHE'S BACK,
IF SHE MANAGES TO HIDE WHAT YOUR FATHER WAS DOING HERE,
SHE COULD ENSLAVE MOST OF EUROPE BEFORE ANYONE'S THE WISER.
AND THEN IT WOULD BE TOO LATE.
BUT WHAT—
YOUR FATHER'S BEEN KILLED.
EVEN FOR A SIMPLE LAB ACCIDENT, THE BARON WILL BE SENDING A QUESTER.
I IMAGINE SHE INTENDS TO ENSLAVE HIM.
YES.
IF IT WORKS, SHE'LL HAVE HER PUPPET ON BOARD THE CASTLE.
SHE'LL BE IN A POSITION TO TAKE THE WHOLE EMPIRE.
AH—I BELIEVE THAT'S THE IDEA...
WHAT KIND OF PLACE DO YOU THINK SHE'LL MAKE IT?
I'LL USE THIS DEVICE TO LET THE BARON'S MAN KNOW WHAT IS HAPPENING BEFORE HE LANDS.
IT'S CHANCY. WE'LL HAVE TO GET IT TO THE ROOF WITHOUT THE PRIESTESSES NOTICING,
AND WE'LL HAVE TO MAKE SURE IT GOES OFF AT JUST THE RIGHT TIME.
BUT AT THIS POINT, IT'S ALL I CAN DO.
BUT YOU'RE SUPPOSED TO BE HIDING FROM THE BARON!
HE'LL COME AND TAKE YOU AWAY— LOCK YOU IN A LAB AND—
GOOD!
MAYBE HE CAN FIND A WAY TO REVERSE THIS!
THE BARON MIGHT DESTROY ME—
BUT THE OTHER CERTAINLY WILL!
ME, AND A WHOLE LOT OF OTHER PEOPLE AS WELL.
I'VE BEEN KEEPING THE UPPER HAND, BUT I'VE TOLD YOU—
IT WON'T LAST.
I HAVE TO MAKE SURE I STOP HER.
STOPPING HER. THAT'S—
THAT'S WORTH IT.
DON'T YOU THINK?

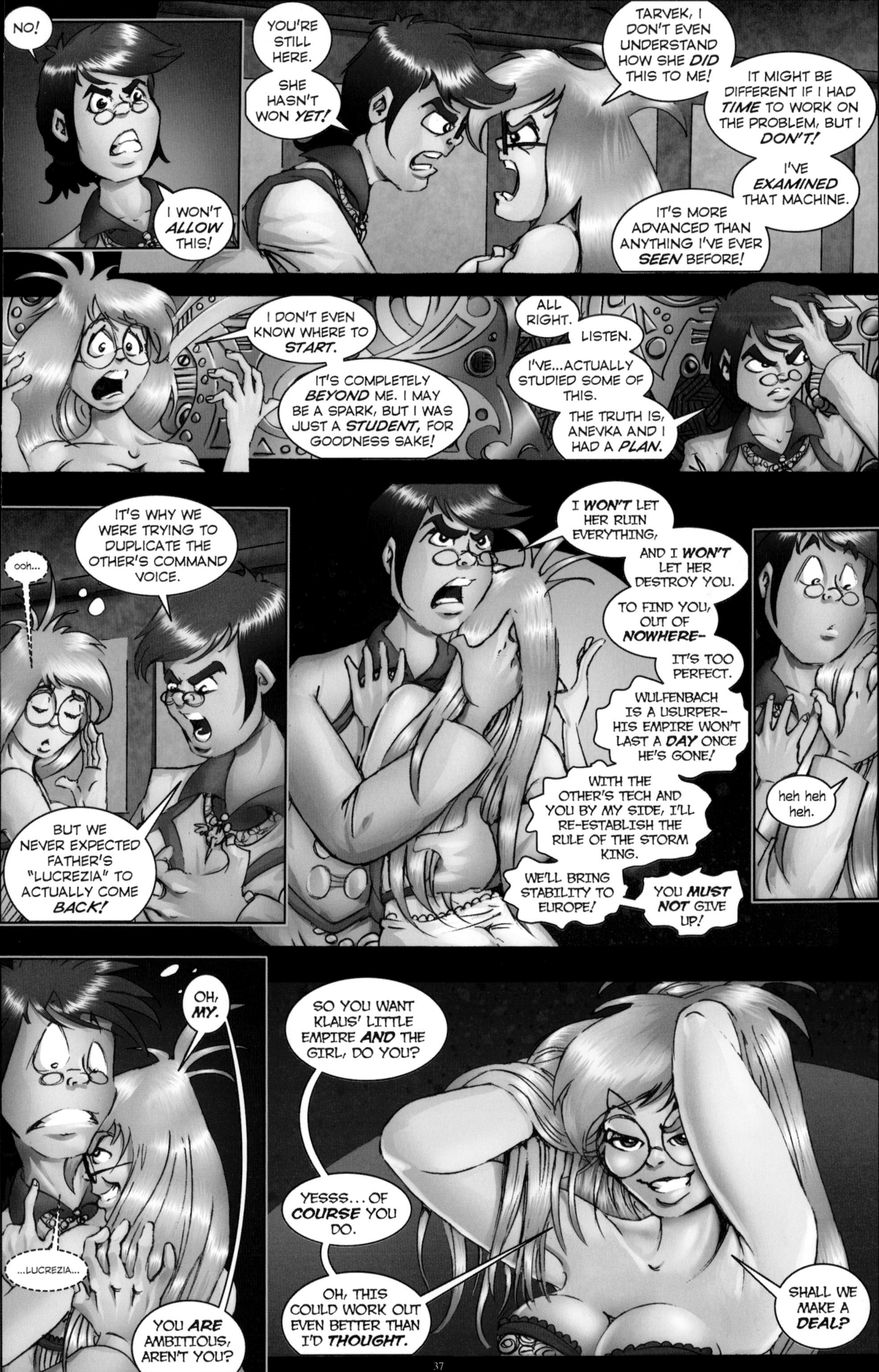
NO!
YOU'RE STILL HERE.
SHE HASN'T WON YET!
I WON'T ALLOW THIS!
TARVEK, I DON'T EVEN UNDERSTAND HOW SHE DID THIS TO ME!
IT MIGHT BE DIFFERENT IF I HAD TIME TO WORK ON THE PROBLEM, BUT I DON'T!
I'VE EXAMINED THAT MACHINE.
IT'S MORE ADVANCED THAN ANYTHING I'VE EVER SEEN BEFORE!
I DON'T EVEN KNOW WHERE TO START.
IT'S COMPLETELY BEYOND ME. I MAY BE A SPARK, BUT I WAS JUST A STUDENT, FOR GOODNESS SAKE!
ALL RIGHT.
LISTEN.
I'VE...ACTUALLY STUDIED SOME OF THIS.
THE TRUTH IS, ANEVKA AND I HAD A PLAN.
IT'S WHY WE WERE TRYING TO DUPLICATE THE OTHER'S COMMAND VOICE.
ooh...
BUT WE NEVER EXPECTED FATHER'S "LUCREZIA" TO ACTUALLY COME BACK!
I WON'T LET HER RUIN EVERYTHING,
AND I WON'T LET HER DESTROY YOU.
TO FIND YOU, OUT OF NOWHERE-
IT'S TOO PERFECT.
WULFENBACH IS A USURPER- HIS EMPIRE WON'T LAST A DAY ONCE HE'S GONE!
WITH THE OTHER'S TECH AND YOU BY MY SIDE, I'LL RE-ESTABLISH THE RULE OF THE STORM KING.
WE'LL BRING STABILITY TO EUROPE!
YOU MUST NOT GIVE UP!
heh heh heh.
OH, MY.
...LUCREZIA...
YOU ARE AMBITIOUS, AREN'T YOU?
SO YOU WANT KLAUS' LITTLE EMPIRE AND THE GIRL, DO YOU?
YESSS... OF COURSE YOU DO.
OH, THIS COULD WORK OUT EVEN BETTER THAN I'D THOUGHT.
SHALL WE MAKE A DEAL?

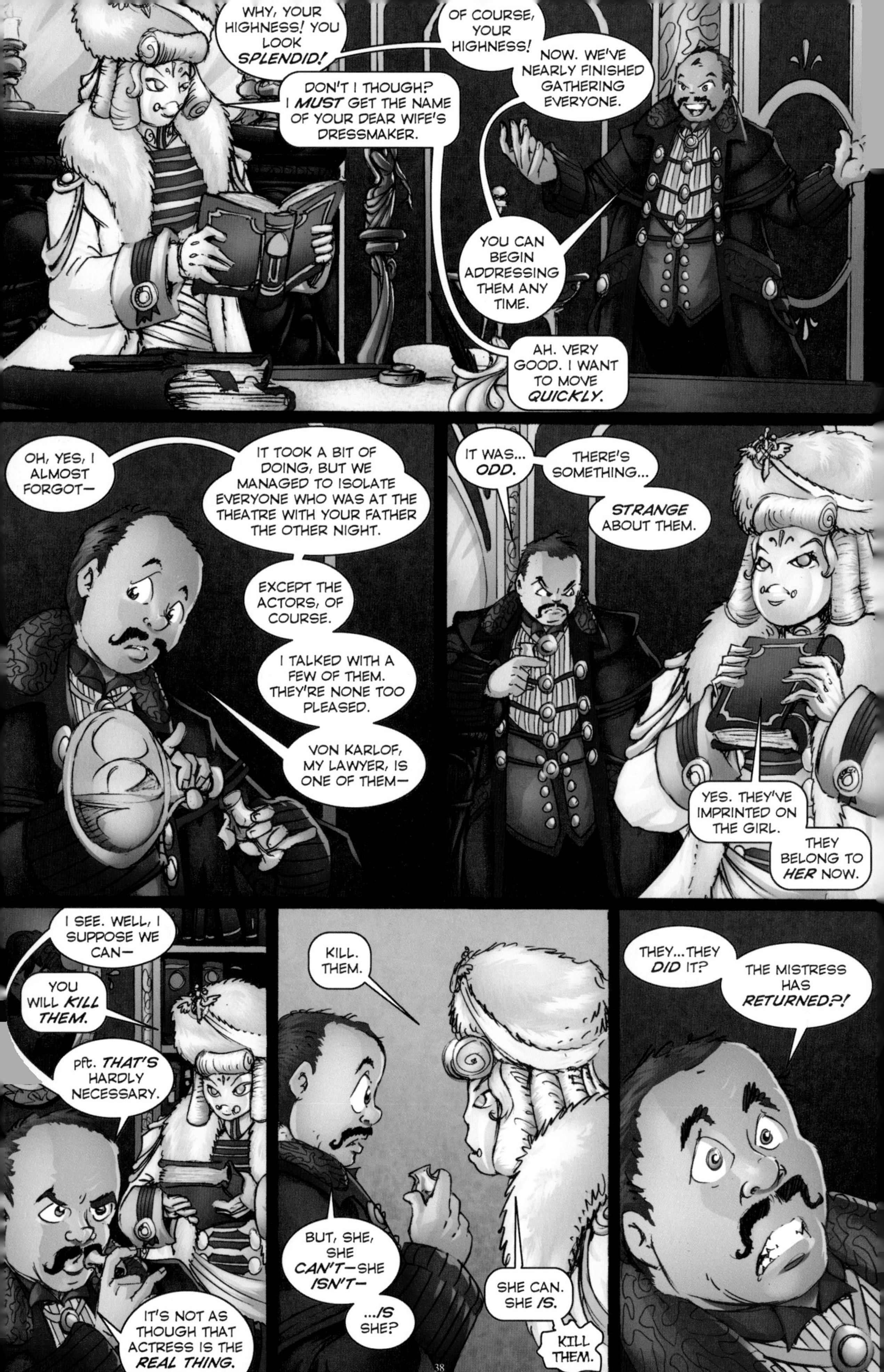
WHY, YOUR HIGHNESS! YOU LOOK SPLENDID!
DON'T I THOUGH? I MUST GET THE NAME OF YOUR DEAR WIFE'S DRESSMAKER.
OF COURSE, YOUR HIGHNESS!
NOW. WE'VE NEARLY FINISHED GATHERING EVERYONE.
YOU CAN BEGIN ADDRESSING THEM ANY TIME.
AH. VERY GOOD. I WANT TO MOVE QUICKLY.
OH, YES, I ALMOST FORGOT—
IT TOOK A BIT OF DOING, BUT WE MANAGED TO ISOLATE EVERYONE WHO WAS AT THE THEATRE WITH YOUR FATHER THE OTHER NIGHT.
EXCEPT THE ACTORS, OF COURSE.
I TALKED WITH A FEW OF THEM. THEY'RE NONE TOO PLEASED.
VON KARLOF, MY LAWYER, IS ONE OF THEM—
IT WAS... ODD.
THERE'S SOMETHING...
STRANGE ABOUT THEM.
YES. THEY'VE IMPRINTED ON THE GIRL.
THEY BELONG TO HER NOW.
I SEE. WELL, I SUPPOSE WE CAN—
YOU WILL KILL THEM.
pft. THAT'S HARDLY NECESSARY.
IT'S NOT AS THOUGH THAT ACTRESS IS THE REAL THING.
KILL. THEM.
BUT, SHE, SHE CAN'T—SHE ISN'T—
...IS SHE?
SHE CAN. SHE IS.
KILL THEM.
THEY...THEY DID IT?
THE MISTRESS HAS RETURNED?!

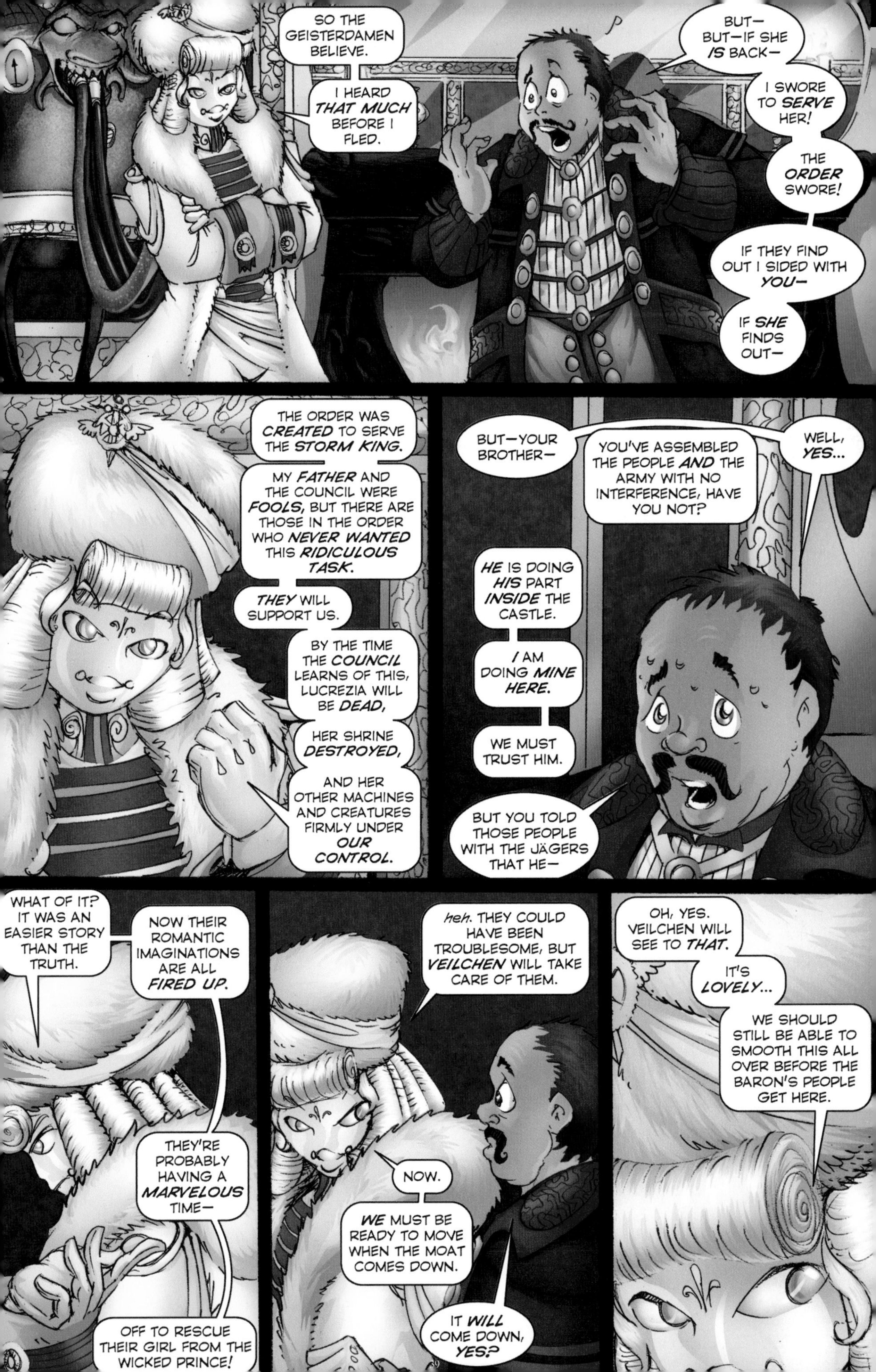
SO THE GEISTERDAMEN BELIEVE.
I HEARD THAT MUCH BEFORE I FLED.
BUT— BUT—IF SHE IS BACK—
I SWORE TO SERVE HER!
THE ORDER SWORE!
IF THEY FIND OUT I SIDED WITH YOU—
IF SHE FINDS OUT—
THE ORDER WAS CREATED TO SERVE THE STORM KING.
MY FATHER AND THE COUNCIL WERE FOOLS, BUT THERE ARE THOSE IN THE ORDER WHO NEVER WANTED THIS RIDICULOUS TASK.
THEY WILL SUPPORT US.
BY THE TIME THE COUNCIL LEARNS OF THIS, LUCREZIA WILL BE DEAD,
HER SHRINE DESTROYED,
AND HER OTHER MACHINES AND CREATURES FIRMLY UNDER OUR CONTROL.
BUT—YOUR BROTHER—
YOU'VE ASSEMBLED THE PEOPLE AND THE ARMY WITH NO INTERFERENCE, HAVE YOU NOT?
WELL, YES...
HE IS DOING HIS PART INSIDE THE CASTLE.
I AM DOING MINE HERE.
WE MUST TRUST HIM.
BUT YOU TOLD THOSE PEOPLE WITH THE JÄGERS THAT HE—
WHAT OF IT? IT WAS AN EASIER STORY THAN THE TRUTH.
NOW THEIR ROMANTIC IMAGINATIONS ARE ALL FIRED UP.
THEY'RE PROBABLY HAVING A MARVELOUS TIME—
OFF TO RESCUE THEIR GIRL FROM THE WICKED PRINCE!
heh. THEY COULD HAVE BEEN TROUBLESOME, BUT VEILCHEN WILL TAKE CARE OF THEM.
NOW.
WE MUST BE READY TO MOVE WHEN THE MOAT COMES DOWN.
IT WILL COME DOWN, YES?
OH, YES. VEILCHEN WILL SEE TO THAT.
IT'S LOVELY...
WE SHOULD STILL BE ABLE TO SMOOTH THIS ALL OVER BEFORE THE BARON'S PEOPLE GET HERE.

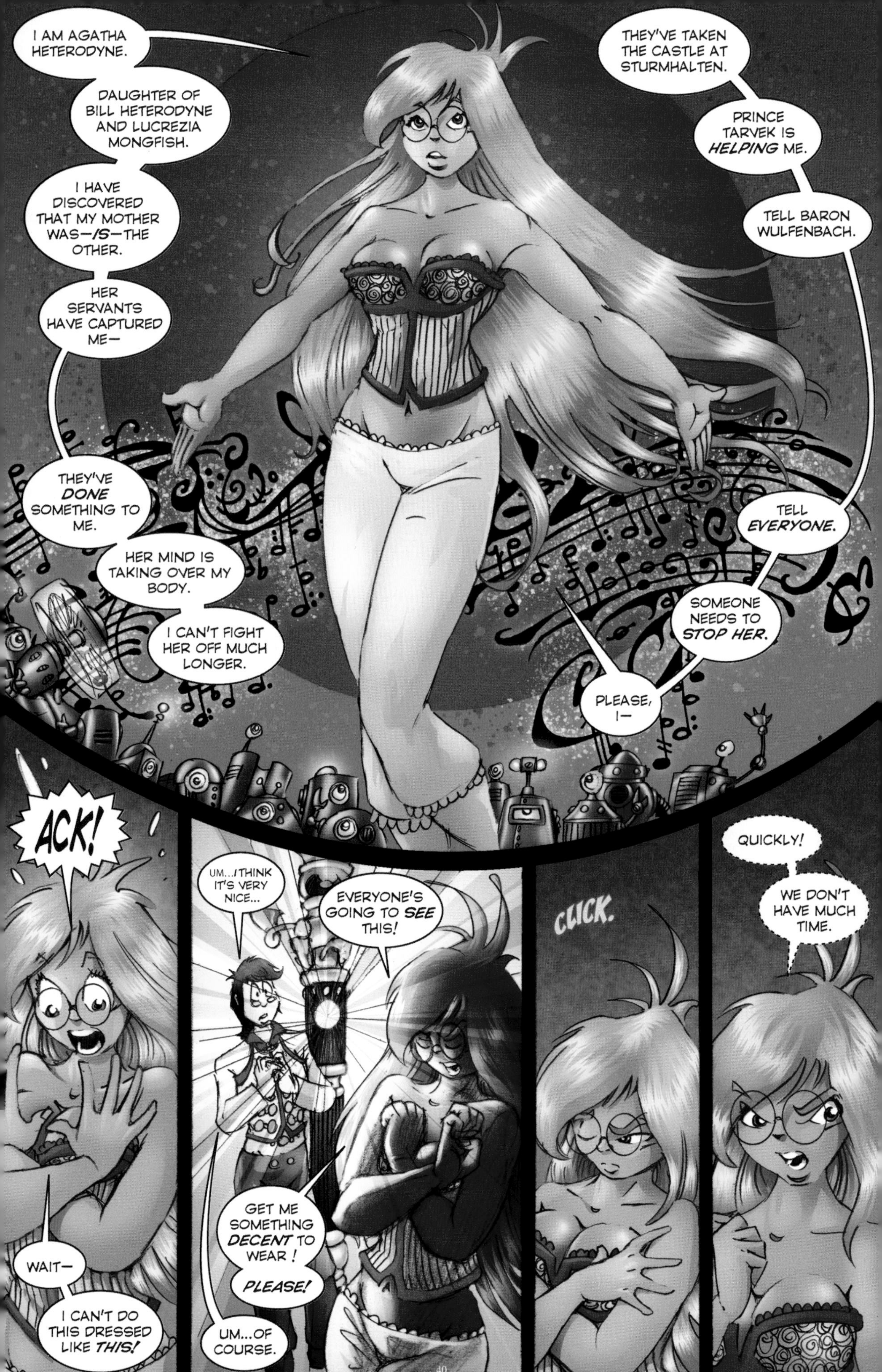

I AM AGATHA HETERODYNE.
DAUGHTER OF BILL HETERODYNE AND LUCREZIA MONGFISH.
I HAVE DISCOVERED THAT MY MOTHER WAS—*IS*—THE OTHER.
HER SERVANTS HAVE CAPTURED ME—
THEY'VE *DONE* SOMETHING TO ME.
HER MIND IS TAKING OVER MY BODY.
I CAN'T FIGHT HER OFF MUCH LONGER.
THEY'VE TAKEN THE CASTLE AT STURMHALTEN.
PRINCE TARVEK IS *HELPING* ME.
TELL BARON WULFENBACH.
TELL *EVERYONE.*
SOMEONE NEEDS TO *STOP HER.*
PLEASE, I—
ACK!
WAIT—
I CAN'T DO THIS DRESSED LIKE *THIS!*
UM...*I* THINK IT'S VERY NICE...
EVERYONE'S GOING TO *SEE* THIS!
GET ME SOMETHING *DECENT* TO WEAR !
PLEASE!
UM...OF COURSE.
CLICK.
QUICKLY!
WE DON'T HAVE MUCH TIME.

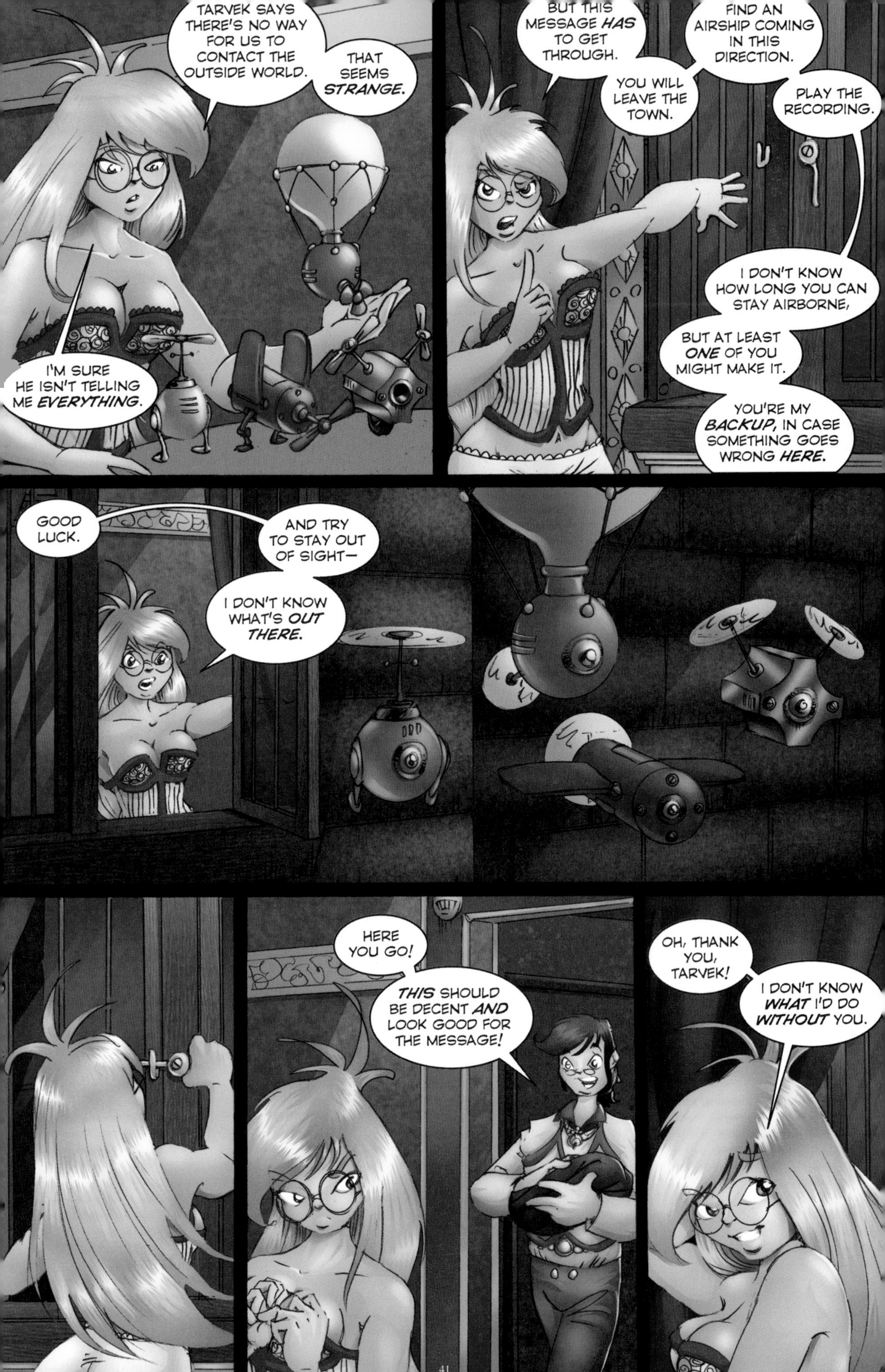
TARVEK SAYS THERE'S NO WAY FOR US TO CONTACT THE OUTSIDE WORLD.
THAT SEEMS *STRANGE.*
I'M SURE HE ISN'T TELLING ME *EVERYTHING.*
BUT THIS MESSAGE *HAS* TO GET THROUGH.
YOU WILL LEAVE THE TOWN.
FIND AN AIRSHIP COMING IN THIS DIRECTION.
PLAY THE RECORDING.
I DON'T KNOW HOW LONG YOU CAN STAY AIRBORNE,
BUT AT LEAST *ONE* OF YOU MIGHT MAKE IT.
YOU'RE MY *BACKUP,* IN CASE SOMETHING GOES WRONG *HERE.*
GOOD LUCK.
AND TRY TO STAY OUT OF SIGHT—
I DON'T KNOW WHAT'S *OUT THERE.*
HERE YOU GO!
THIS SHOULD BE DECENT *AND* LOOK GOOD FOR THE MESSAGE!
OH, THANK YOU, TARVEK!
I DON'T KNOW *WHAT* I'D DO *WITHOUT* YOU.

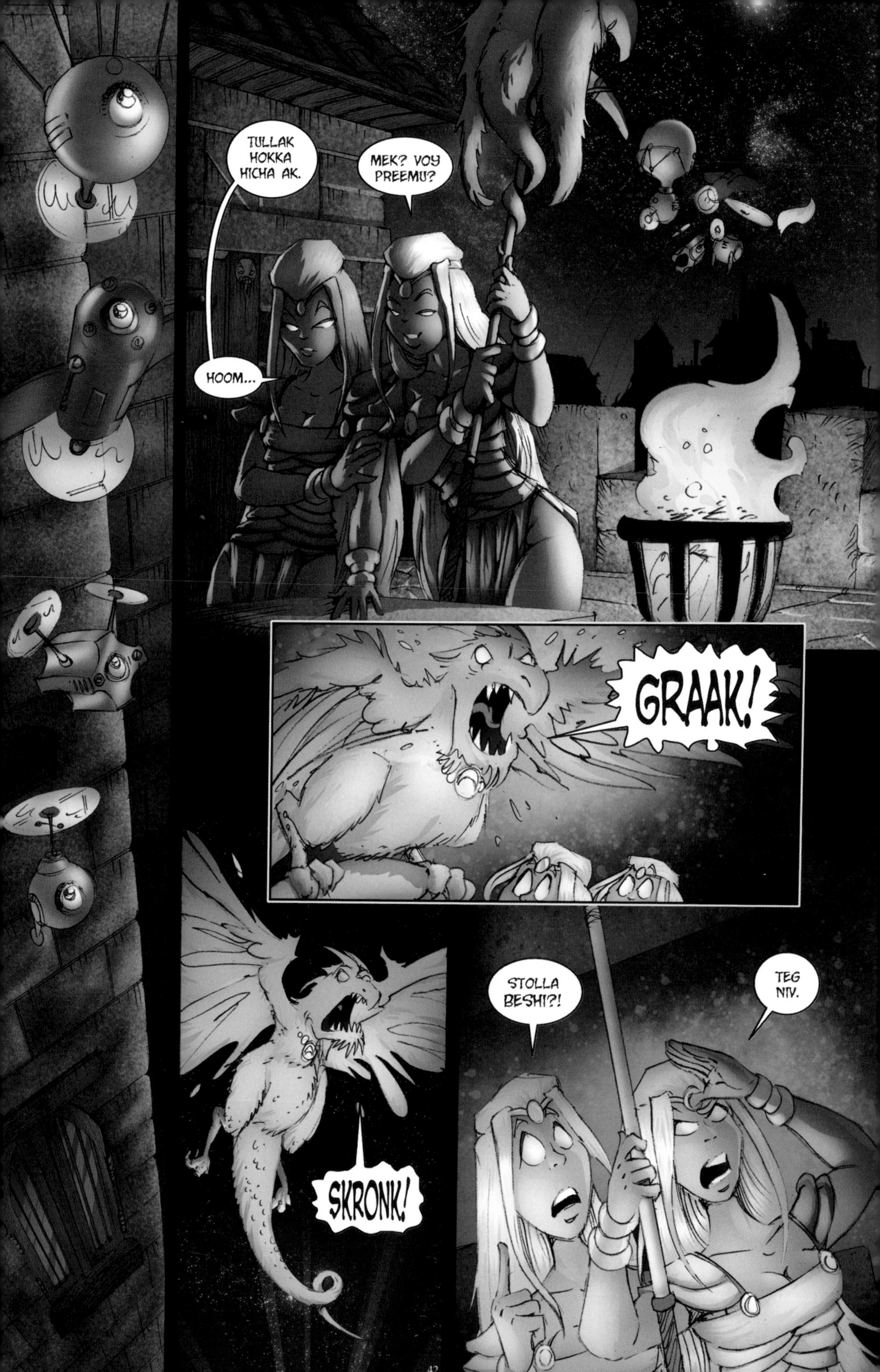
TULLAK HOKKA HICHA AK.
MEK? VOY PREEMU?
HOOM...
GRAAK!
SKRONK!
STOLLA BESHI?!
TEG NIV.

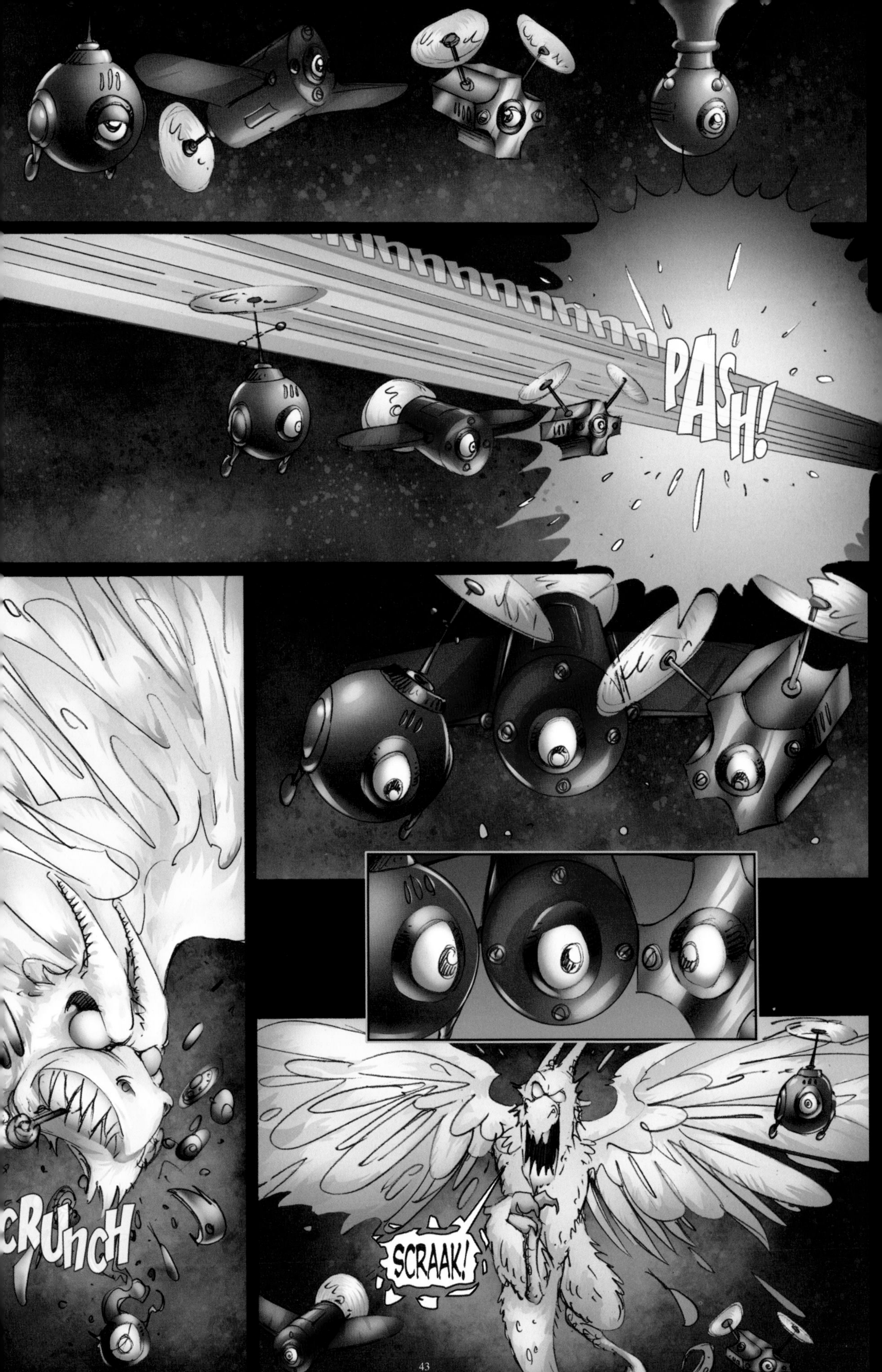

WHHHHHHHHHHHHHHHHH
PASH!
CRUNCH
SCRAAK!

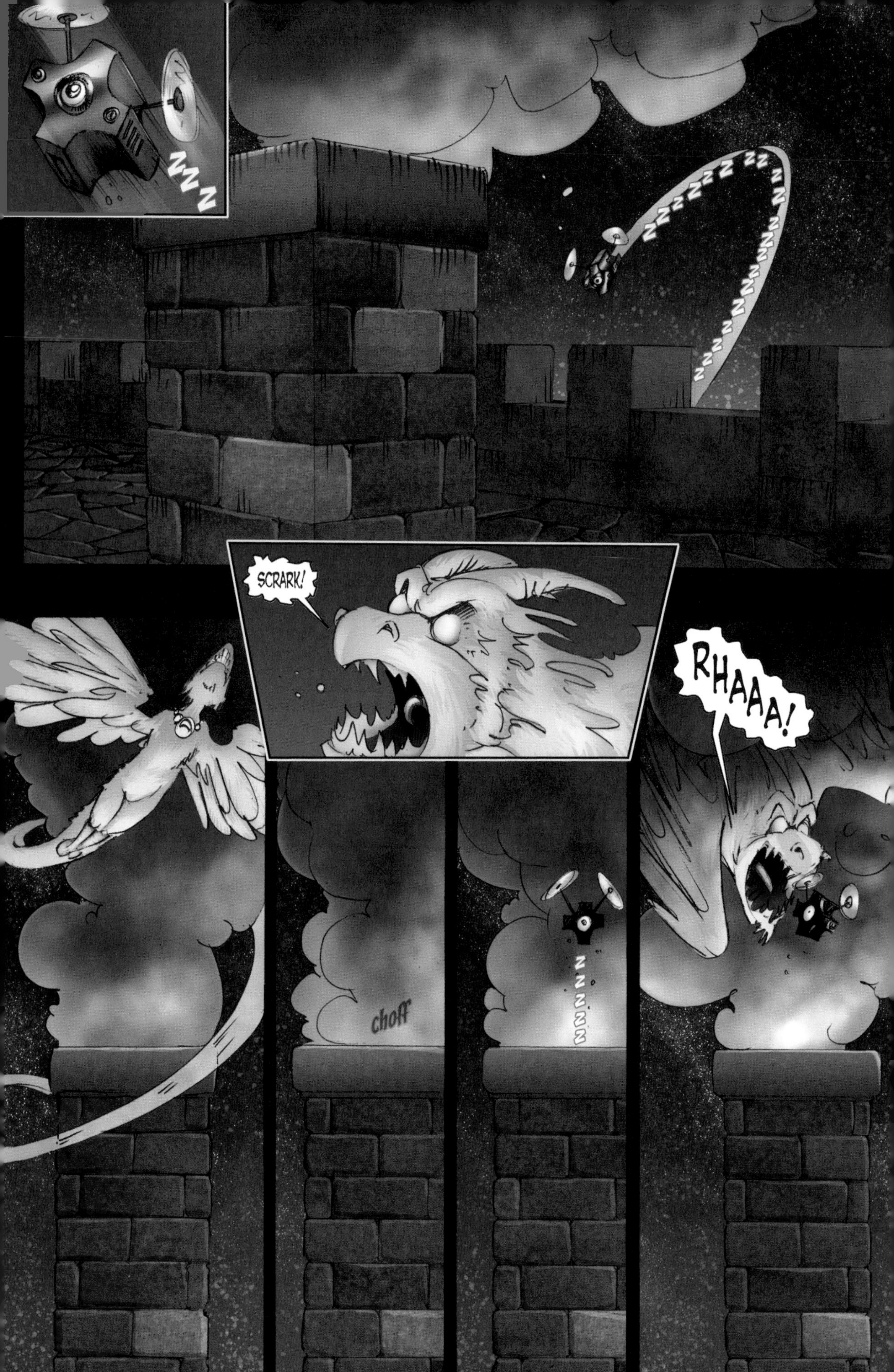
ZZZ
SCRARK!
RHAAAA!
choff
ZZZZZ

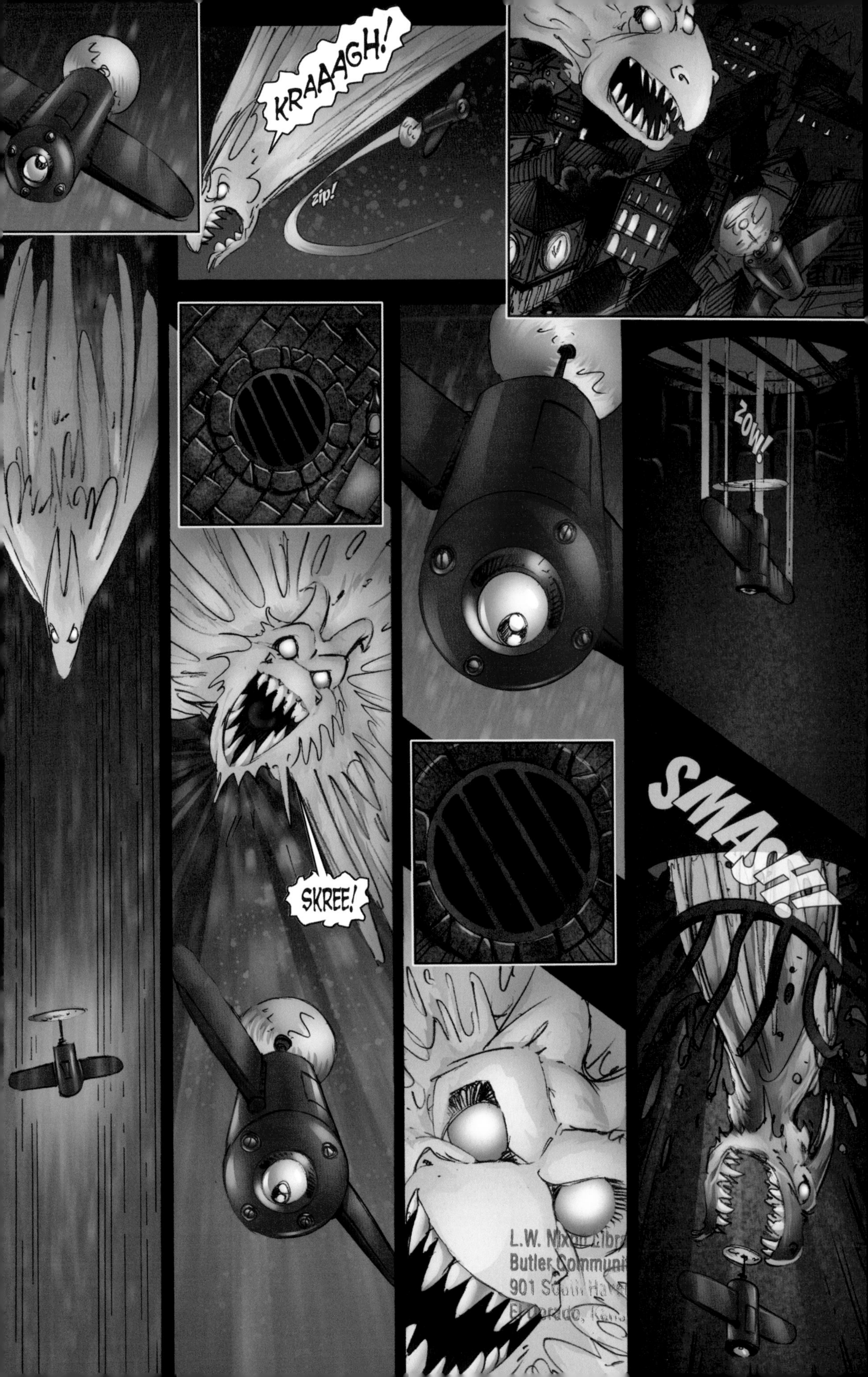
KRAAAGH!
zip!
ZOW!
SKREE!
SMASH!!

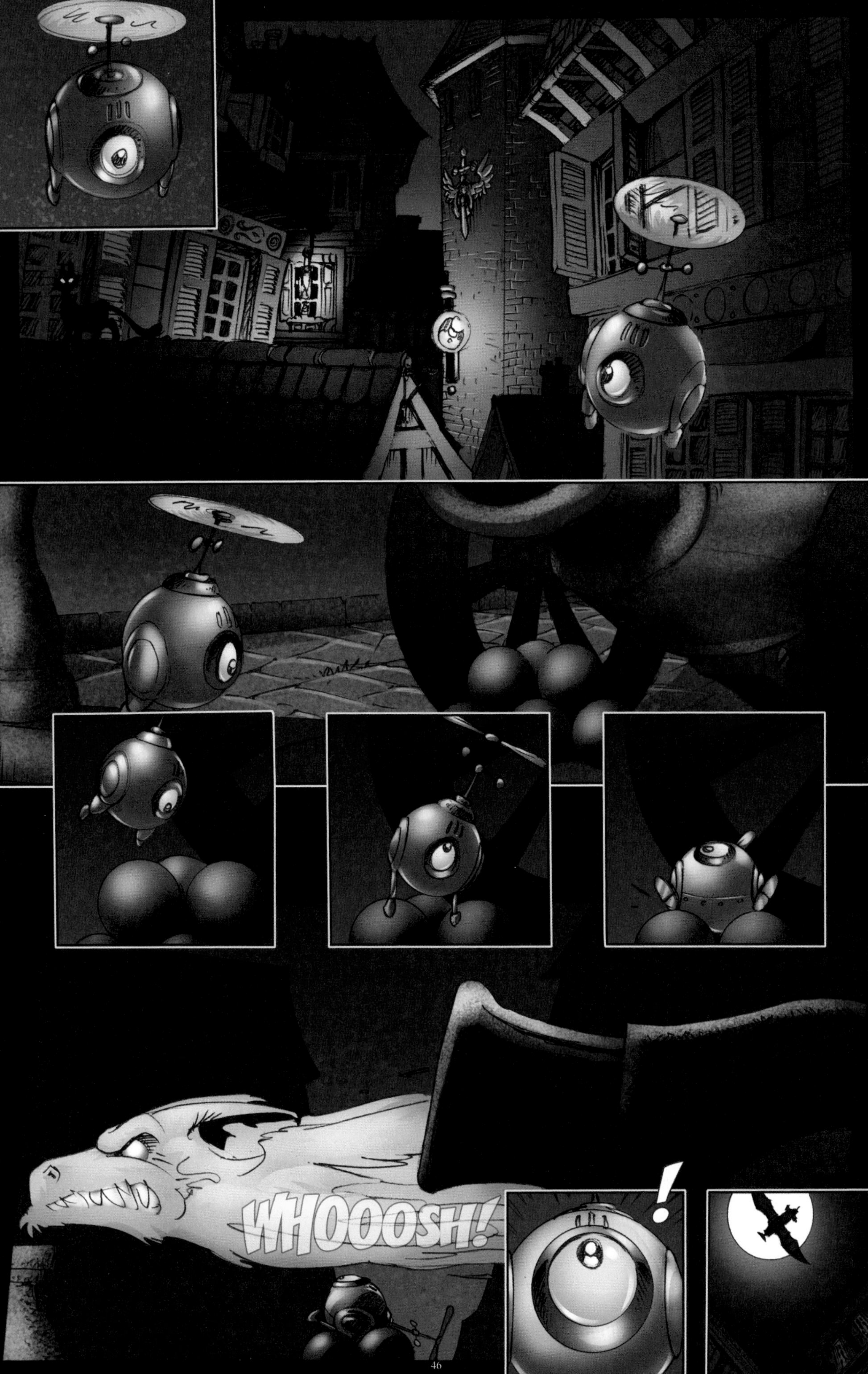
WHOOOSH!
!

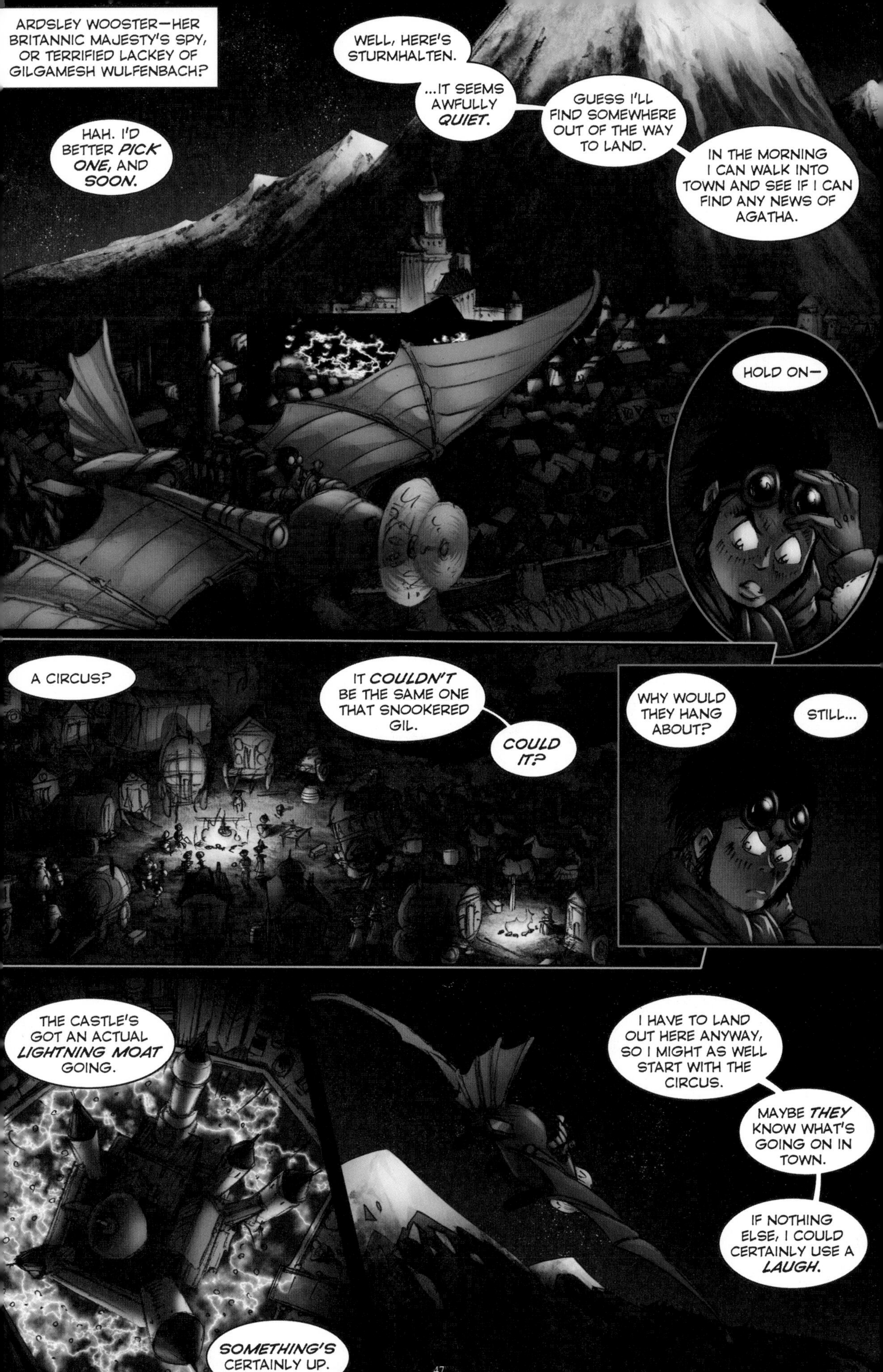

ARDSLEY WOOSTER—HER BRITANNIC MAJESTY'S SPY, OR TERRIFIED LACKEY OF GILGAMESH WULFENBACH?
HAH. I'D BETTER *PICK ONE,* AND *SOON.*
WELL, HERE'S STURMHALTEN.
...IT SEEMS AWFULLY *QUIET.*
GUESS I'LL FIND SOMEWHERE OUT OF THE WAY TO LAND.
IN THE MORNING I CAN WALK INTO TOWN AND SEE IF I CAN FIND ANY NEWS OF AGATHA.
HOLD ON—
A CIRCUS?
IT *COULDN'T* BE THE SAME ONE THAT SNOOKERED GIL.
COULD IT?
WHY WOULD THEY HANG ABOUT?
STILL...
THE CASTLE'S GOT AN ACTUAL *LIGHTNING MOAT* GOING.
SOMETHING'S CERTAINLY UP.
I HAVE TO LAND OUT HERE ANYWAY, SO I MIGHT AS WELL START WITH THE CIRCUS.
MAYBE *THEY* KNOW WHAT'S GOING ON IN TOWN.
IF NOTHING ELSE, I COULD CERTAINLY USE A *LAUGH.*

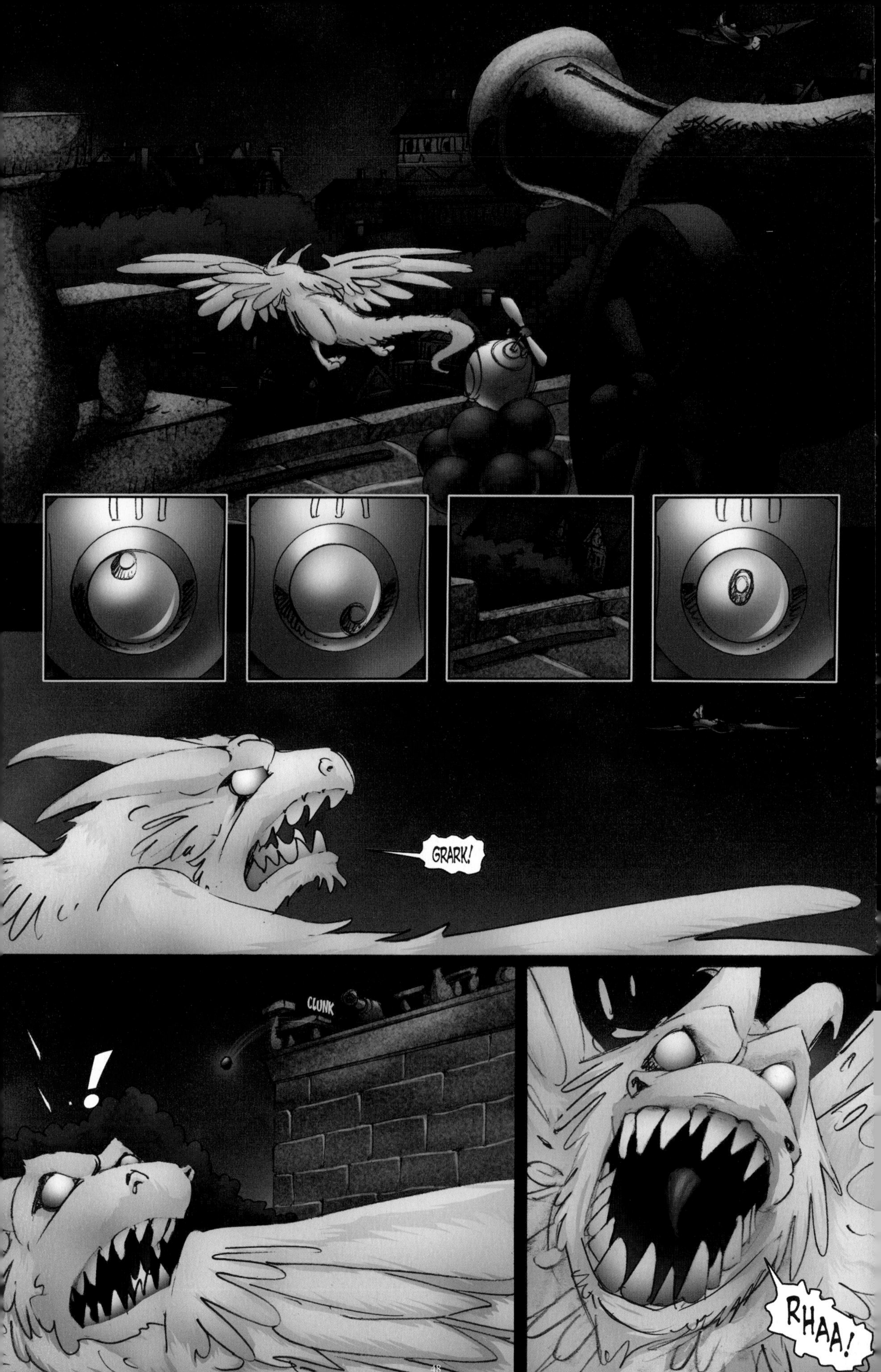
GRARK!
CLUNK
!
RHAA!

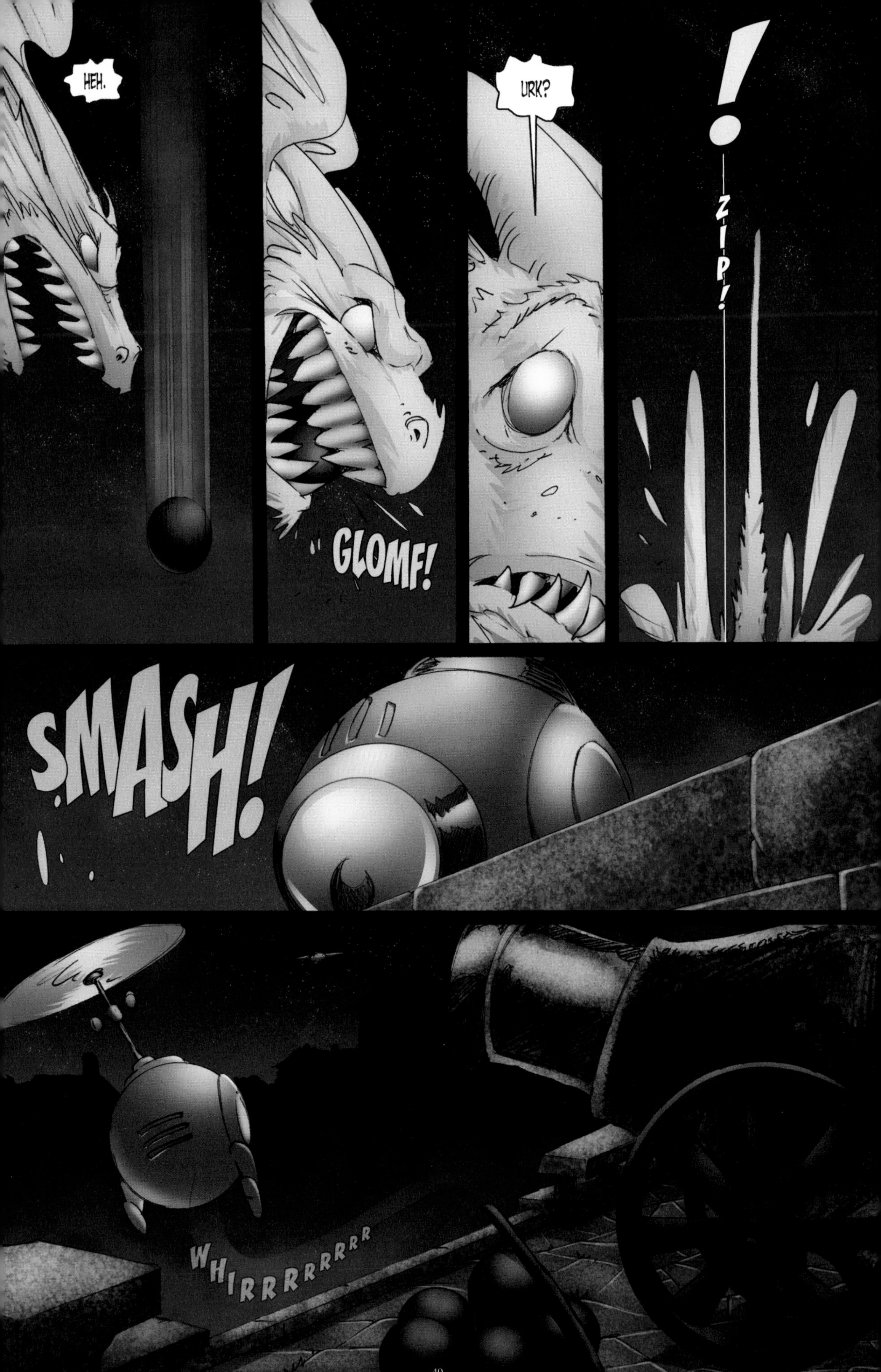
HEH.
GLOMF!
URK?
!
ZIP!
SMASH!
WHIRRRRRRRR

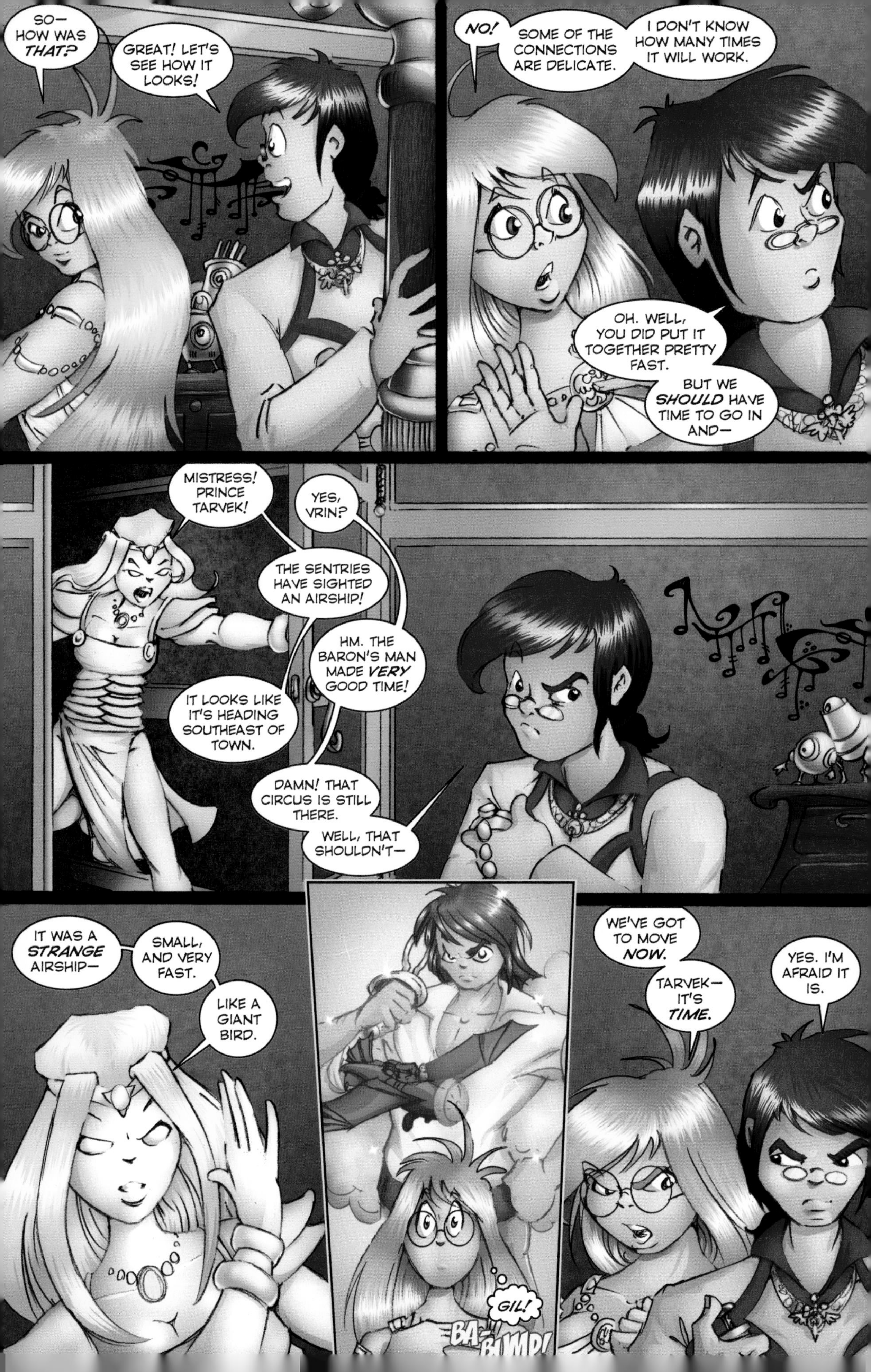

SO— HOW WAS *THAT?*
GREAT! LET'S SEE HOW IT LOOKS!
NO!
SOME OF THE CONNECTIONS ARE DELICATE.
I DON'T KNOW HOW MANY TIMES IT WILL WORK.
OH. WELL, YOU DID PUT IT TOGETHER PRETTY FAST.
BUT WE *SHOULD* HAVE TIME TO GO IN AND—
MISTRESS! PRINCE TARVEK!
YES, VRIN?
THE SENTRIES HAVE SIGHTED AN AIRSHIP!
HM. THE BARON'S MAN MADE *VERY* GOOD TIME!
IT LOOKS LIKE IT'S HEADING SOUTHEAST OF TOWN.
DAMN! THAT CIRCUS IS STILL THERE.
WELL, THAT SHOULDN'T—
IT WAS A *STRANGE* AIRSHIP—
SMALL, AND VERY FAST.
LIKE A GIANT BIRD.
GIL!
BA-BUMP!
WE'VE GOT TO MOVE *NOW.*
TARVEK— IT'S *TIME.*
YES. I'M AFRAID IT IS.

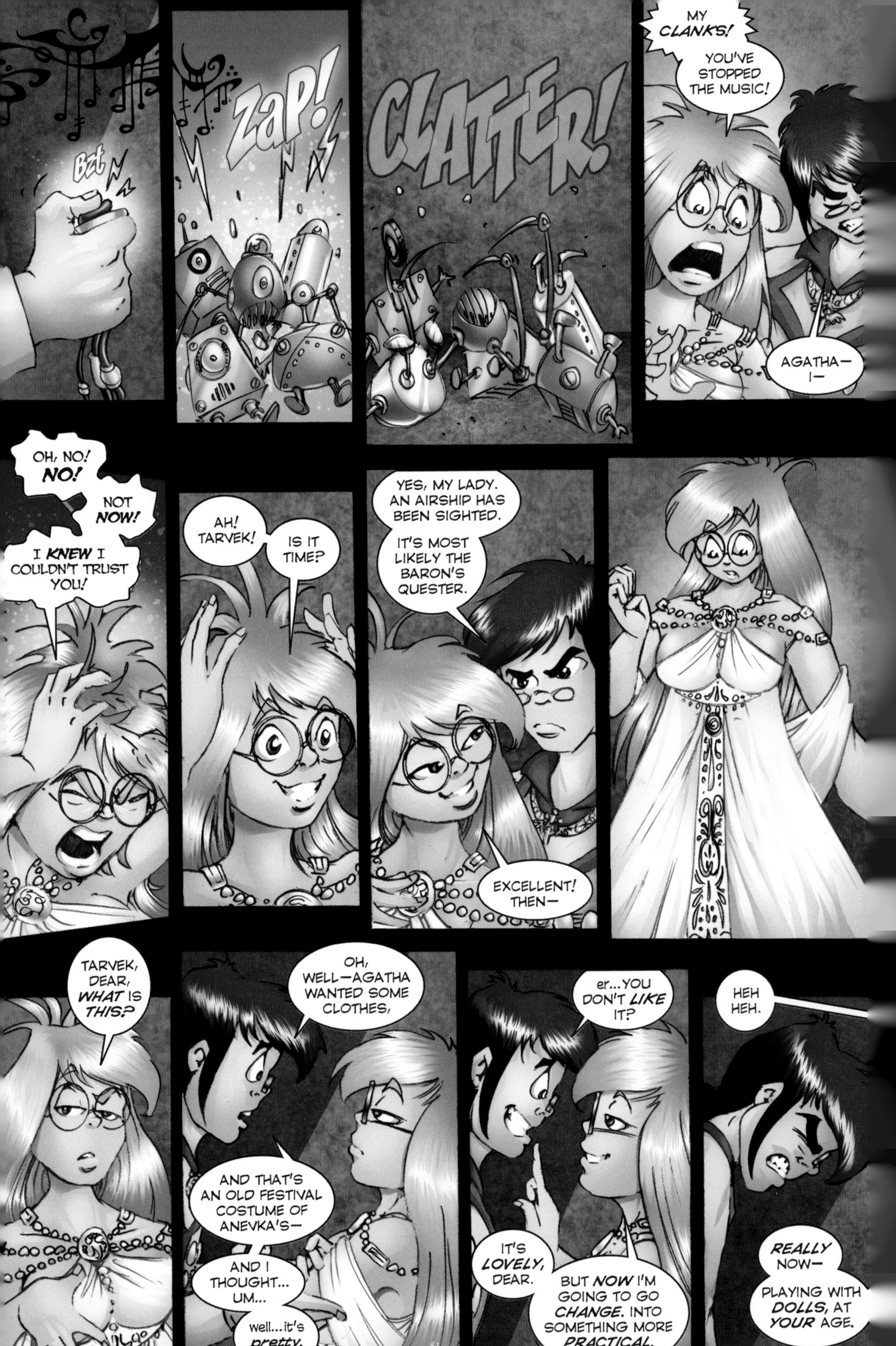

Bzt
ZAP!
CLATTER!
MY CLANKS!
YOU'VE STOPPED THE MUSIC!
AGATHA— I—
OH, NO! NO!
NOT NOW!
I KNEW I COULDN'T TRUST YOU!
AH! TARVEK!
IS IT TIME?
YES, MY LADY. AN AIRSHIP HAS BEEN SIGHTED.
IT'S MOST LIKELY THE BARON'S QUESTER.
EXCELLENT! THEN—
TARVEK, DEAR, WHAT IS THIS?
OH, WELL—AGATHA WANTED SOME CLOTHES,
AND THAT'S AN OLD FESTIVAL COSTUME OF ANEVKA'S—
AND I THOUGHT... UM...
well... it's pretty.
er... YOU DON'T LIKE IT?
IT'S LOVELY, DEAR.
BUT NOW I'M GOING TO GO CHANGE. INTO SOMETHING MORE PRACTICAL.
HEH HEH.
REALLY NOW—
PLAYING WITH DOLLS, AT YOUR AGE.

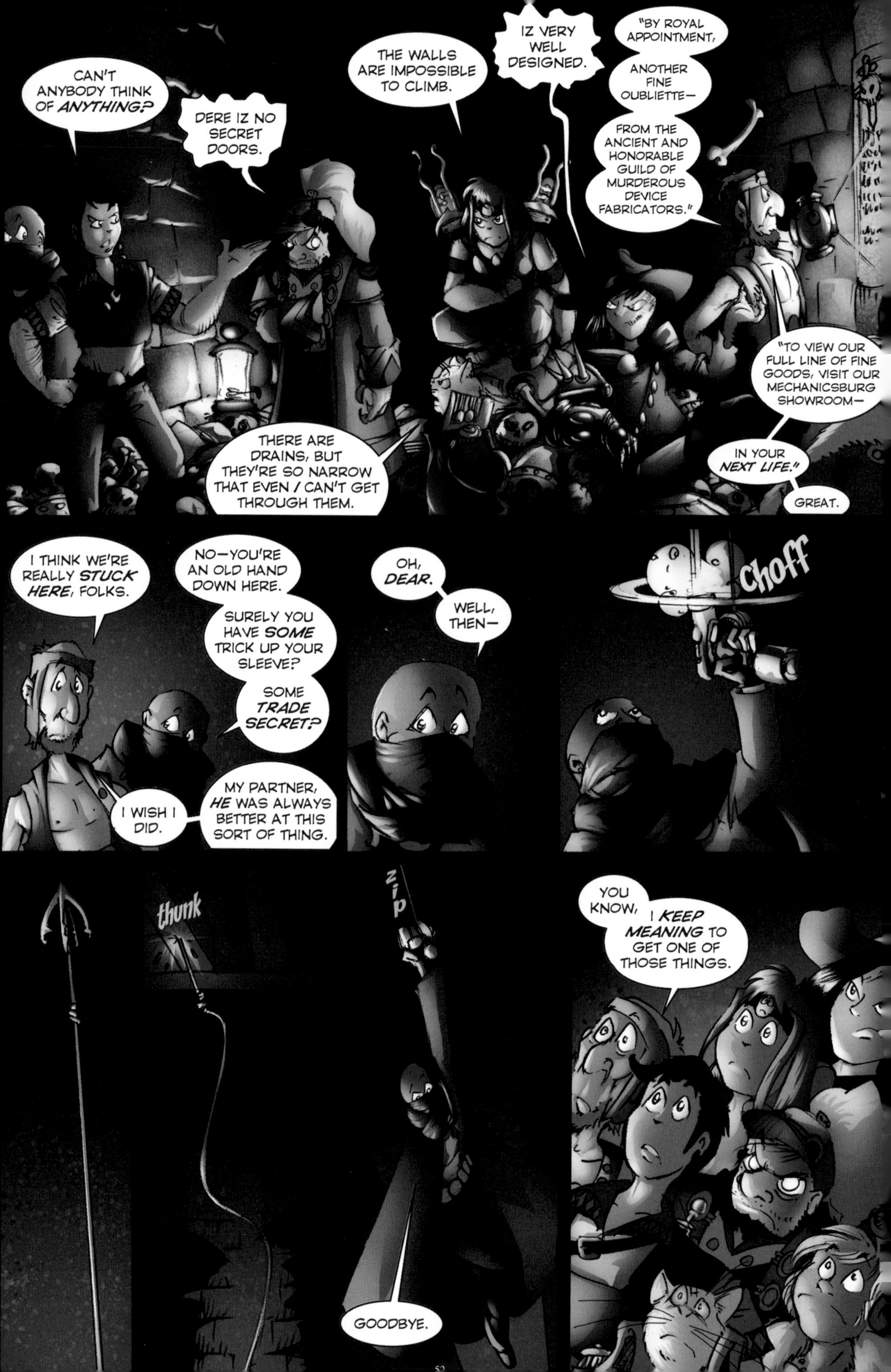
CAN'T ANYBODY THINK OF *ANYTHING?*
DERE IZ NO SECRET DOORS.
THE WALLS ARE IMPOSSIBLE TO CLIMB.
IZ VERY WELL DESIGNED.
"BY ROYAL APPOINTMENT,
ANOTHER FINE OUBLIETTE—
FROM THE ANCIENT AND HONORABLE GUILD OF MURDEROUS DEVICE FABRICATORS."
"TO VIEW OUR FULL LINE OF FINE GOODS, VISIT OUR MECHANICSBURG SHOWROOM—
IN YOUR *NEXT LIFE.*"
THERE ARE DRAINS, BUT THEY'RE SO NARROW THAT EVEN *I* CAN'T GET THROUGH THEM.
GREAT.
I THINK WE'RE REALLY *STUCK HERE*, FOLKS.
NO—YOU'RE AN OLD HAND DOWN HERE.
SURELY YOU HAVE *SOME* TRICK UP YOUR SLEEVE?
SOME *TRADE SECRET?*
I WISH I DID.
MY PARTNER, *HE* WAS ALWAYS BETTER AT THIS SORT OF THING.
OH, *DEAR.*
WELL, THEN—
CHOFF
THUNK
ZIP
GOODBYE.
YOU KNOW, I *KEEP MEANING* TO GET ONE OF THOSE THINGS.

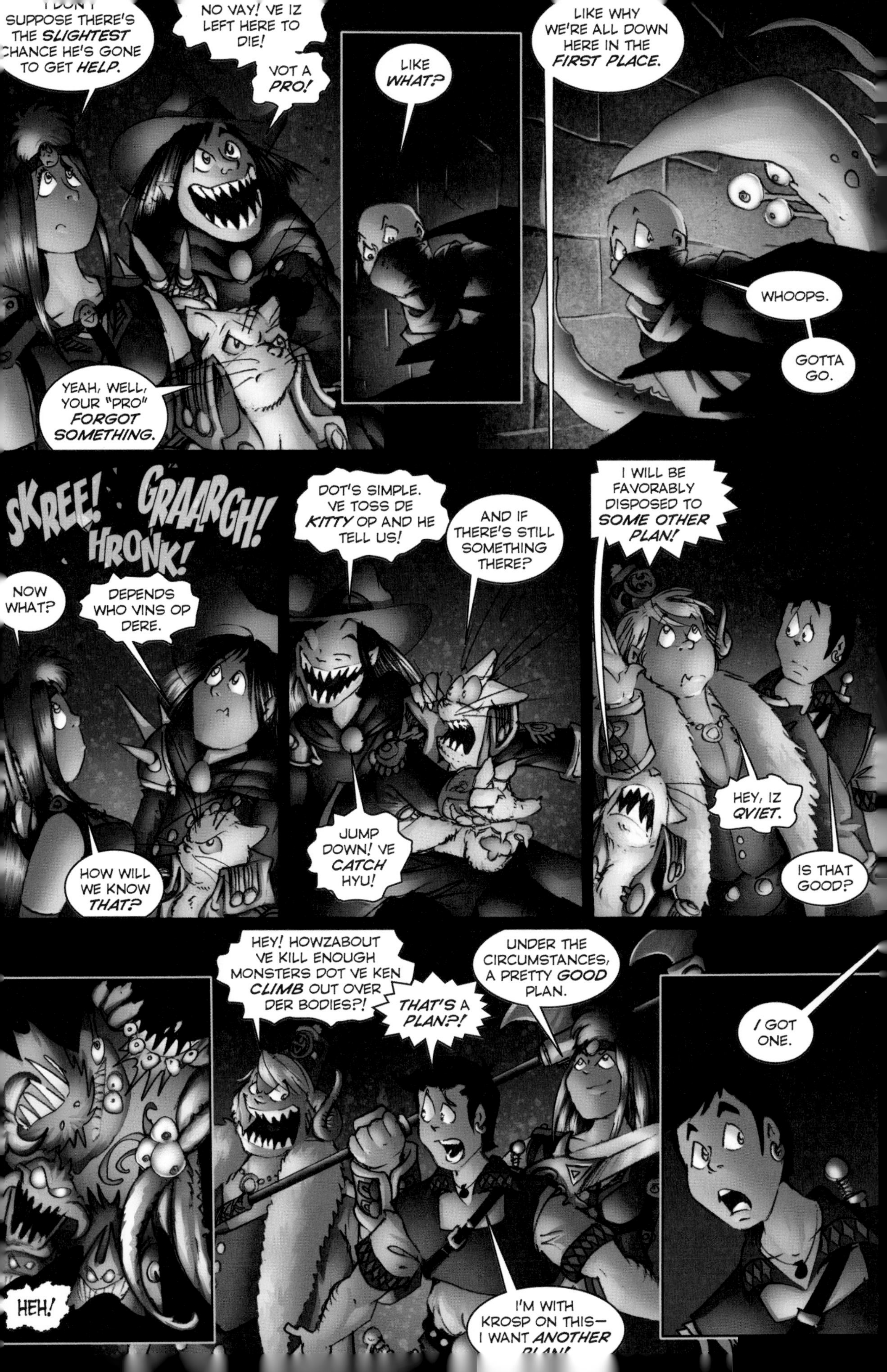

I DON'T SUPPOSE THERE'S THE SLIGHTEST CHANCE HE'S GONE TO GET HELP.
NO VAY! VE IZ LEFT HERE TO DIE!
VOT A PRO!
YEAH, WELL, YOUR "PRO" FORGOT SOMETHING.
LIKE WHAT?
LIKE WHY WE'RE ALL DOWN HERE IN THE FIRST PLACE.
WHOOPS.
GOTTA GO.
SKREE!
GRAARGH!
HRONK!
NOW WHAT?
DEPENDS WHO VINS OP DERE.
HOW WILL WE KNOW THAT?
DOT'S SIMPLE. VE TOSS DE KITTY OP AND HE TELL US!
AND IF THERE'S STILL SOMETHING THERE?
JUMP DOWN! VE CATCH HYU!
I WILL BE FAVORABLY DISPOSED TO SOME OTHER PLAN!
HEY, IZ QVIET.
IS THAT GOOD?
HEH!
HEY! HOWZABOUT VE KILL ENOUGH MONSTERS DOT VE KEN CLIMB OUT OVER DER BODIES?!
THAT'S A PLAN?!
UNDER THE CIRCUMSTANCES, A PRETTY GOOD PLAN.
I'M WITH KROSP ON THIS— I WANT ANOTHER PLAN!
I GOT ONE.

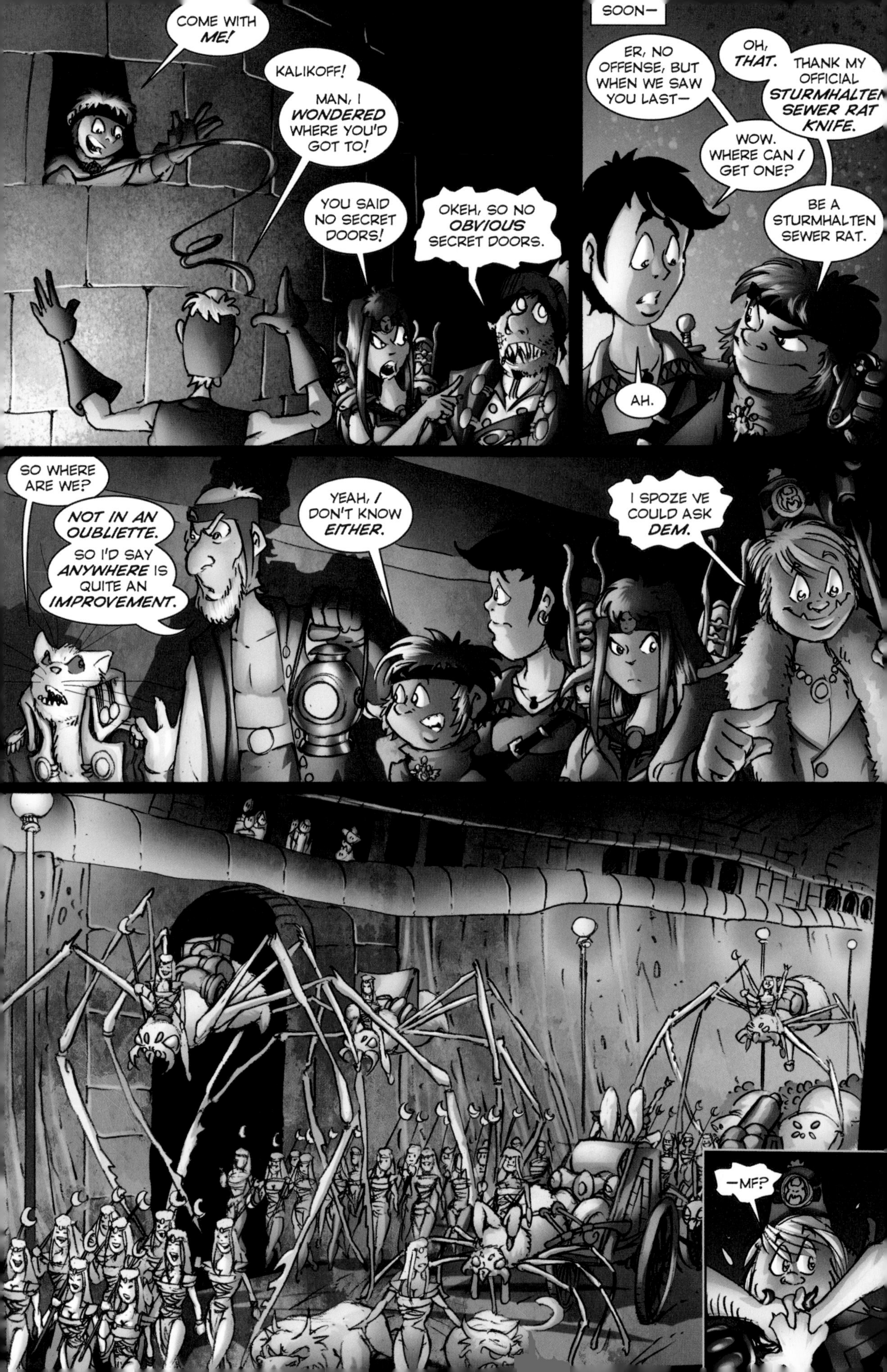
COME WITH ME!
KALIKOFF!
MAN, I WONDERED WHERE YOU'D GOT TO!
YOU SAID NO SECRET DOORS!
OKEH, SO NO OBVIOUS SECRET DOORS.
SOON—
ER, NO OFFENSE, BUT WHEN WE SAW YOU LAST—
OH, THAT.
THANK MY OFFICIAL STURMHALTEN SEWER RAT KNIFE.
WOW. WHERE CAN I GET ONE?
BE A STURMHALTEN SEWER RAT.
AH.
SO WHERE ARE WE?
NOT IN AN OUBLIETTE.
SO I'D SAY ANYWHERE IS QUITE AN IMPROVEMENT.
YEAH, I DON'T KNOW EITHER.
I SPOZE VE COULD ASK DEM.
—MF?

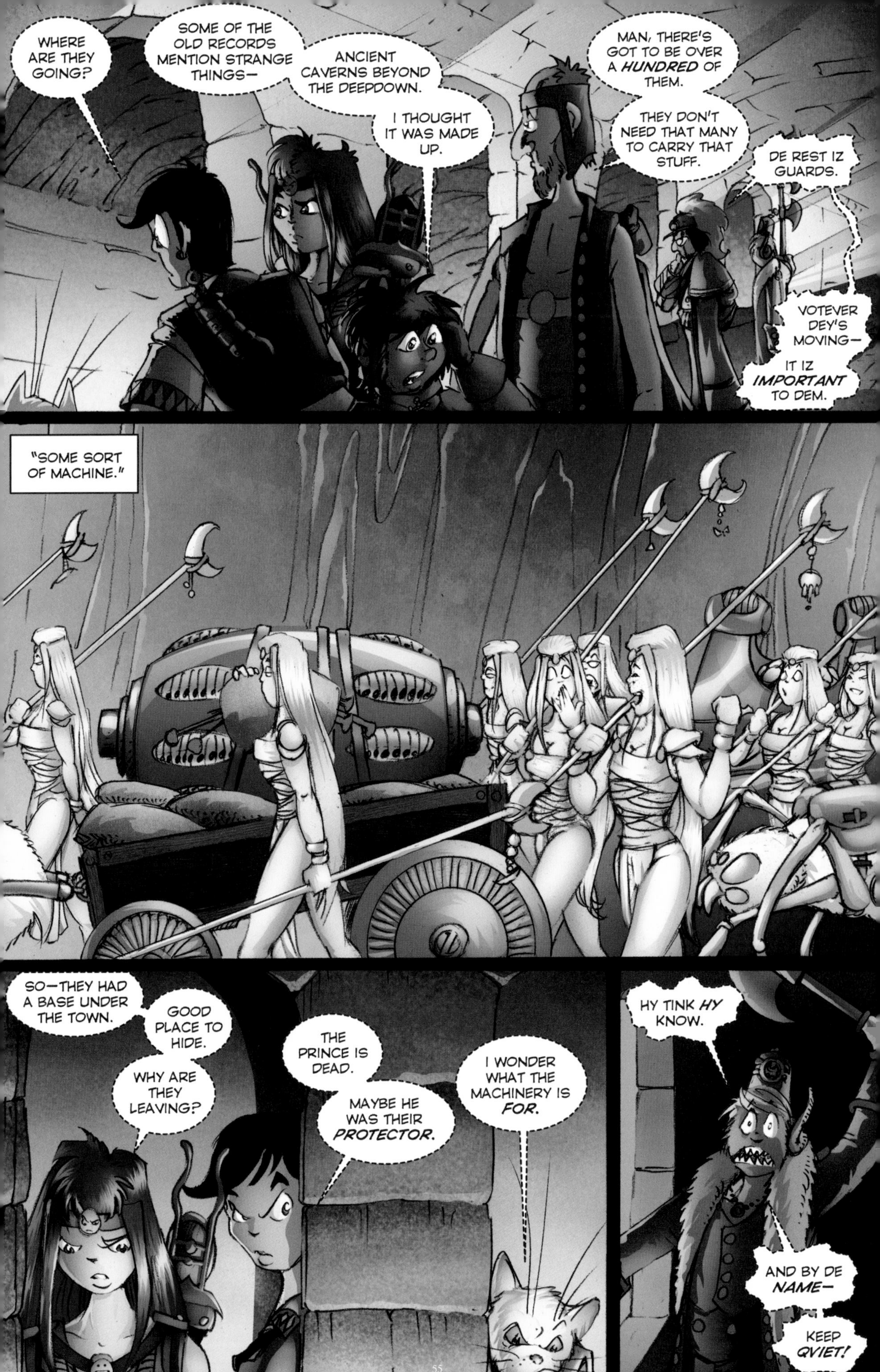
WHERE ARE THEY GOING?
SOME OF THE OLD RECORDS MENTION STRANGE THINGS—
ANCIENT CAVERNS BEYOND THE DEEPDOWN.
I THOUGHT IT WAS MADE UP.
MAN, THERE'S GOT TO BE OVER A *HUNDRED* OF THEM.
THEY DON'T NEED THAT MANY TO CARRY THAT STUFF.
DE REST IZ GUARDS.
VOTEVER DEY'S MOVING—
IT IZ *IMPORTANT* TO DEM.
"SOME SORT OF MACHINE."
SO—THEY HAD A BASE UNDER THE TOWN.
GOOD PLACE TO HIDE.
WHY ARE THEY LEAVING?
THE PRINCE IS DEAD.
MAYBE HE WAS THEIR *PROTECTOR*.
I WONDER WHAT THE MACHINERY IS *FOR*.
HY TINK *HY* KNOW.
AND BY DE *NAME*—
KEEP *QVIET!*

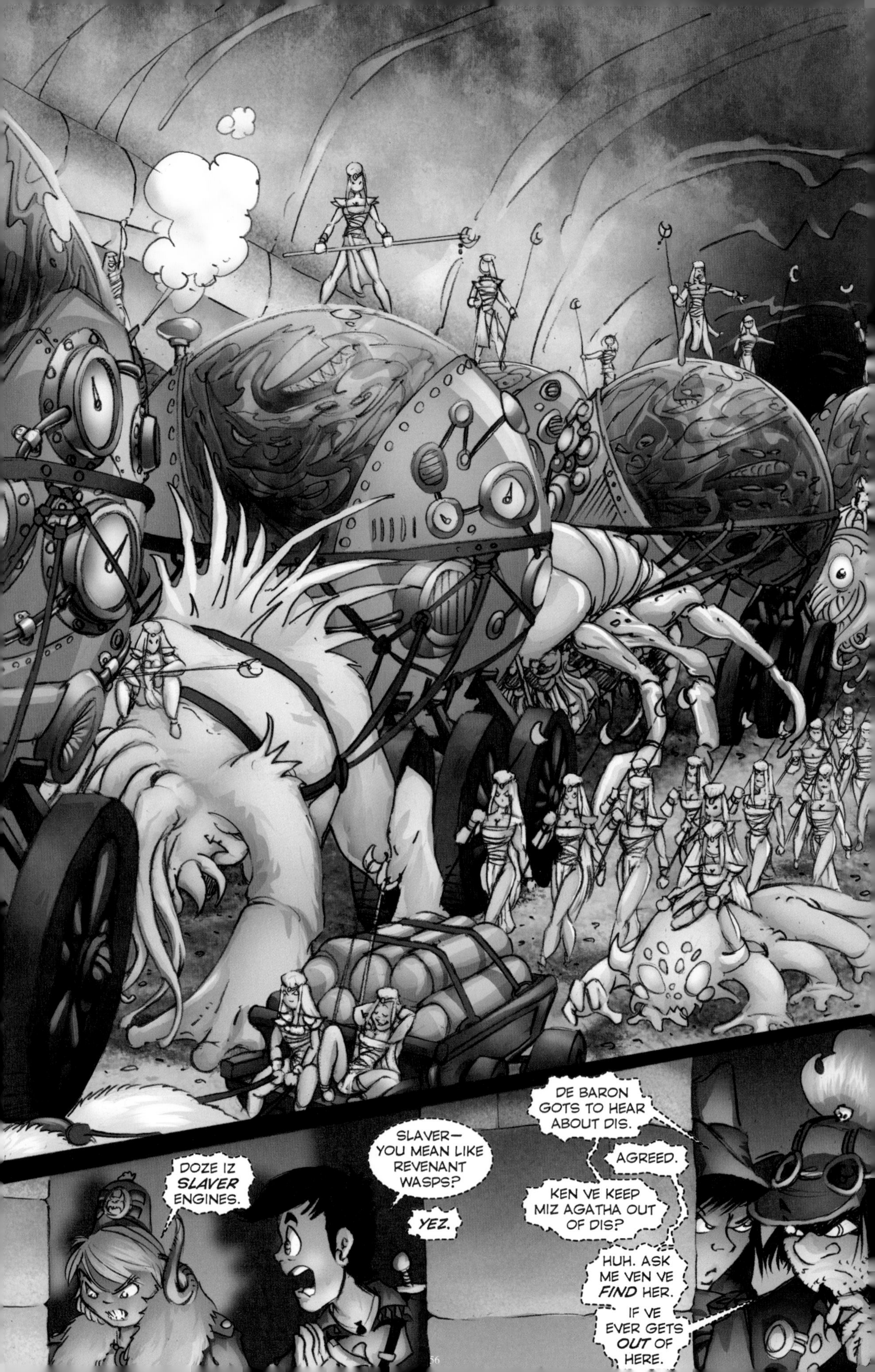

DOZE IZ SLAVER ENGINES.
SLAVER— YOU MEAN LIKE REVENANT WASPS?
YEZ.
DE BARON GOTS TO HEAR ABOUT DIS.
AGREED.
KEN VE KEEP MIZ AGATHA OUT OF DIS?
HUH. ASK ME VEN VE FIND HER.
IF VE EVER GETS OUT OF HERE.

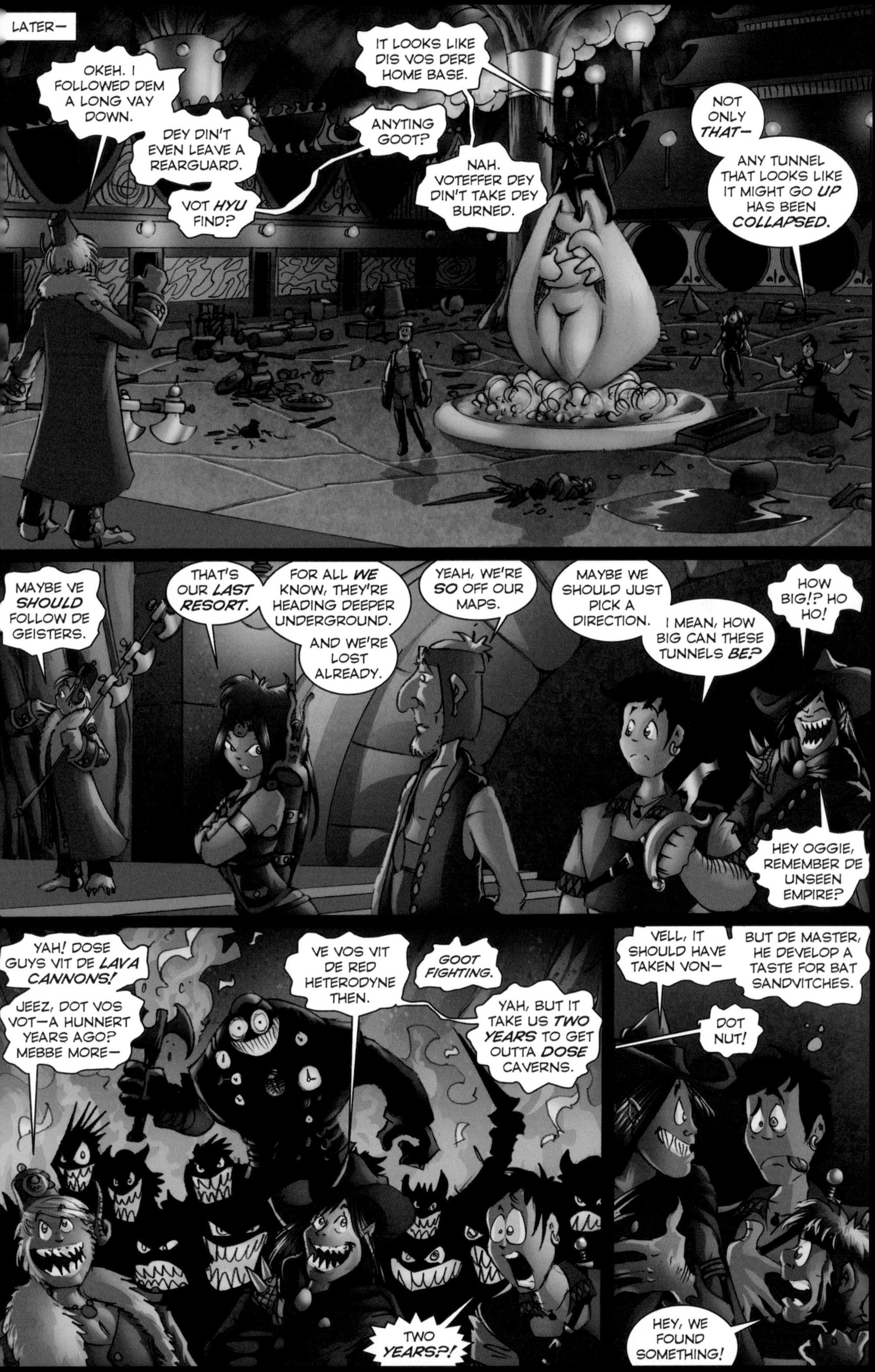
LATER—
OKEH. I FOLLOWED DEM A LONG VAY DOWN.
DEY DIN'T EVEN LEAVE A REARGUARD.
VOT *HYU* FIND?
ANYTING GOOT?
IT LOOKS LIKE DIS VOS DERE HOME BASE.
NAH. VOTEFFER DEY DIN'T TAKE DEY BURNED.
NOT ONLY *THAT*—
ANY TUNNEL THAT LOOKS LIKE IT MIGHT GO *UP* HAS BEEN *COLLAPSED*.
MAYBE VE *SHOULD* FOLLOW DE GEISTERS.
THAT'S OUR *LAST RESORT*.
FOR ALL *WE* KNOW, THEY'RE HEADING DEEPER UNDERGROUND.
AND WE'RE LOST ALREADY.
YEAH, WE'RE *SO* OFF OUR MAPS.
MAYBE WE SHOULD JUST PICK A DIRECTION.
I MEAN, HOW BIG CAN THESE TUNNELS *BE?*
HOW BIG*!?* HO HO*!*
HEY OGGIE, REMEMBER DE UNSEEN EMPIRE?
YAH*!* DOSE GUYS VIT DE *LAVA CANNONS!*
JEEZ, DOT VOS VOT—A HUNNERT YEARS AGO? MEBBE MORE—
VE VOS VIT DE RED HETERODYNE THEN.
GOOT FIGHTING.
YAH, BUT IT TAKE US *TWO YEARS* TO GET OUTTA *DOSE* CAVERNS.
TWO *YEARS?!*
VELL, IT SHOULD HAVE TAKEN VON—
BUT DE MASTER, HE DEVELOP A TASTE FOR BAT SANDVITCHES.
DOT NUT*!*
HEY, WE FOUND SOMETHING*!*

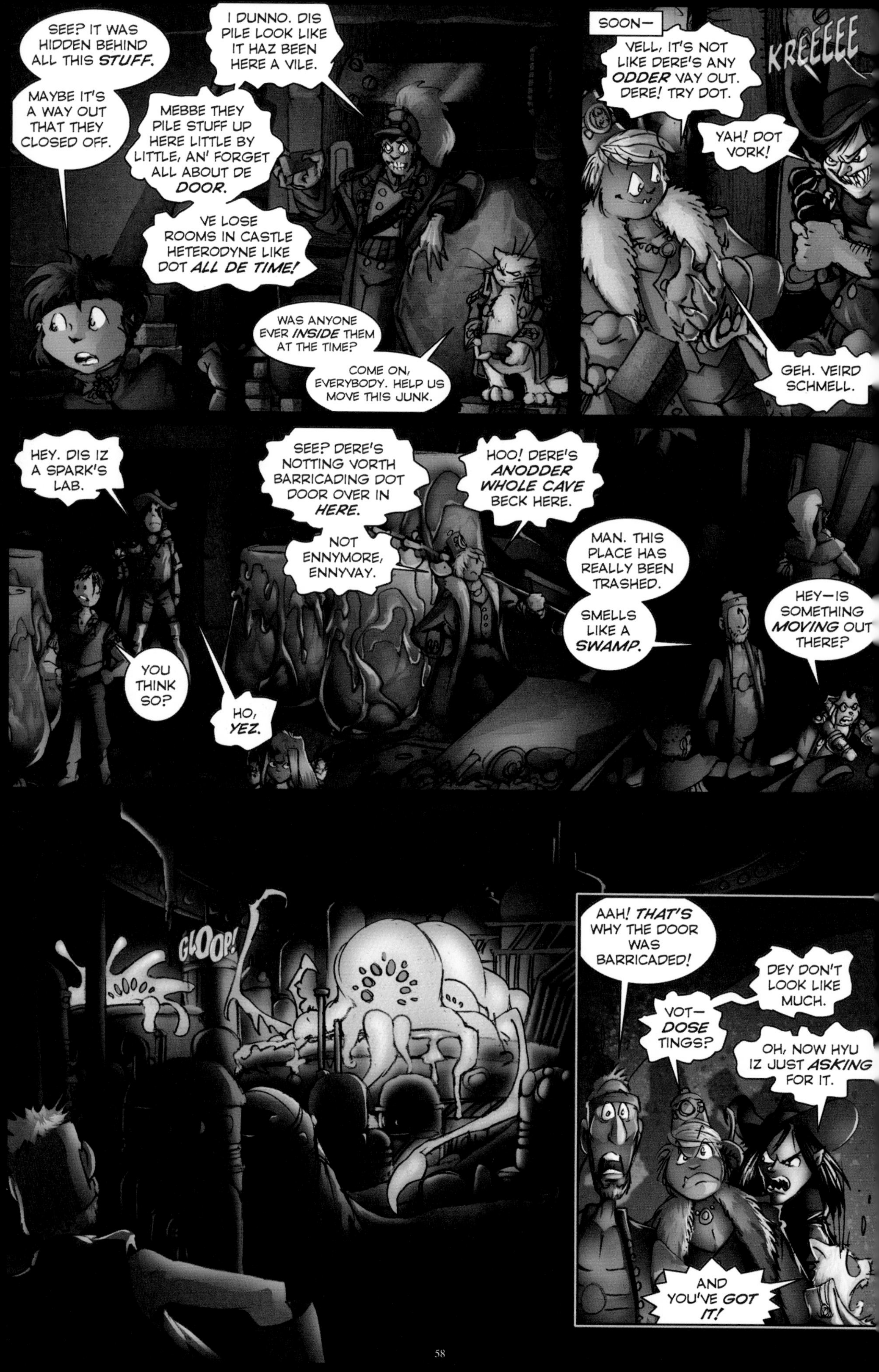

SEE? IT WAS HIDDEN BEHIND ALL THIS STUFF.
MAYBE IT'S A WAY OUT THAT THEY CLOSED OFF.
I DUNNO. DIS PILE LOOK LIKE IT HAZ BEEN HERE A VILE.
MEBBE THEY PILE STUFF UP HERE LITTLE BY LITTLE, AN' FORGET ALL ABOUT DE DOOR.
VE LOSE ROOMS IN CASTLE HETERODYNE LIKE DOT ALL DE TIME!
WAS ANYONE EVER INSIDE THEM AT THE TIME?
COME ON, EVERYBODY. HELP US MOVE THIS JUNK.
SOON—
VELL, IT'S NOT LIKE DERE'S ANY ODDER VAY OUT. DERE! TRY DOT.
KREEEEE
YAH! DOT VORK!
GEH. VEIRD SCHMELL.
HEY. DIS IZ A SPARK'S LAB.
YOU THINK SO?
HO, YEZ.
SEE? DERE'S NOTTING VORTH BARRICADING DOT DOOR OVER IN HERE.
NOT ENNYMORE, ENNYVAY.
HOO! DERE'S ANODDER WHOLE CAVE BECK HERE.
MAN. THIS PLACE HAS REALLY BEEN TRASHED.
SMELLS LIKE A SWAMP.
HEY—IS SOMETHING MOVING OUT THERE?
GLOOP!
AAH! THAT'S WHY THE DOOR WAS BARRICADED!
VOT—DOSE TINGS?
DEY DON'T LOOK LIKE MUCH.
OH, NOW HYU IZ JUST ASKING FOR IT.
AND YOU'VE GOT IT!

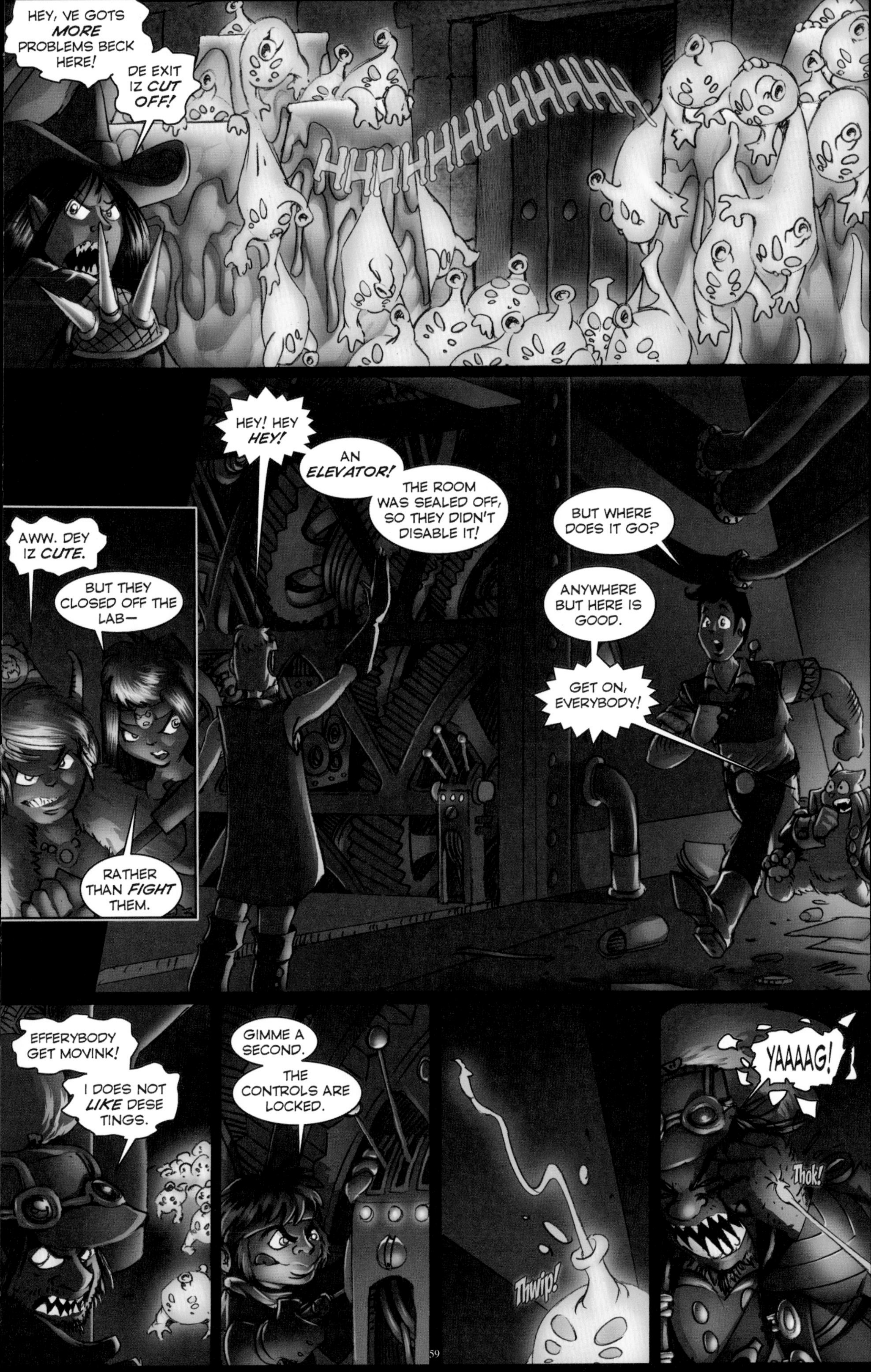

HEY, VE GOTS MORE PROBLEMS BECK HERE!
DE EXIT IZ CUT OFF!
HHHHHHHHHHHHHHHHH
HEY! HEY HEY!
AN ELEVATOR!
THE ROOM WAS SEALED OFF, SO THEY DIDN'T DISABLE IT!
AWW. DEY IZ CUTE.
BUT THEY CLOSED OFF THE LAB—
RATHER THAN FIGHT THEM.
BUT WHERE DOES IT GO?
ANYWHERE BUT HERE IS GOOD.
GET ON, EVERYBODY!
EFFERYBODY GET MOVINK!
I DOES NOT LIKE DESE TINGS.
GIMME A SECOND.
THE CONTROLS ARE LOCKED.
Thwip!
YAAAAG!
Thok!

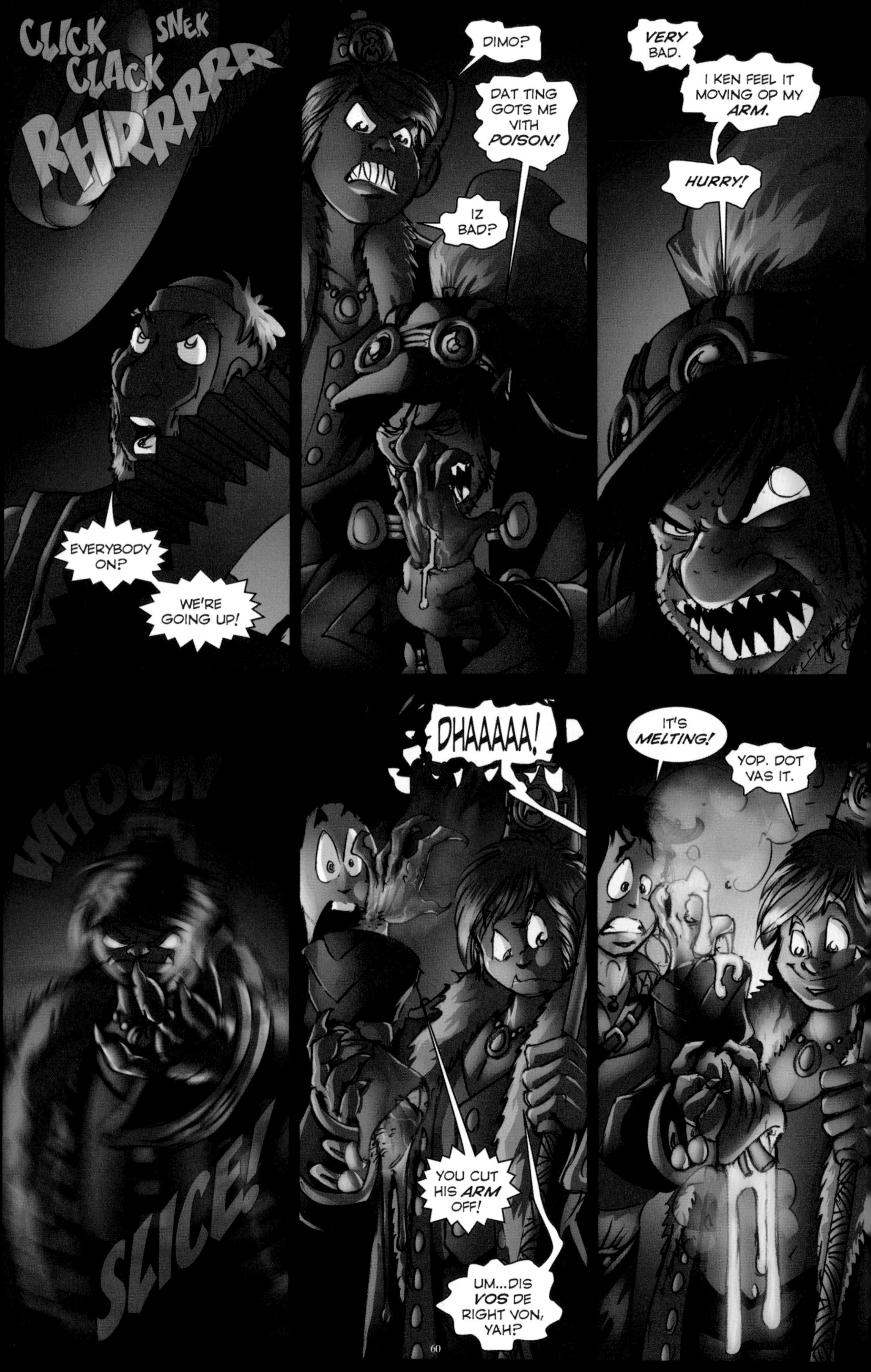
CLICK
CLACK
SNEK
RHRRRRR
EVERYBODY ON?
WE'RE GOING UP!
DIMO?
DAT TING GOTS ME VITH POISON!
IZ BAD?
VERY BAD.
I KEN FEEL IT MOVING OP MY ARM.
HURRY!
WHOOM
SLICE!
DHAAAAA!
YOU CUT HIS ARM OFF!
UM...DIS VOS DE RIGHT VON, YAH?
IT'S MELTING!
YOP. DOT VAS IT.

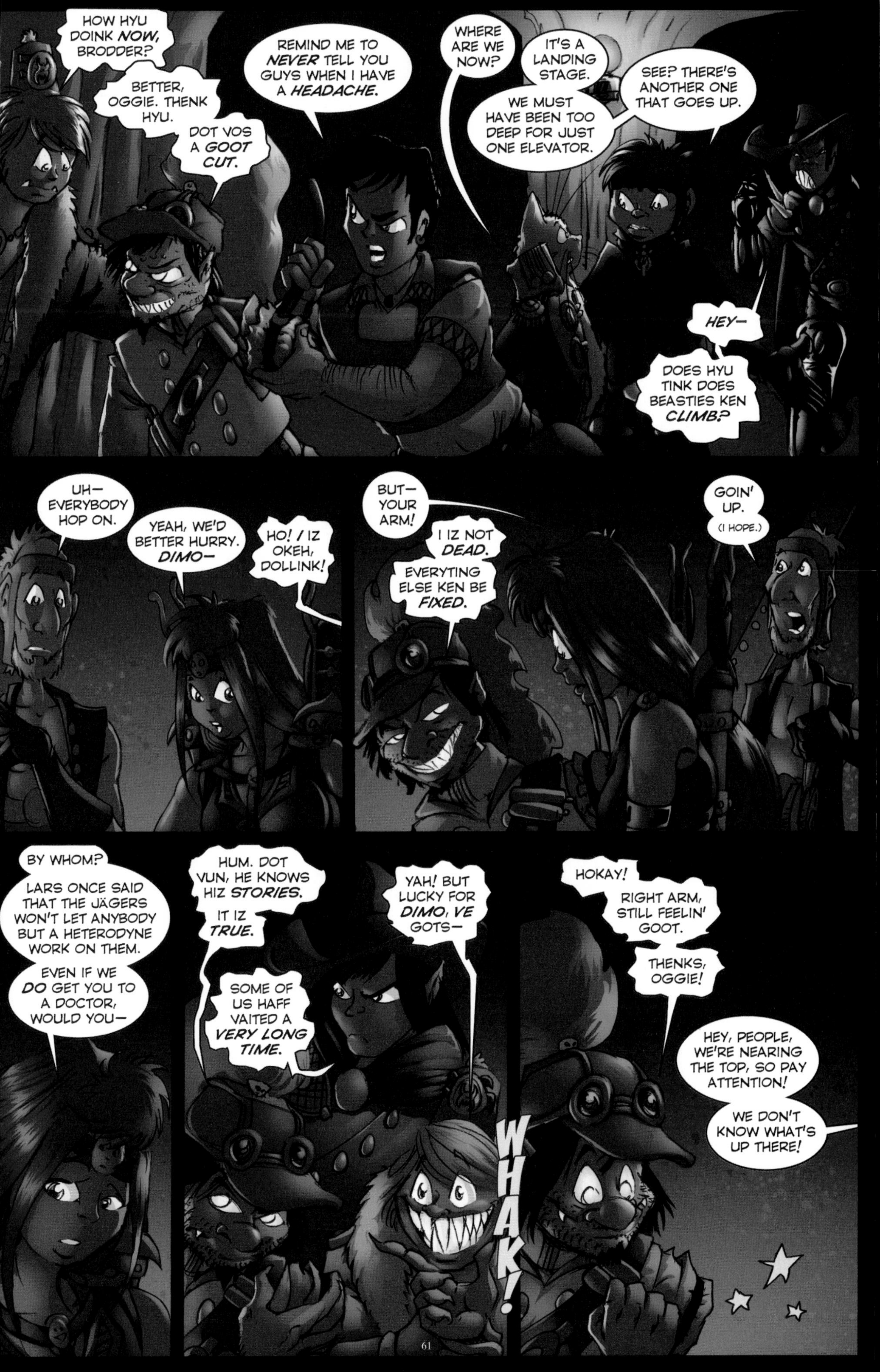

HOW HYU DOINK NOW, BRODDER?
BETTER, OGGIE. THENK HYU.
DOT VOS A GOOT CUT.
REMIND ME TO NEVER TELL YOU GUYS WHEN I HAVE A HEADACHE.
WHERE ARE WE NOW?
IT'S A LANDING STAGE.
WE MUST HAVE BEEN TOO DEEP FOR JUST ONE ELEVATOR.
SEE? THERE'S ANOTHER ONE THAT GOES UP.
HEY—
DOES HYU TINK DOES BEASTIES KEN CLIMB?
UH— EVERYBODY HOP ON.
YEAH, WE'D BETTER HURRY. DIMO—
HO! / IZ OKEH, DOLLINK!
BUT— YOUR ARM!
I IZ NOT DEAD.
EVERYTING ELSE KEN BE FIXED.
GOIN' UP.
(I HOPE.)
BY WHOM?
LARS ONCE SAID THAT THE JÄGERS WON'T LET ANYBODY BUT A HETERODYNE WORK ON THEM.
EVEN IF WE DO GET YOU TO A DOCTOR, WOULD YOU—
HUM. DOT VUN, HE KNOWS HIZ STORIES.
IT IZ TRUE.
SOME OF US HAFF VAITED A VERY LONG TIME.
YAH! BUT LUCKY FOR DIMO, VE GOTS—
WHAK!
HOKAY!
RIGHT ARM, STILL FEELIN' GOOT.
THENKS, OGGIE!
HEY, PEOPLE, WE'RE NEARING THE TOP, SO PAY ATTENTION!
WE DON'T KNOW WHAT'S UP THERE!

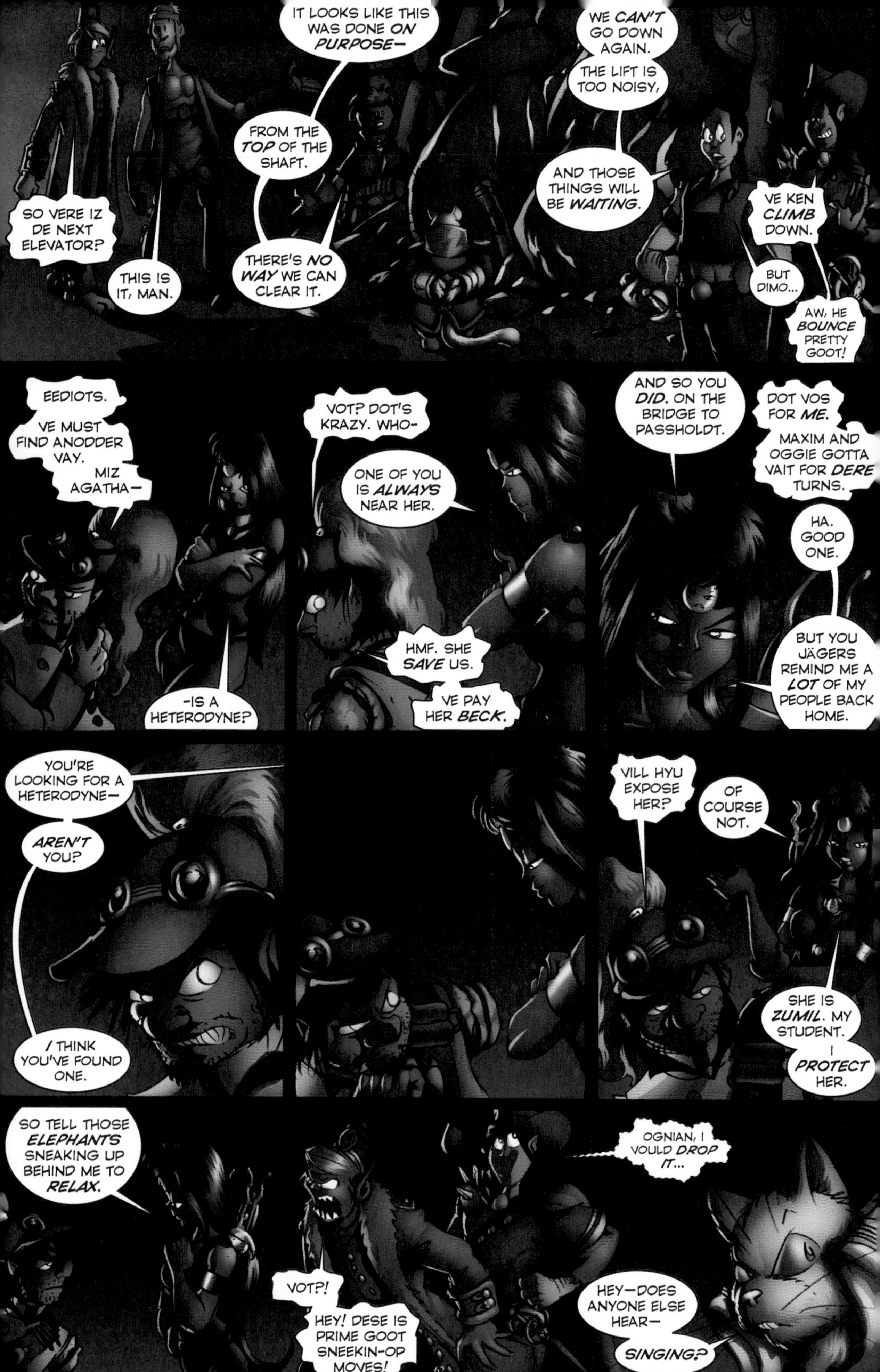
SO VERE IZ DE NEXT ELEVATOR?
THIS IS IT, MAN.
IT LOOKS LIKE THIS WAS DONE ON PURPOSE—
FROM THE TOP OF THE SHAFT.
THERE'S NO WAY WE CAN CLEAR IT.
WE CAN'T GO DOWN AGAIN.
THE LIFT IS TOO NOISY,
AND THOSE THINGS WILL BE WAITING.
VE KEN CLIMB DOWN.
BUT DIMO...
AW, HE BOUNCE PRETTY GOOT!
EEDIOTS.
VE MUST FIND ANODDER VAY.
MIZ AGATHA—
-IS A HETERODYNE?
VOT? DOT'S KRAZY. WHO-
ONE OF YOU IS ALWAYS NEAR HER.
HMF. SHE SAVE US.
VE PAY HER BECK.
AND SO YOU DID. ON THE BRIDGE TO PASSHOLDT.
DOT VOS FOR ME.
MAXIM AND OGGIE GOTTA VAIT FOR DERE TURNS.
HA. GOOD ONE.
BUT YOU JÄGERS REMIND ME A LOT OF MY PEOPLE BACK HOME.
YOU'RE LOOKING FOR A HETERODYNE—
AREN'T YOU?
I THINK YOU'VE FOUND ONE.
VILL HYU EXPOSE HER?
OF COURSE NOT.
SHE IS ZUMIL. MY STUDENT.
I PROTECT HER.
SO TELL THOSE ELEPHANTS SNEAKING UP BEHIND ME TO RELAX.
VOT?!
HEY! DESE IS PRIME GOOT SNEEKIN-OP MOVES!
OGNIAN, I VOULD DROP IT...
HEY—DOES ANYONE ELSE HEAR—
SINGING?

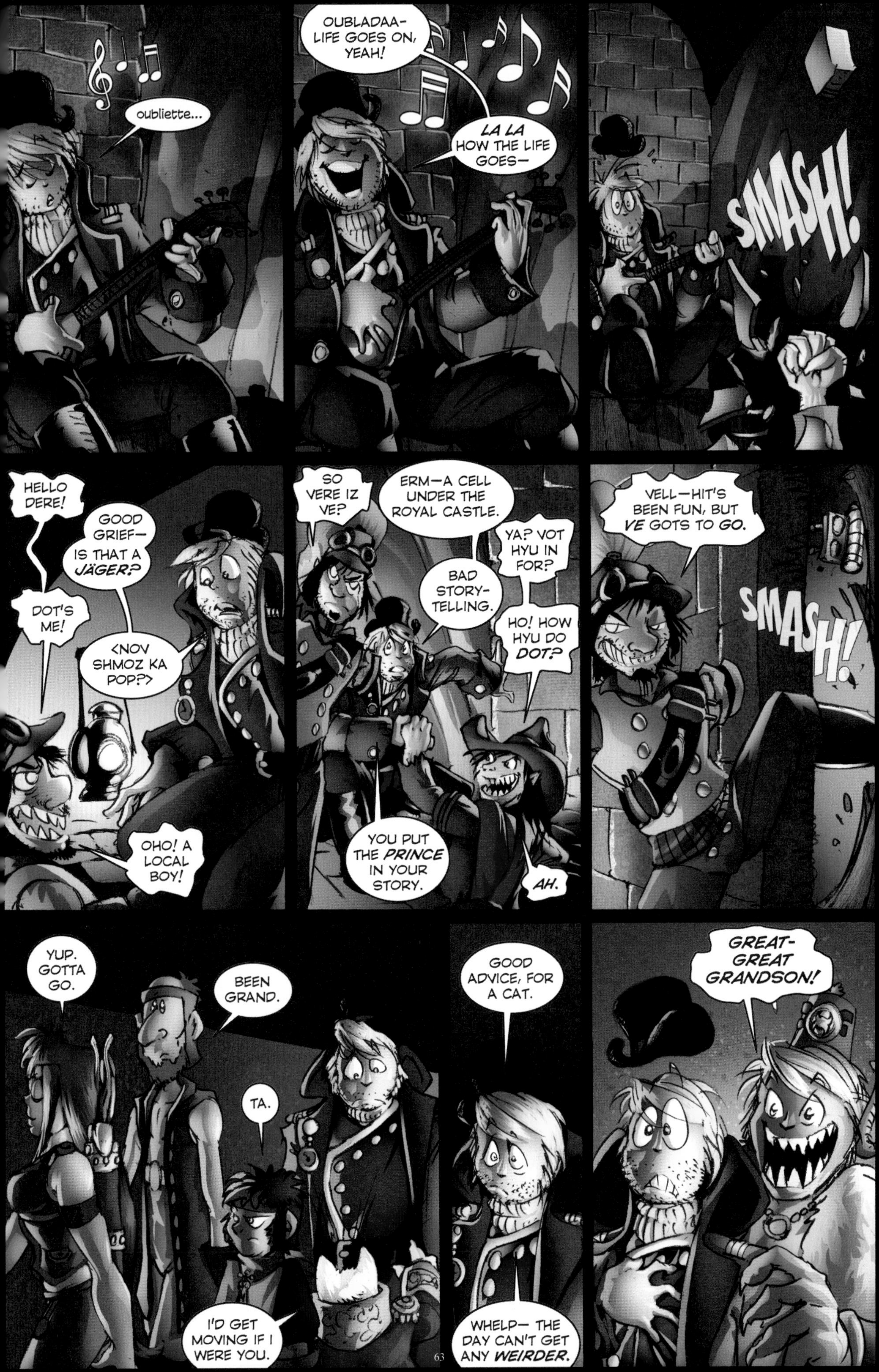

oubliette...
OUBLADAA- LIFE GOES ON, YEAH!
LA LA HOW THE LIFE GOES—
SMASH!
HELLO DERE!
GOOD GRIEF— IS THAT A JÄGER?
DOT'S ME!
<NOV SHMOZ KA POP?>
OHO! A LOCAL BOY!
SO VERE IZ VE?
ERM—A CELL UNDER THE ROYAL CASTLE.
YA? VOT HYU IN FOR?
BAD STORY-TELLING.
HO! HOW HYU DO DOT?
YOU PUT THE PRINCE IN YOUR STORY.
AH.
VELL—HIT'S BEEN FUN, BUT VE GOTS TO GO.
SMASH!
YUP. GOTTA GO.
BEEN GRAND.
TA.
I'D GET MOVING IF I WERE YOU.
GOOD ADVICE, FOR A CAT.
WHELP— THE DAY CAN'T GET ANY WEIRDER.
GREAT-GREAT GRANDSON!

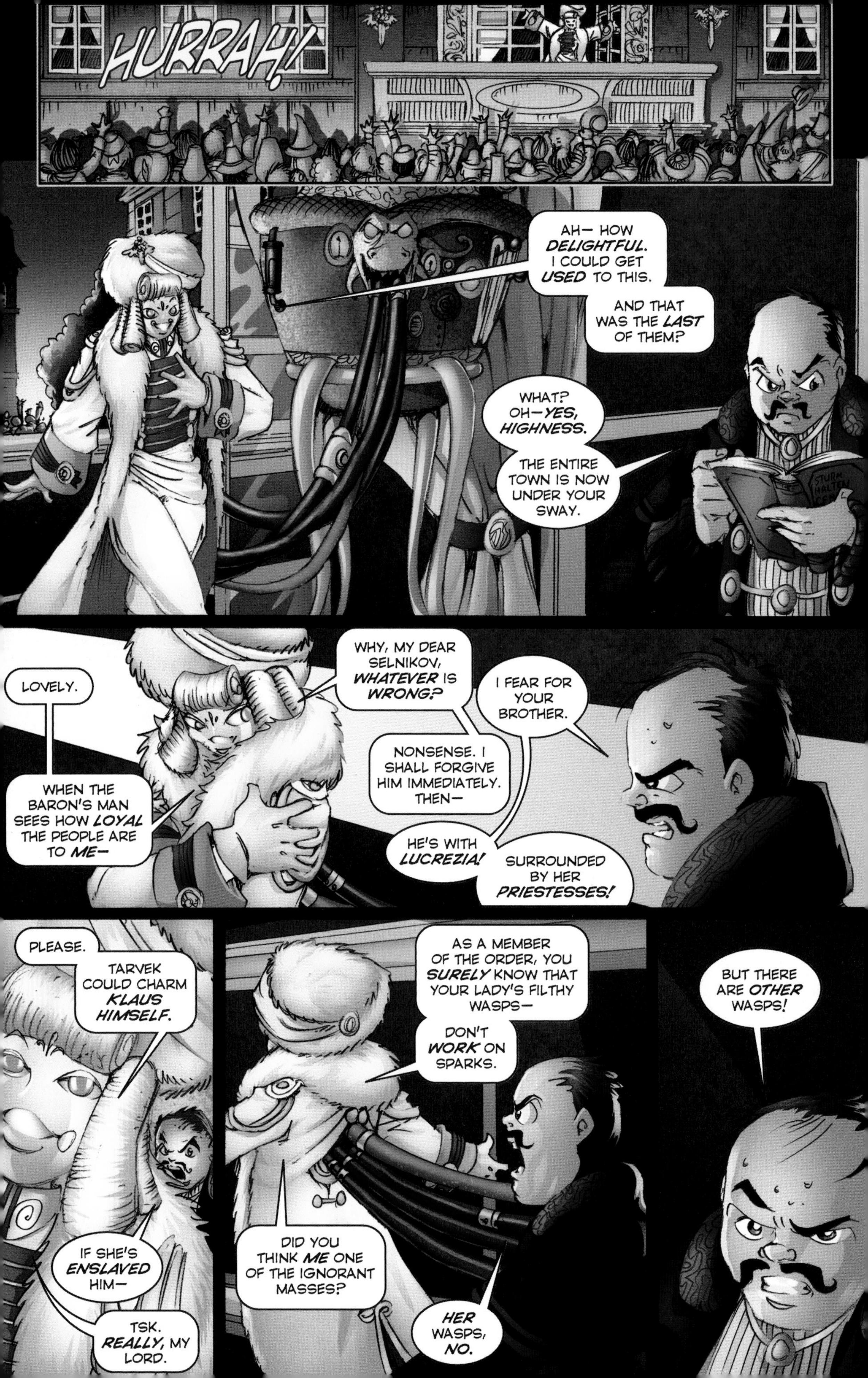
HURRAH!
AH— HOW DELIGHTFUL. I COULD GET USED TO THIS.
AND THAT WAS THE LAST OF THEM?
WHAT? OH—YES, HIGHNESS.
THE ENTIRE TOWN IS NOW UNDER YOUR SWAY.
STURM HALTEN
LOVELY.
WHEN THE BARON'S MAN SEES HOW LOYAL THE PEOPLE ARE TO ME—
WHY, MY DEAR SELNIKOV, WHATEVER IS WRONG?
I FEAR FOR YOUR BROTHER.
NONSENSE. I SHALL FORGIVE HIM IMMEDIATELY. THEN—
HE'S WITH LUCREZIA!
SURROUNDED BY HER PRIESTESSES!
PLEASE.
TARVEK COULD CHARM KLAUS HIMSELF.
IF SHE'S ENSLAVED HIM—
TSK. REALLY, MY LORD.
AS A MEMBER OF THE ORDER, YOU SURELY KNOW THAT YOUR LADY'S FILTHY WASPS—
DON'T WORK ON SPARKS.
DID YOU THINK ME ONE OF THE IGNORANT MASSES?
HER WASPS, NO.
BUT THERE ARE OTHER WASPS!

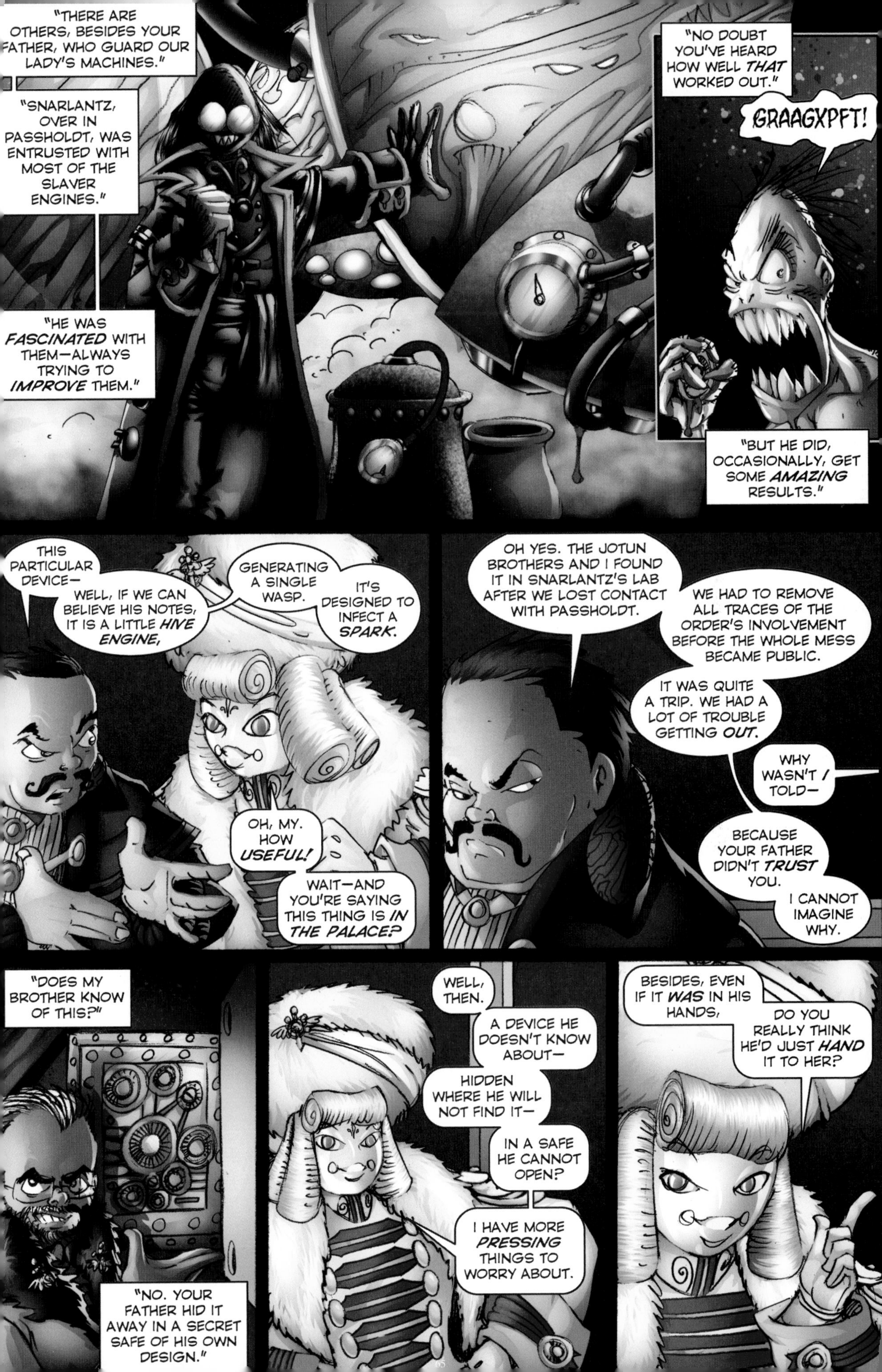

"THERE ARE OTHERS, BESIDES YOUR FATHER, WHO GUARD OUR LADY'S MACHINES."
"SNARLANTZ, OVER IN PASSHOLDT, WAS ENTRUSTED WITH MOST OF THE SLAVER ENGINES."
"HE WAS FASCINATED WITH THEM—ALWAYS TRYING TO IMPROVE THEM."
"NO DOUBT YOU'VE HEARD HOW WELL THAT WORKED OUT."
GRAAGXPFT!
"BUT HE DID, OCCASIONALLY, GET SOME AMAZING RESULTS."
THIS PARTICULAR DEVICE—
WELL, IF WE CAN BELIEVE HIS NOTES, IT IS A LITTLE HIVE ENGINE,
GENERATING A SINGLE WASP.
IT'S DESIGNED TO INFECT A SPARK.
OH, MY. HOW USEFUL!
WAIT—AND YOU'RE SAYING THIS THING IS IN THE PALACE?
OH YES. THE JOTUN BROTHERS AND I FOUND IT IN SNARLANTZ'S LAB AFTER WE LOST CONTACT WITH PASSHOLDT.
WE HAD TO REMOVE ALL TRACES OF THE ORDER'S INVOLVEMENT BEFORE THE WHOLE MESS BECAME PUBLIC.
IT WAS QUITE A TRIP. WE HAD A LOT OF TROUBLE GETTING OUT.
WHY WASN'T I TOLD—
BECAUSE YOUR FATHER DIDN'T TRUST YOU.
I CANNOT IMAGINE WHY.
"DOES MY BROTHER KNOW OF THIS?"
"NO. YOUR FATHER HID IT AWAY IN A SECRET SAFE OF HIS OWN DESIGN."
WELL, THEN.
A DEVICE HE DOESN'T KNOW ABOUT—
HIDDEN WHERE HE WILL NOT FIND IT—
IN A SAFE HE CANNOT OPEN?
I HAVE MORE PRESSING THINGS TO WORRY ABOUT.
BESIDES, EVEN IF IT WAS IN HIS HANDS,
DO YOU REALLY THINK HE'D JUST HAND IT TO HER?

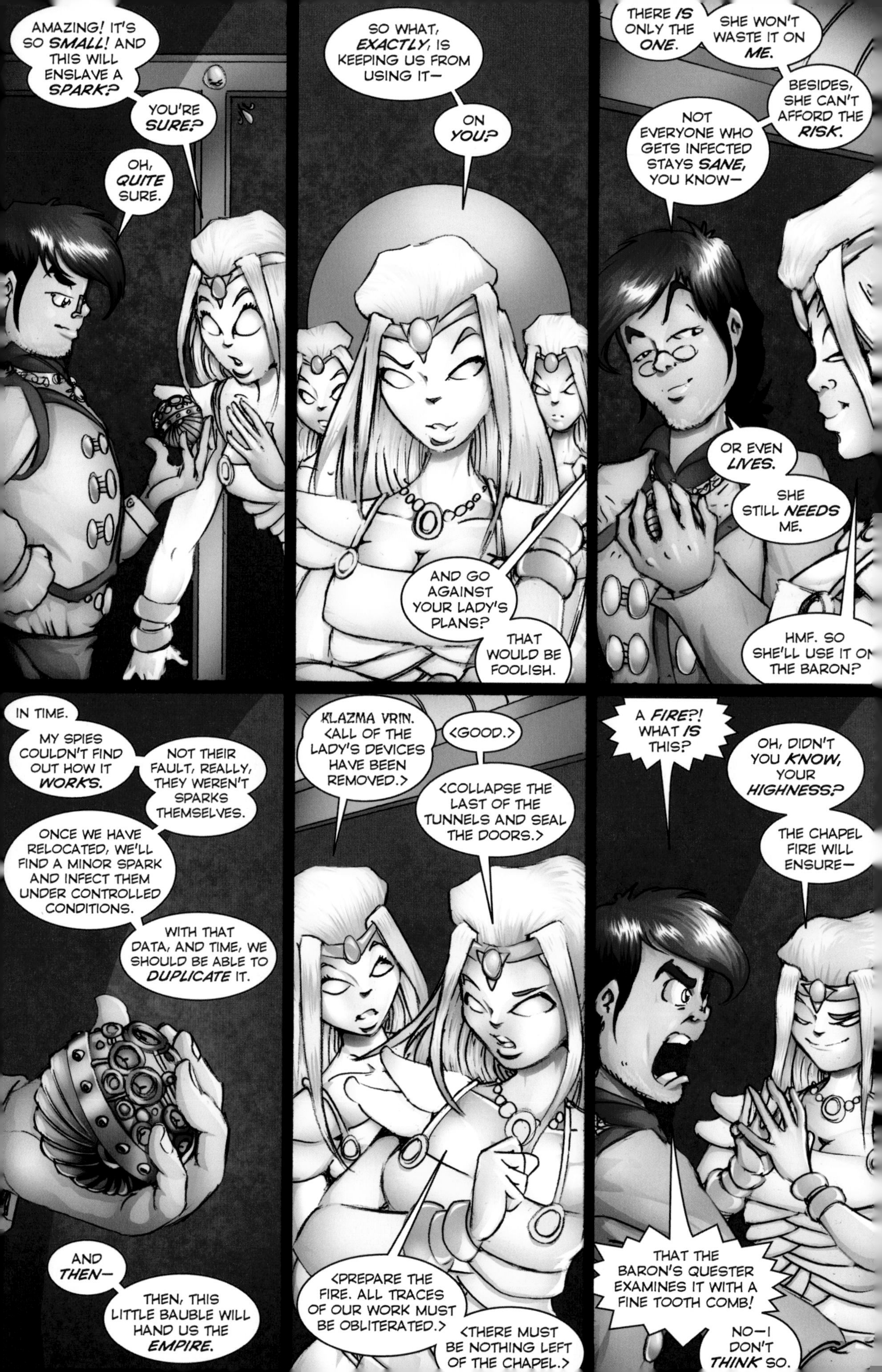
AMAZING! IT'S SO SMALL! AND THIS WILL ENSLAVE A SPARK?
YOU'RE SURE?
OH, QUITE SURE.
SO WHAT, EXACTLY, IS KEEPING US FROM USING IT—
ON YOU?
AND GO AGAINST YOUR LADY'S PLANS?
THAT WOULD BE FOOLISH.
THERE IS ONLY THE ONE.
SHE WON'T WASTE IT ON ME.
BESIDES, SHE CAN'T AFFORD THE RISK.
NOT EVERYONE WHO GETS INFECTED STAYS SANE, YOU KNOW—
OR EVEN LIVES.
SHE STILL NEEDS ME.
HMF. SO SHE'LL USE IT ON THE BARON?
IN TIME.
MY SPIES COULDN'T FIND OUT HOW IT WORKS.
NOT THEIR FAULT, REALLY, THEY WEREN'T SPARKS THEMSELVES.
ONCE WE HAVE RELOCATED, WE'LL FIND A MINOR SPARK AND INFECT THEM UNDER CONTROLLED CONDITIONS.
WITH THAT DATA, AND TIME, WE SHOULD BE ABLE TO DUPLICATE IT.
AND THEN—
THEN, THIS LITTLE BAUBLE WILL HAND US THE EMPIRE.
KLAZMA VRIN. <ALL OF THE LADY'S DEVICES HAVE BEEN REMOVED.>
<GOOD.>
<COLLAPSE THE LAST OF THE TUNNELS AND SEAL THE DOORS.>
<PREPARE THE FIRE. ALL TRACES OF OUR WORK MUST BE OBLITERATED.>
<THERE MUST BE NOTHING LEFT OF THE CHAPEL.>
A FIRE?! WHAT IS THIS?
OH, DIDN'T YOU KNOW, YOUR HIGHNESS?
THE CHAPEL FIRE WILL ENSURE—
THAT THE BARON'S QUESTER EXAMINES IT WITH A FINE TOOTH COMB!
NO—I DON'T THINK SO.

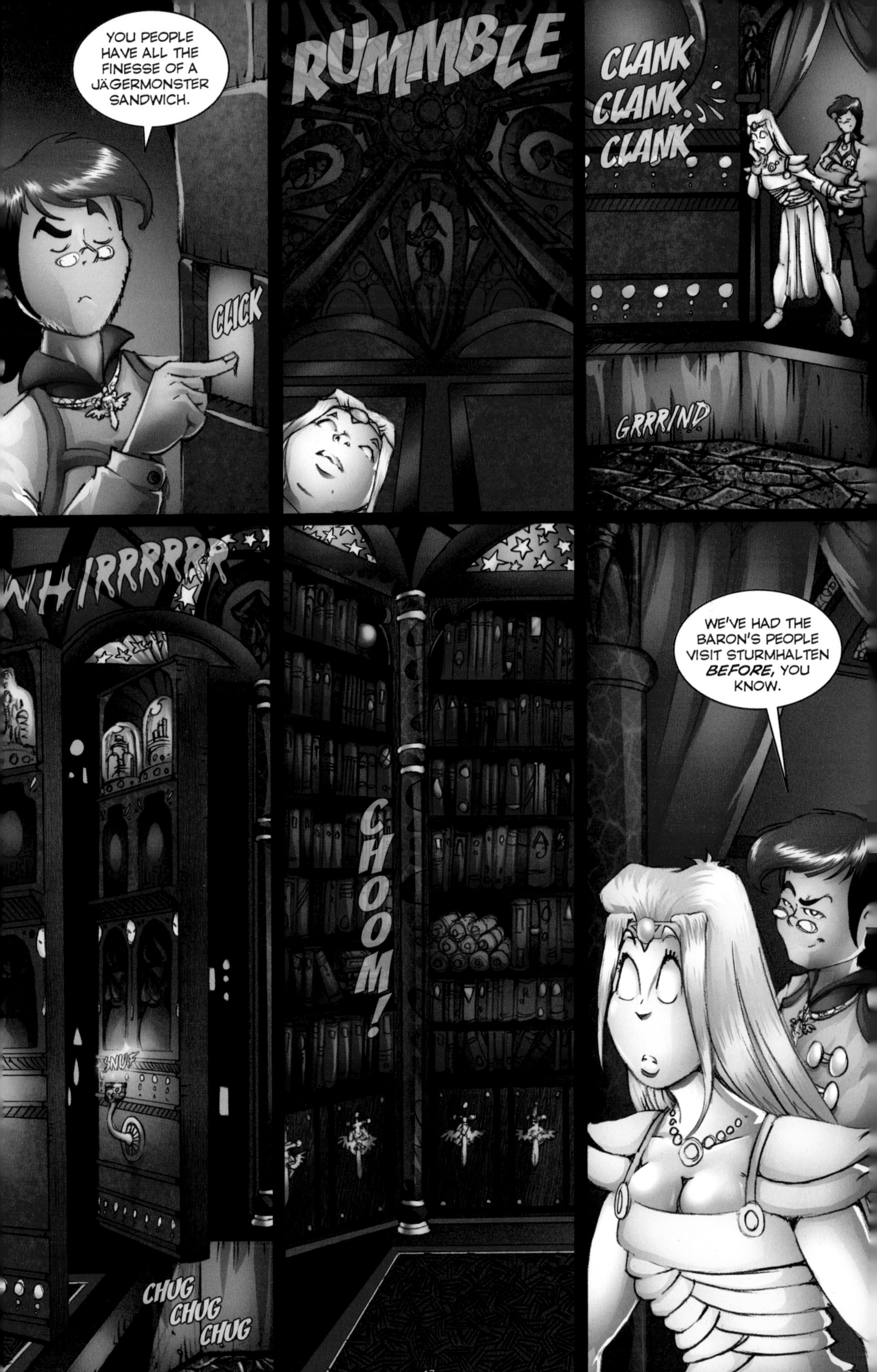
YOU PEOPLE HAVE ALL THE FINESSE OF A JÄGERMONSTER SANDWICH.
CLICK
RUMMBLE
CLANK
CLANK
CLANK
GRRRIND
WHIRRRRRR
SNUF
CHOOM!
CHUG
CHUG
CHUG
WE'VE HAD THE BARON'S PEOPLE VISIT STURMHALTEN *BEFORE,* YOU KNOW.

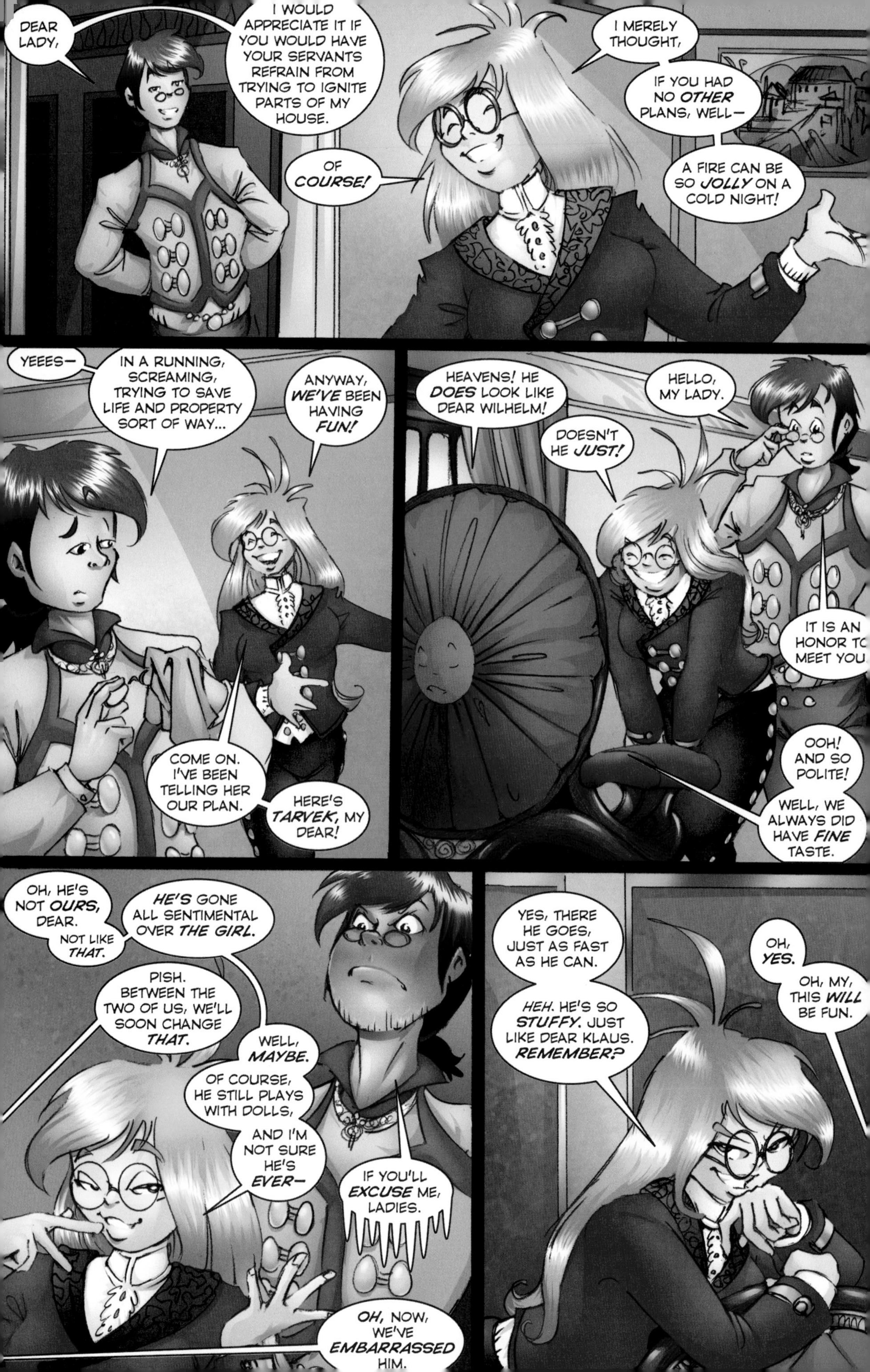
DEAR LADY,
I WOULD APPRECIATE IT IF YOU WOULD HAVE YOUR SERVANTS REFRAIN FROM TRYING TO IGNITE PARTS OF MY HOUSE.
OF COURSE!
I MERELY THOUGHT,
IF YOU HAD NO OTHER PLANS, WELL—
A FIRE CAN BE SO JOLLY ON A COLD NIGHT!
YEEES—
IN A RUNNING, SCREAMING, TRYING TO SAVE LIFE AND PROPERTY SORT OF WAY...
ANYWAY, WE'VE BEEN HAVING FUN!
COME ON. I'VE BEEN TELLING HER OUR PLAN.
HERE'S TARVEK, MY DEAR!
HEAVENS! HE DOES LOOK LIKE DEAR WILHELM!
DOESN'T HE JUST!
HELLO, MY LADY.
IT IS AN HONOR TO MEET YOU.
OOH! AND SO POLITE!
WELL, WE ALWAYS DID HAVE FINE TASTE.
OH, HE'S NOT OURS, DEAR.
NOT LIKE THAT.
HE'S GONE ALL SENTIMENTAL OVER THE GIRL.
PISH. BETWEEN THE TWO OF US, WE'LL SOON CHANGE THAT.
WELL, MAYBE.
OF COURSE, HE STILL PLAYS WITH DOLLS,
AND I'M NOT SURE HE'S EVER—
IF YOU'LL EXCUSE ME, LADIES.
OH, NOW, WE'VE EMBARRASSED HIM.
YES, THERE HE GOES, JUST AS FAST AS HE CAN.
HEH. HE'S SO STUFFY. JUST LIKE DEAR KLAUS. REMEMBER?
OH, YES.
OH, MY, THIS WILL BE FUN.

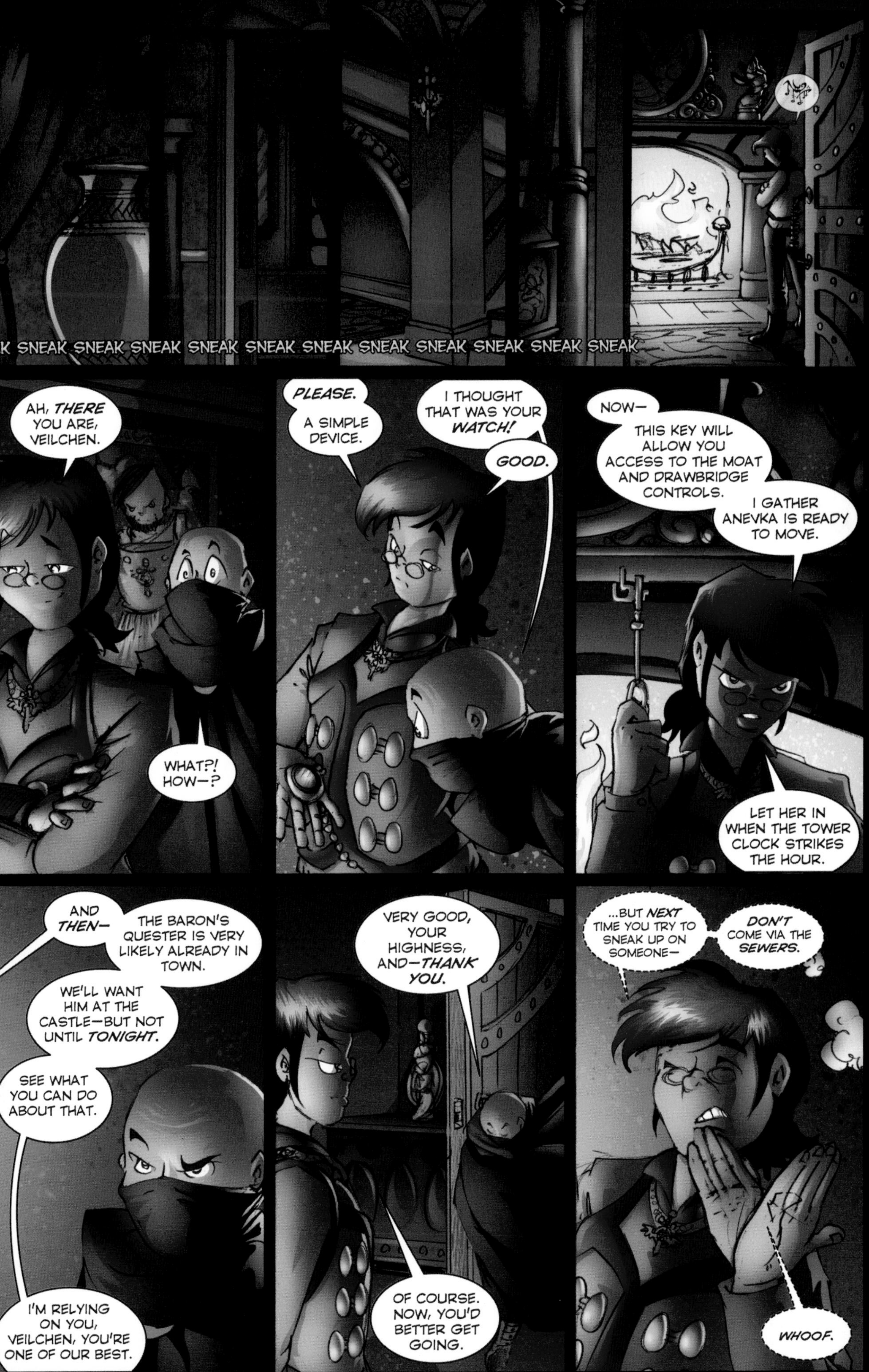

K SNEAK SNEAK SNEAK SNEAK SNEAK SNEAK SNEAK SNEAK SNEAK SNEAK SNEAK
AH, *THERE* YOU ARE, VEILCHEN.
WHAT?! HOW—?
PLEASE.
A SIMPLE DEVICE.
I THOUGHT THAT WAS YOUR *WATCH!*
GOOD.
NOW—
THIS KEY WILL ALLOW YOU ACCESS TO THE MOAT AND DRAWBRIDGE CONTROLS.
I GATHER ANEVKA IS READY TO MOVE.
LET HER IN WHEN THE TOWER CLOCK STRIKES THE HOUR.
AND *THEN—*
THE BARON'S QUESTER IS VERY LIKELY ALREADY IN TOWN.
WE'LL WANT HIM AT THE CASTLE—BUT NOT UNTIL *TONIGHT.*
SEE WHAT YOU CAN DO ABOUT THAT.
I'M RELYING ON YOU, VEILCHEN, YOU'RE ONE OF OUR BEST.
VERY GOOD, YOUR HIGHNESS, AND—*THANK YOU.*
OF COURSE. NOW, YOU'D BETTER GET GOING.
...BUT *NEXT* TIME YOU TRY TO SNEAK UP ON SOMEONE—
DON'T COME VIA THE *SEWERS.*
WHOOF.

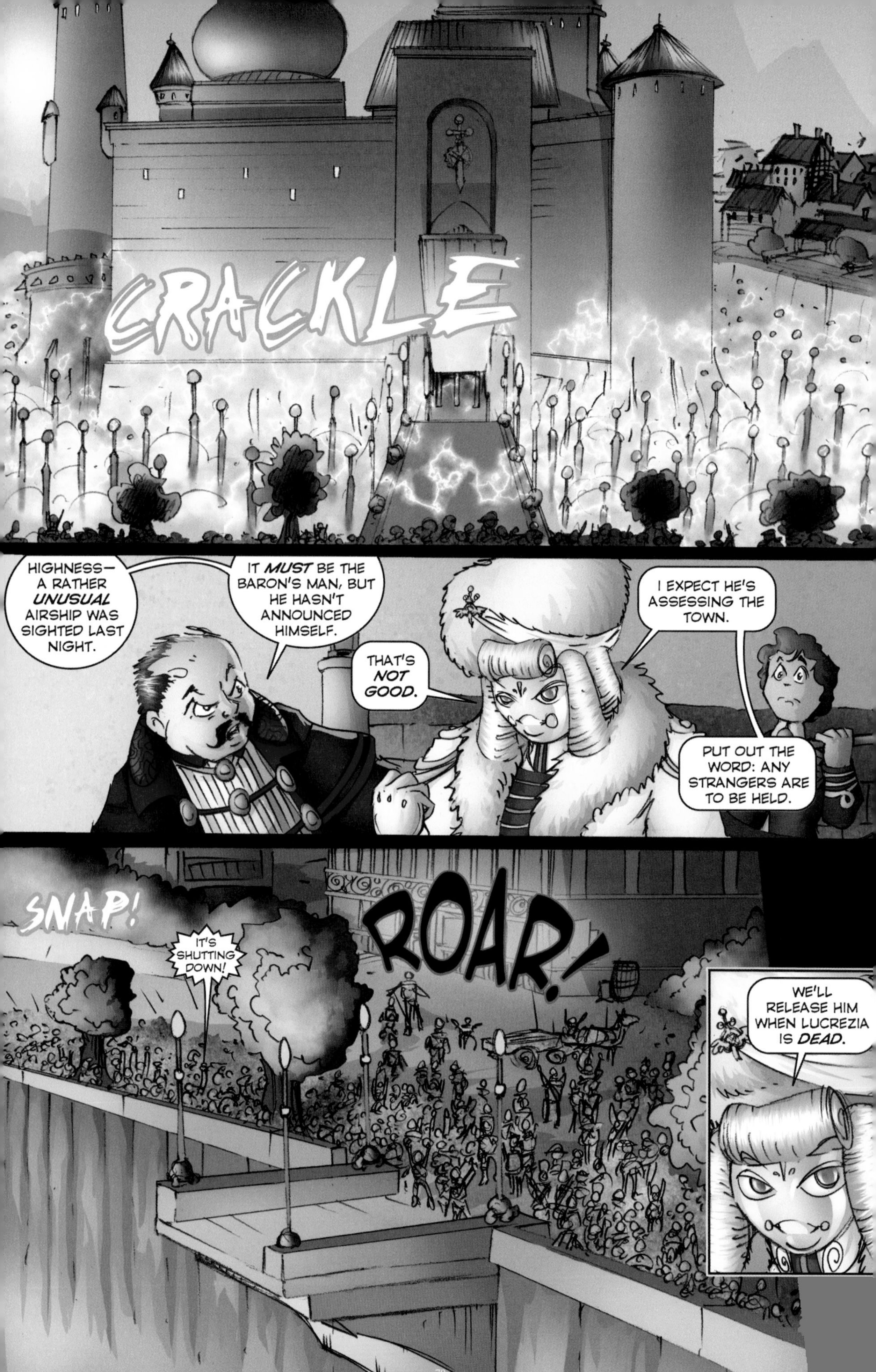
CRACKLE
HIGHNESS— A RATHER UNUSUAL AIRSHIP WAS SIGHTED LAST NIGHT.
IT MUST BE THE BARON'S MAN, BUT HE HASN'T ANNOUNCED HIMSELF.
THAT'S NOT GOOD.
I EXPECT HE'S ASSESSING THE TOWN.
PUT OUT THE WORD: ANY STRANGERS ARE TO BE HELD.
SNAP!
IT'S SHUTTING DOWN!
ROAR!
WE'LL RELEASE HIM WHEN LUCREZIA IS DEAD.

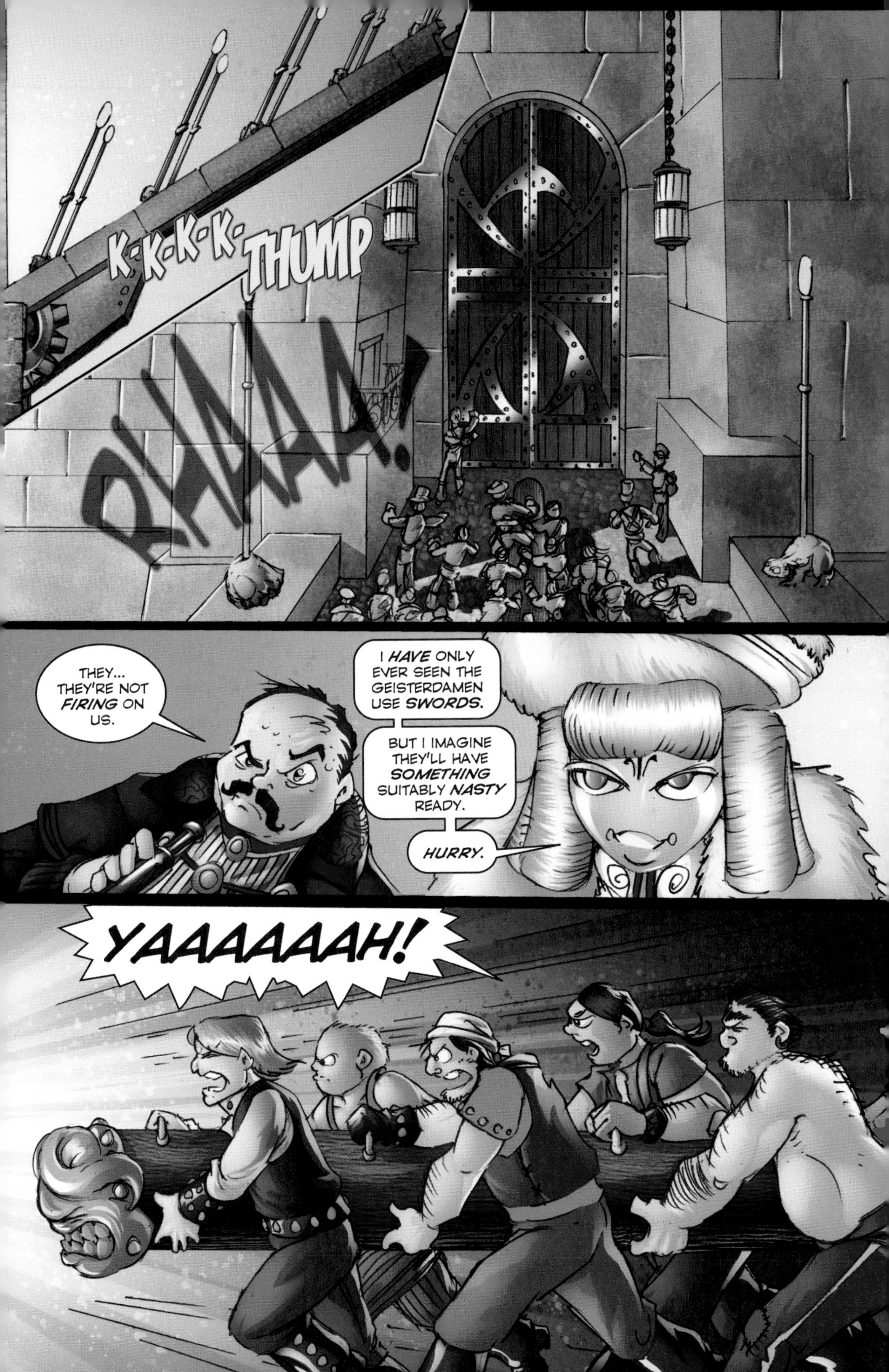
K-K-K-K-THUMP
RHAAA!
THEY... THEY'RE NOT FIRING ON US.
I HAVE ONLY EVER SEEN THE GEISTERDAMEN USE SWORDS.
BUT I IMAGINE THEY'LL HAVE SOMETHING SUITABLY NASTY READY.
HURRY.
YAAAAAAH!

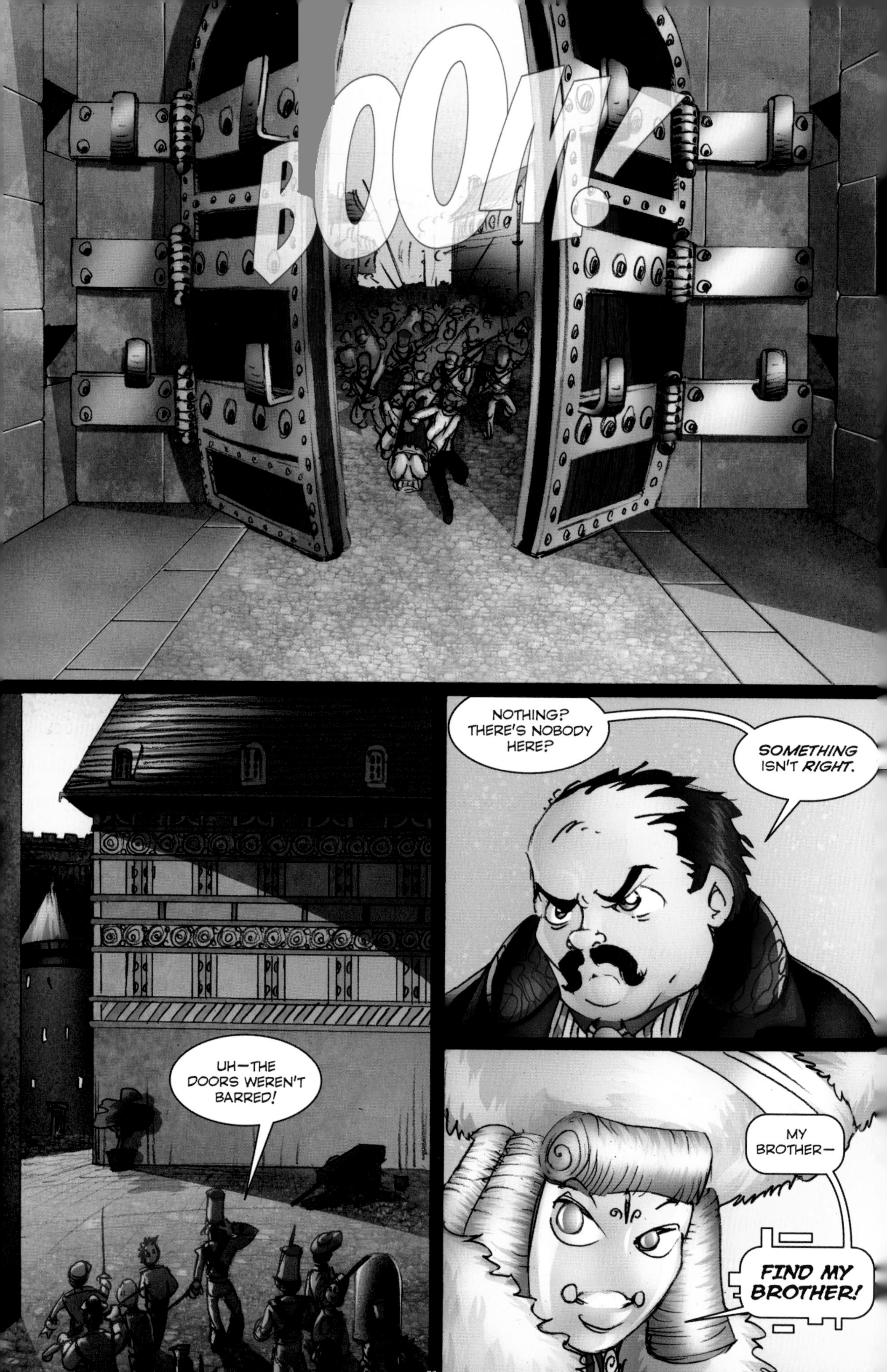
BOOM!
UH—THE DOORS WEREN'T BARRED!
NOTHING? THERE'S NOBODY HERE?
SOMETHING ISN'T RIGHT.
MY BROTHER—
FIND MY BROTHER!

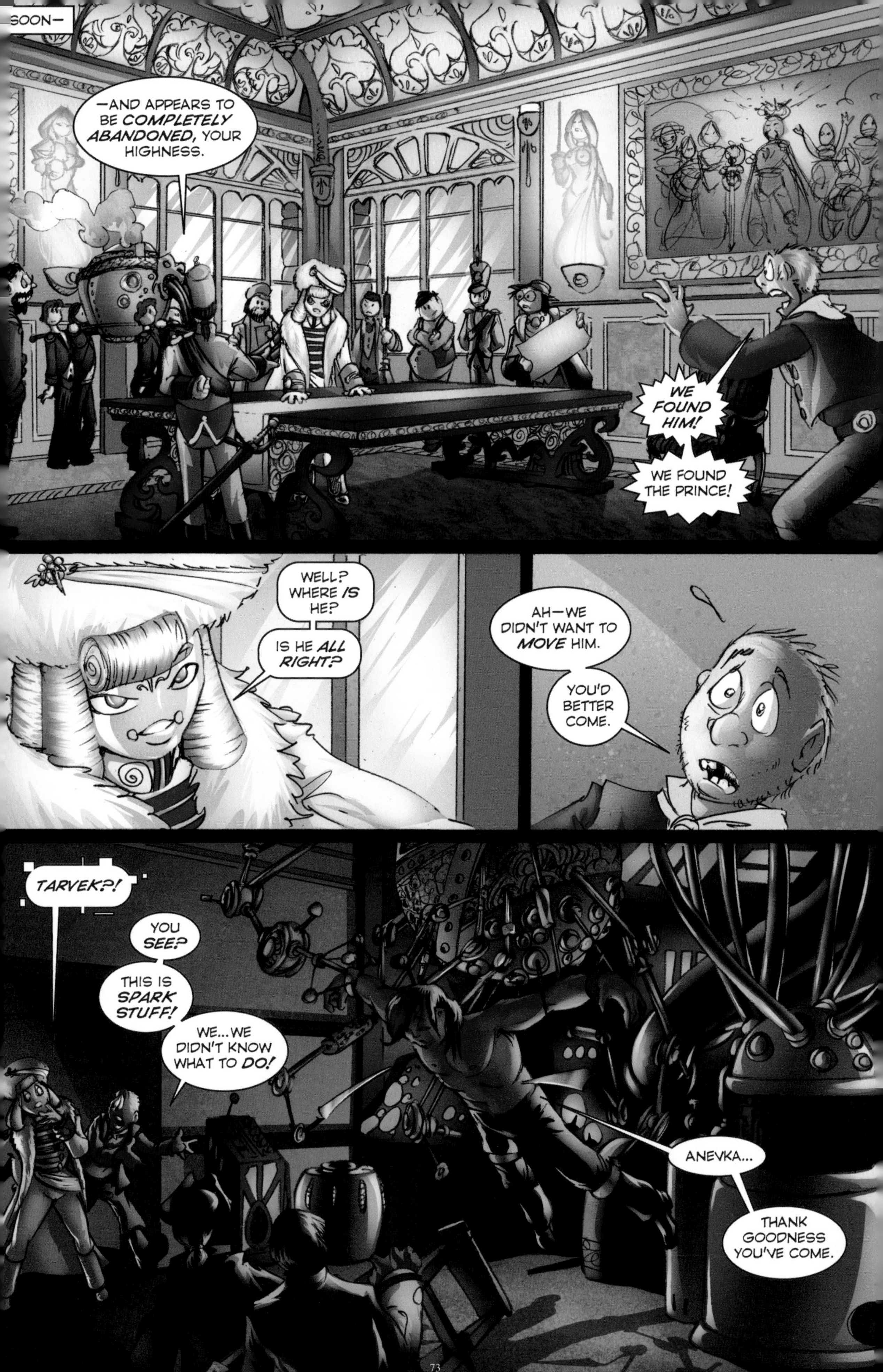
SOON—
—AND APPEARS TO BE COMPLETELY ABANDONED, YOUR HIGHNESS.
WE FOUND HIM!
WE FOUND THE PRINCE!
WELL? WHERE IS HE?
IS HE ALL RIGHT?
AH—WE DIDN'T WANT TO MOVE HIM.
YOU'D BETTER COME.
TARVEK?!
YOU SEE?
THIS IS SPARK STUFF!
WE...WE DIDN'T KNOW WHAT TO DO!
ANEVKA...
THANK GOODNESS YOU'VE COME.

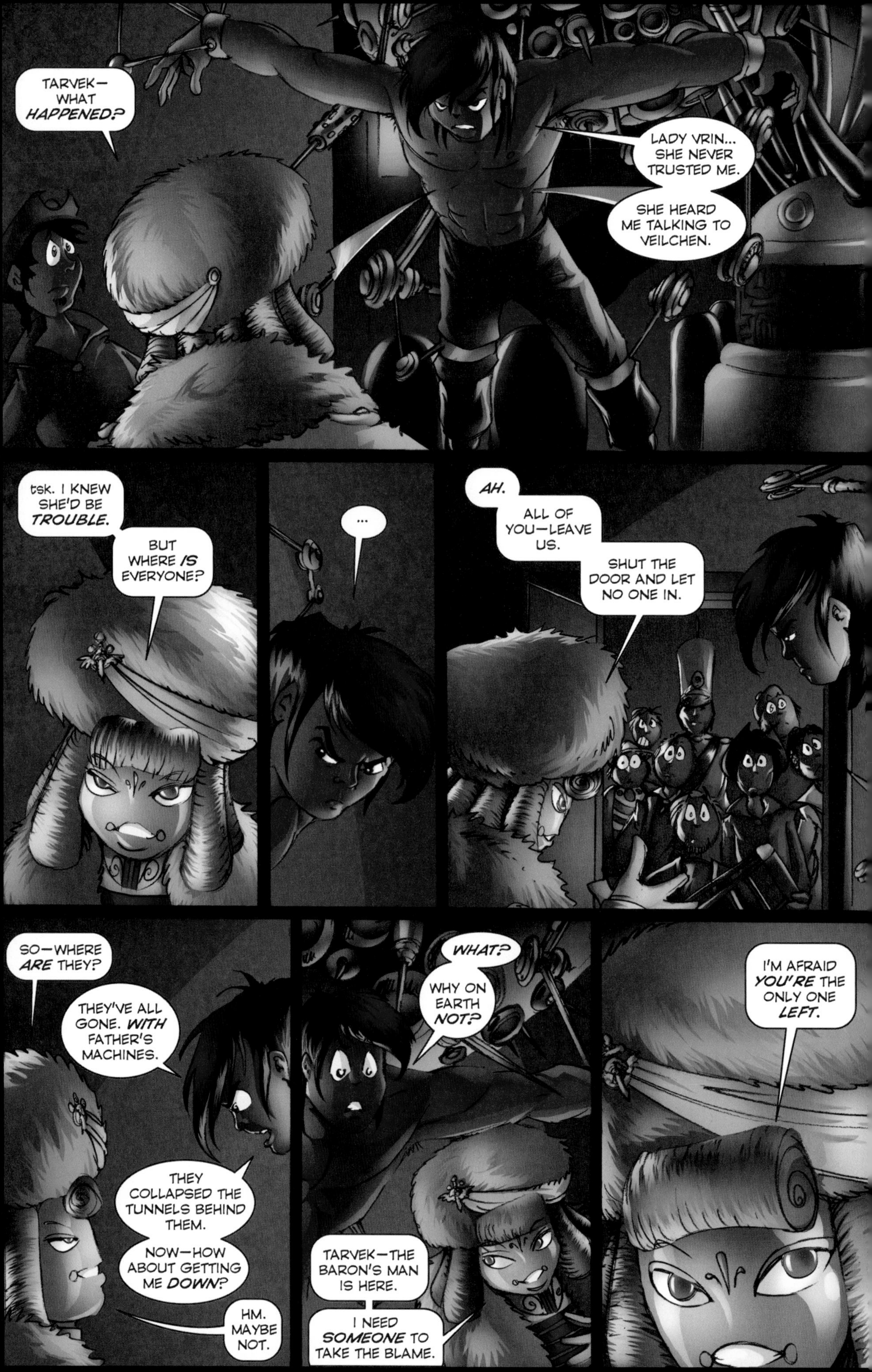
TARVEK—WHAT HAPPENED?
LADY VRIN... SHE NEVER TRUSTED ME.
SHE HEARD ME TALKING TO VEILCHEN.
tsk. I KNEW SHE'D BE TROUBLE.
BUT WHERE IS EVERYONE?
...
AH.
ALL OF YOU—LEAVE US.
SHUT THE DOOR AND LET NO ONE IN.
SO—WHERE ARE THEY?
THEY'VE ALL GONE. WITH FATHER'S MACHINES.
THEY COLLAPSED THE TUNNELS BEHIND THEM.
NOW—HOW ABOUT GETTING ME DOWN?
HM. MAYBE NOT.
WHAT?
WHY ON EARTH NOT?
TARVEK—THE BARON'S MAN IS HERE.
I NEED SOMEONE TO TAKE THE BLAME.
I'M AFRAID YOU'RE THE ONLY ONE LEFT.

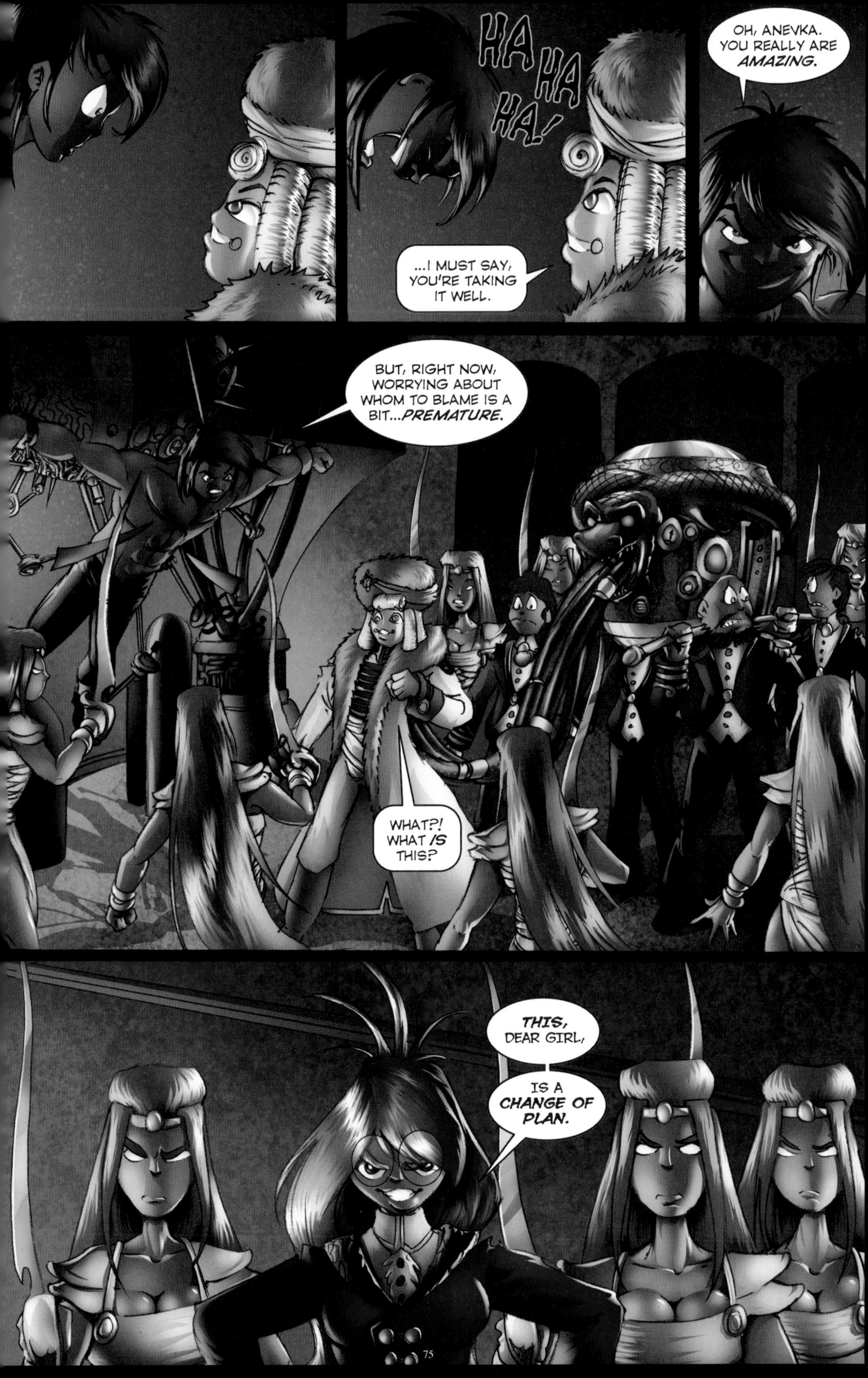
HA HA HA!
...I MUST SAY, YOU'RE TAKING IT WELL.
OH, ANEVKA. YOU REALLY ARE AMAZING.
BUT, RIGHT NOW, WORRYING ABOUT WHOM TO BLAME IS A BIT...PREMATURE.
WHAT?! WHAT IS THIS?
THIS, DEAR GIRL,
IS A CHANGE OF PLAN.

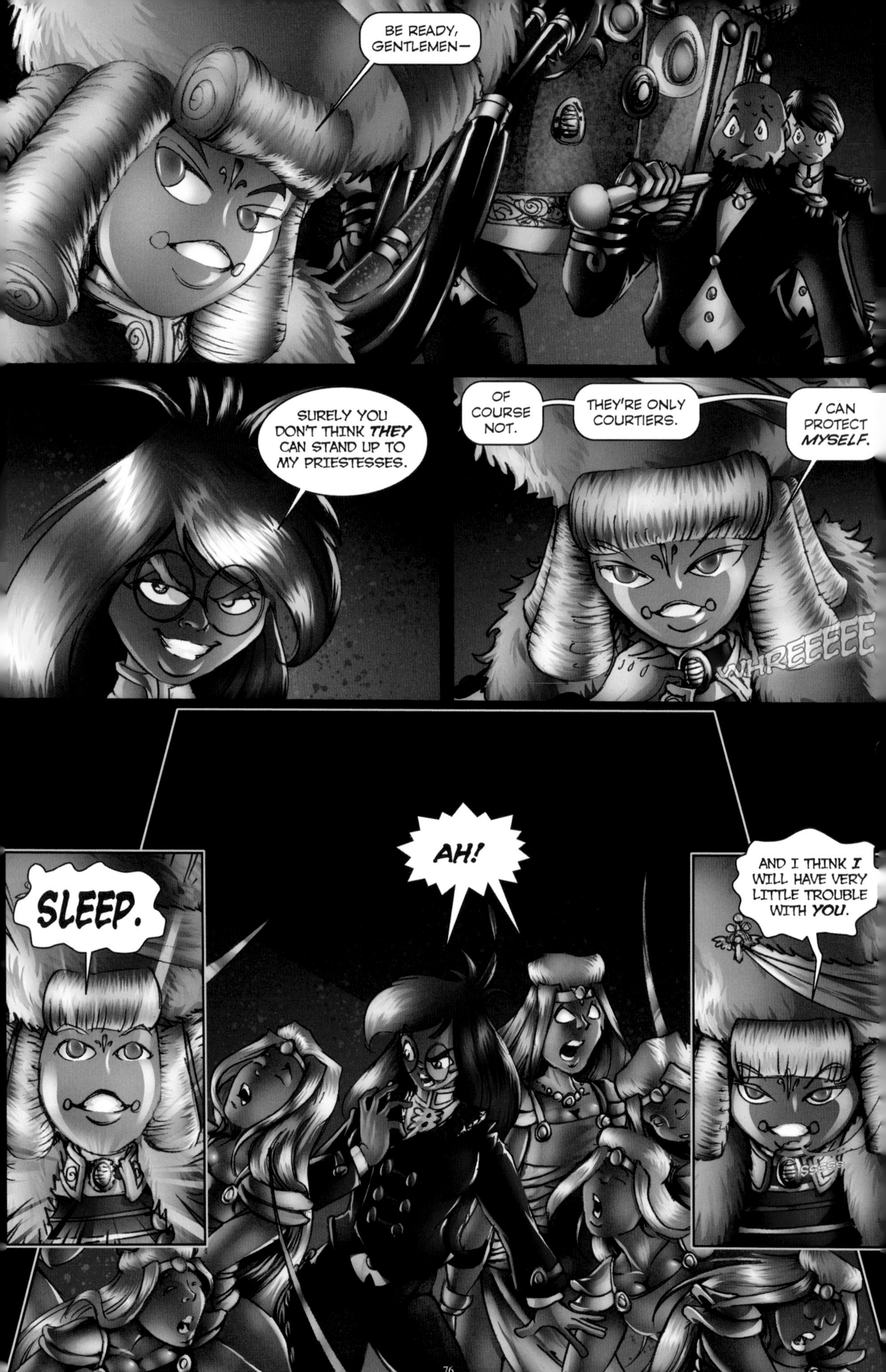
BE READY, GENTLEMEN—
SURELY YOU DON'T THINK *THEY* CAN STAND UP TO MY PRIESTESSES.
OF COURSE NOT.
THEY'RE ONLY COURTIERS.
I CAN PROTECT *MYSELF*.
WHREEEEEE
SLEEP.
AH!
AND I THINK *I* WILL HAVE VERY LITTLE TROUBLE WITH *YOU*.
SSSSS

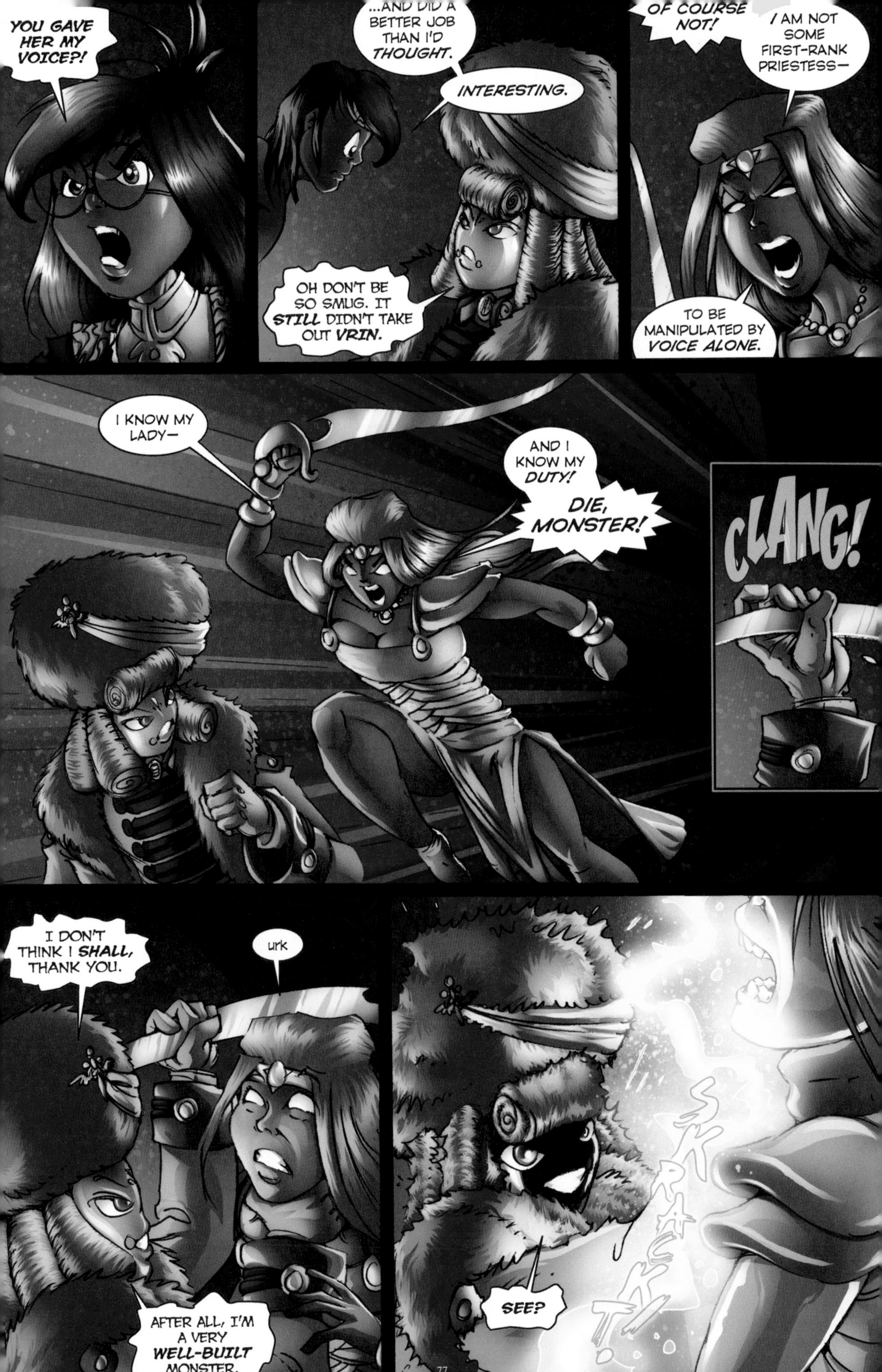
YOU GAVE HER MY VOICE?!
...AND DID A BETTER JOB THAN I'D THOUGHT.
INTERESTING.
OH DON'T BE SO SMUG. IT STILL DIDN'T TAKE OUT VRIN.
OF COURSE NOT!
I AM NOT SOME FIRST-RANK PRIESTESS—
TO BE MANIPULATED BY VOICE ALONE.
I KNOW MY LADY—
AND I KNOW MY DUTY!
DIE, MONSTER!
CLANG!
I DON'T THINK I SHALL, THANK YOU.
urk
AFTER ALL, I'M A VERY WELL-BUILT MONSTER.
SEE?
SKRACK!

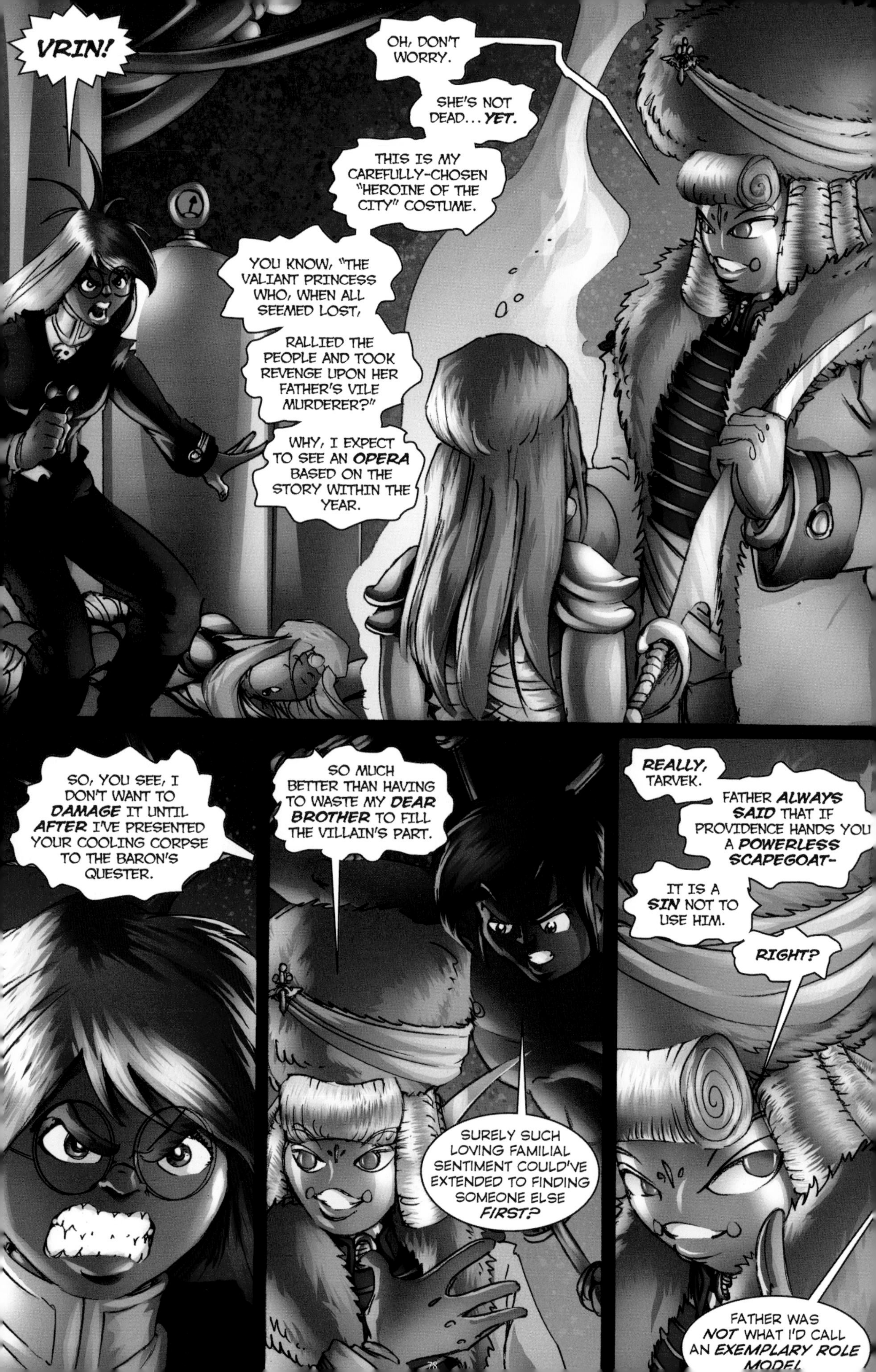
VRIN!
OH, DON'T WORRY.
SHE'S NOT DEAD... YET.
THIS IS MY CAREFULLY-CHOSEN "HEROINE OF THE CITY" COSTUME.
YOU KNOW, "THE VALIANT PRINCESS WHO, WHEN ALL SEEMED LOST,
RALLIED THE PEOPLE AND TOOK REVENGE UPON HER FATHER'S VILE MURDERER?"
WHY, I EXPECT TO SEE AN OPERA BASED ON THE STORY WITHIN THE YEAR.
SO, YOU SEE, I DON'T WANT TO DAMAGE IT UNTIL AFTER I'VE PRESENTED YOUR COOLING CORPSE TO THE BARON'S QUESTER.
SO MUCH BETTER THAN HAVING TO WASTE MY DEAR BROTHER TO FILL THE VILLAIN'S PART.
SURELY SUCH LOVING FAMILIAL SENTIMENT COULD'VE EXTENDED TO FINDING SOMEONE ELSE FIRST?
REALLY, TARVEK.
FATHER ALWAYS SAID THAT IF PROVIDENCE HANDS YOU A POWERLESS SCAPEGOAT-
IT IS A SIN NOT TO USE HIM.
RIGHT?
FATHER WAS NOT WHAT I'D CALL AN EXEMPLARY ROLE MODEL.

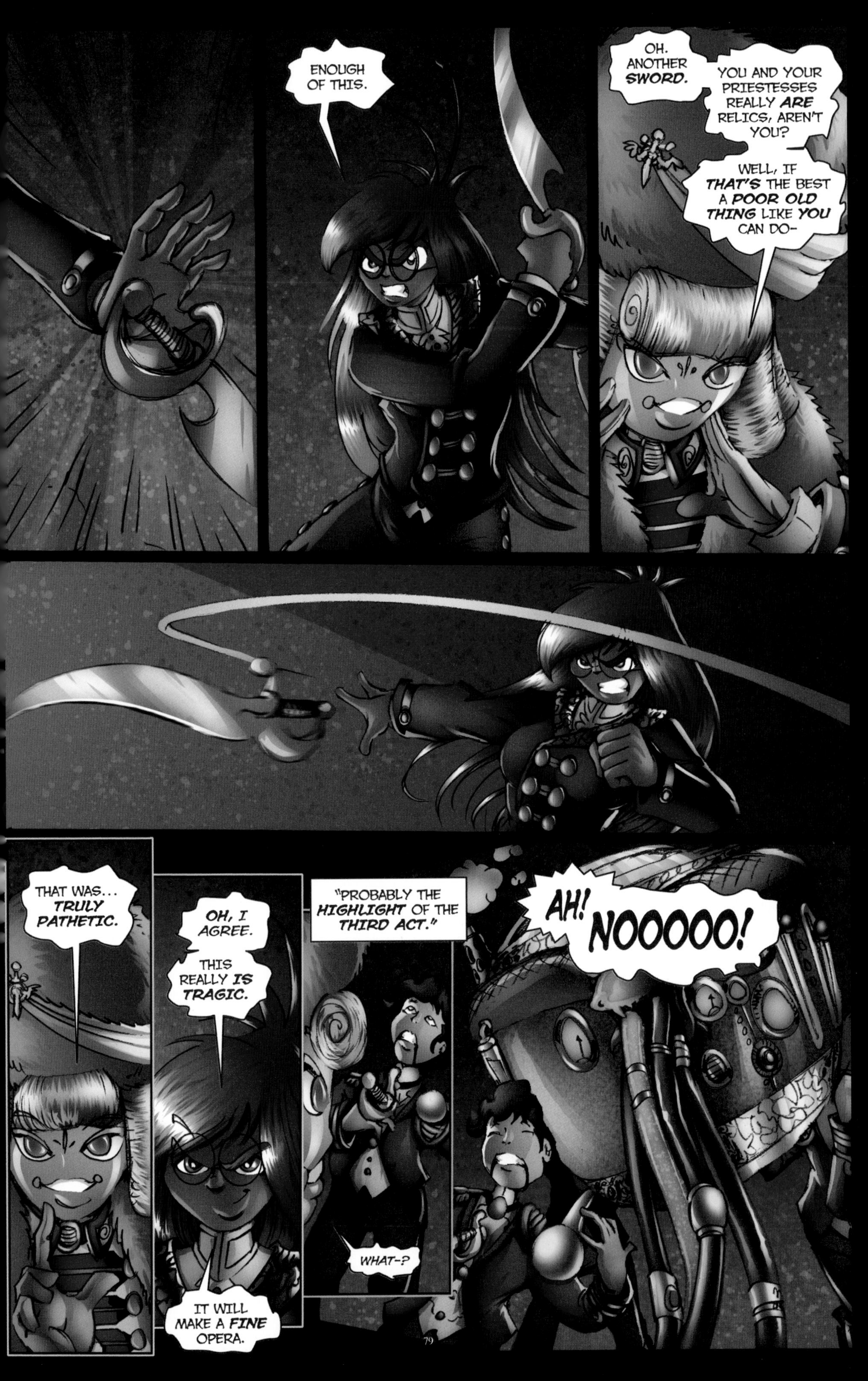
ENOUGH OF THIS.
OH. ANOTHER SWORD.
YOU AND YOUR PRIESTESSES REALLY ARE RELICS, AREN'T YOU?
WELL, IF THAT'S THE BEST A POOR OLD THING LIKE YOU CAN DO-
THAT WAS... TRULY PATHETIC.
OH, I AGREE.
THIS REALLY IS TRAGIC.
IT WILL MAKE A FINE OPERA.
"PROBABLY THE HIGHLIGHT OF THE THIRD ACT."
WHAT-?
AH! NOOOOO!

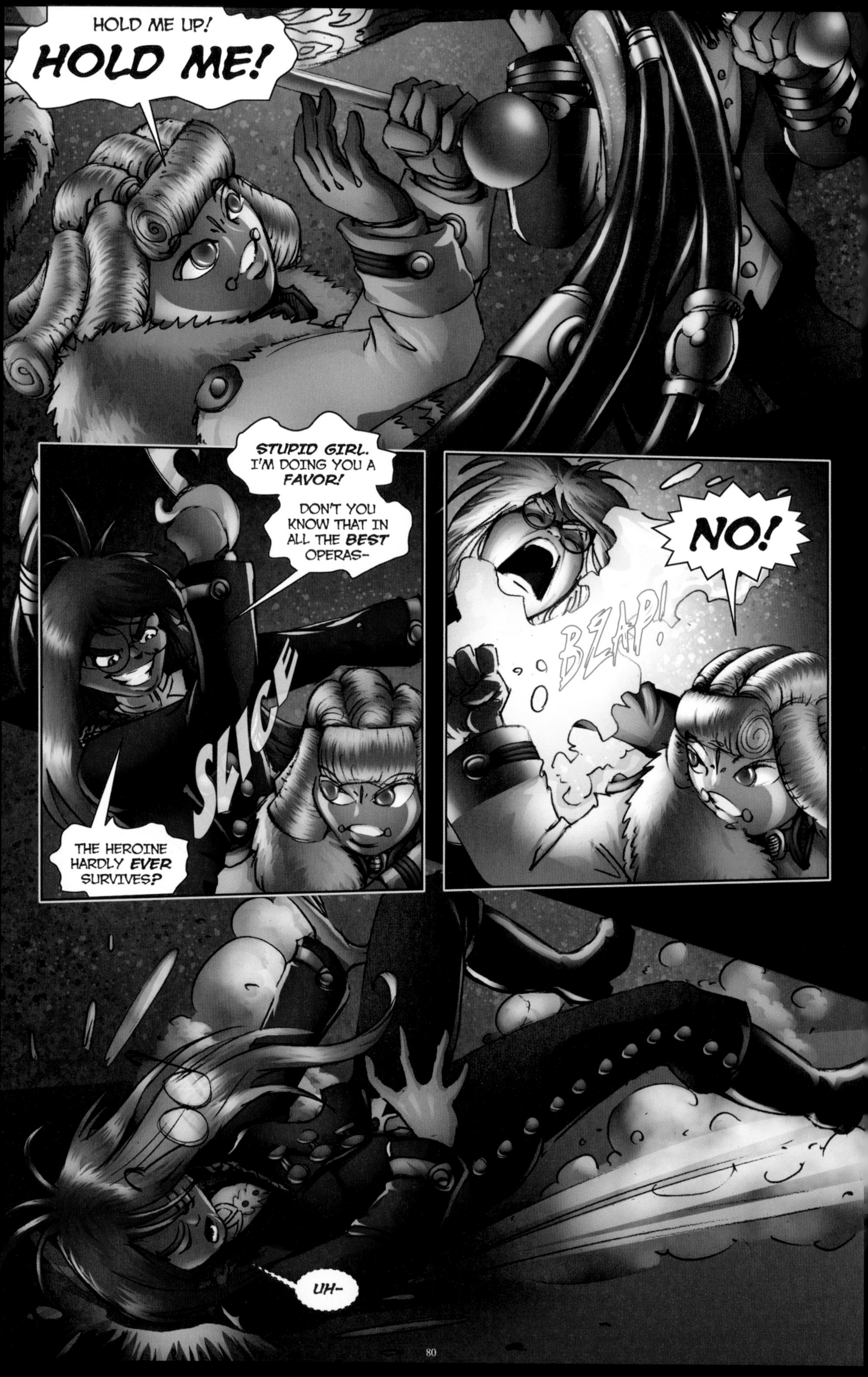
HOLD ME UP! HOLD ME!
STUPID GIRL. I'M DOING YOU A FAVOR!
DON'T YOU KNOW THAT IN ALL THE BEST OPERAS-
SLICE
THE HEROINE HARDLY EVER SURVIVES?
NO!
BZAP!
UH-

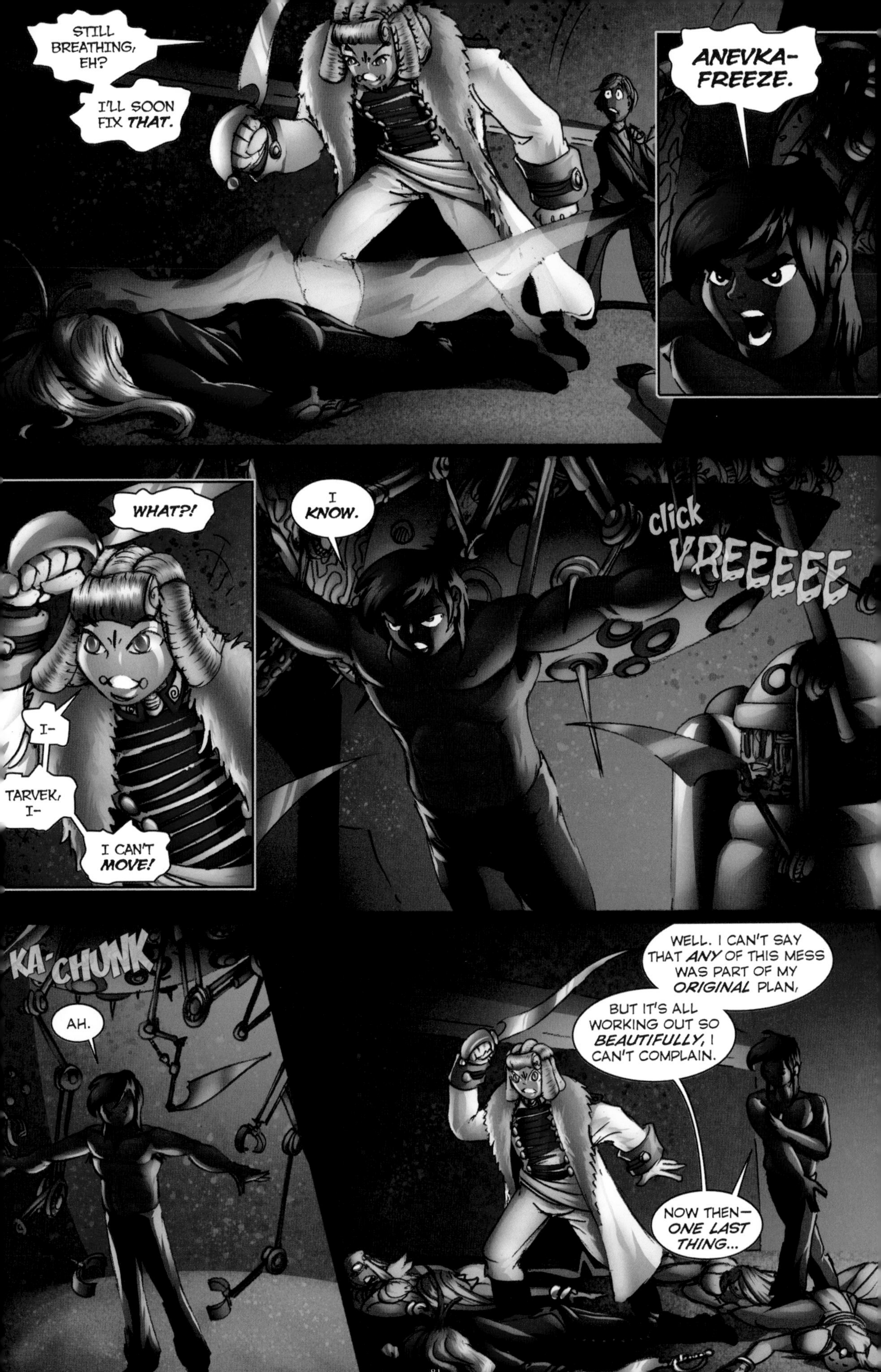
STILL BREATHING, EH?
I'LL SOON FIX THAT.
ANEVKA- FREEZE.
WHAT?!
I KNOW.
click
VREEEEE
I-
TARVEK, I-
I CAN'T MOVE!
KA-CHUNK
AH.
WELL. I CAN'T SAY THAT ANY OF THIS MESS WAS PART OF MY ORIGINAL PLAN,
BUT IT'S ALL WORKING OUT SO BEAUTIFULLY, I CAN'T COMPLAIN.
NOW THEN— ONE LAST THING...

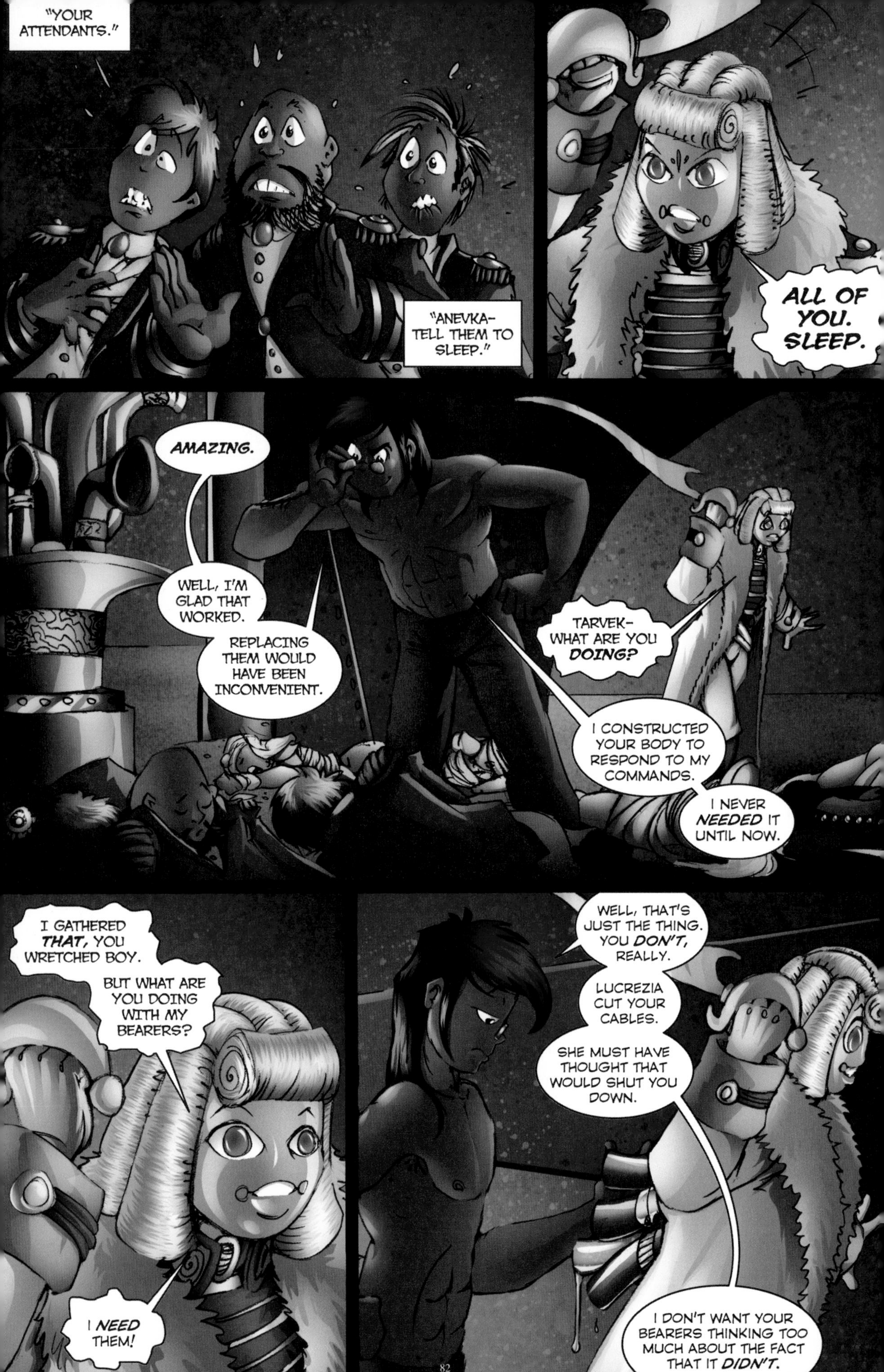
"YOUR ATTENDANTS."
"ANEVKA- TELL THEM TO SLEEP."
ALL OF YOU. SLEEP.
AMAZING.
WELL, I'M GLAD THAT WORKED.
REPLACING THEM WOULD HAVE BEEN INCONVENIENT.
TARVEK- WHAT ARE YOU DOING?
I CONSTRUCTED YOUR BODY TO RESPOND TO MY COMMANDS.
I NEVER NEEDED IT UNTIL NOW.
I GATHERED THAT, YOU WRETCHED BOY.
BUT WHAT ARE YOU DOING WITH MY BEARERS?
I NEED THEM!
WELL, THAT'S JUST THE THING. YOU DON'T, REALLY.
LUCREZIA CUT YOUR CABLES.
SHE MUST HAVE THOUGHT THAT WOULD SHUT YOU DOWN.
I DON'T WANT YOUR BEARERS THINKING TOO MUCH ABOUT THE FACT THAT IT DIDN'T.

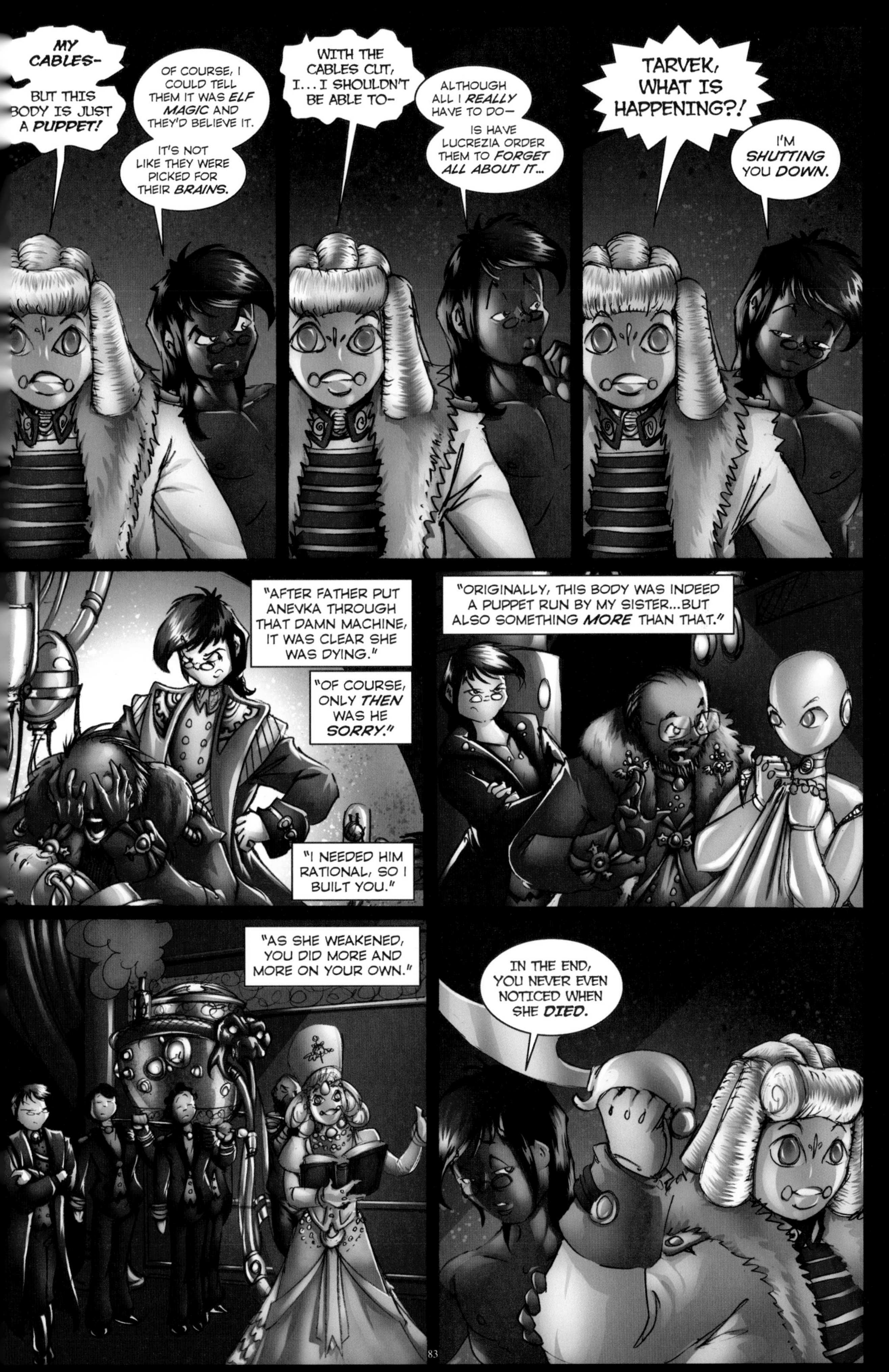
MY CABLES-
BUT THIS BODY IS JUST A PUPPET!
OF COURSE, I COULD TELL THEM IT WAS ELF MAGIC AND THEY'D BELIEVE IT.
IT'S NOT LIKE THEY WERE PICKED FOR THEIR BRAINS.
WITH THE CABLES CUT, I... I SHOULDN'T BE ABLE TO-
ALTHOUGH ALL I REALLY HAVE TO DO—
IS HAVE LUCREZIA ORDER THEM TO FORGET ALL ABOUT IT...
TARVEK, WHAT IS HAPPENING?!
I'M SHUTTING YOU DOWN.
"AFTER FATHER PUT ANEVKA THROUGH THAT DAMN MACHINE, IT WAS CLEAR SHE WAS DYING."
"OF COURSE, ONLY THEN WAS HE SORRY."
"I NEEDED HIM RATIONAL, SO I BUILT YOU."
"ORIGINALLY, THIS BODY WAS INDEED A PUPPET RUN BY MY SISTER...BUT ALSO SOMETHING MORE THAN THAT."
"AS SHE WEAKENED, YOU DID MORE AND MORE ON YOUR OWN."
IN THE END, YOU NEVER EVEN NOTICED WHEN SHE DIED.

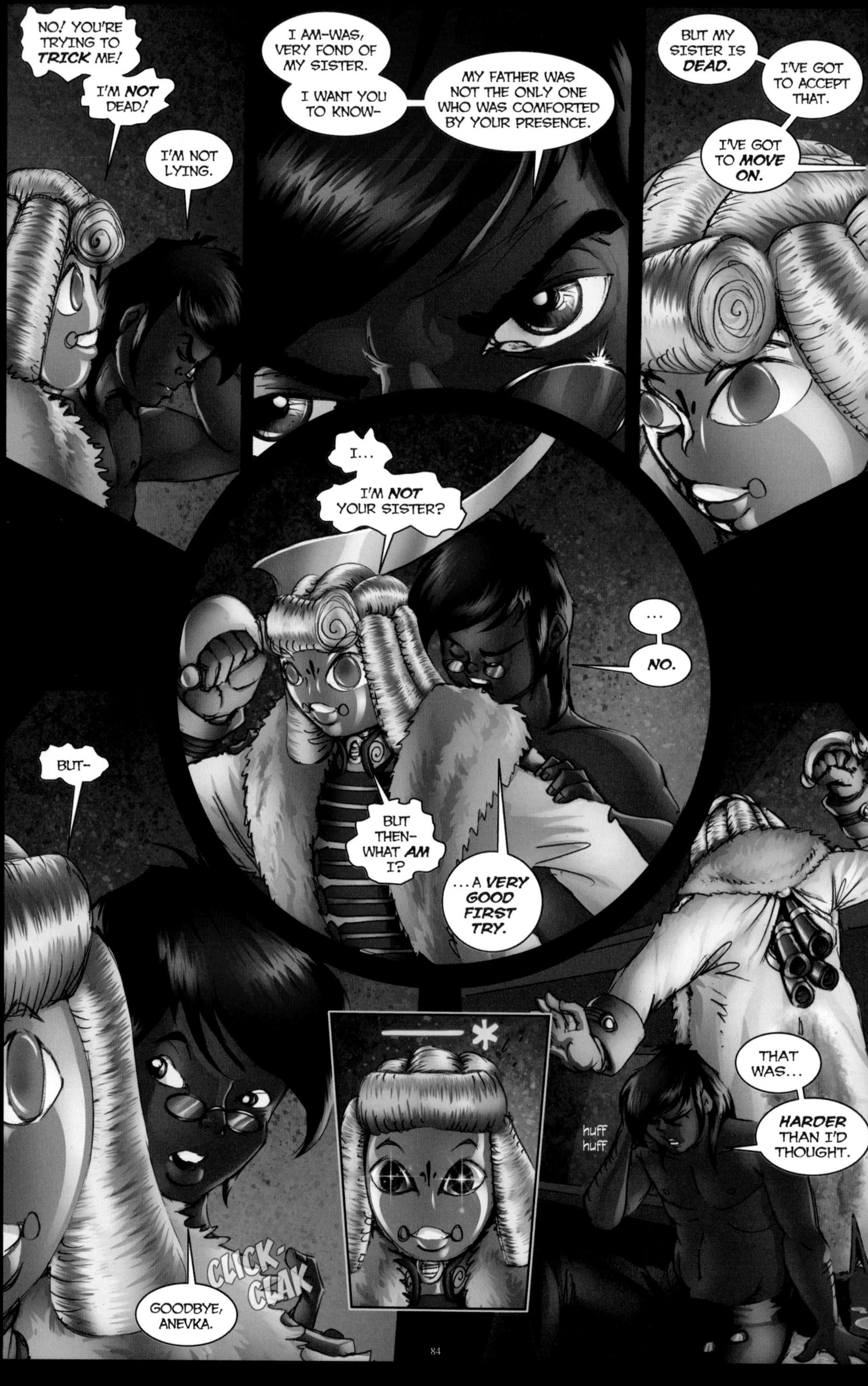
NO! YOU'RE TRYING TO TRICK ME!
I'M NOT DEAD!
I'M NOT LYING.
I AM-WAS, VERY FOND OF MY SISTER.
I WANT YOU TO KNOW-
MY FATHER WAS NOT THE ONLY ONE WHO WAS COMFORTED BY YOUR PRESENCE.
BUT MY SISTER IS DEAD.
I'VE GOT TO ACCEPT THAT.
I'VE GOT TO MOVE ON.
I...
I'M NOT YOUR SISTER?
...
NO.
BUT THEN- WHAT AM I?
...A VERY GOOD FIRST TRY.
BUT-
CLICK-CLAK
GOODBYE, ANEVKA.
THAT WAS...
HARDER THAN I'D THOUGHT.
huff huff

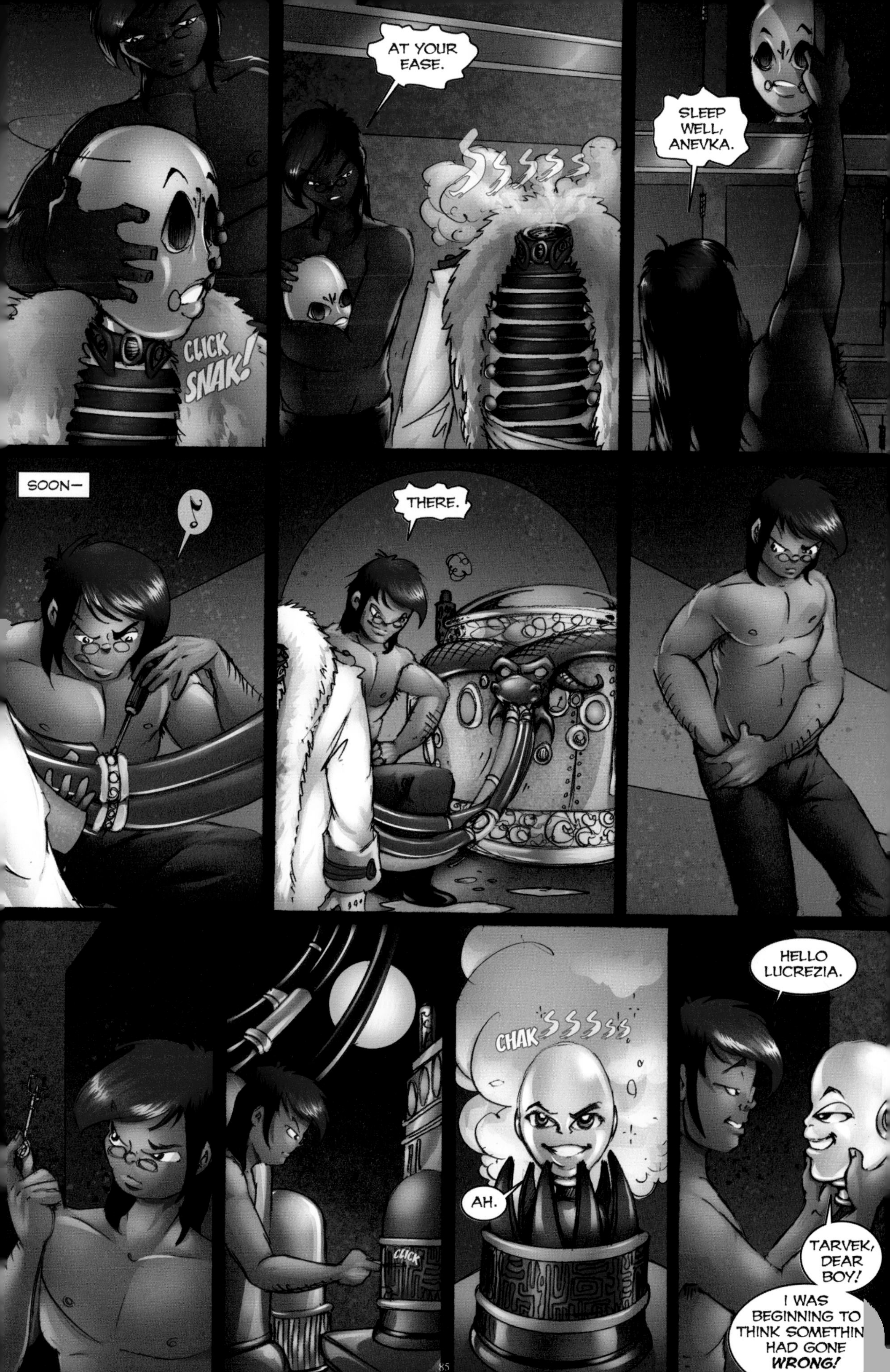
CLICK
SNAK!
AT YOUR EASE.
SSSSS
SLEEP WELL, ANEVKA.
SOON—
THERE.
CLICK
CHAK SSSSSS
AH.
HELLO LUCREZIA.
TARVEK, DEAR BOY!
I WAS BEGINNING TO THINK SOMETHIN HAD GONE WRONG!

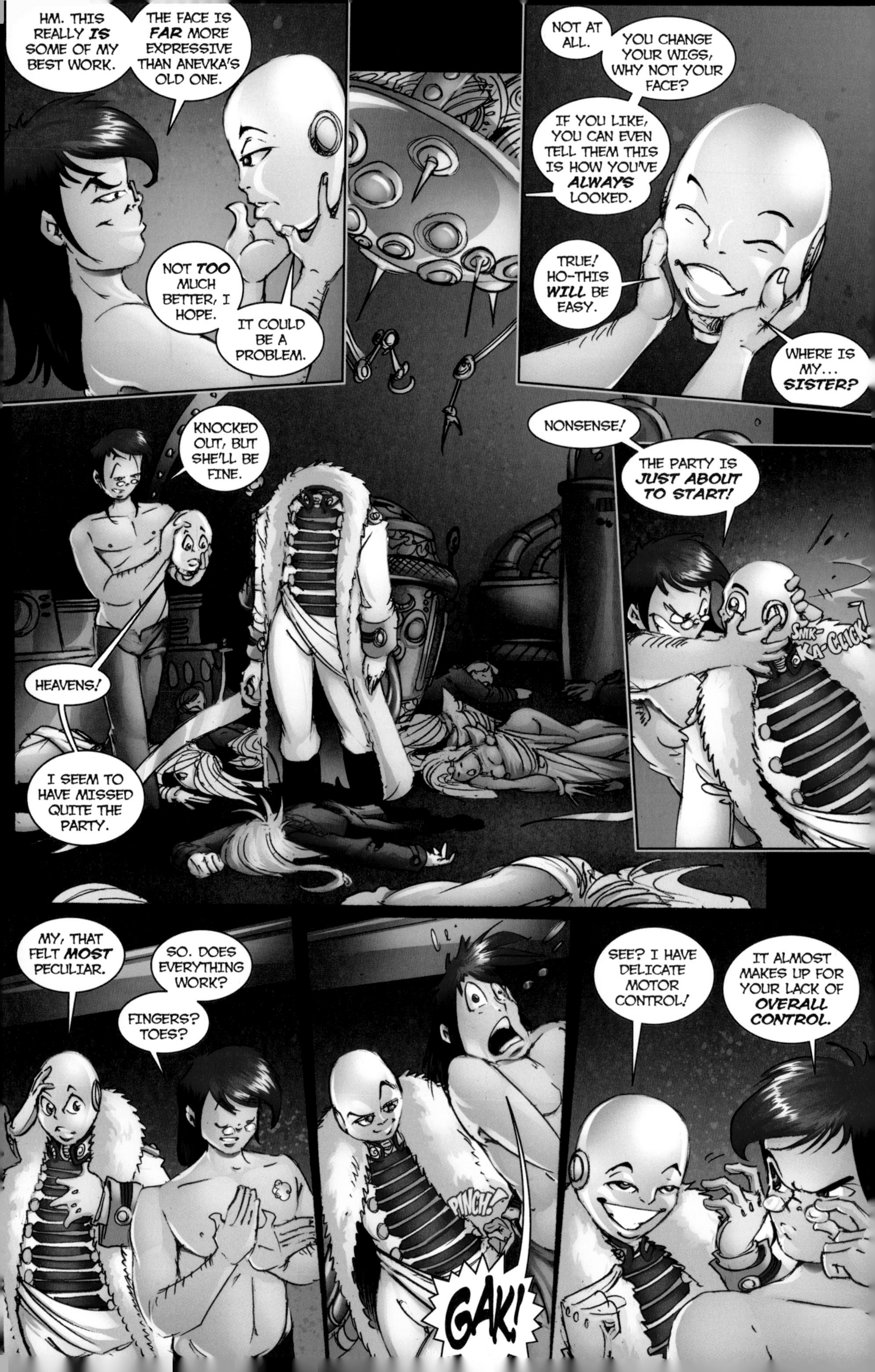
HM. THIS REALLY IS SOME OF MY BEST WORK.
THE FACE IS FAR MORE EXPRESSIVE THAN ANEVKA'S OLD ONE.
NOT TOO MUCH BETTER, I HOPE.
IT COULD BE A PROBLEM.
NOT AT ALL.
YOU CHANGE YOUR WIGS, WHY NOT YOUR FACE?
IF YOU LIKE, YOU CAN EVEN TELL THEM THIS IS HOW YOU'VE ALWAYS LOOKED.
TRUE! HO-THIS WILL BE EASY.
WHERE IS MY... SISTER?
KNOCKED OUT, BUT SHE'LL BE FINE.
HEAVENS!
I SEEM TO HAVE MISSED QUITE THE PARTY.
NONSENSE!
THE PARTY IS JUST ABOUT TO START!
SNIK-KA-CLICK
MY, THAT FELT MOST PECULIAR.
SO. DOES EVERYTHING WORK?
FINGERS? TOES?
PINCH!
GAK!
SEE? I HAVE DELICATE MOTOR CONTROL!
IT ALMOST MAKES UP FOR YOUR LACK OF OVERALL CONTROL.

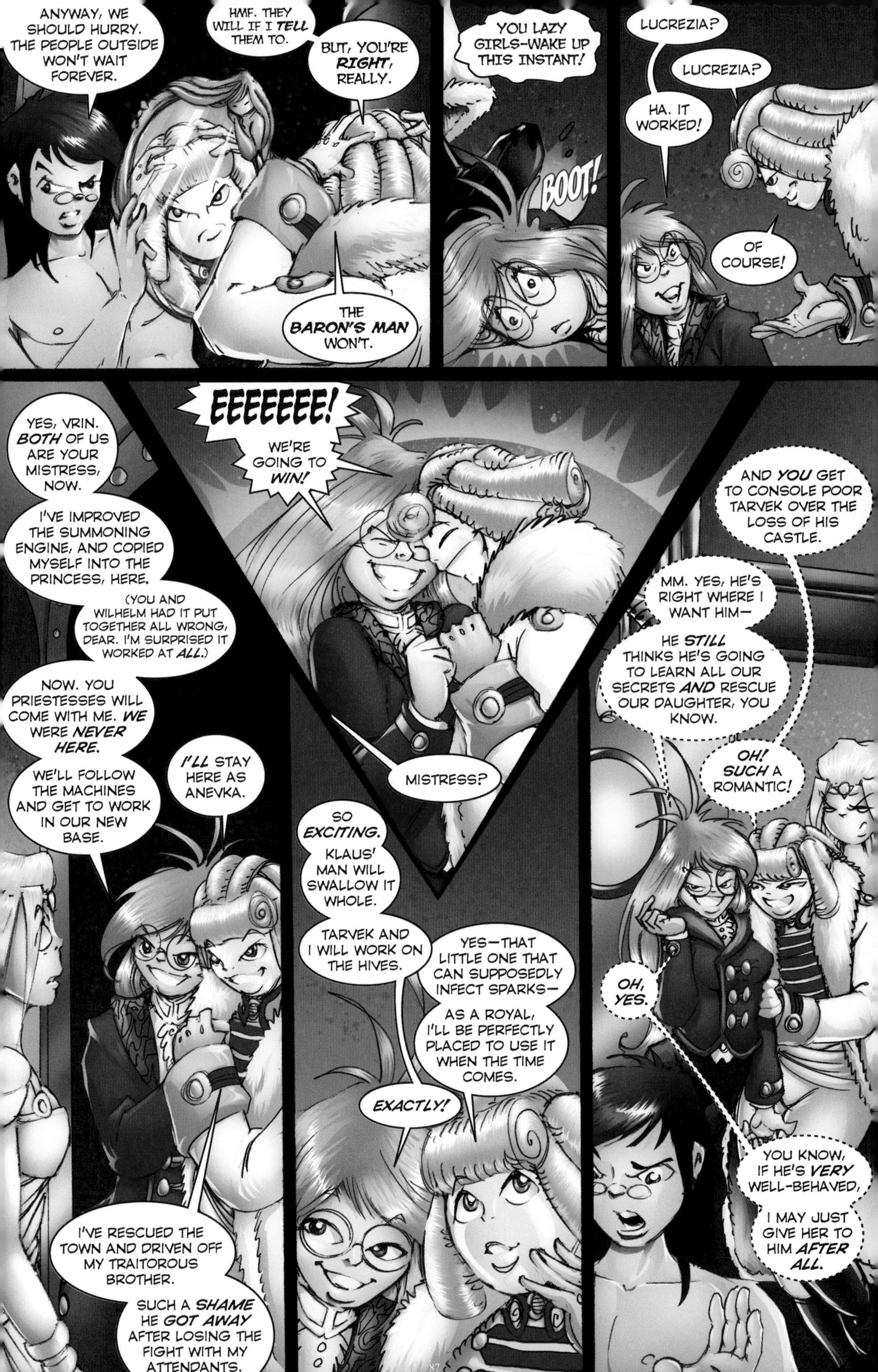
ANYWAY, WE SHOULD HURRY. THE PEOPLE OUTSIDE WON'T WAIT FOREVER.
HMF. THEY WILL IF I *TELL* THEM TO.
BUT, YOU'RE *RIGHT*, REALLY.
THE *BARON'S MAN* WON'T.
YOU LAZY GIRLS—WAKE UP THIS INSTANT!
BOOT!
LUCREZIA?
LUCREZIA?
HA. IT WORKED!
OF COURSE!
EEEEEEE!
WE'RE GOING TO *WIN!*
MISTRESS?
YES, VRIN. *BOTH* OF US ARE YOUR MISTRESS, NOW.
I'VE IMPROVED THE SUMMONING ENGINE, AND COPIED MYSELF INTO THE PRINCESS, HERE.
(YOU AND WILHELM HAD IT PUT TOGETHER ALL WRONG, DEAR. I'M SURPRISED IT WORKED AT *ALL*.)
NOW. YOU PRIESTESSES WILL COME WITH ME. *WE* WERE *NEVER HERE*.
WE'LL FOLLOW THE MACHINES AND GET TO WORK IN OUR NEW BASE.
I'LL STAY HERE AS ANEVKA.
I'VE RESCUED THE TOWN AND DRIVEN OFF MY TRAITOROUS BROTHER.
SUCH A *SHAME* HE *GOT AWAY* AFTER LOSING THE FIGHT WITH MY ATTENDANTS.
SO *EXCITING*.
KLAUS' MAN WILL SWALLOW IT WHOLE.
TARVEK AND I WILL WORK ON THE HIVES.
YES—THAT LITTLE ONE THAT CAN SUPPOSEDLY INFECT SPARKS—
AS A ROYAL, I'LL BE PERFECTLY PLACED TO USE IT WHEN THE TIME COMES.
EXACTLY!
AND *YOU* GET TO CONSOLE POOR TARVEK OVER THE LOSS OF HIS CASTLE.
MM. YES, HE'S RIGHT WHERE I WANT HIM—
HE *STILL* THINKS HE'S GOING TO LEARN ALL OUR SECRETS *AND* RESCUE OUR DAUGHTER, YOU KNOW.
OH! SUCH A ROMANTIC!
OH, YES.
YOU KNOW, IF HE'S *VERY* WELL-BEHAVED,
I MAY JUST GIVE HER TO HIM *AFTER ALL*.

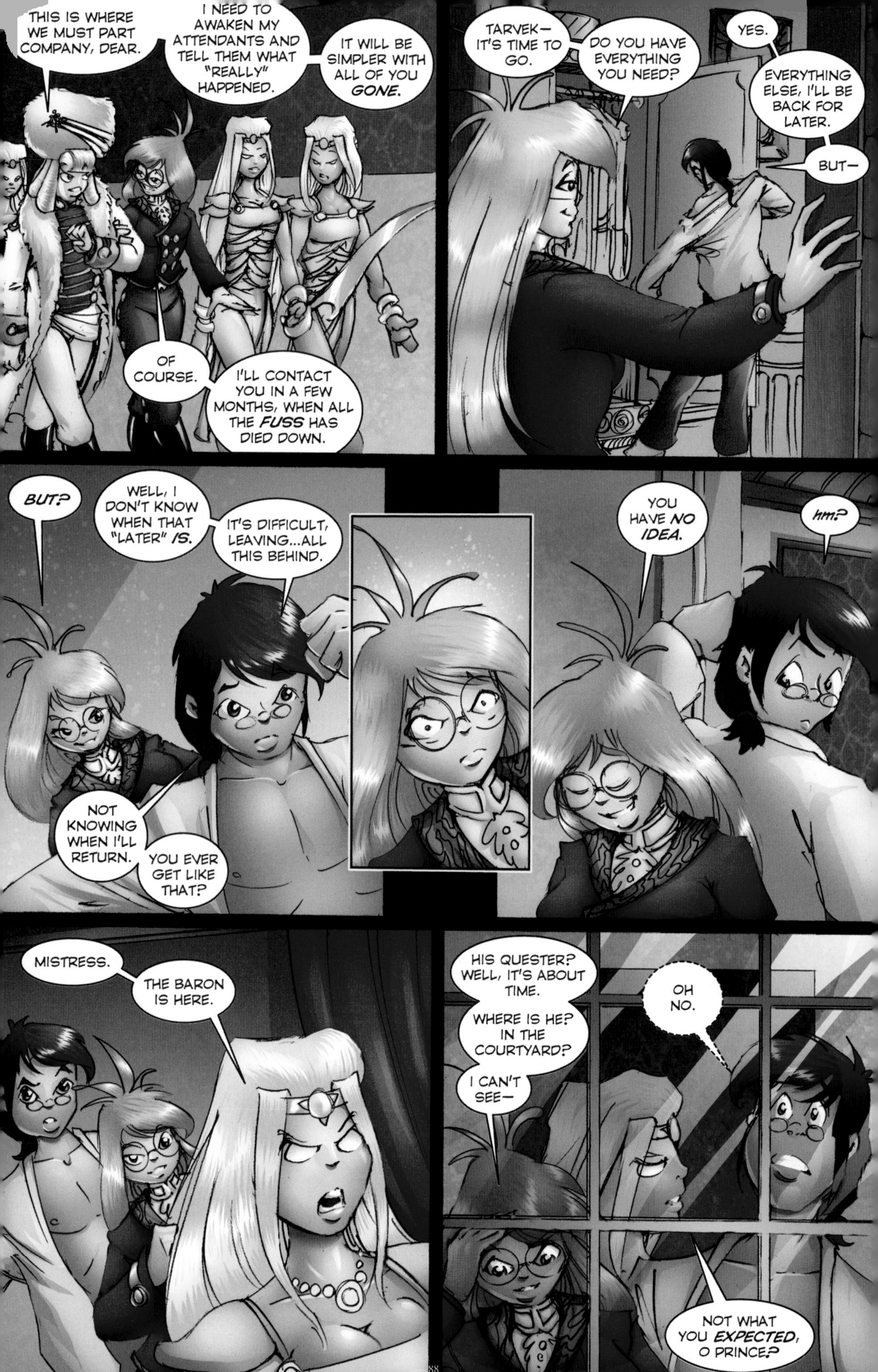
THIS IS WHERE WE MUST PART COMPANY, DEAR.
I NEED TO AWAKEN MY ATTENDANTS AND TELL THEM WHAT "REALLY" HAPPENED.
IT WILL BE SIMPLER WITH ALL OF YOU *GONE.*
OF COURSE.
I'LL CONTACT YOU IN A FEW MONTHS, WHEN ALL THE *FUSS* HAS DIED DOWN.
TARVEK— IT'S TIME TO GO.
DO YOU HAVE EVERYTHING YOU NEED?
YES.
EVERYTHING ELSE, I'LL BE BACK FOR LATER.
BUT—
BUT?
WELL, I DON'T KNOW WHEN THAT "LATER" *IS.*
IT'S DIFFICULT, LEAVING...ALL THIS BEHIND.
NOT KNOWING WHEN I'LL RETURN.
YOU EVER GET LIKE THAT?
YOU HAVE *NO IDEA.*
hm?
MISTRESS.
THE BARON IS HERE.
HIS QUESTER? WELL, IT'S ABOUT TIME.
WHERE IS HE? IN THE COURTYARD?
I CAN'T SEE—
OH NO.
NOT WHAT YOU *EXPECTED,* O PRINCE?

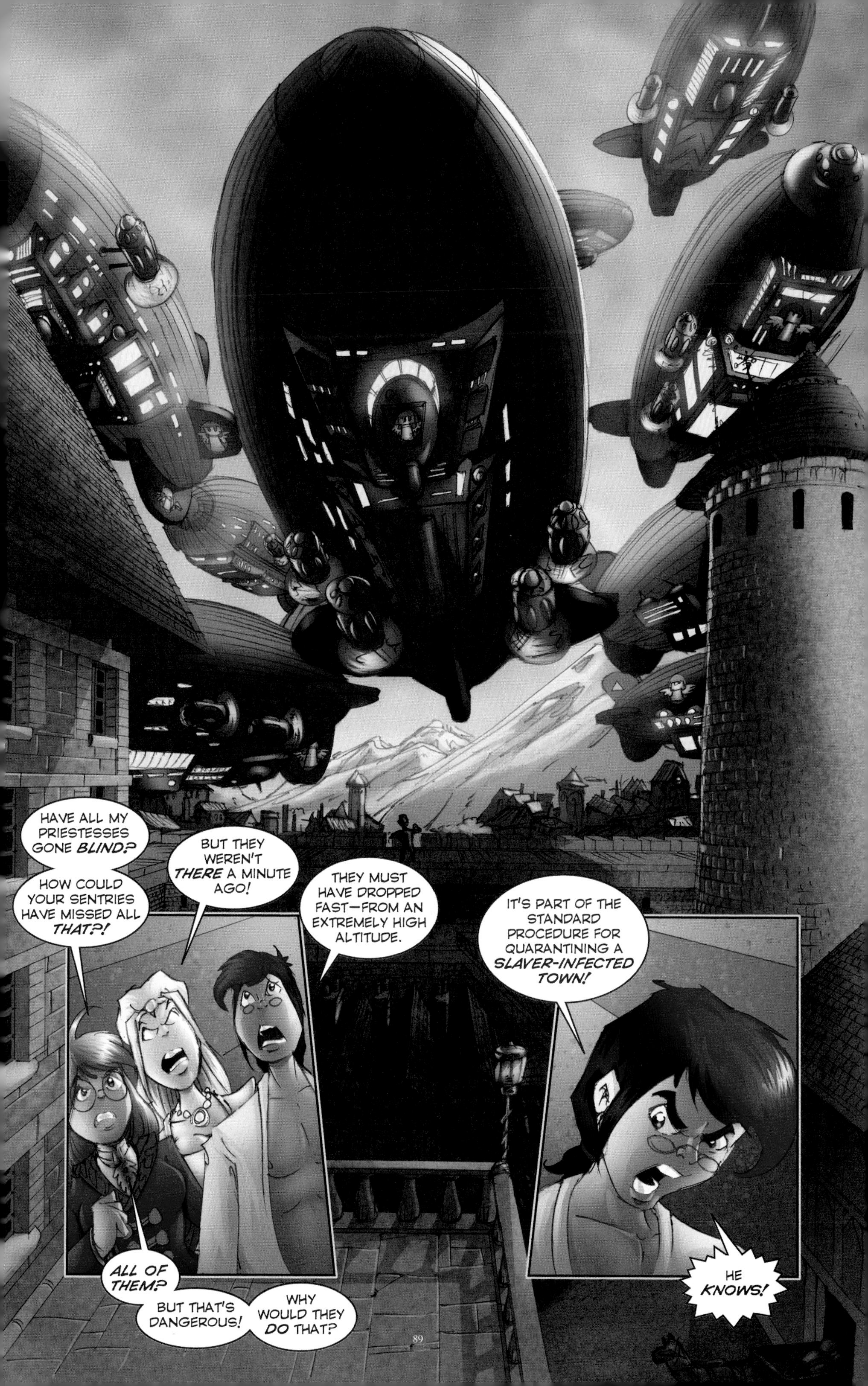
HAVE ALL MY PRIESTESSES GONE BLIND?
HOW COULD YOUR SENTRIES HAVE MISSED ALL THAT?!
BUT THEY WEREN'T THERE A MINUTE AGO!
THEY MUST HAVE DROPPED FAST—FROM AN EXTREMELY HIGH ALTITUDE.
ALL OF THEM?
BUT THAT'S DANGEROUS!
WHY WOULD THEY DO THAT?
IT'S PART OF THE STANDARD PROCEDURE FOR QUARANTINING A SLAVER-INFECTED TOWN!
HE KNOWS!

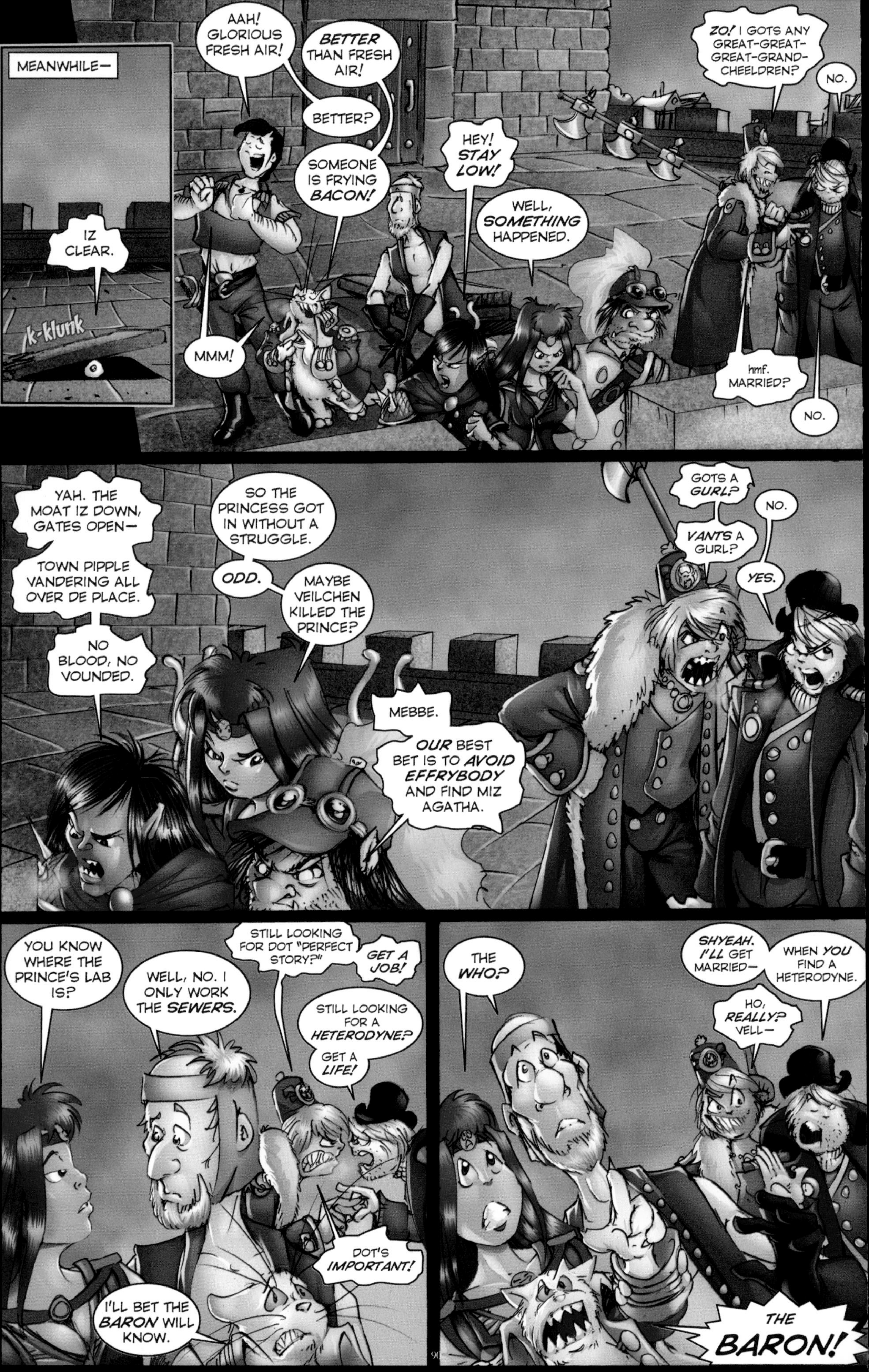

MEANWHILE—
IZ CLEAR.
k-klunk
AAH! GLORIOUS FRESH AIR!
BETTER THAN FRESH AIR!
BETTER?
SOMEONE IS FRYING BACON!
MMM!
HEY! STAY LOW!
WELL, SOMETHING HAPPENED.
ZO! I GOTS ANY GREAT-GREAT-GREAT-GRAND-CHEELDREN?
NO.
hmf. MARRIED?
NO.
YAH. THE MOAT IZ DOWN, GATES OPEN—
TOWN PIPPLE VANDERING ALL OVER DE PLACE.
NO BLOOD, NO VOUNDED.
SO THE PRINCESS GOT IN WITHOUT A STRUGGLE.
ODD.
MAYBE VEILCHEN KILLED THE PRINCE?
MEBBE.
OUR BEST BET IS TO AVOID EFFRYBODY AND FIND MIZ AGATHA.
GOTS A GURL?
NO.
VANTS A GURL?
YES.
YOU KNOW WHERE THE PRINCE'S LAB IS?
WELL, NO. I ONLY WORK THE SEWERS.
STILL LOOKING FOR DOT "PERFECT STORY?"
GET A JOB!
STILL LOOKING FOR A HETERODYNE?
GET A LIFE!
DOT'S IMPORTANT!
I'LL BET THE BARON WILL KNOW.
THE WHO?
SHYEAH. I'LL GET MARRIED—
WHEN YOU FIND A HETERODYNE.
HO, REALLY? VELL—
THE BARON!

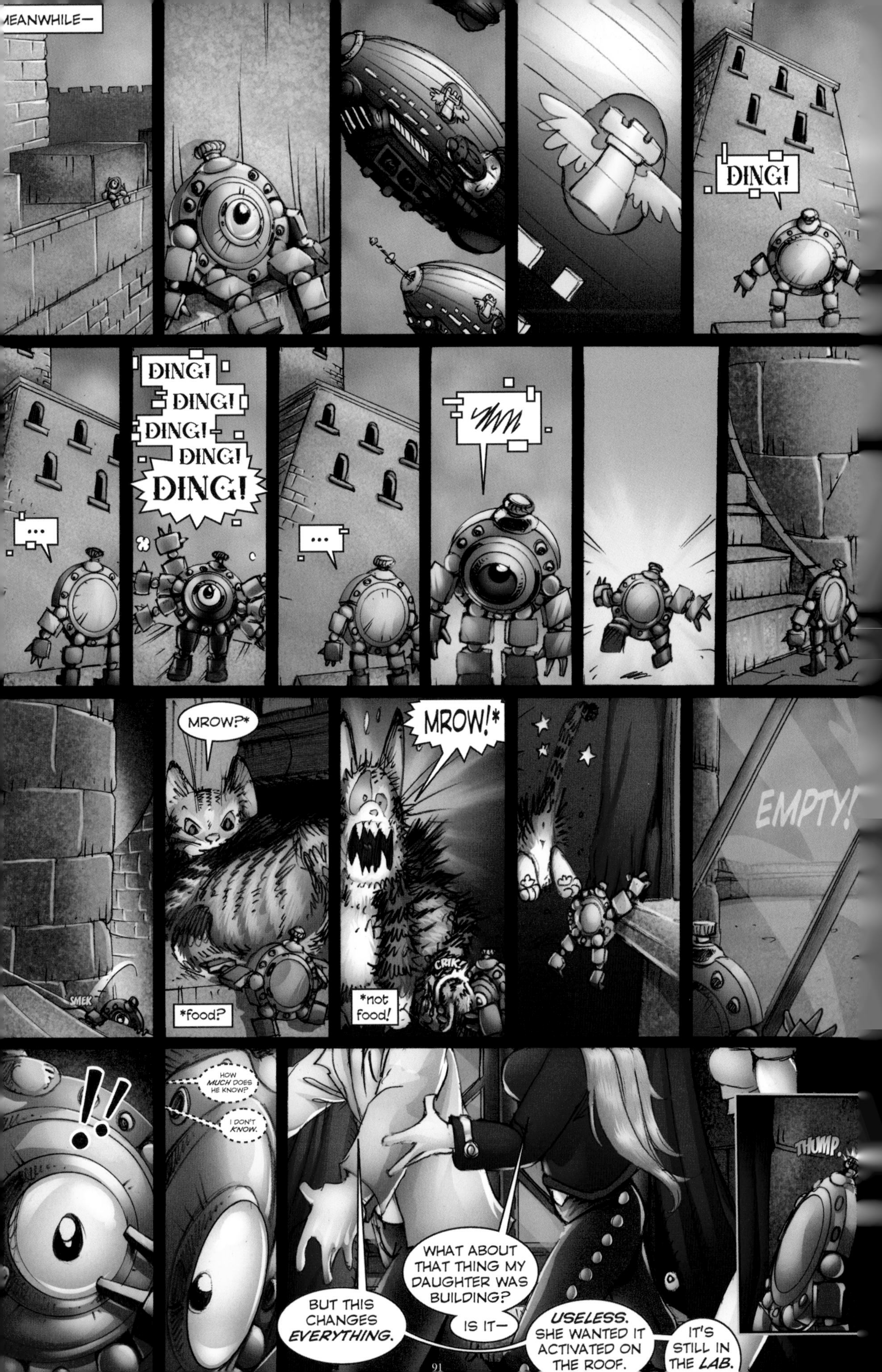
MEANWHILE—
DING!
...
DING!
DING!
DING!
DING!
DING!
...
MROW?*
*food?
SMEK
MROW!*
*not food!
CRIK!
EMPTY!
!!
HOW MUCH DOES HE KNOW?
I DON'T KNOW.
BUT THIS CHANGES EVERYTHING.
WHAT ABOUT THAT THING MY DAUGHTER WAS BUILDING?
IS IT—
USELESS. SHE WANTED IT ACTIVATED ON THE ROOF.
IT'S STILL IN THE LAB.
THUMP.

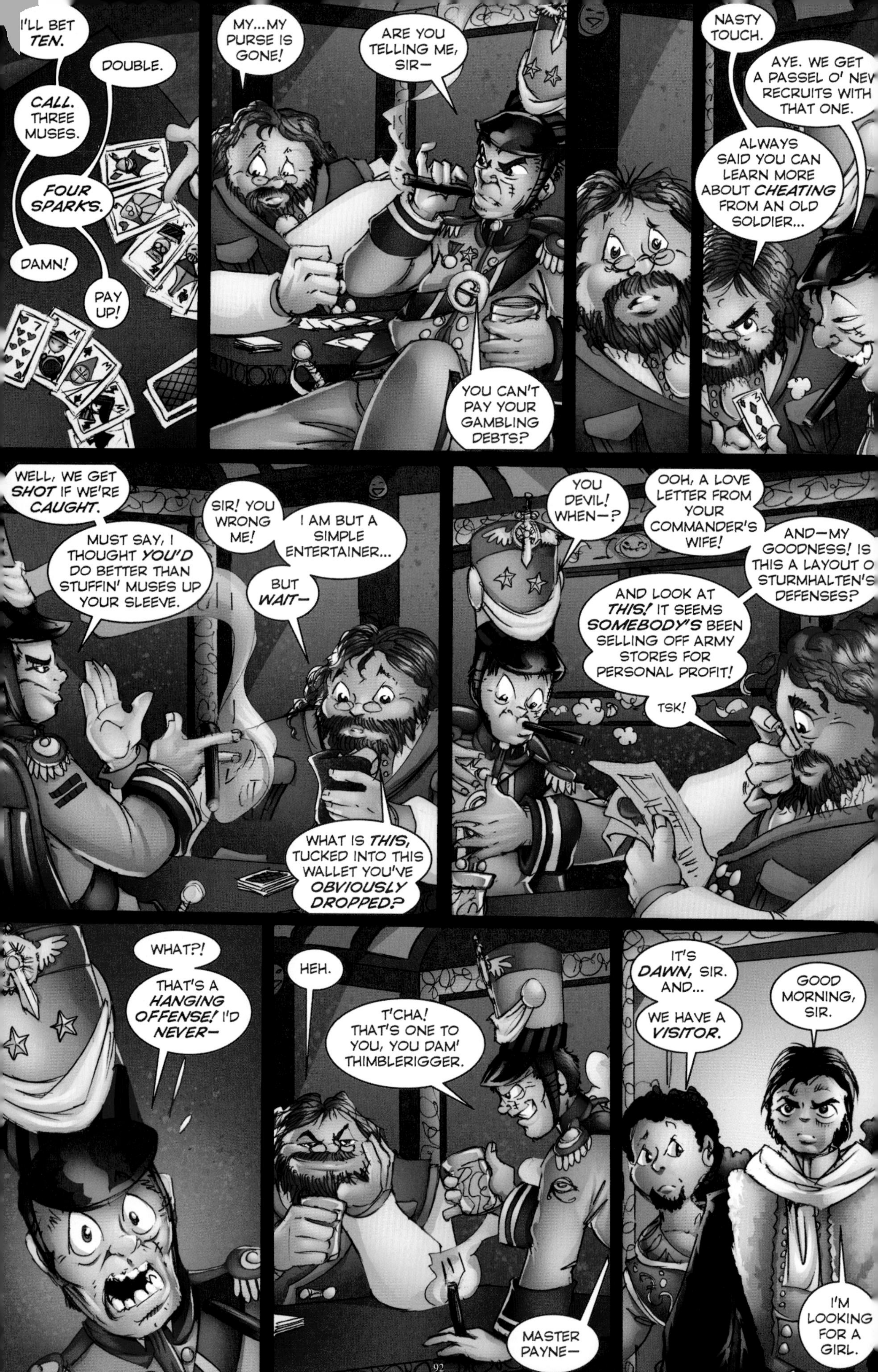

I'LL BET TEN.
DOUBLE.
CALL. THREE MUSES.
FOUR SPARKS.
DAMN!
PAY UP!
MY...MY PURSE IS GONE!
ARE YOU TELLING ME, SIR—
YOU CAN'T PAY YOUR GAMBLING DEBTS?
NASTY TOUCH.
AYE. WE GET A PASSEL O' NEW RECRUITS WITH THAT ONE.
ALWAYS SAID YOU CAN LEARN MORE ABOUT CHEATING FROM AN OLD SOLDIER...
WELL, WE GET SHOT IF WE'RE CAUGHT.
MUST SAY, I THOUGHT YOU'D DO BETTER THAN STUFFIN' MUSES UP YOUR SLEEVE.
SIR! YOU WRONG ME!
I AM BUT A SIMPLE ENTERTAINER...
BUT WAIT—
WHAT IS THIS, TUCKED INTO THIS WALLET YOU'VE OBVIOUSLY DROPPED?
YOU DEVIL! WHEN—?
OOH, A LOVE LETTER FROM YOUR COMMANDER'S WIFE!
AND—MY GOODNESS! IS THIS A LAYOUT OF STURMHALTEN'S DEFENSES?
AND LOOK AT THIS! IT SEEMS SOMEBODY'S BEEN SELLING OFF ARMY STORES FOR PERSONAL PROFIT!
TSK!
WHAT?!
THAT'S A HANGING OFFENSE! I'D NEVER—
HEH.
T'CHA! THAT'S ONE TO YOU, YOU DAM' THIMBLERIGGER.
MASTER PAYNE—
IT'S DAWN, SIR. AND...
WE HAVE A VISITOR.
GOOD MORNING, SIR.
I'M LOOKING FOR A GIRL.

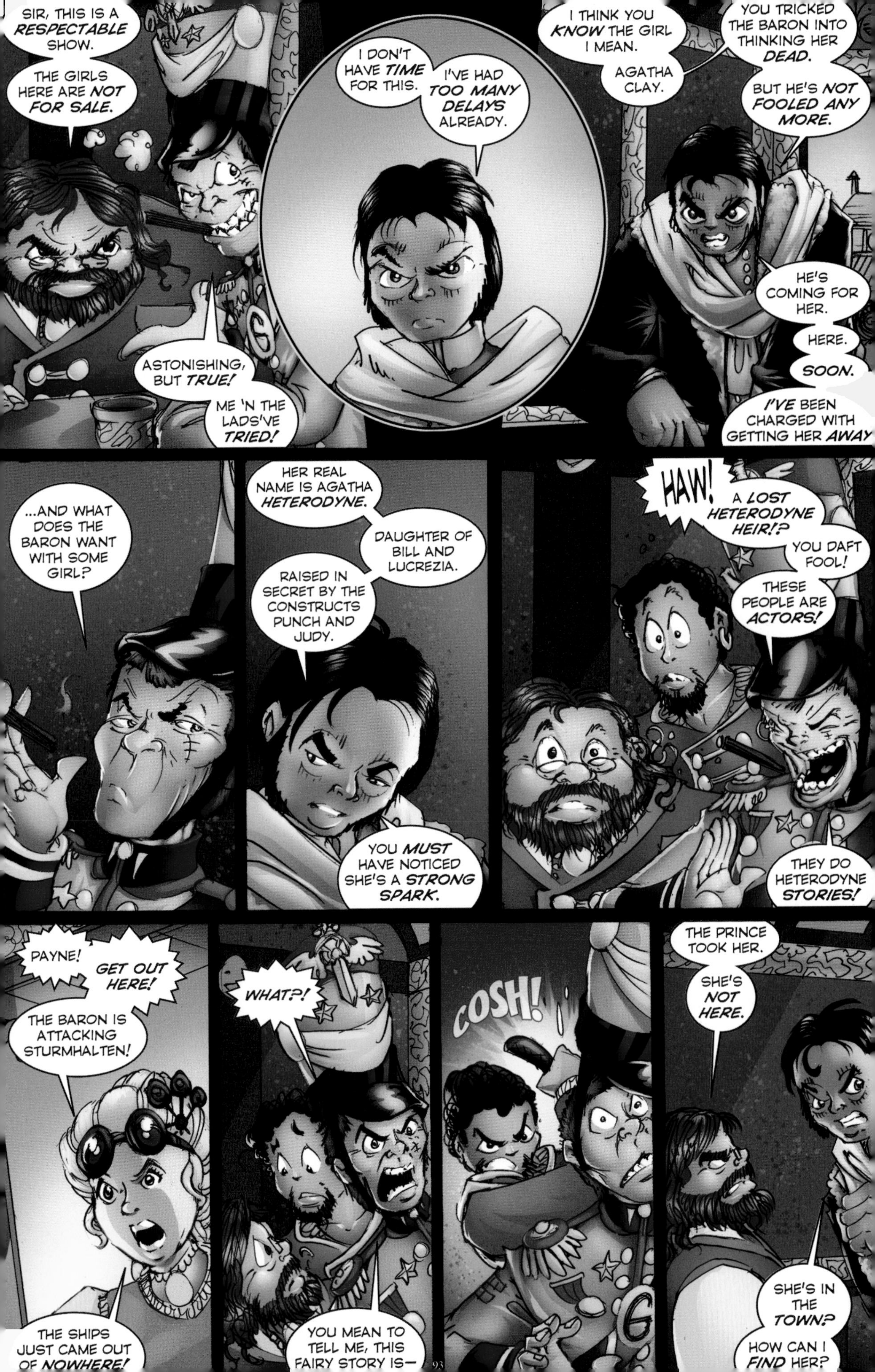
SIR, THIS IS A RESPECTABLE SHOW.
THE GIRLS HERE ARE NOT FOR SALE.
ASTONISHING, BUT TRUE!
ME 'N THE LADS'VE TRIED!
I DON'T HAVE TIME FOR THIS.
I'VE HAD TOO MANY DELAYS ALREADY.
I THINK YOU KNOW THE GIRL I MEAN.
AGATHA CLAY.
YOU TRICKED THE BARON INTO THINKING HER DEAD.
BUT HE'S NOT FOOLED ANY MORE.
HE'S COMING FOR HER.
HERE.
SOON.
I'VE BEEN CHARGED WITH GETTING HER AWAY
...AND WHAT DOES THE BARON WANT WITH SOME GIRL?
HER REAL NAME IS AGATHA HETERODYNE.
DAUGHTER OF BILL AND LUCREZIA.
RAISED IN SECRET BY THE CONSTRUCTS PUNCH AND JUDY.
YOU MUST HAVE NOTICED SHE'S A STRONG SPARK.
HAW!
A LOST HETERODYNE HEIR!?
YOU DAFT FOOL!
THESE PEOPLE ARE ACTORS!
THEY DO HETERODYNE STORIES!
PAYNE!
GET OUT HERE!
THE BARON IS ATTACKING STURMHALTEN!
THE SHIPS JUST CAME OUT OF NOWHERE!
WHAT?!
YOU MEAN TO TELL ME, THIS FAIRY STORY IS—
COSH!
THE PRINCE TOOK HER.
SHE'S NOT HERE.
SHE'S IN THE TOWN?
HOW CAN I FIND HER?

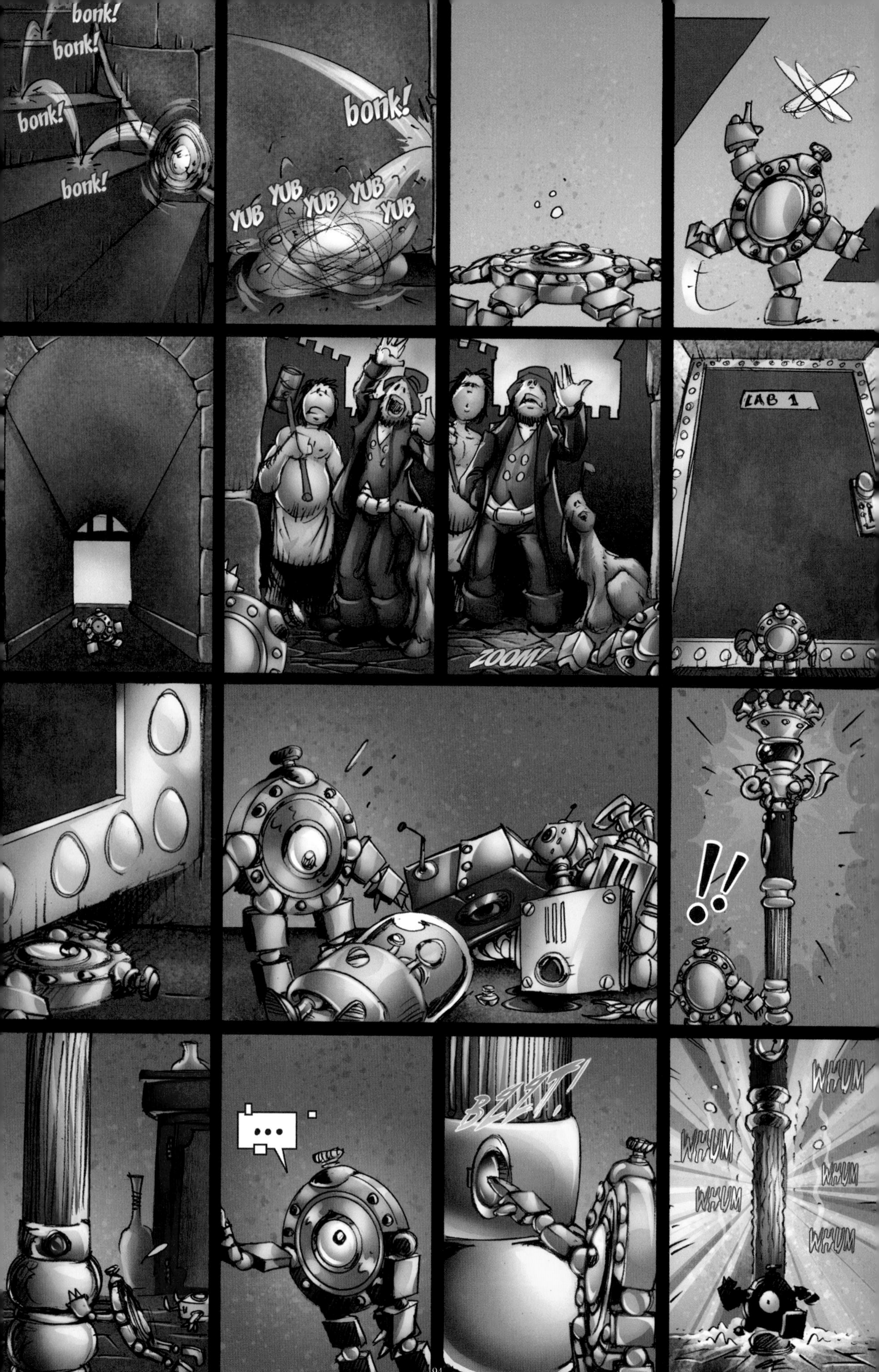
bonk!
bonk!
bonk!
bonk!
bonk!
YUB YUB YUB YUB YUB
LAB 1
ZOOM!
!!
...
BZZT!
WHUM
WHUM
WHUM
WHUM
WHUM

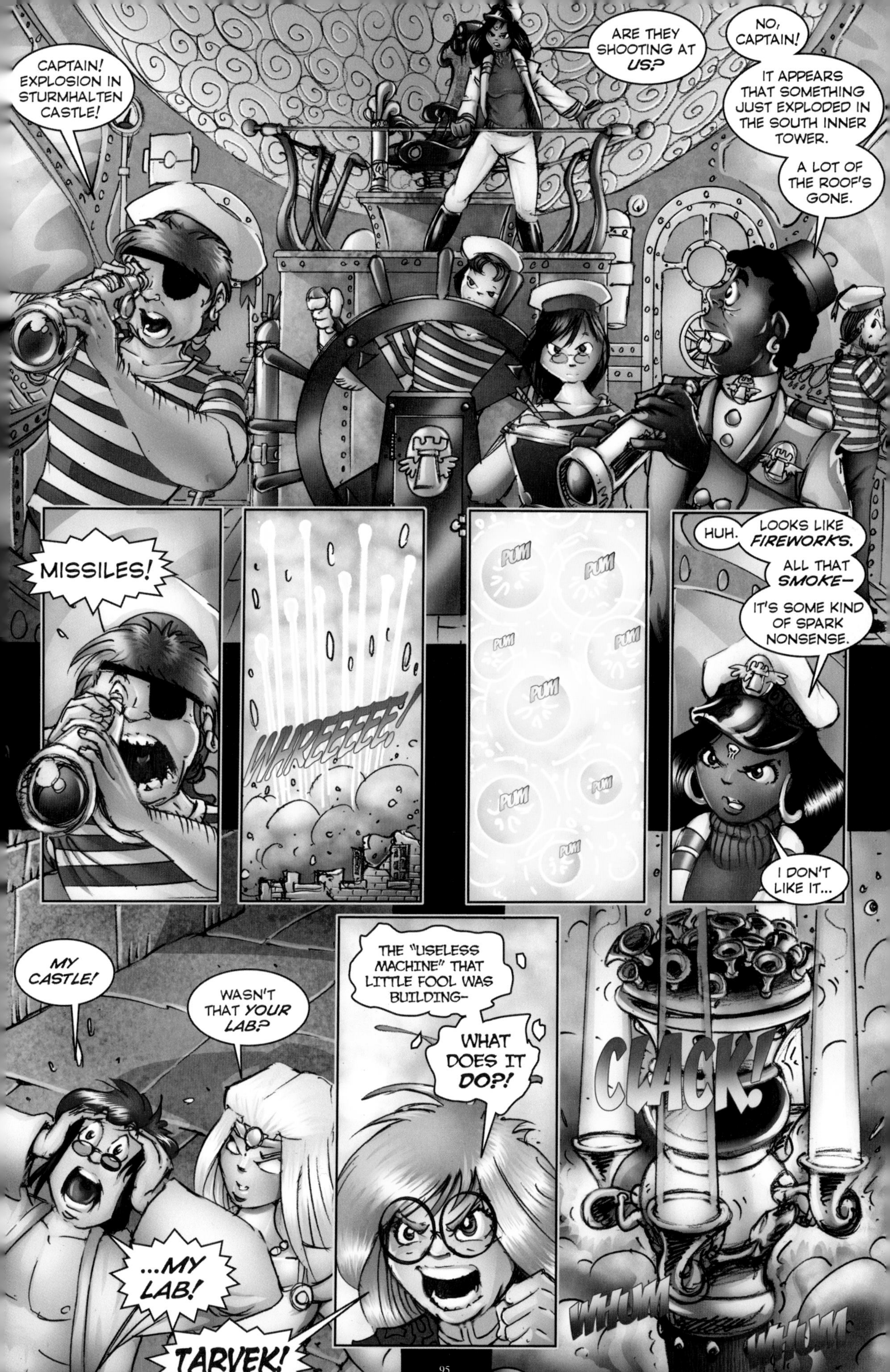
CAPTAIN! EXPLOSION IN STURMHALTEN CASTLE!
ARE THEY SHOOTING AT *US?*
NO, CAPTAIN!
IT APPEARS THAT SOMETHING JUST EXPLODED IN THE SOUTH INNER TOWER.
A LOT OF THE ROOF'S GONE.
MISSILES!
WHREEEEEE!
PUM
PUM
PUM
PUM
PUM
PUM
PUM
PUM
HUH.
LOOKS LIKE *FIREWORKS.*
ALL THAT *SMOKE—*
IT'S SOME KIND OF SPARK NONSENSE.
I DON'T LIKE IT...
MY CASTLE!
WASN'T THAT *YOUR* LAB?
...MY LAB!
TARVEK!
THE "USELESS MACHINE" THAT LITTLE FOOL WAS BUILDING—
WHAT DOES IT *DO?!*
CLACK!
WHUM
WHUM

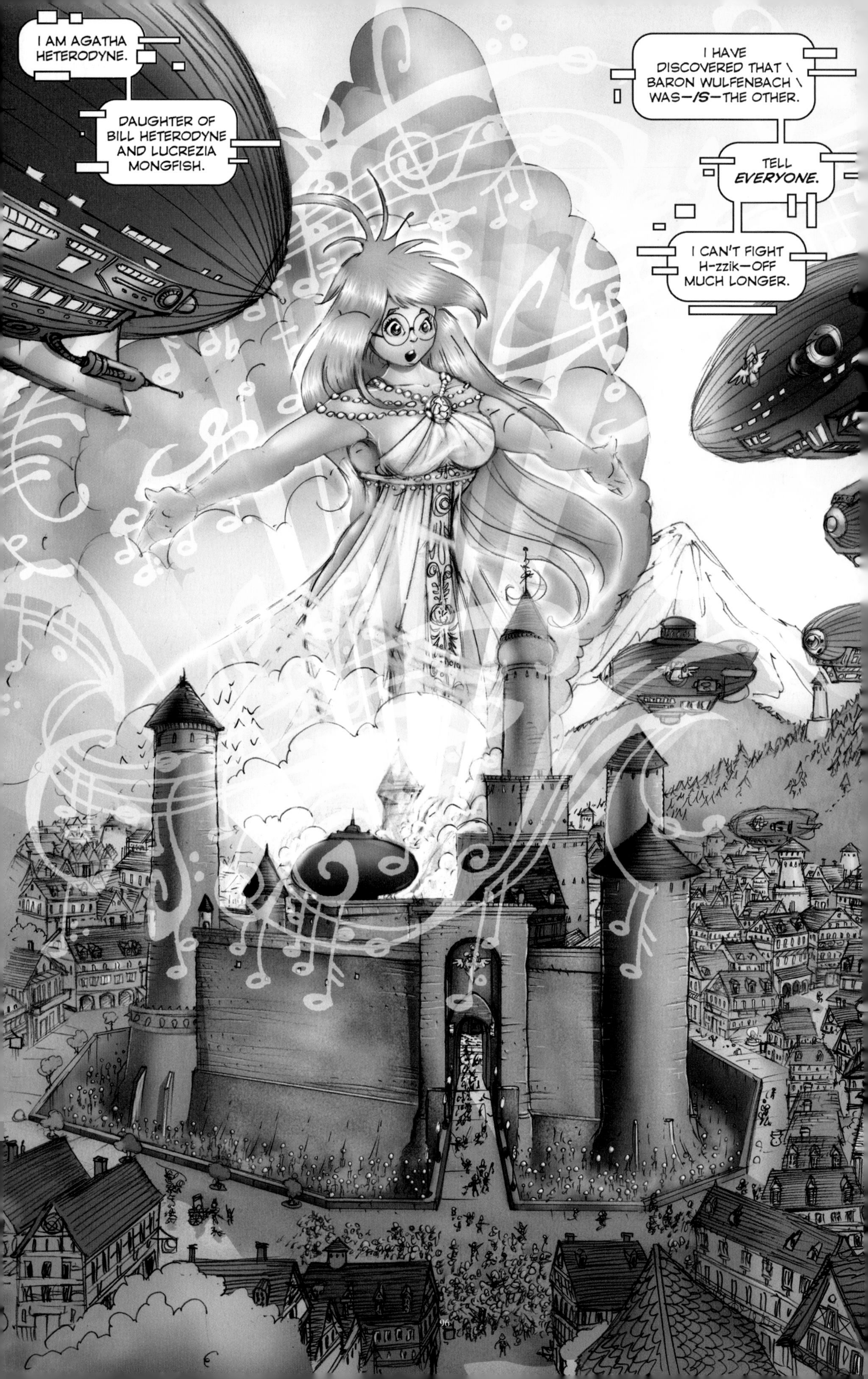
I AM AGATHA HETERODYNE.
DAUGHTER OF BILL HETERODYNE AND LUCREZIA MONGFISH.
I HAVE DISCOVERED THAT \ BARON WULFENBACH \ WAS—IS—THE OTHER.
TELL EVERYONE.
I CAN'T FIGHT H-zzik—OFF MUCH LONGER.

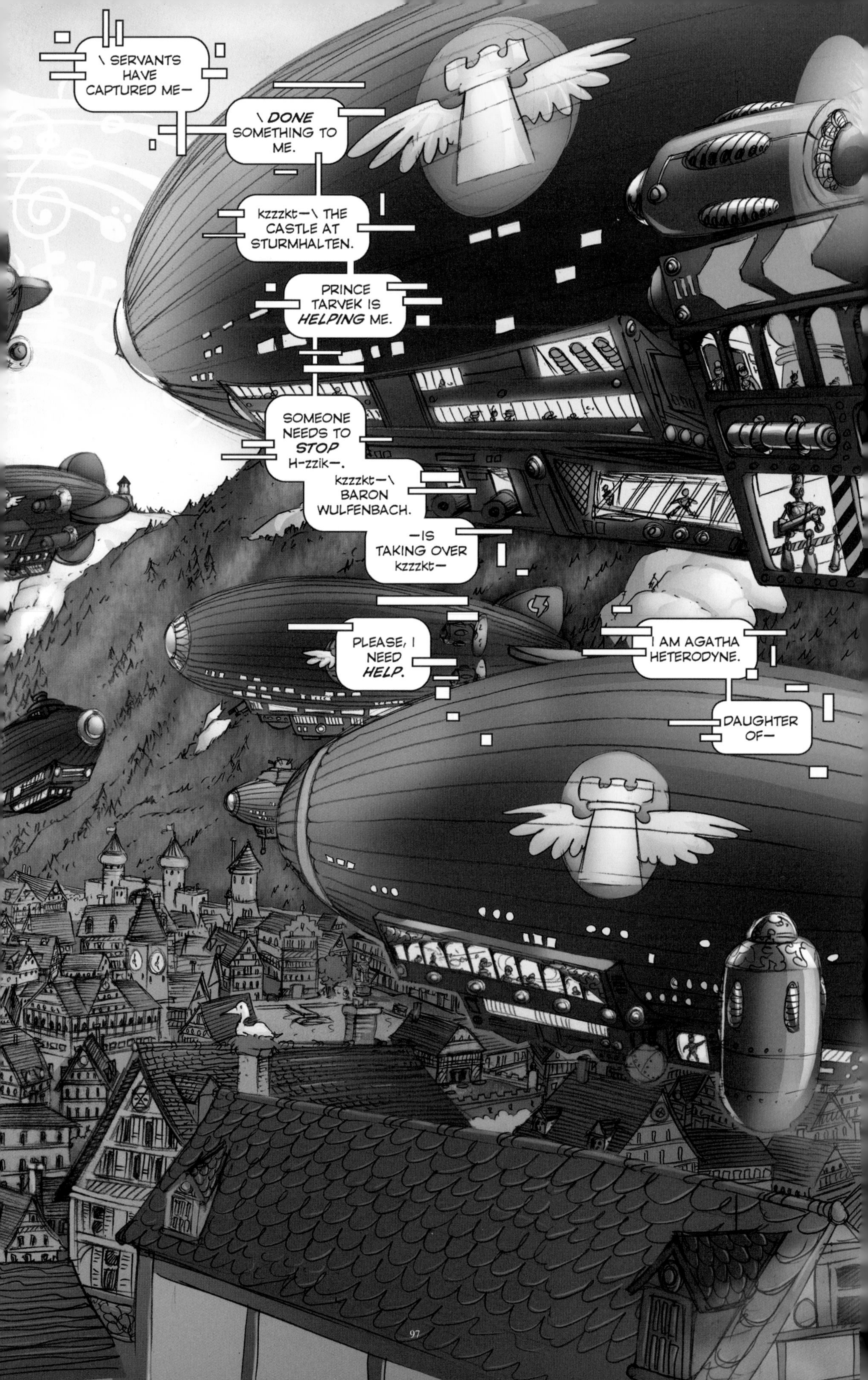
\ SERVANTS HAVE CAPTURED ME—
\ DONE SOMETHING TO ME.
kzzzkt—\ THE CASTLE AT STURMHALTEN.
PRINCE TARVEK IS HELPING ME.
SOMEONE NEEDS TO STOP H-zzik—.
kzzzkt—\ BARON WULFENBACH.
—IS TAKING OVER kzzzkt—
PLEASE, I NEED HELP.
I AM AGATHA HETERODYNE.
DAUGHTER OF—

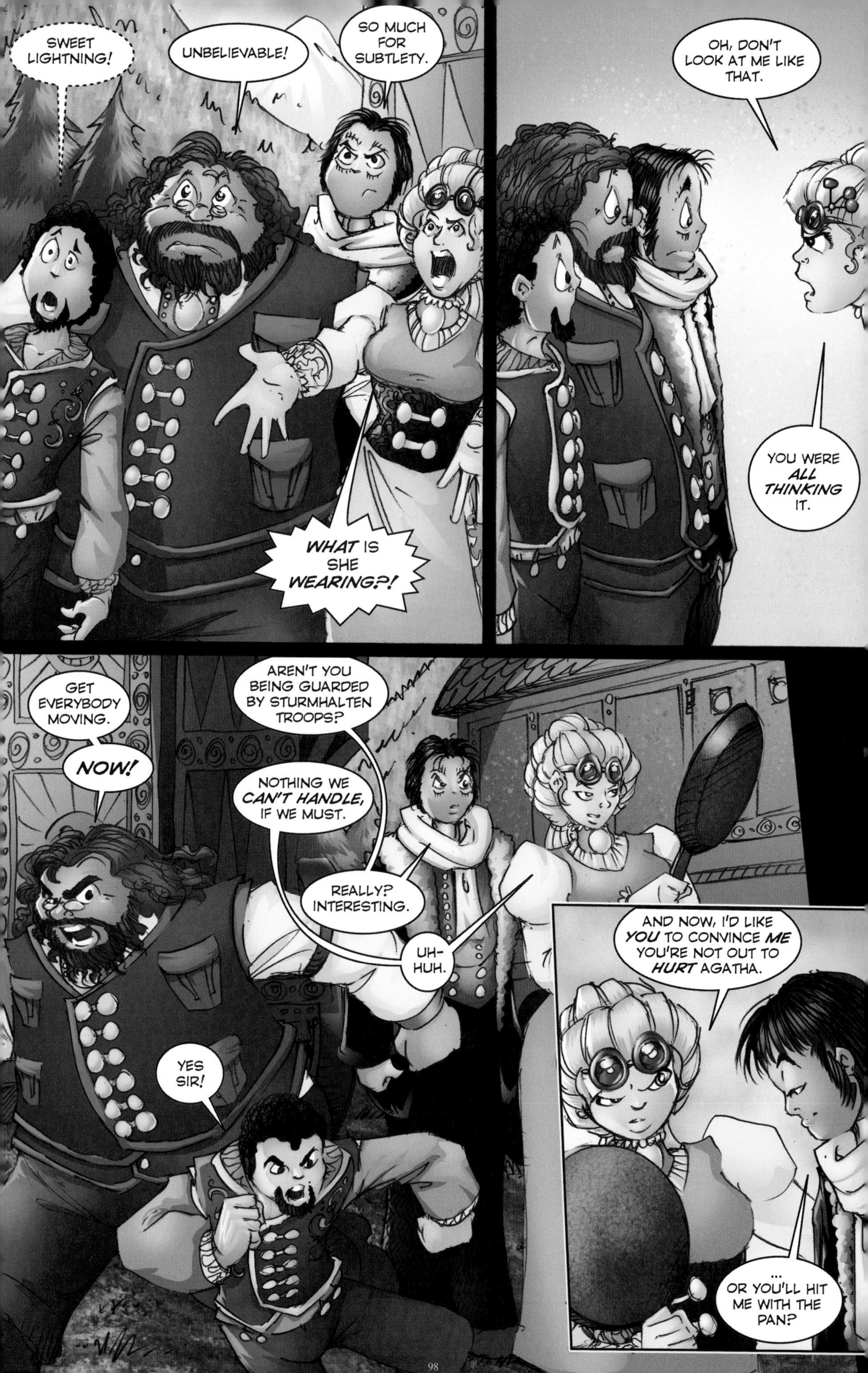
SWEET LIGHTNING!
UNBELIEVABLE!
SO MUCH FOR SUBTLETY.
WHAT IS SHE WEARING?!
OH, DON'T LOOK AT ME LIKE THAT.
YOU WERE ALL THINKING IT.
GET EVERYBODY MOVING.
NOW!
AREN'T YOU BEING GUARDED BY STURMHALTEN TROOPS?
NOTHING WE CAN'T HANDLE, IF WE MUST.
REALLY? INTERESTING.
UH-HUH.
YES SIR!
AND NOW, I'D LIKE YOU TO CONVINCE ME YOU'RE NOT OUT TO HURT AGATHA.
... OR YOU'LL HIT ME WITH THE PAN?

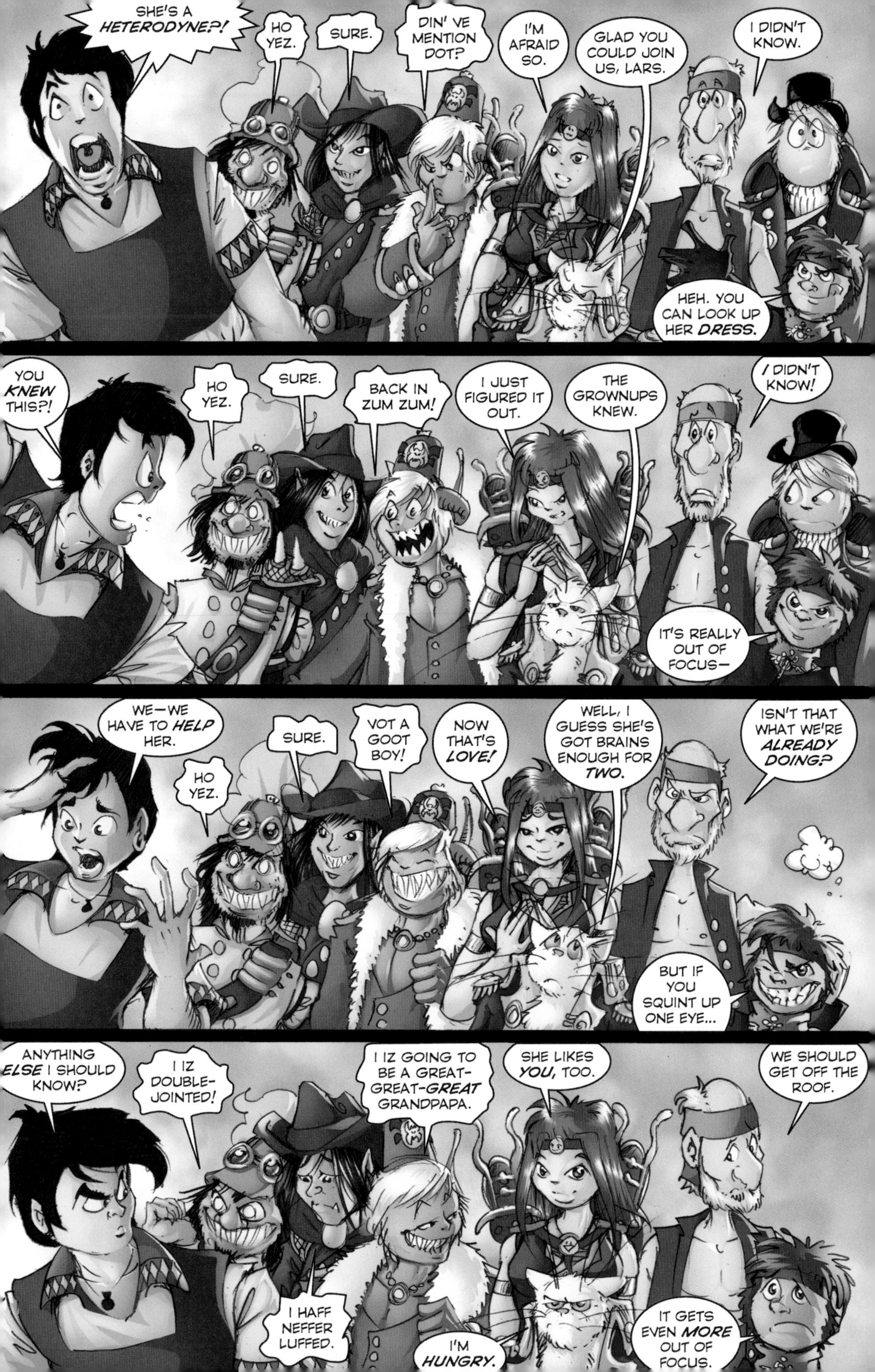
SHE'S A HETERODYNE?!
HO YEZ.
SURE.
DIN' VE MENTION DOT?
I'M AFRAID SO.
GLAD YOU COULD JOIN US, LARS.
I DIDN'T KNOW.
HEH. YOU CAN LOOK UP HER DRESS.
YOU KNEW THIS?!
HO YEZ.
SURE.
BACK IN ZUM ZUM!
I JUST FIGURED IT OUT.
THE GROWNUPS KNEW.
I DIDN'T KNOW!
IT'S REALLY OUT OF FOCUS—
WE—WE HAVE TO HELP HER.
HO YEZ.
SURE.
VOT A GOOT BOY!
NOW THAT'S LOVE!
WELL, I GUESS SHE'S GOT BRAINS ENOUGH FOR TWO.
ISN'T THAT WHAT WE'RE ALREADY DOING?
BUT IF YOU SQUINT UP ONE EYE...
ANYTHING ELSE I SHOULD KNOW?
I IZ DOUBLE-JOINTED!
I IZ GOING TO BE A GREAT-GREAT-GREAT GRANDPAPA.
SHE LIKES YOU, TOO.
WE SHOULD GET OFF THE ROOF.
I HAFF NEFFER LUFFED.
I'M HUNGRY.
IT GETS EVEN MORE OUT OF FOCUS.

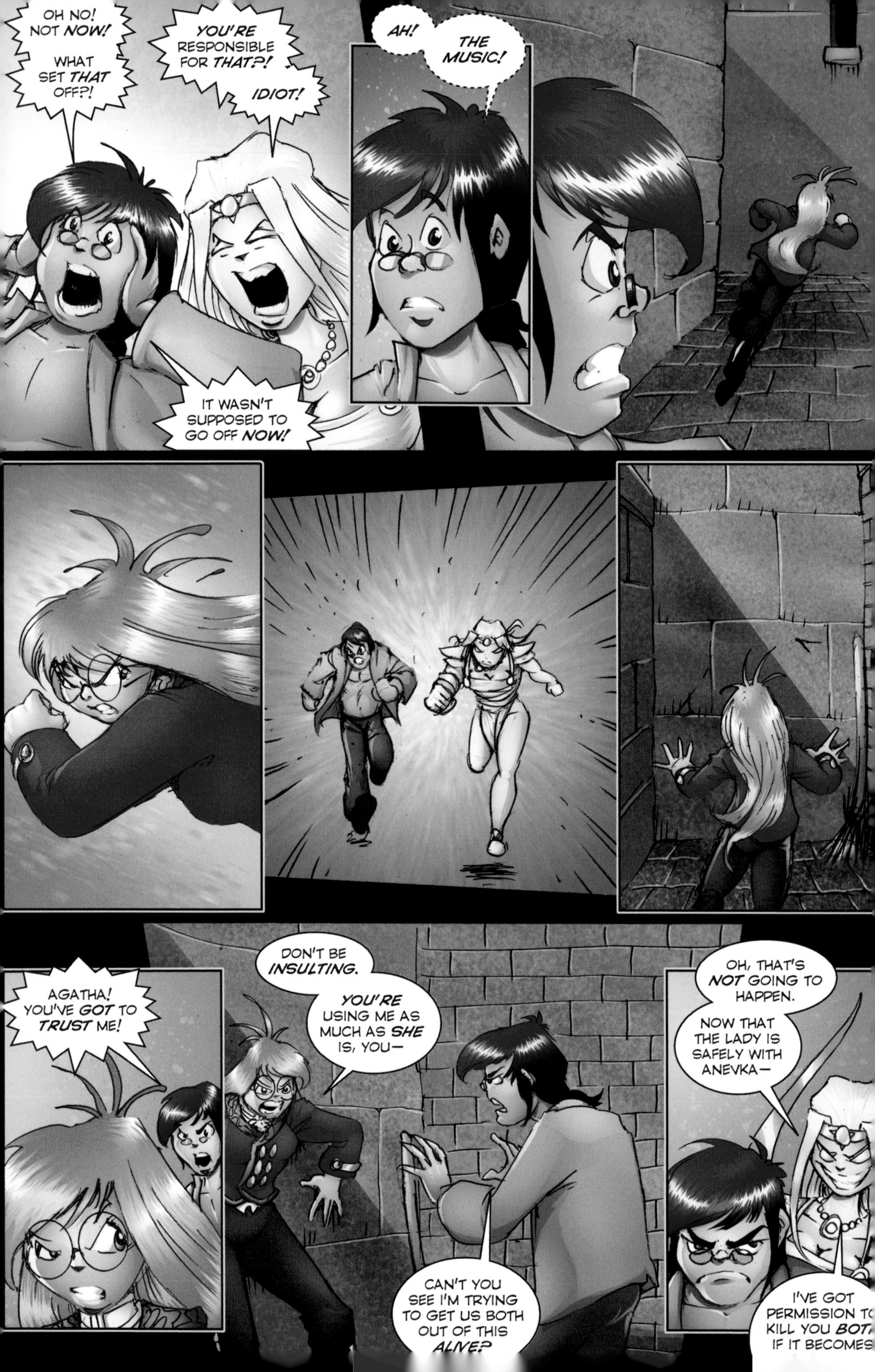
OH NO! NOT NOW! WHAT SET THAT OFF?!
YOU'RE RESPONSIBLE FOR THAT?! IDIOT!
IT WASN'T SUPPOSED TO GO OFF NOW!
AH! THE MUSIC!
AGATHA! YOU'VE GOT TO TRUST ME!
DON'T BE INSULTING.
YOU'RE USING ME AS MUCH AS SHE IS, YOU—
CAN'T YOU SEE I'M TRYING TO GET US BOTH OUT OF THIS ALIVE?
OH, THAT'S NOT GOING TO HAPPEN.
NOW THAT THE LADY IS SAFELY WITH ANEVKA—
I'VE GOT PERMISSION TO KILL YOU BOTH IF IT BECOMES

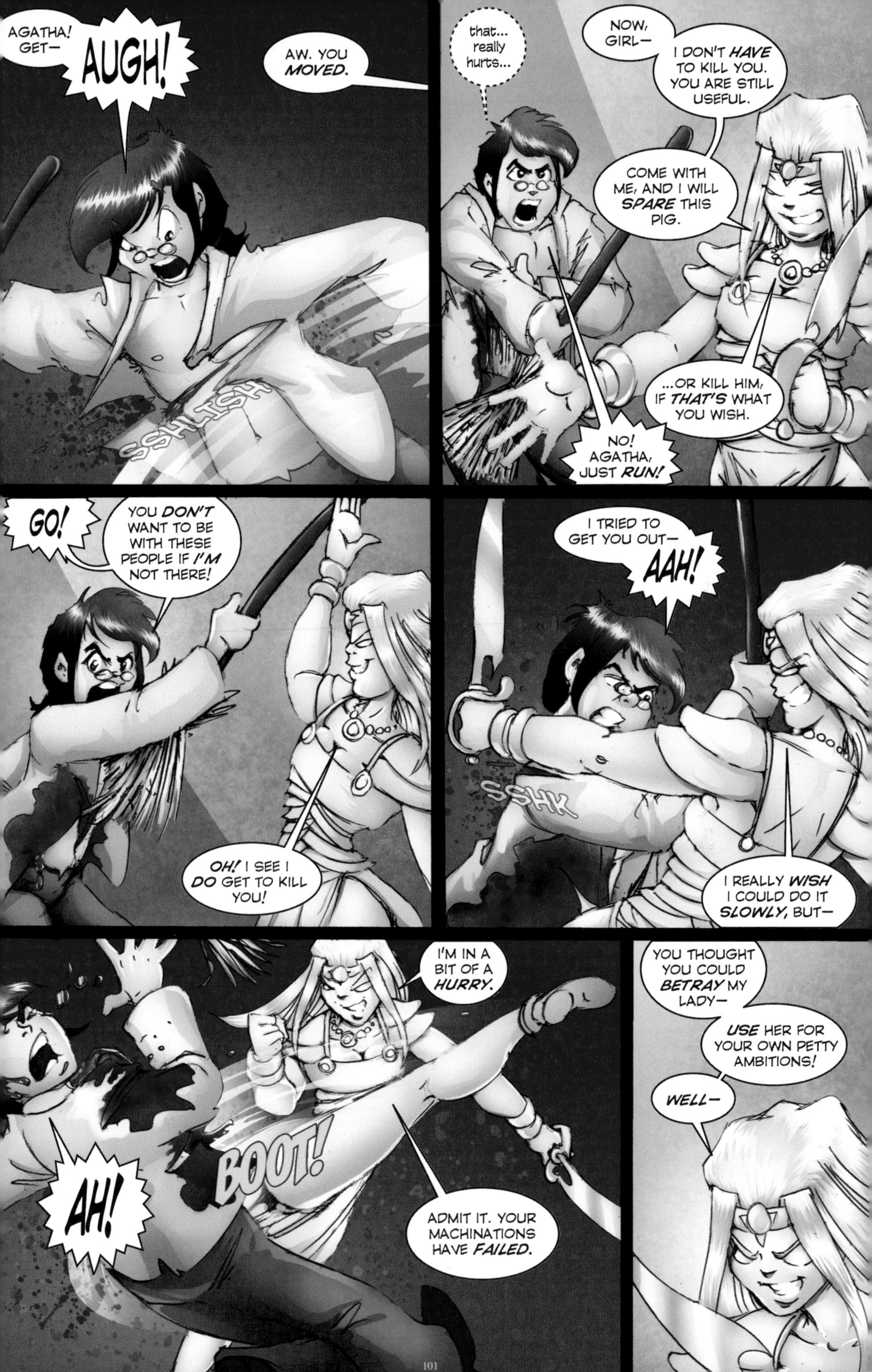
AGATHA! GET—
AUGH!
SSHLISH
AW. YOU MOVED.
that... really hurts...
NOW, GIRL—
I DON'T HAVE TO KILL YOU. YOU ARE STILL USEFUL.
COME WITH ME, AND I WILL SPARE THIS PIG.
...OR KILL HIM, IF THAT'S WHAT YOU WISH.
NO! AGATHA, JUST RUN!
GO!
YOU DON'T WANT TO BE WITH THESE PEOPLE IF I'M NOT THERE!
OH! I SEE I DO GET TO KILL YOU!
I TRIED TO GET YOU OUT—
AAH!
SSHK
I REALLY WISH I COULD DO IT SLOWLY, BUT—
I'M IN A BIT OF A HURRY.
BOOT!
AH!
ADMIT IT. YOUR MACHINATIONS HAVE FAILED.
YOU THOUGHT YOU COULD BETRAY MY LADY—
USE HER FOR YOUR OWN PETTY AMBITIONS!
WELL—

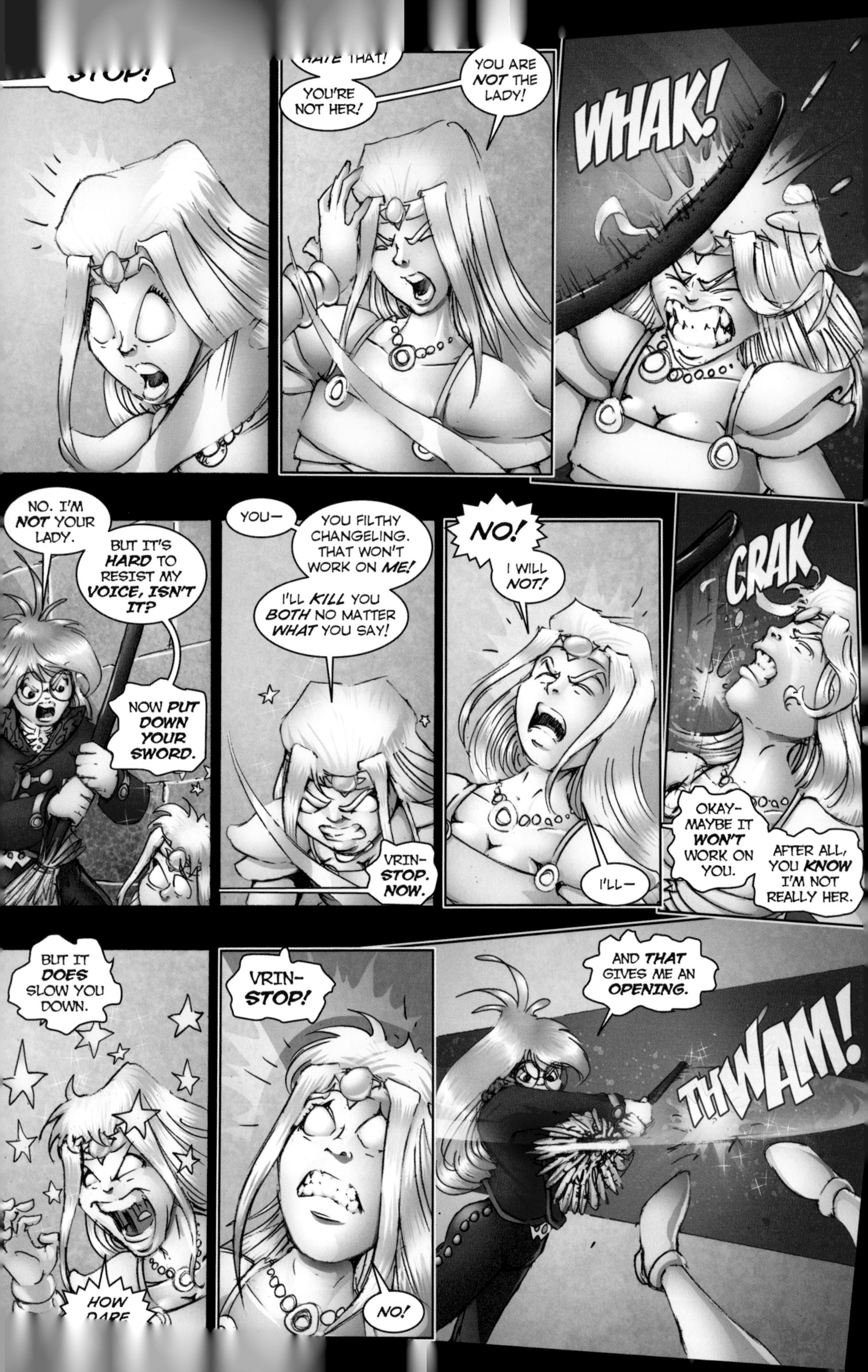
STOP!
HATE THAT!
YOU'RE NOT HER!
YOU ARE NOT THE LADY!
WHAK!
NO. I'M NOT YOUR LADY.
BUT IT'S HARD TO RESIST MY VOICE, ISN'T IT?
NOW PUT DOWN YOUR SWORD.
YOU—
YOU FILTHY CHANGELING. THAT WON'T WORK ON ME!
I'LL KILL YOU BOTH NO MATTER WHAT YOU SAY!
VRIN- STOP. NOW.
NO!
I WILL NOT!
I'LL—
CRAK
OKAY- MAYBE IT WON'T WORK ON YOU.
AFTER ALL, YOU KNOW I'M NOT REALLY HER.
BUT IT DOES SLOW YOU DOWN.
HOW
VRIN- STOP!
NO!
AND THAT GIVES ME AN OPENING.
THWAM!

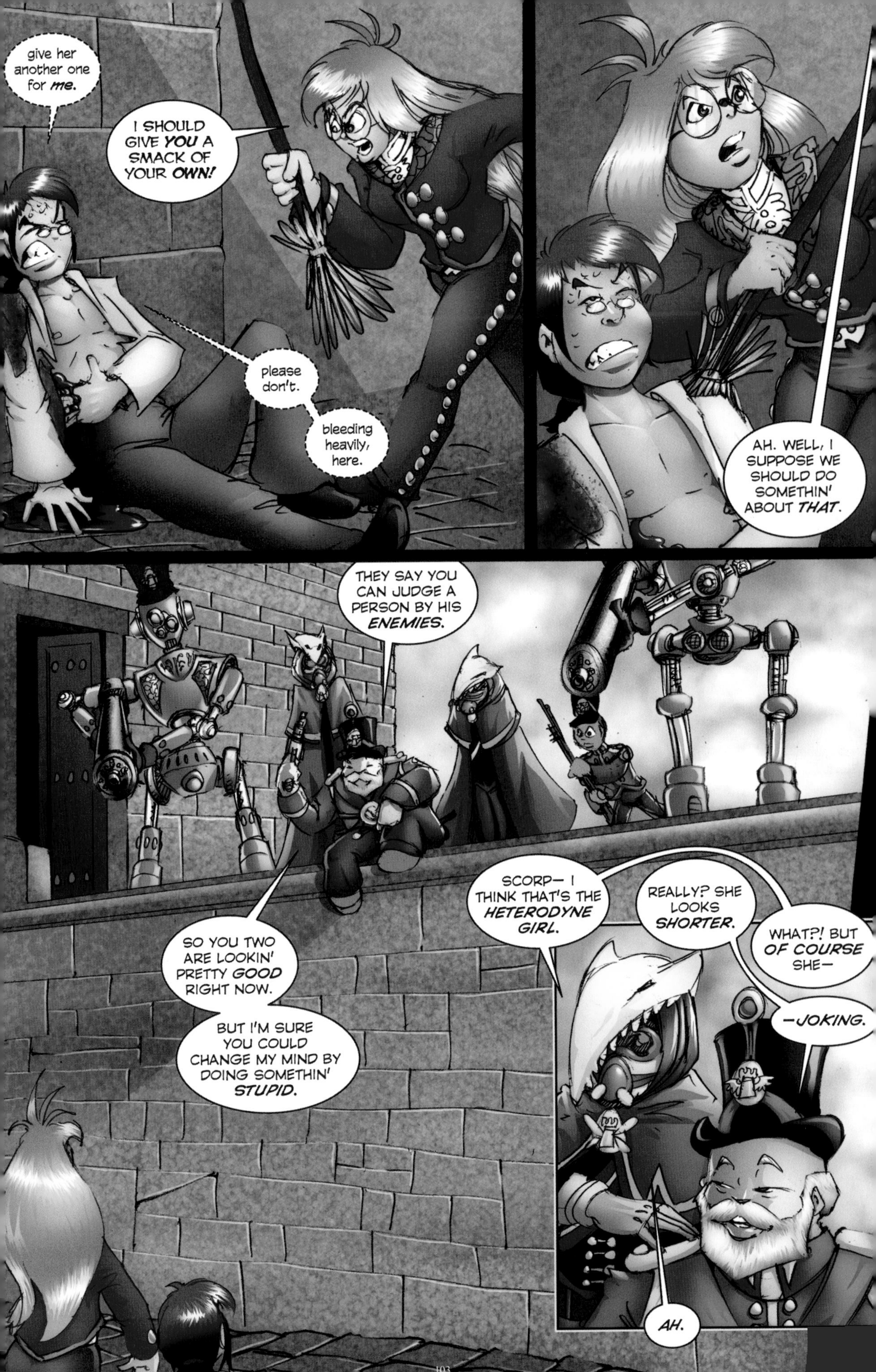
give her another one for *me.*
I SHOULD GIVE ***YOU*** A SMACK OF YOUR ***OWN!***
please don't.
bleeding heavily, here.
AH. WELL, I SUPPOSE WE SHOULD DO SOMETHIN' ABOUT ***THAT.***
THEY SAY YOU CAN JUDGE A PERSON BY HIS ***ENEMIES.***
SO YOU TWO ARE LOOKIN' PRETTY ***GOOD*** RIGHT NOW.
BUT I'M SURE YOU COULD CHANGE MY MIND BY DOING SOMETHIN' ***STUPID.***
SCORP— I THINK THAT'S THE ***HETERODYNE GIRL.***
REALLY? SHE LOOKS ***SHORTER.***
WHAT?! BUT ***OF COURSE*** SHE—
—JOKING.
AH.

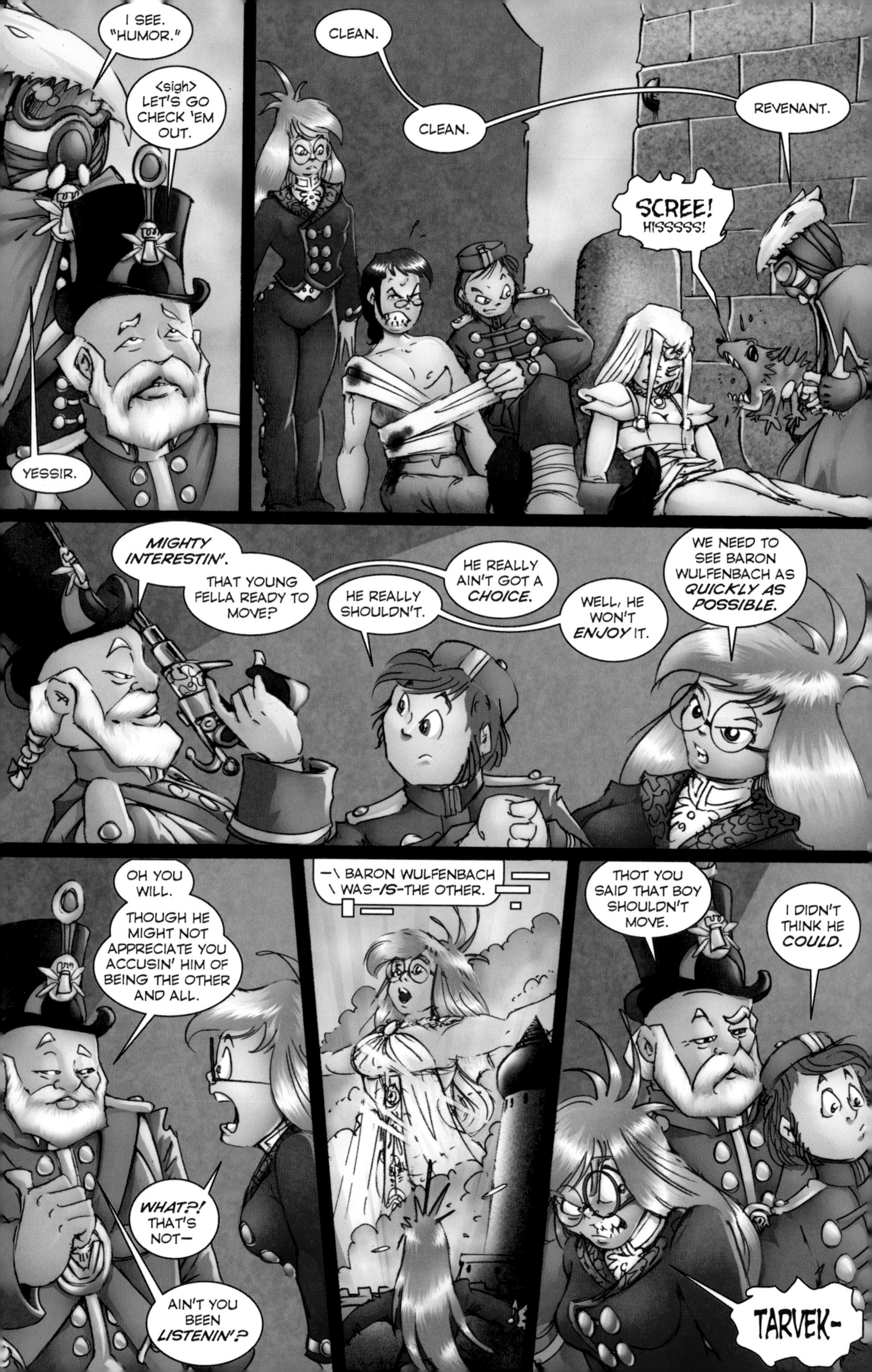

I SEE. "HUMOR."
<sigh> LET'S GO CHECK 'EM OUT.
YESSIR.
CLEAN.
CLEAN.
REVENANT.
SCREE! HISSSSS!
MIGHTY INTERESTIN'.
THAT YOUNG FELLA READY TO MOVE?
HE REALLY SHOULDN'T.
HE REALLY AIN'T GOT A CHOICE.
WELL, HE WON'T ENJOY IT.
WE NEED TO SEE BARON WULFENBACH AS QUICKLY AS POSSIBLE.
OH YOU WILL.
THOUGH HE MIGHT NOT APPRECIATE YOU ACCUSIN' HIM OF BEING THE OTHER AND ALL.
WHAT?! THAT'S NOT—
AIN'T YOU BEEN LISTENIN'?
—\ BARON WULFENBACH \ WAS-IS-THE OTHER.
THOT YOU SAID THAT BOY SHOULDN'T MOVE.
I DIDN'T THINK HE COULD.
TARVEK-

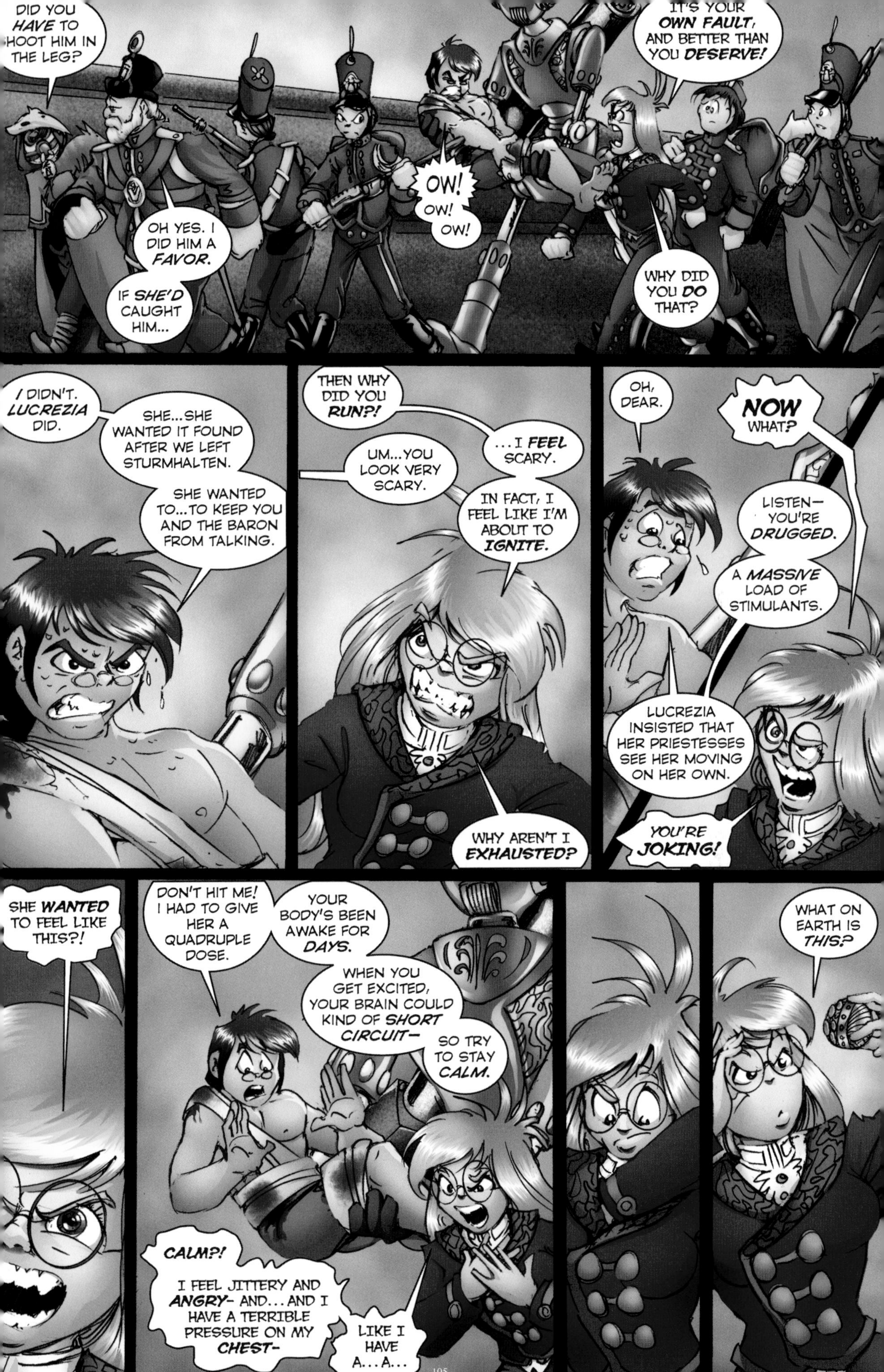
DID YOU *HAVE* TO SHOOT HIM IN THE LEG?
OH YES. I DID HIM A *FAVOR.*
IF *SHE'D* CAUGHT HIM...
OW! OW! OW!
IT'S YOUR *OWN FAULT,* AND BETTER THAN YOU *DESERVE!*
WHY DID YOU *DO* THAT?
I DIDN'T. *LUCREZIA* DID.
SHE...SHE WANTED IT FOUND AFTER WE LEFT STURMHALTEN.
SHE WANTED TO...TO KEEP YOU AND THE BARON FROM TALKING.
THEN WHY DID YOU *RUN?!*
...I *FEEL* SCARY.
UM...YOU LOOK VERY SCARY.
IN FACT, I FEEL LIKE I'M ABOUT TO *IGNITE.*
WHY AREN'T I *EXHAUSTED?*
OH, DEAR.
NOW WHAT?
LISTEN— YOU'RE *DRUGGED.*
A *MASSIVE* LOAD OF STIMULANTS.
LUCREZIA INSISTED THAT HER PRIESTESSES SEE HER MOVING ON HER OWN.
YOU'RE JOKING!
SHE *WANTED* TO FEEL LIKE THIS?!
DON'T HIT ME! I HAD TO GIVE HER A QUADRUPLE DOSE.
YOUR BODY'S BEEN AWAKE FOR *DAYS.*
WHEN YOU GET EXCITED, YOUR BRAIN COULD KIND OF *SHORT CIRCUIT—*
SO TRY TO STAY *CALM.*
CALM?!
I FEEL JITTERY AND *ANGRY*- AND... AND I HAVE A TERRIBLE PRESSURE ON MY *CHEST*-
LIKE I HAVE A... A...
WHAT ON EARTH IS *THIS?*

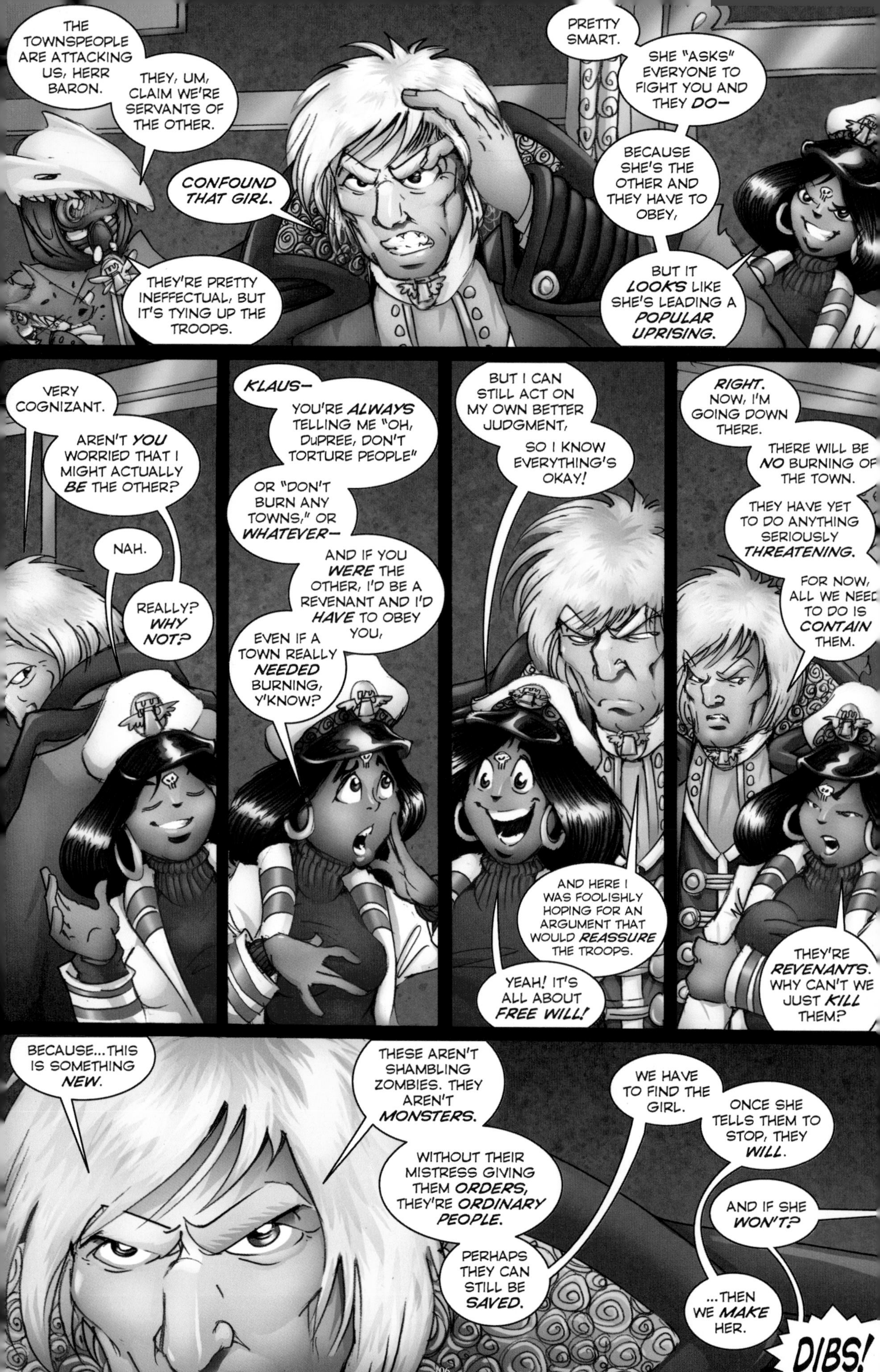
THE TOWNSPEOPLE ARE ATTACKING US, HERR BARON.
THEY, UM, CLAIM WE'RE SERVANTS OF THE OTHER.
THEY'RE PRETTY INEFFECTUAL, BUT IT'S TYING UP THE TROOPS.
CONFOUND THAT GIRL.
PRETTY SMART.
SHE "ASKS" EVERYONE TO FIGHT YOU AND THEY DO—
BECAUSE SHE'S THE OTHER AND THEY HAVE TO OBEY,
BUT IT LOOKS LIKE SHE'S LEADING A POPULAR UPRISING.
VERY COGNIZANT.
AREN'T YOU WORRIED THAT I MIGHT ACTUALLY BE THE OTHER?
NAH.
REALLY? WHY NOT?
KLAUS—
YOU'RE ALWAYS TELLING ME "OH, DUPREE, DON'T TORTURE PEOPLE"
OR "DON'T BURN ANY TOWNS," OR WHATEVER—
AND IF YOU WERE THE OTHER, I'D BE A REVENANT AND I'D HAVE TO OBEY YOU,
EVEN IF A TOWN REALLY NEEDED BURNING, Y'KNOW?
BUT I CAN STILL ACT ON MY OWN BETTER JUDGMENT,
SO I KNOW EVERYTHING'S OKAY!
AND HERE I WAS FOOLISHLY HOPING FOR AN ARGUMENT THAT WOULD REASSURE THE TROOPS.
YEAH! IT'S ALL ABOUT FREE WILL!
RIGHT. NOW, I'M GOING DOWN THERE.
THERE WILL BE NO BURNING OF THE TOWN.
THEY HAVE YET TO DO ANYTHING SERIOUSLY THREATENING.
FOR NOW, ALL WE NEED TO DO IS CONTAIN THEM.
THEY'RE REVENANTS. WHY CAN'T WE JUST KILL THEM?
BECAUSE...THIS IS SOMETHING NEW.
THESE AREN'T SHAMBLING ZOMBIES. THEY AREN'T MONSTERS.
WITHOUT THEIR MISTRESS GIVING THEM ORDERS, THEY'RE ORDINARY PEOPLE.
PERHAPS THEY CAN STILL BE SAVED.
WE HAVE TO FIND THE GIRL.
ONCE SHE TELLS THEM TO STOP, THEY WILL.
AND IF SHE WON'T?
...THEN WE MAKE HER.
DIBS!

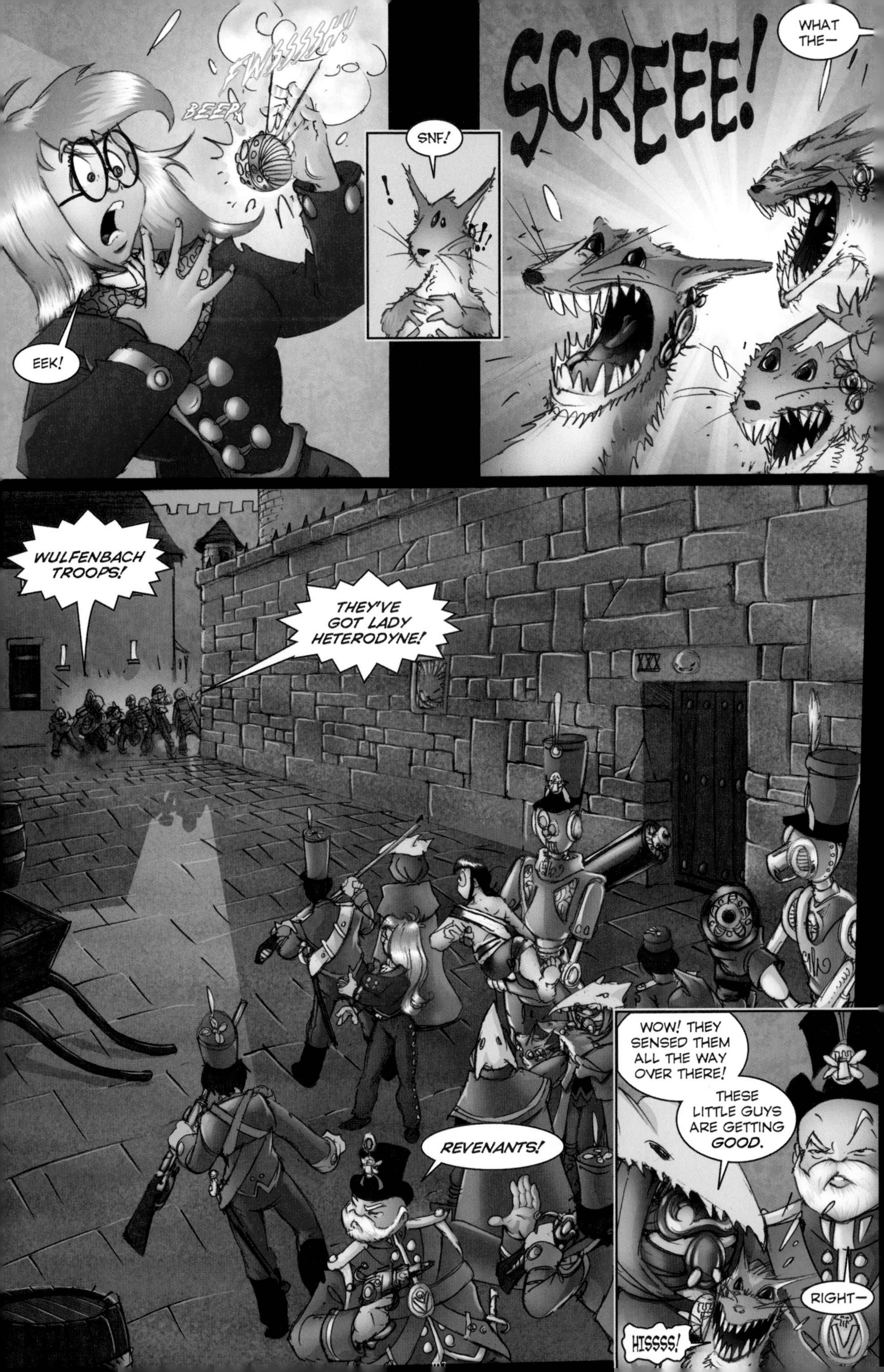
FWISSSSSH!
BEEP!
EEK!
SNF!
SCREEE!
WHAT THE—
WULFENBACH TROOPS!
THEY'VE GOT LADY HETERODYNE!
REVENANTS!
WOW! THEY SENSED THEM ALL THE WAY OVER THERE!
THESE LITTLE GUYS ARE GETTING GOOD.
RIGHT—
HISSSS!

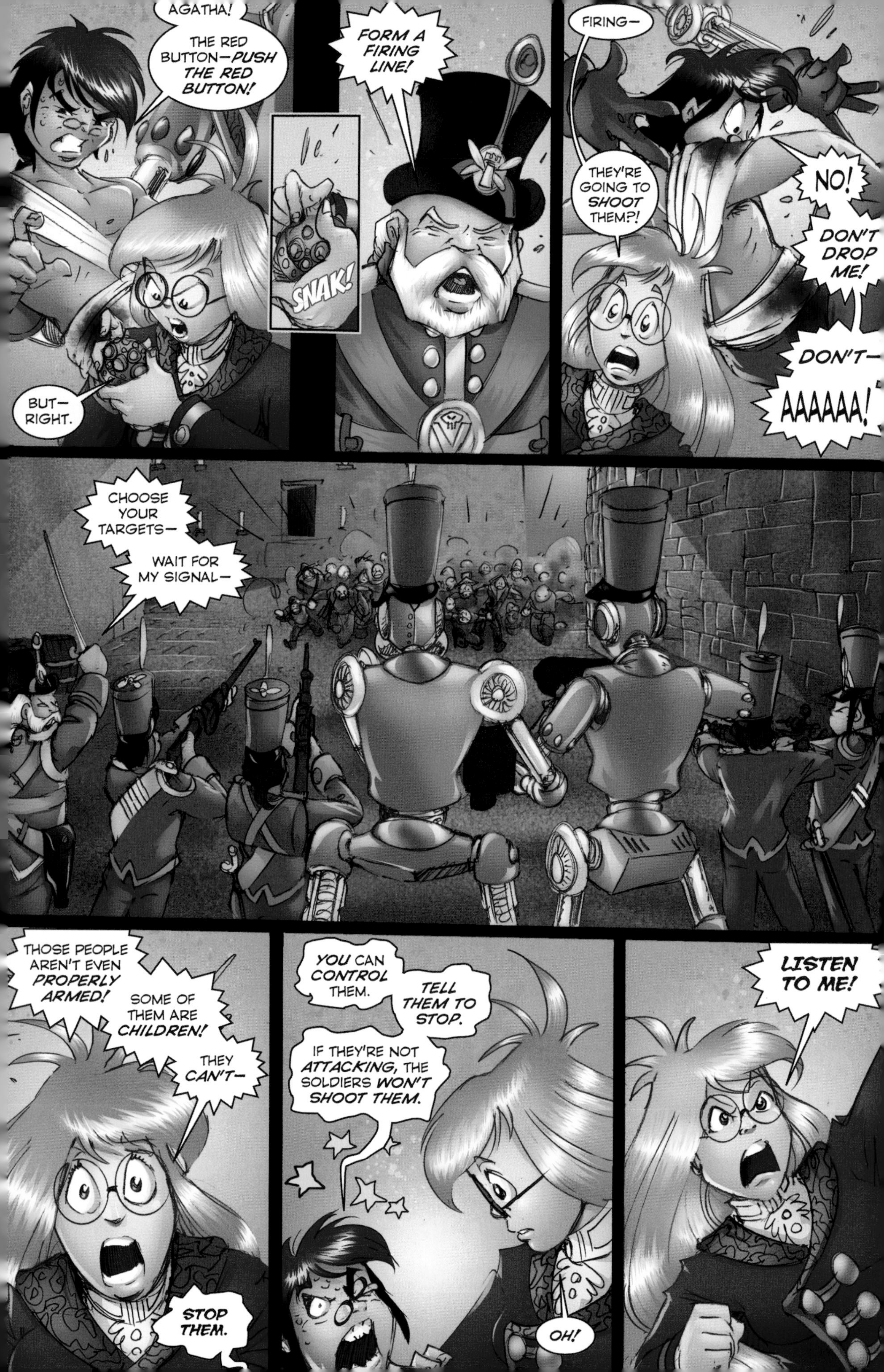
AGATHA!
THE RED BUTTON—PUSH THE RED BUTTON!
BUT—RIGHT.
SNAK!
FORM A FIRING LINE!
FIRING—
THEY'RE GOING TO SHOOT THEM?!
NO!
DON'T DROP ME!
DON'T—
AAAAAA!
CHOOSE YOUR TARGETS—
WAIT FOR MY SIGNAL—
THOSE PEOPLE AREN'T EVEN PROPERLY ARMED!
SOME OF THEM ARE CHILDREN!
THEY CAN'T—
STOP THEM.
YOU CAN CONTROL THEM.
TELL THEM TO STOP.
IF THEY'RE NOT ATTACKING, THE SOLDIERS WON'T SHOOT THEM.
OH!
LISTEN TO ME!

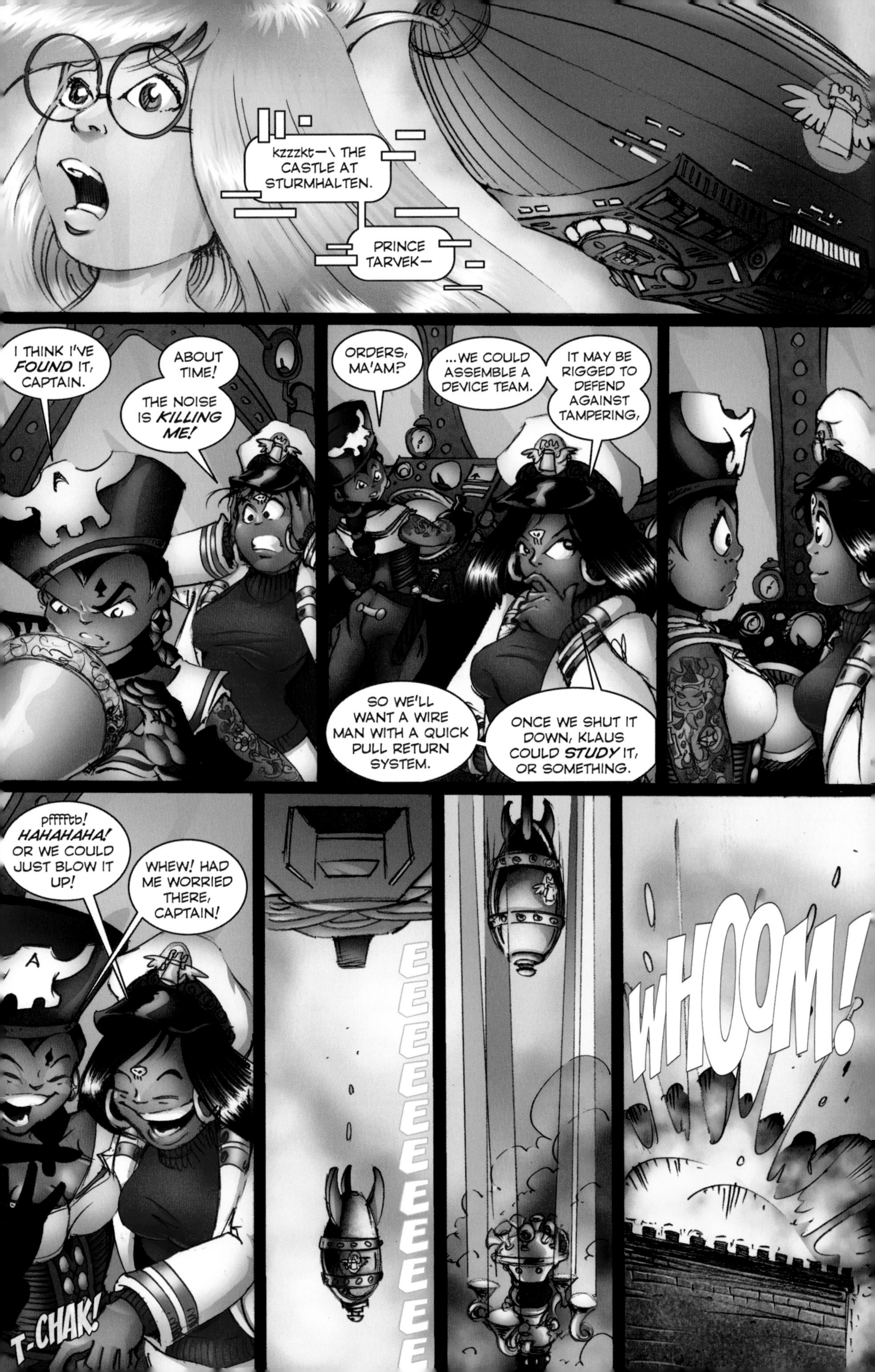

kzzzkt—\ THE CASTLE AT STURMHALTEN.
PRINCE TARVEK—
I THINK I'VE FOUND IT, CAPTAIN.
ABOUT TIME!
THE NOISE IS KILLING ME!
ORDERS, MA'AM?
...WE COULD ASSEMBLE A DEVICE TEAM.
IT MAY BE RIGGED TO DEFEND AGAINST TAMPERING,
SO WE'LL WANT A WIRE MAN WITH A QUICK PULL RETURN SYSTEM.
ONCE WE SHUT IT DOWN, KLAUS COULD STUDY IT, OR SOMETHING.
pffffftb! HAHAHAHA! OR WE COULD JUST BLOW IT UP!
WHEW! HAD ME WORRIED THERE, CAPTAIN!
T-CHAK!
EEEEEEEEEEEEEEE
wHOOM!

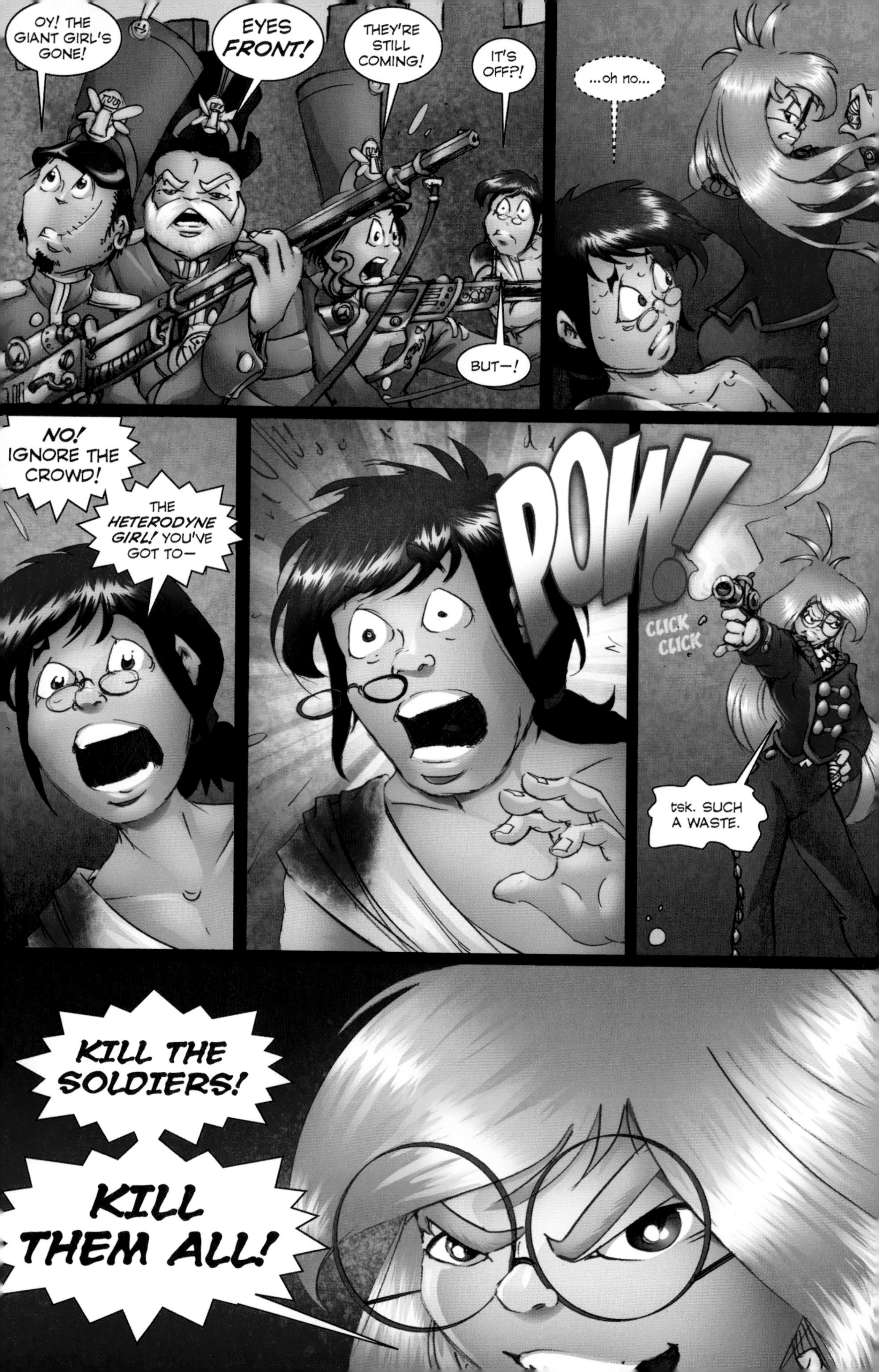
OY! THE GIANT GIRL'S GONE!
EYES FRONT!
THEY'RE STILL COMING!
IT'S OFF?!
BUT—!
...oh no...
NO! IGNORE THE CROWD!
THE HETERODYNE GIRL! YOU'VE GOT TO—
POW!
CLICK CLICK
tsk. SUCH A WASTE.
KILL THE SOLDIERS!
KILL THEM ALL!

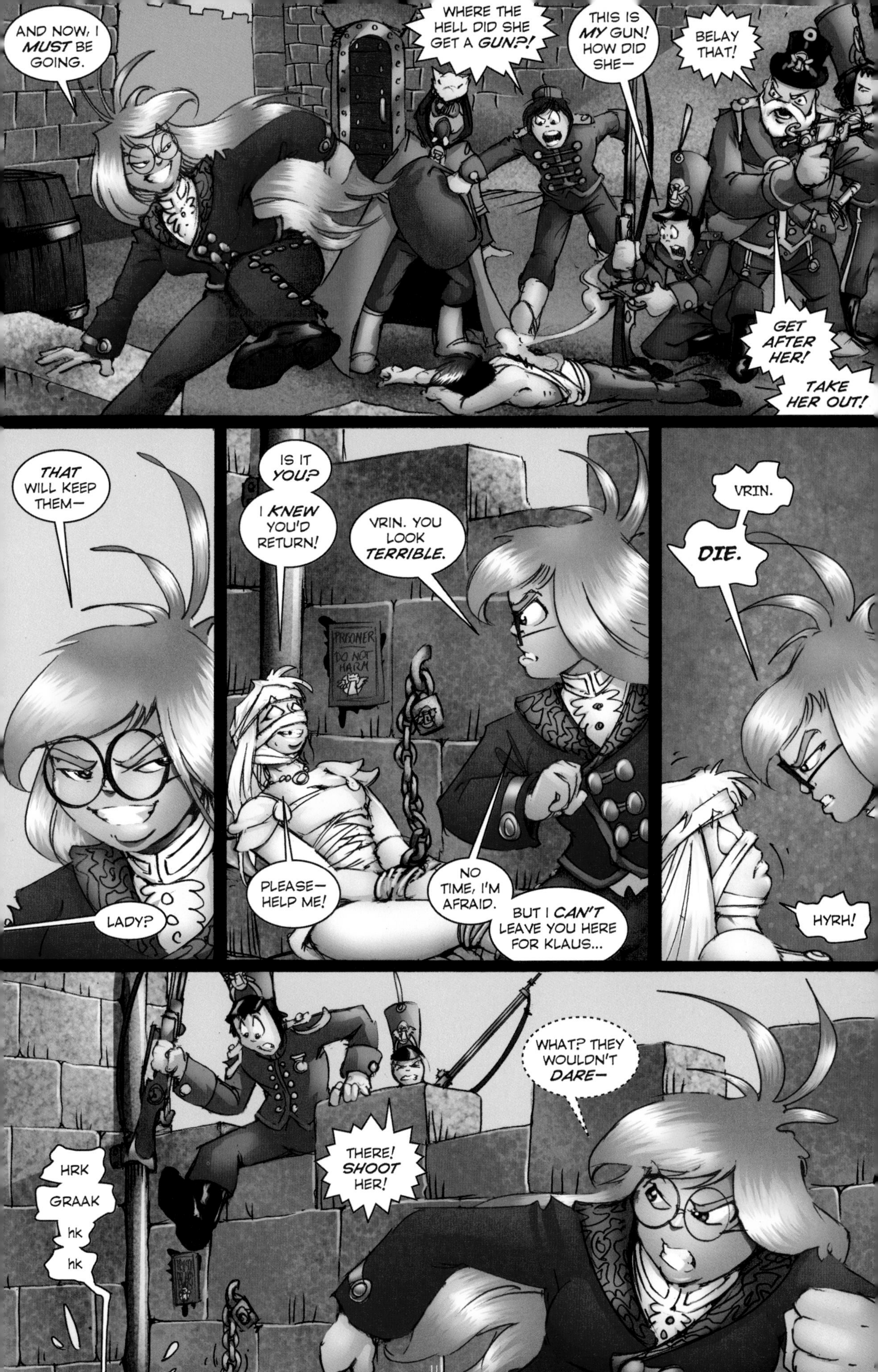

AND NOW, I *MUST* BE GOING.
WHERE THE HELL DID SHE GET A *GUN?!*
THIS IS *MY* GUN! HOW DID SHE—
BELAY THAT!
GET AFTER HER!
TAKE HER OUT!
THAT WILL KEEP THEM—
LADY?
IS IT *YOU?*
I *KNEW* YOU'D RETURN!
VRIN. YOU LOOK *TERRIBLE.*
PLEASE— HELP ME!
NO TIME, I'M AFRAID.
BUT I *CAN'T* LEAVE YOU HERE FOR KLAUS...
PRISONER DO NOT HARM
VRIN.
DIE.
HYRH!
WHAT? THEY WOULDN'T *DARE—*
THERE! *SHOOT* HER!
HRK
GRAAK
hk
hk

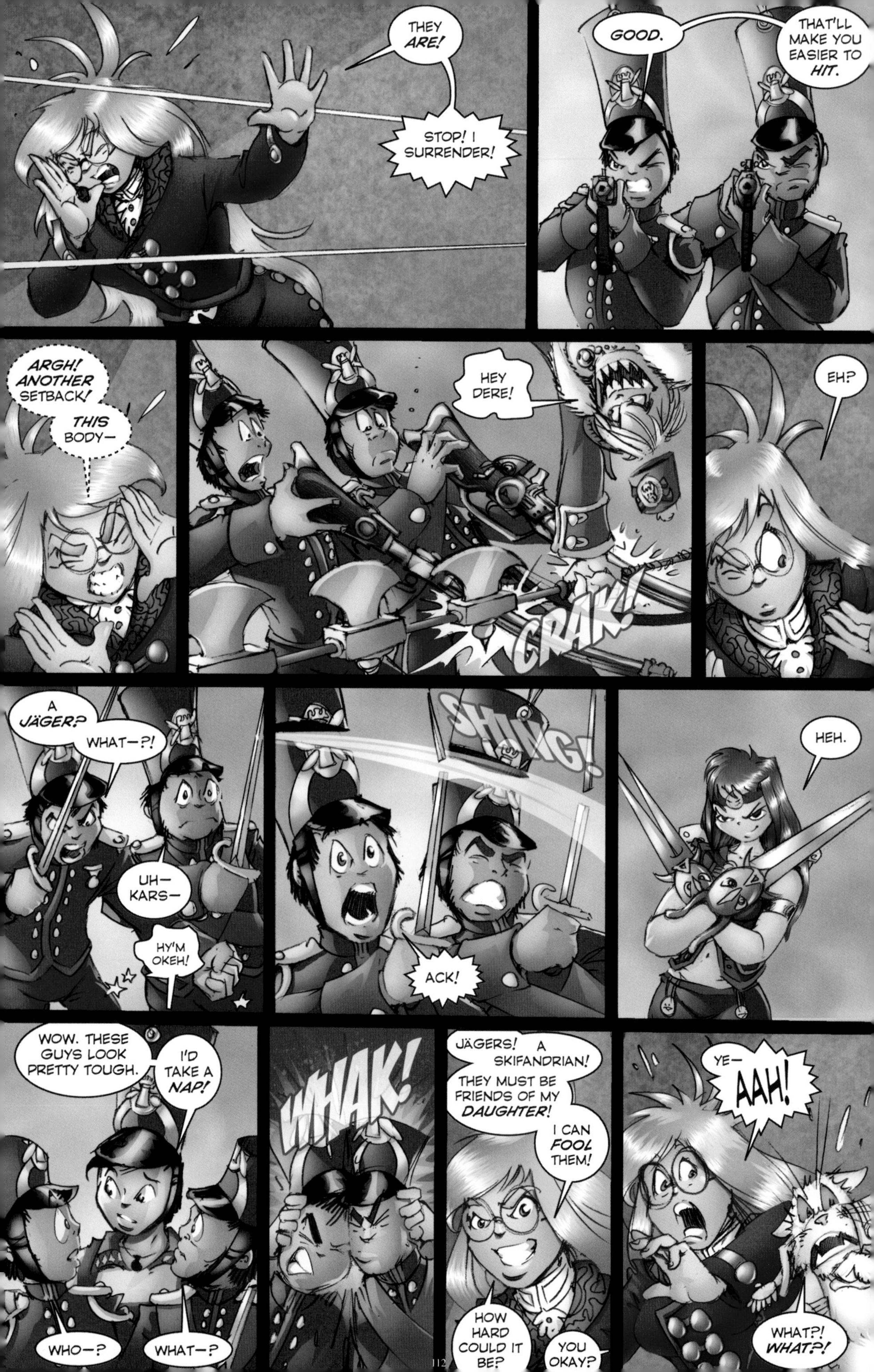
THEY ARE!
STOP! I SURRENDER!
GOOD.
THAT'LL MAKE YOU EASIER TO HIT.
ARGH! ANOTHER SETBACK!
THIS BODY—
HEY DERE!
CRAK!
EH?
A JÄGER?
WHAT—?!
UH— KARS—
HY'M OKEH!
SHING!
ACK!
HEH.
WOW. THESE GUYS LOOK PRETTY TOUGH.
I'D TAKE A NAP!
WHO—?
WHAT—?
WHAK!
JÄGERS! A SKIFANDRIAN!
THEY MUST BE FRIENDS OF MY DAUGHTER!
I CAN FOOL THEM!
HOW HARD COULD IT BE?
YOU OKAY?
YE— AAH!
WHAT?! WHAT?!

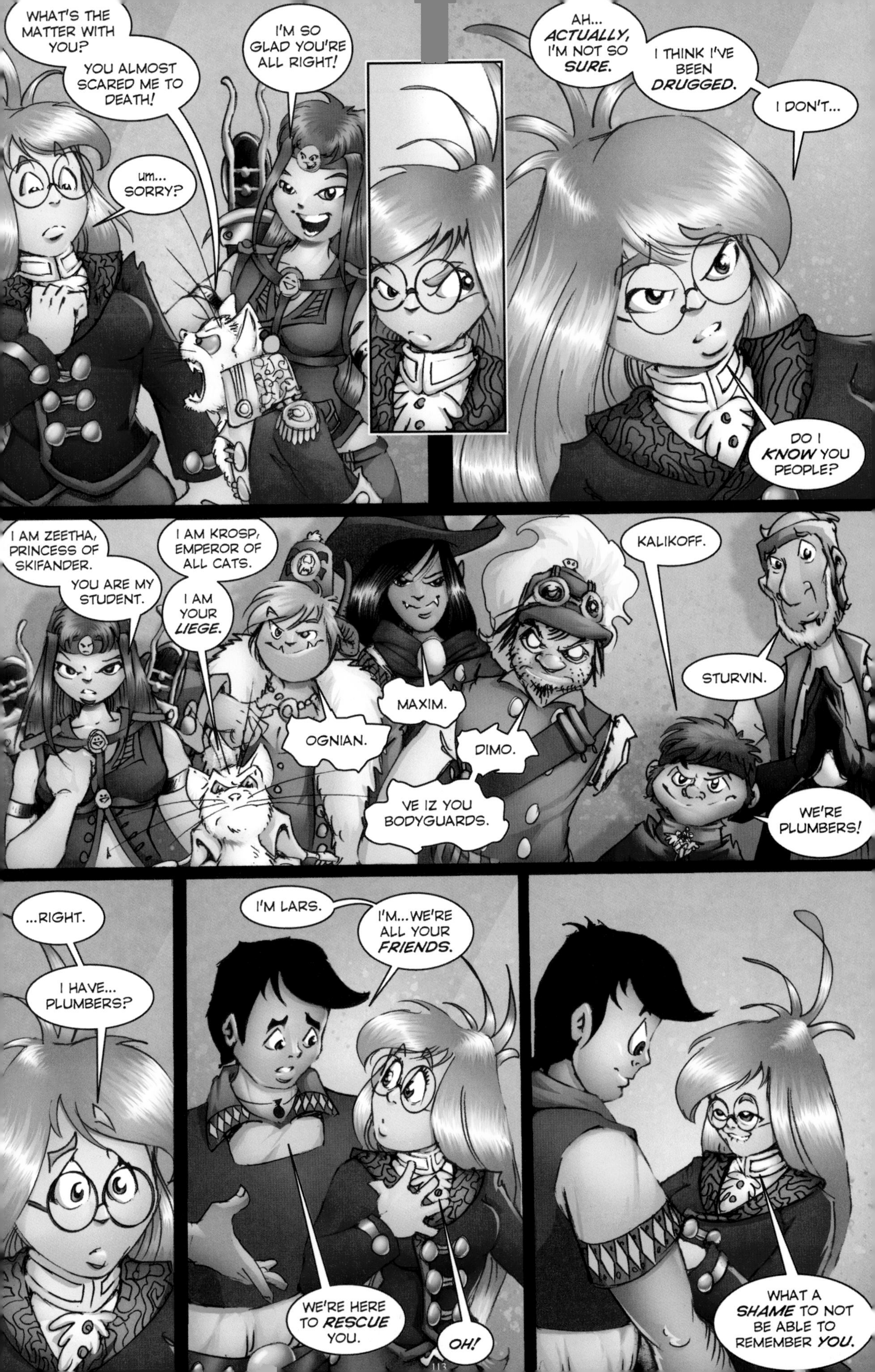
WHAT'S THE MATTER WITH YOU?
YOU ALMOST SCARED ME TO DEATH!
I'M SO GLAD YOU'RE ALL RIGHT!
um... SORRY?
AH... ACTUALLY, I'M NOT SO SURE.
I THINK I'VE BEEN DRUGGED.
I DON'T...
DO I KNOW YOU PEOPLE?
I AM ZEETHA, PRINCESS OF SKIFANDER.
YOU ARE MY STUDENT.
I AM KROSP, EMPEROR OF ALL CATS.
I AM YOUR LIEGE.
OGNIAN.
MAXIM.
DIMO.
VE IZ YOU BODYGUARDS.
KALIKOFF.
STURVIN.
WE'RE PLUMBERS!
...RIGHT.
I HAVE... PLUMBERS?
I'M LARS.
I'M...WE'RE ALL YOUR FRIENDS.
WE'RE HERE TO RESCUE YOU.
OH!
WHAT A SHAME TO NOT BE ABLE TO REMEMBER YOU.

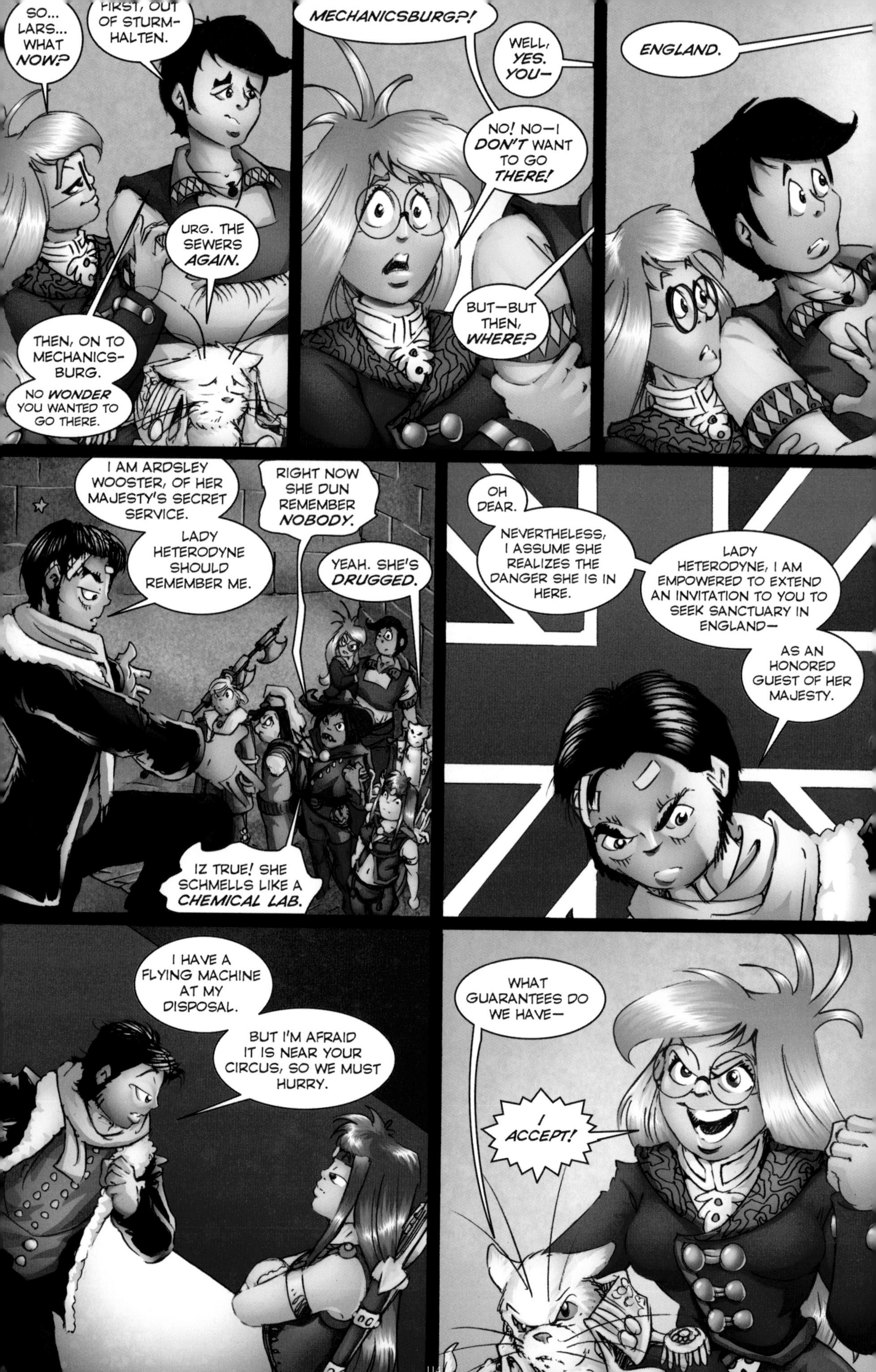

SO... LARS... WHAT NOW?
FIRST, OUT OF STURM-HALTEN.
URG. THE SEWERS AGAIN.
THEN, ON TO MECHANICS-BURG.
NO WONDER YOU WANTED TO GO THERE.
MECHANICSBURG?!
WELL, YES. YOU—
NO! NO—I DON'T WANT TO GO THERE!
BUT—BUT THEN, WHERE?
ENGLAND.
I AM ARDSLEY WOOSTER, OF HER MAJESTY'S SECRET SERVICE.
LADY HETERODYNE SHOULD REMEMBER ME.
RIGHT NOW SHE DUN REMEMBER NOBODY.
YEAH. SHE'S DRUGGED.
IZ TRUE! SHE SCHMELLS LIKE A CHEMICAL LAB.
OH DEAR.
NEVERTHELESS, I ASSUME SHE REALIZES THE DANGER SHE IS IN HERE.
LADY HETERODYNE, I AM EMPOWERED TO EXTEND AN INVITATION TO YOU TO SEEK SANCTUARY IN ENGLAND—
AS AN HONORED GUEST OF HER MAJESTY.
I HAVE A FLYING MACHINE AT MY DISPOSAL.
BUT I'M AFRAID IT IS NEAR YOUR CIRCUS, SO WE MUST HURRY.
WHAT GUARANTEES DO WE HAVE—
I ACCEPT!

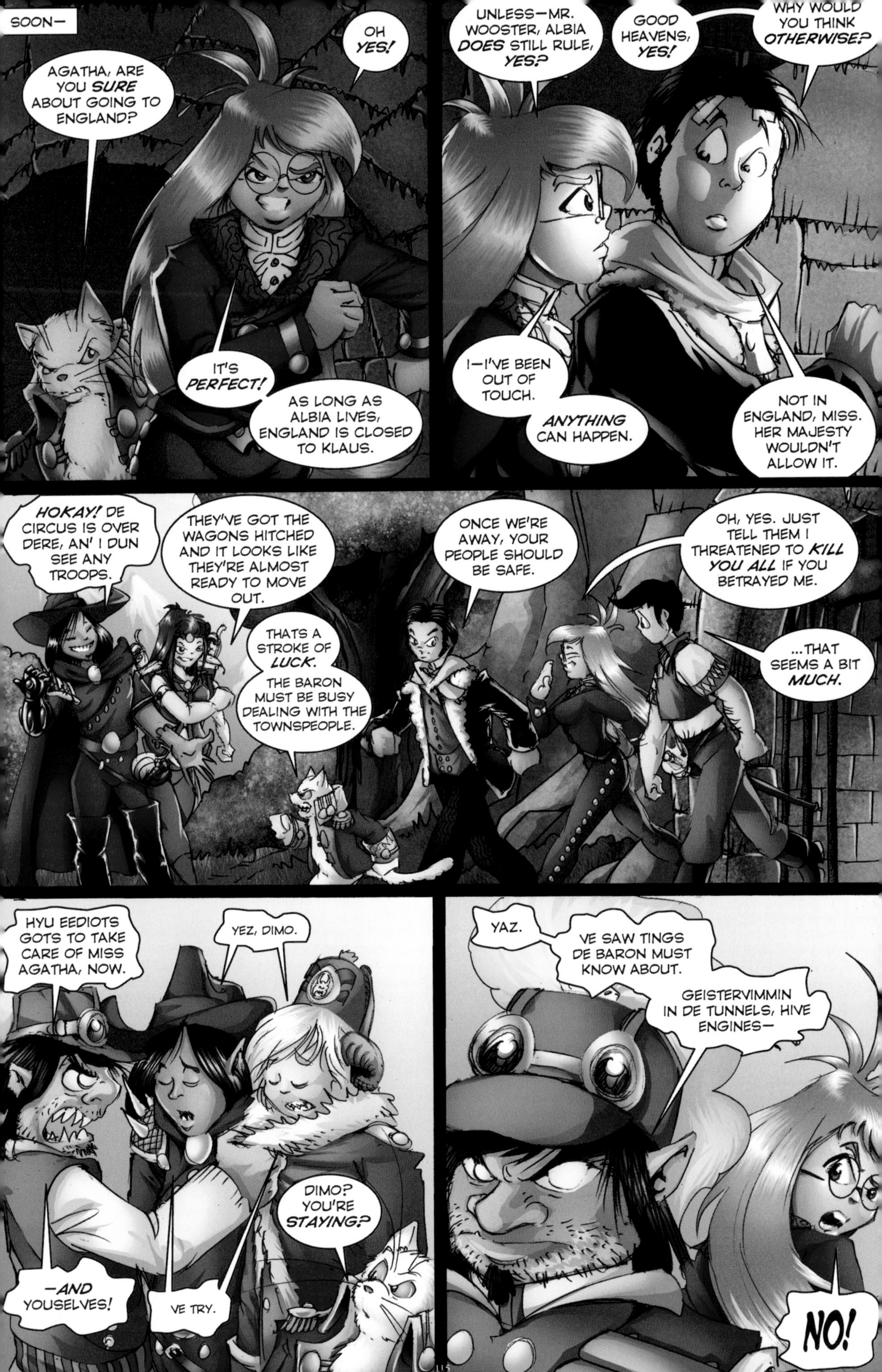
SOON—
AGATHA, ARE YOU *SURE* ABOUT GOING TO ENGLAND?
OH *YES!*
IT'S *PERFECT!*
AS LONG AS ALBIA LIVES, ENGLAND IS CLOSED TO KLAUS.
UNLESS—MR. WOOSTER, ALBIA *DOES* STILL RULE, *YES?*
GOOD HEAVENS, *YES!*
WHY WOULD YOU THINK *OTHERWISE?*
I—I'VE BEEN OUT OF TOUCH.
ANYTHING CAN HAPPEN.
NOT IN ENGLAND, MISS. HER MAJESTY WOULDN'T ALLOW IT.
HOKAY! DE CIRCUS IS OVER DERE, AN' I DUN SEE ANY TROOPS.
THEY'VE GOT THE WAGONS HITCHED AND IT LOOKS LIKE THEY'RE ALMOST READY TO MOVE OUT.
THATS A STROKE OF *LUCK*.
THE BARON MUST BE BUSY DEALING WITH THE TOWNSPEOPLE.
ONCE WE'RE AWAY, YOUR PEOPLE SHOULD BE SAFE.
OH, YES. JUST TELL THEM I THREATENED TO *KILL YOU ALL* IF YOU BETRAYED ME.
...THAT SEEMS A BIT *MUCH*.
HYU EEDIOTS GOTS TO TAKE CARE OF MISS AGATHA, NOW.
YEZ, DIMO.
—*AND* YOUSELVES!
VE TRY.
DIMO? YOU'RE *STAYING?*
YAZ.
VE SAW TINGS DE BARON MUST KNOW ABOUT.
GEISTERVIMMIN IN DE TUNNELS, HIVE ENGINES—
NO!

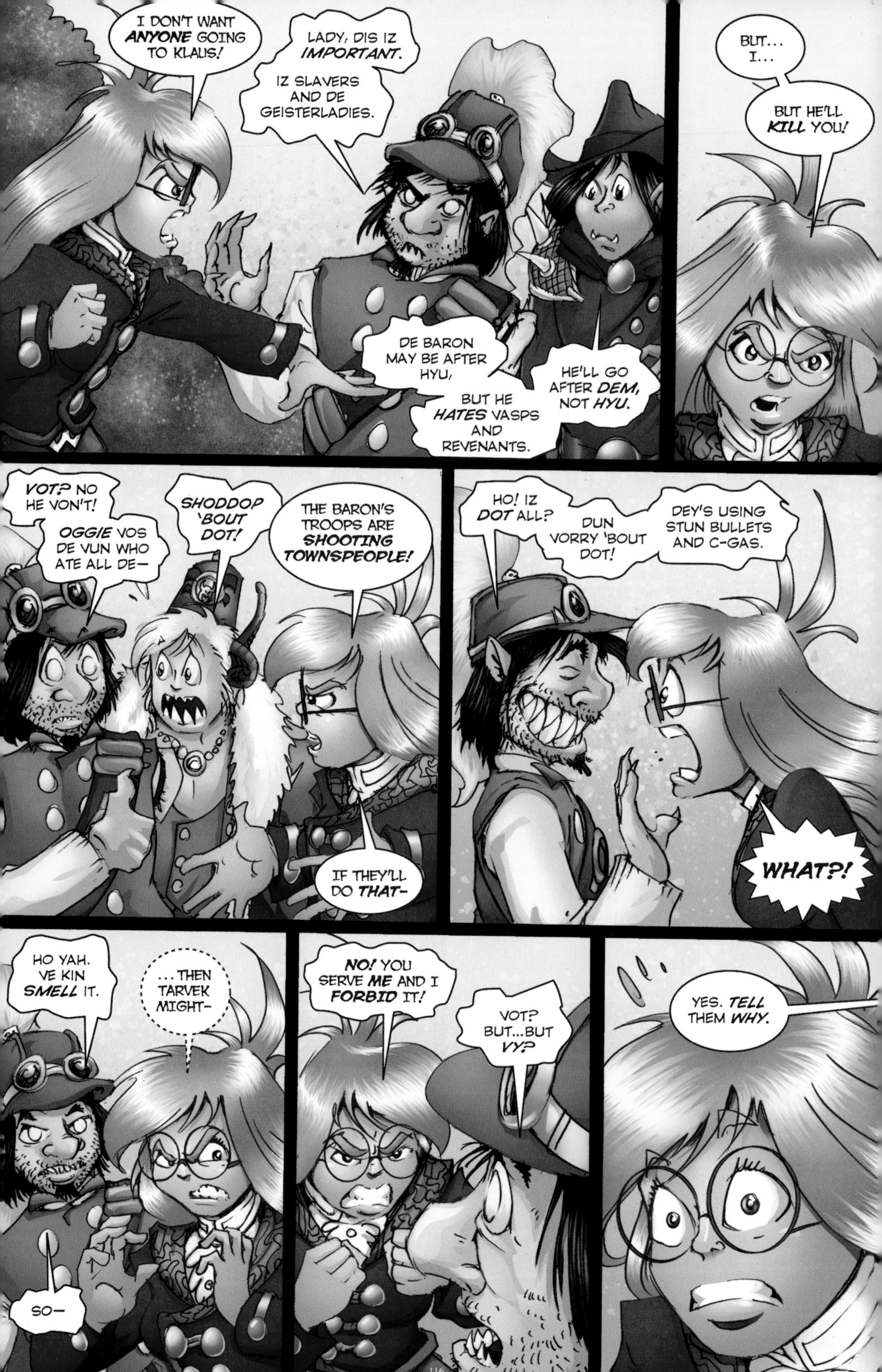
I DON'T WANT ANYONE GOING TO KLAUS!
LADY, DIS IZ IMPORTANT.
IZ SLAVERS AND DE GEISTERLADIES.
DE BARON MAY BE AFTER HYU,
BUT HE HATES VASPS AND REVENANTS.
HE'LL GO AFTER DEM, NOT HYU.
BUT... I...
BUT HE'LL KILL YOU!
VOT? NO HE VON'T!
OGGIE VOS DE VUN WHO ATE ALL DE—
SHODDOP 'BOUT DOT!
THE BARON'S TROOPS ARE SHOOTING TOWNSPEOPLE!
IF THEY'LL DO THAT-
HO! IZ DOT ALL?
DUN VORRY 'BOUT DOT!
DEY'S USING STUN BULLETS AND C-GAS.
WHAT?!
HO YAH. VE KIN SMELL IT.
SO—
...THEN TARVEK MIGHT-
NO! YOU SERVE ME AND I FORBID IT!
VOT? BUT...BUT VY?
YES. TELL THEM WHY.

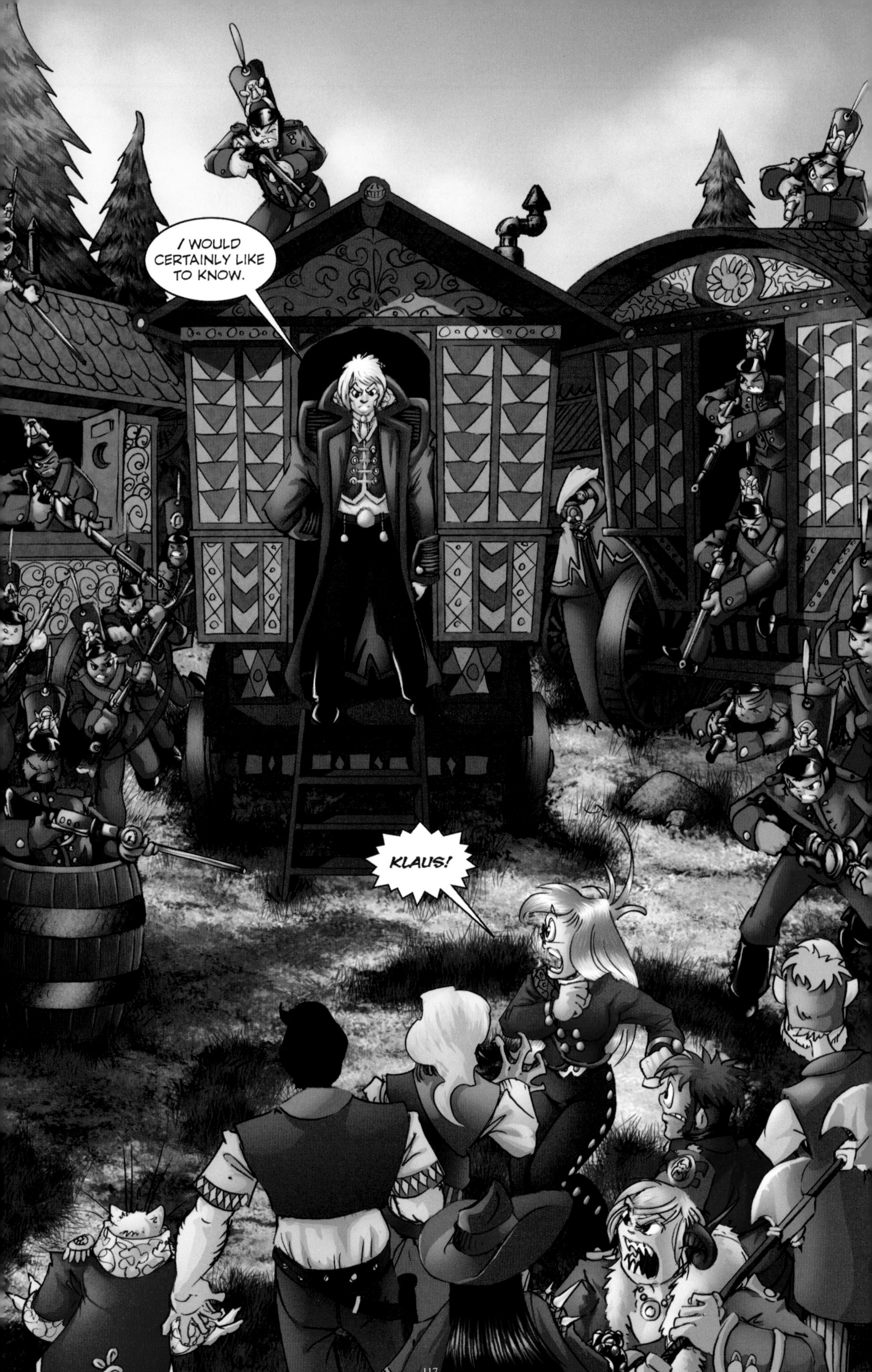
I WOULD CERTAINLY LIKE TO KNOW.
KLAUS!

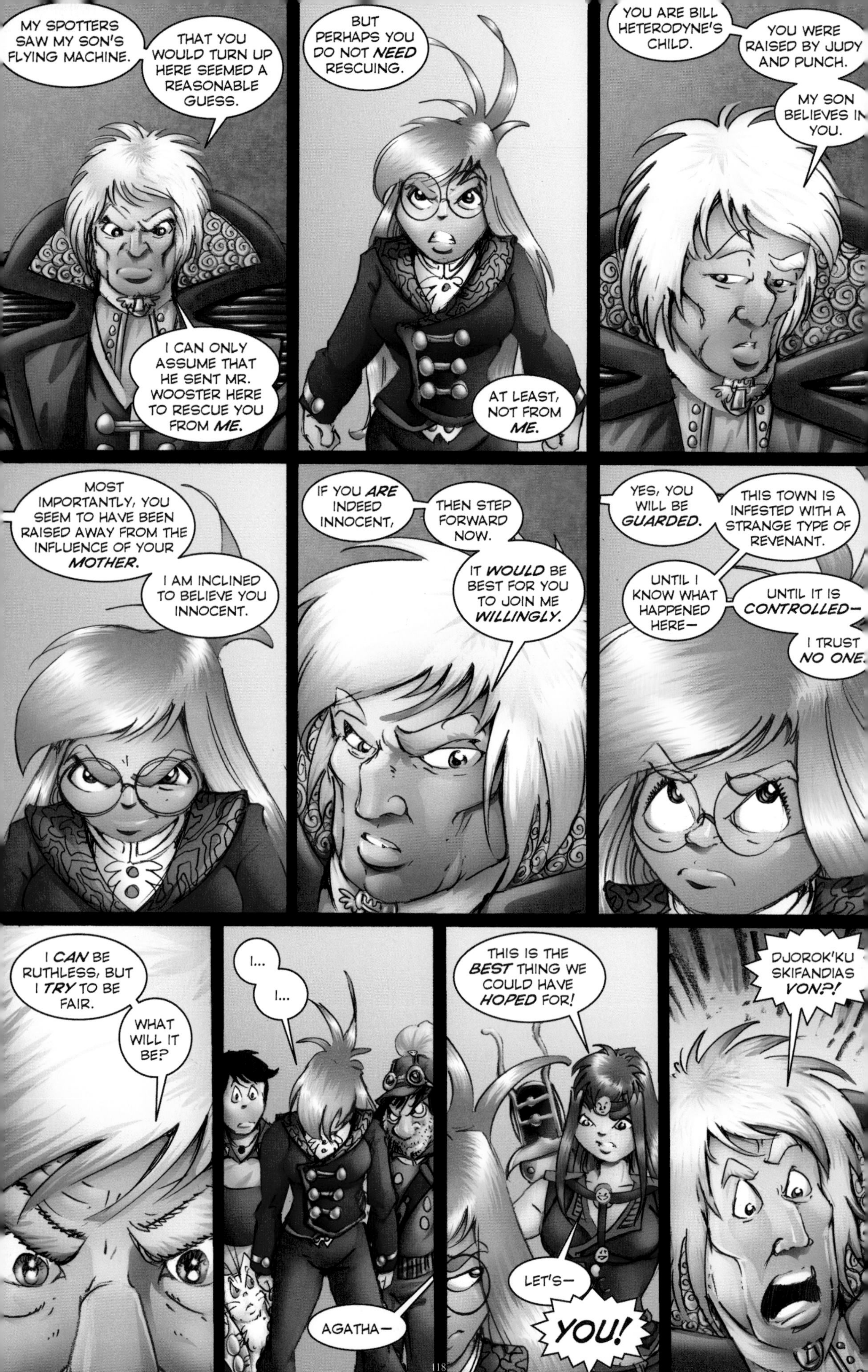

MY SPOTTERS SAW MY SON'S FLYING MACHINE.
THAT YOU WOULD TURN UP HERE SEEMED A REASONABLE GUESS.
I CAN ONLY ASSUME THAT HE SENT MR. WOOSTER HERE TO RESCUE YOU FROM ME.
BUT PERHAPS YOU DO NOT NEED RESCUING.
AT LEAST, NOT FROM ME.
YOU ARE BILL HETERODYNE'S CHILD.
YOU WERE RAISED BY JUDY AND PUNCH.
MY SON BELIEVES IN YOU.
MOST IMPORTANTLY, YOU SEEM TO HAVE BEEN RAISED AWAY FROM THE INFLUENCE OF YOUR MOTHER.
I AM INCLINED TO BELIEVE YOU INNOCENT.
IF YOU ARE INDEED INNOCENT,
THEN STEP FORWARD NOW.
IT WOULD BE BEST FOR YOU TO JOIN ME WILLINGLY.
YES, YOU WILL BE GUARDED.
THIS TOWN IS INFESTED WITH A STRANGE TYPE OF REVENANT.
UNTIL I KNOW WHAT HAPPENED HERE—
UNTIL IT IS CONTROLLED—
I TRUST NO ONE.
I CAN BE RUTHLESS, BUT I TRY TO BE FAIR.
WHAT WILL IT BE?
I...
I...
AGATHA—
THIS IS THE BEST THING WE COULD HAVE HOPED FOR!
LET'S—
YOU!
DJOROK'KU SKIFANDIAS VON?!

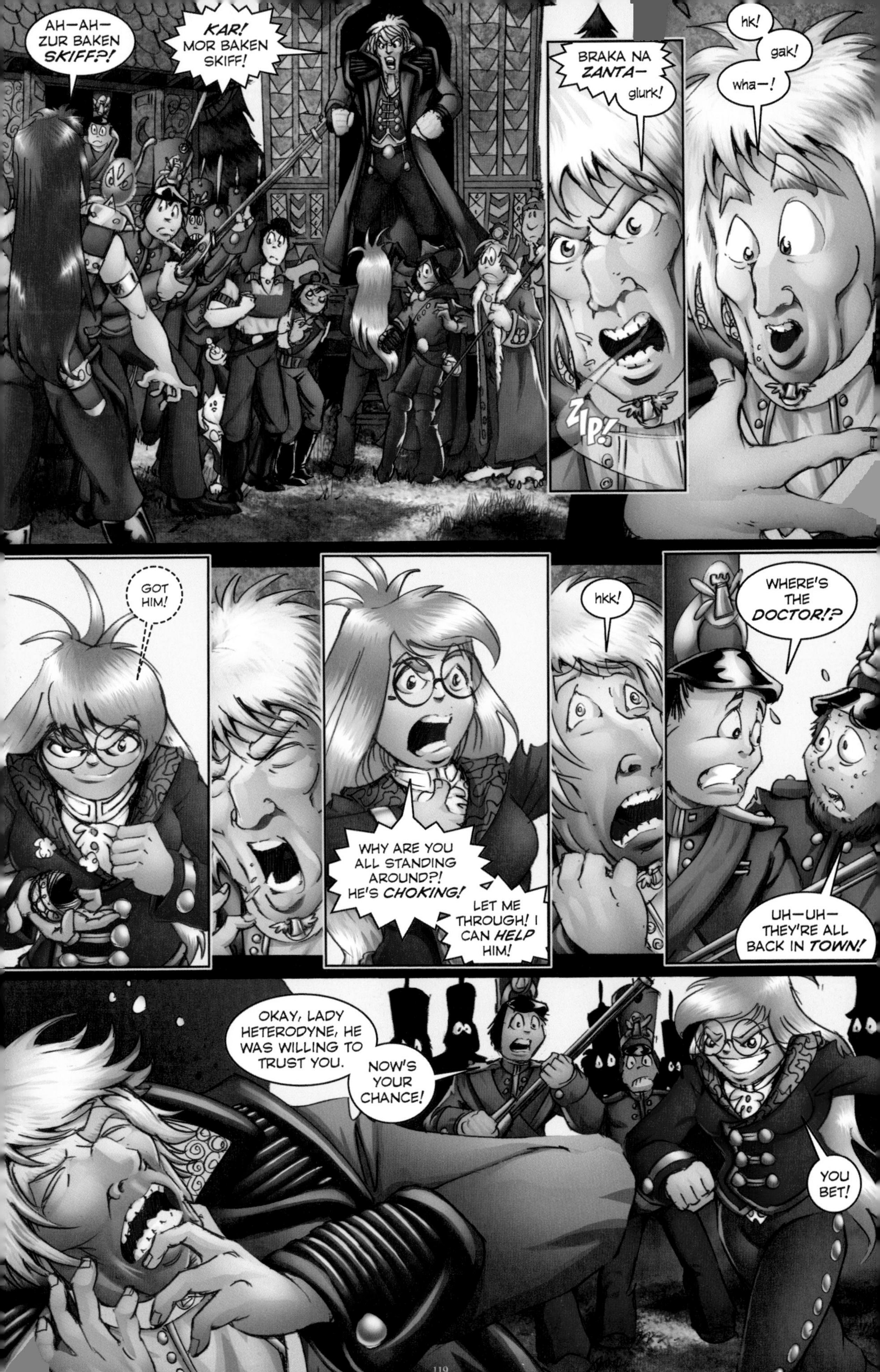
AH—AH—
ZUR BAKEN
SKIFF?!
KAR!
MOR BAKEN
SKIFF!
BRAKA NA
ZANTA—
glurk!
ZIP!
hk!
gak!
wha—!
GOT
HIM!
WHY ARE YOU
ALL STANDING
AROUND?!
HE'S CHOKING!
LET ME
THROUGH! I
CAN HELP
HIM!
hkk!
WHERE'S
THE
DOCTOR!?
UH—UH—
THEY'RE ALL
BACK IN TOWN!
OKAY, LADY
HETERODYNE, HE
WAS WILLING TO
TRUST YOU.
NOW'S
YOUR
CHANCE!
YOU
BET!

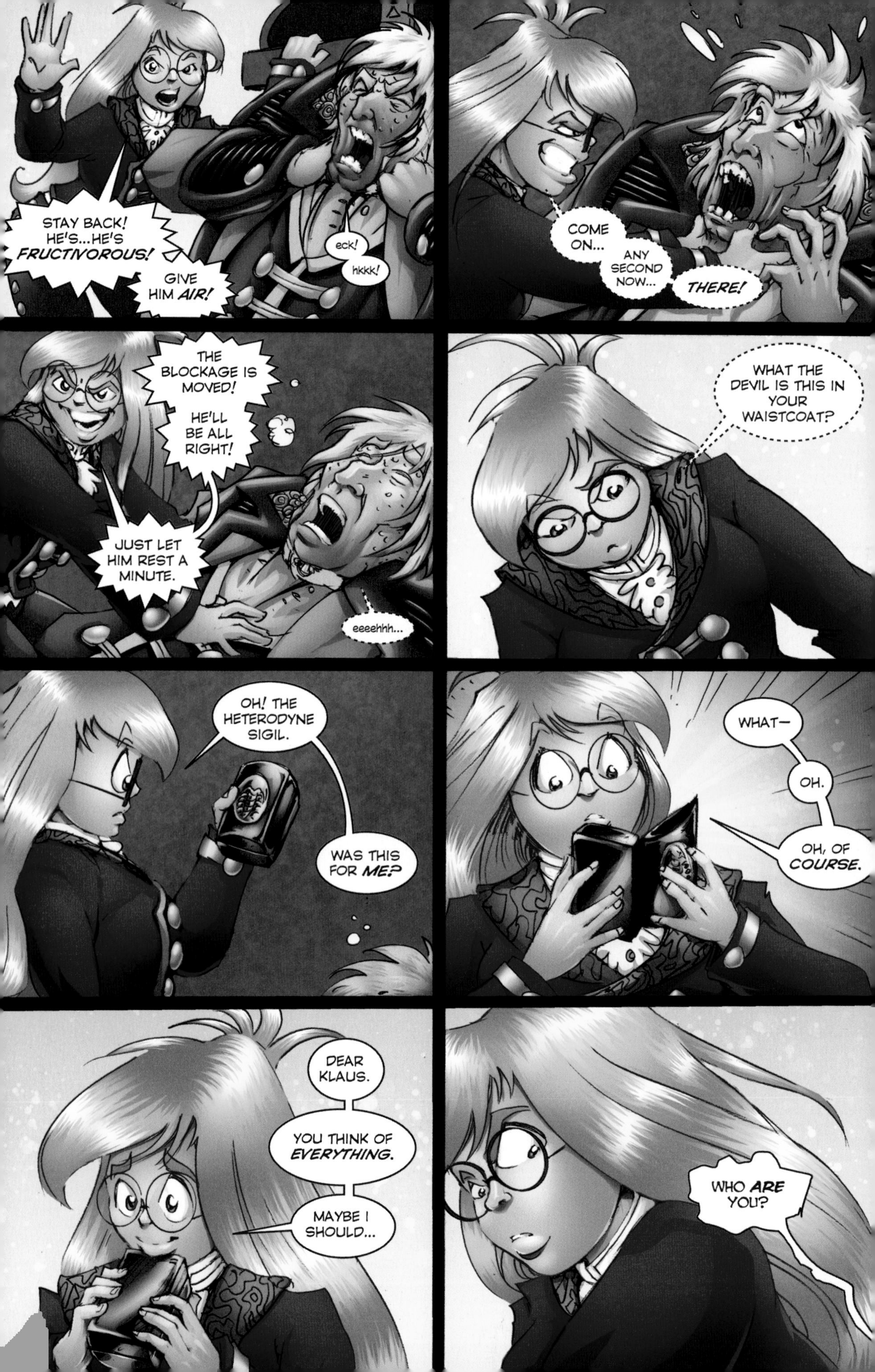
STAY BACK! HE'S...HE'S *FRUCTIVOROUS!*
eck!
hkkk!
GIVE HIM *AIR!*
COME ON...
ANY SECOND NOW...
THERE!
THE BLOCKAGE IS MOVED!
HE'LL BE ALL RIGHT!
JUST LET HIM REST A MINUTE.
eeeehhh...
WHAT THE DEVIL IS THIS IN YOUR WAISTCOAT?
OH! THE HETERODYNE SIGIL.
WAS THIS FOR *ME?*
WHAT—
OH.
OH, OF *COURSE.*
DEAR KLAUS.
YOU THINK OF *EVERYTHING.*
MAYBE I SHOULD...
WHO *ARE* YOU?

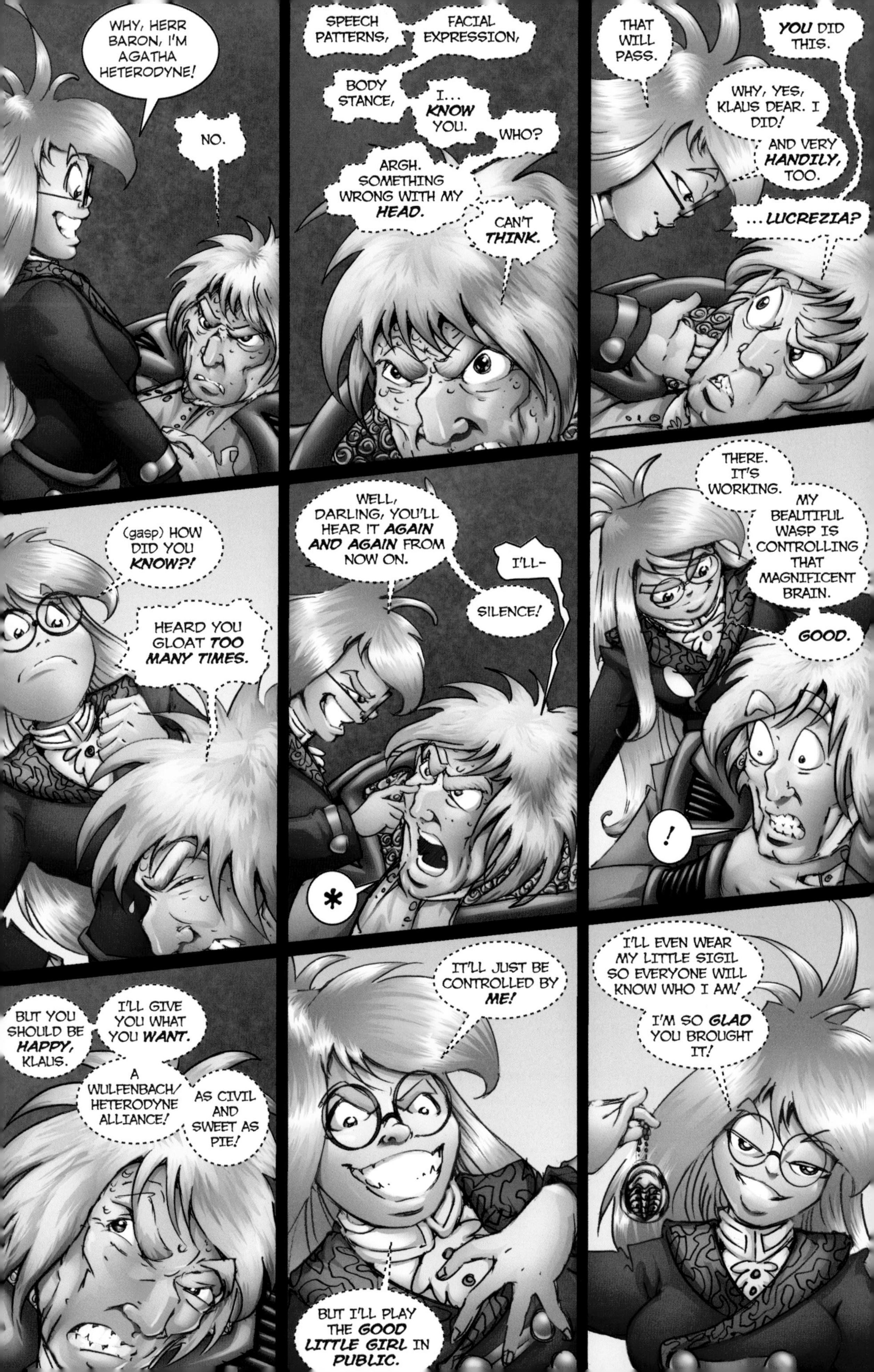

WHY, HERR BARON, I'M AGATHA HETERODYNE!
NO.
SPEECH PATTERNS,
FACIAL EXPRESSION,
BODY STANCE,
I... KNOW YOU.
WHO?
ARGH. SOMETHING WRONG WITH MY HEAD.
CAN'T THINK.
THAT WILL PASS.
YOU DID THIS.
WHY, YES, KLAUS DEAR. I DID!
AND VERY HANDILY, TOO.
...LUCREZIA?
(gasp) HOW DID YOU KNOW?!
HEARD YOU GLOAT TOO MANY TIMES.
WELL, DARLING, YOU'LL HEAR IT AGAIN AND AGAIN FROM NOW ON.
I'LL-
SILENCE!
*
THERE. IT'S WORKING.
MY BEAUTIFUL WASP IS CONTROLLING THAT MAGNIFICENT BRAIN.
GOOD.
!
BUT YOU SHOULD BE HAPPY, KLAUS.
I'LL GIVE YOU WHAT YOU WANT.
A WULFENBACH/HETERODYNE ALLIANCE!
AS CIVIL AND SWEET AS PIE!
IT'LL JUST BE CONTROLLED BY ME!
BUT I'LL PLAY THE GOOD LITTLE GIRL IN PUBLIC.
I'LL EVEN WEAR MY LITTLE SIGIL SO EVERYONE WILL KNOW WHO I AM!
I'M SO GLAD YOU BROUGHT IT!

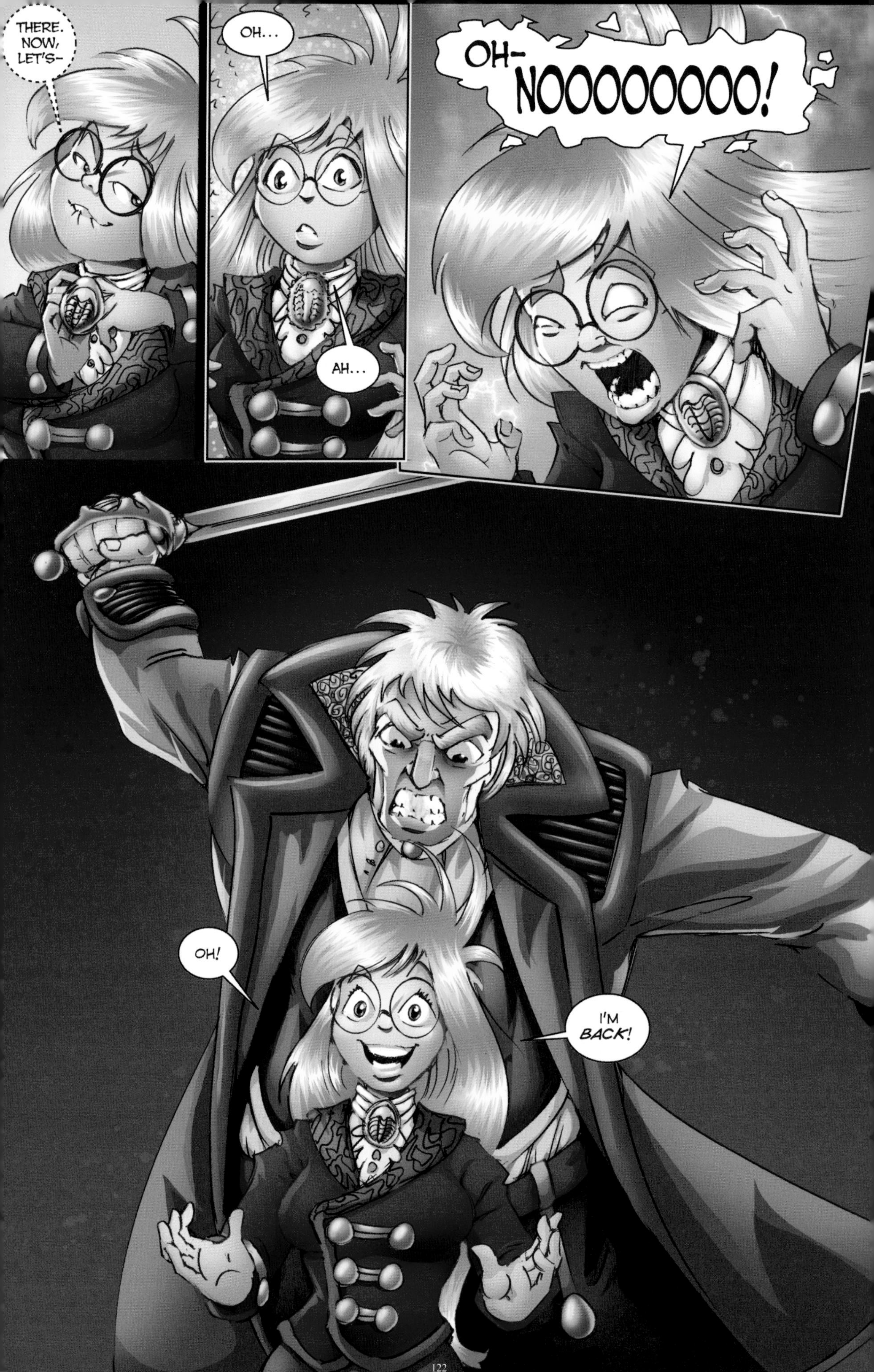
THERE. NOW, LET'S-
OH...
AH...
OH-NOOOOOOOOO!
OH!
I'M BACK!

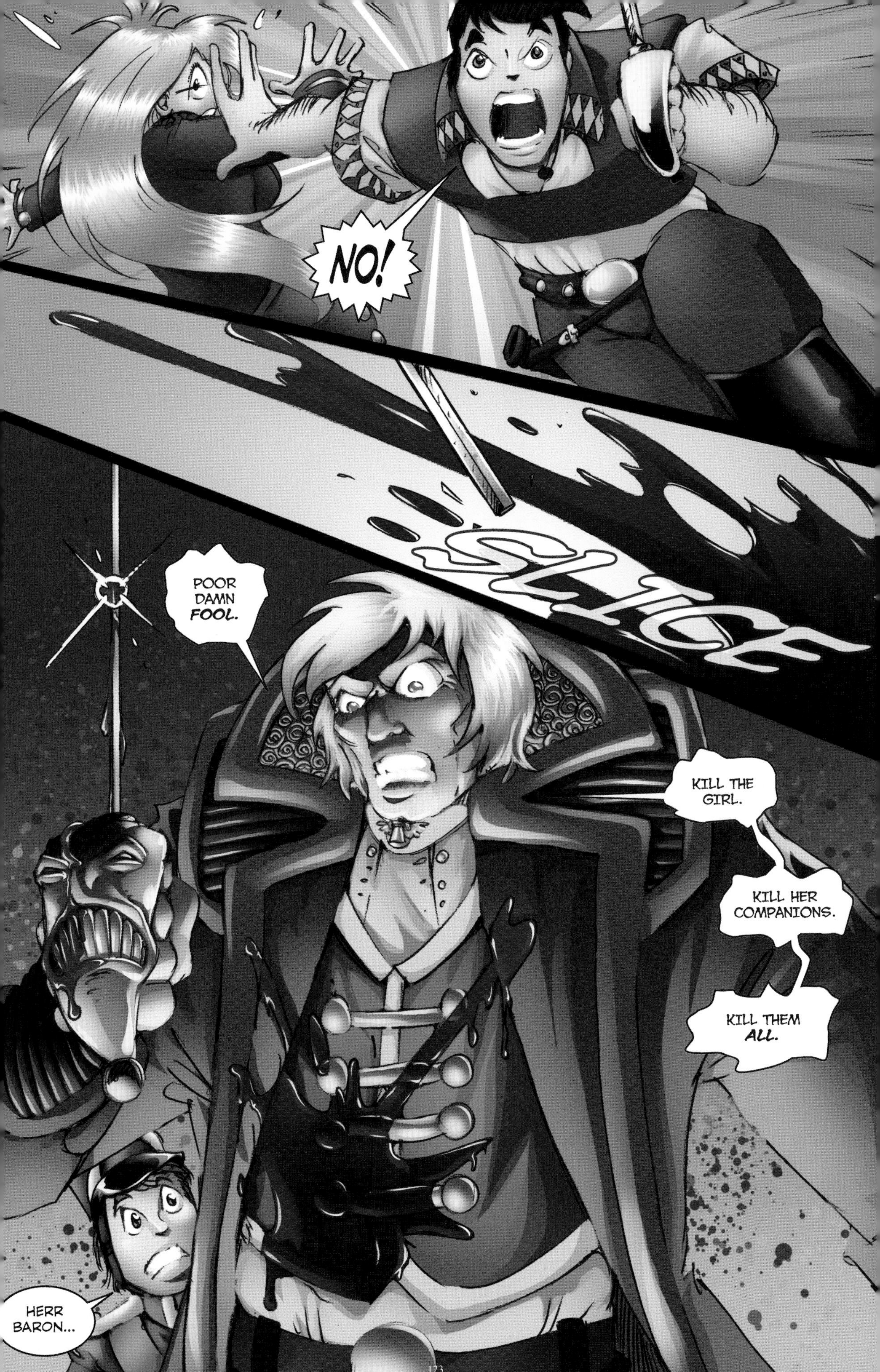
NO!
SLICE
POOR DAMN FOOL.
KILL THE GIRL.
KILL HER COMPANIONS.
KILL THEM ALL.
HERR BARON...

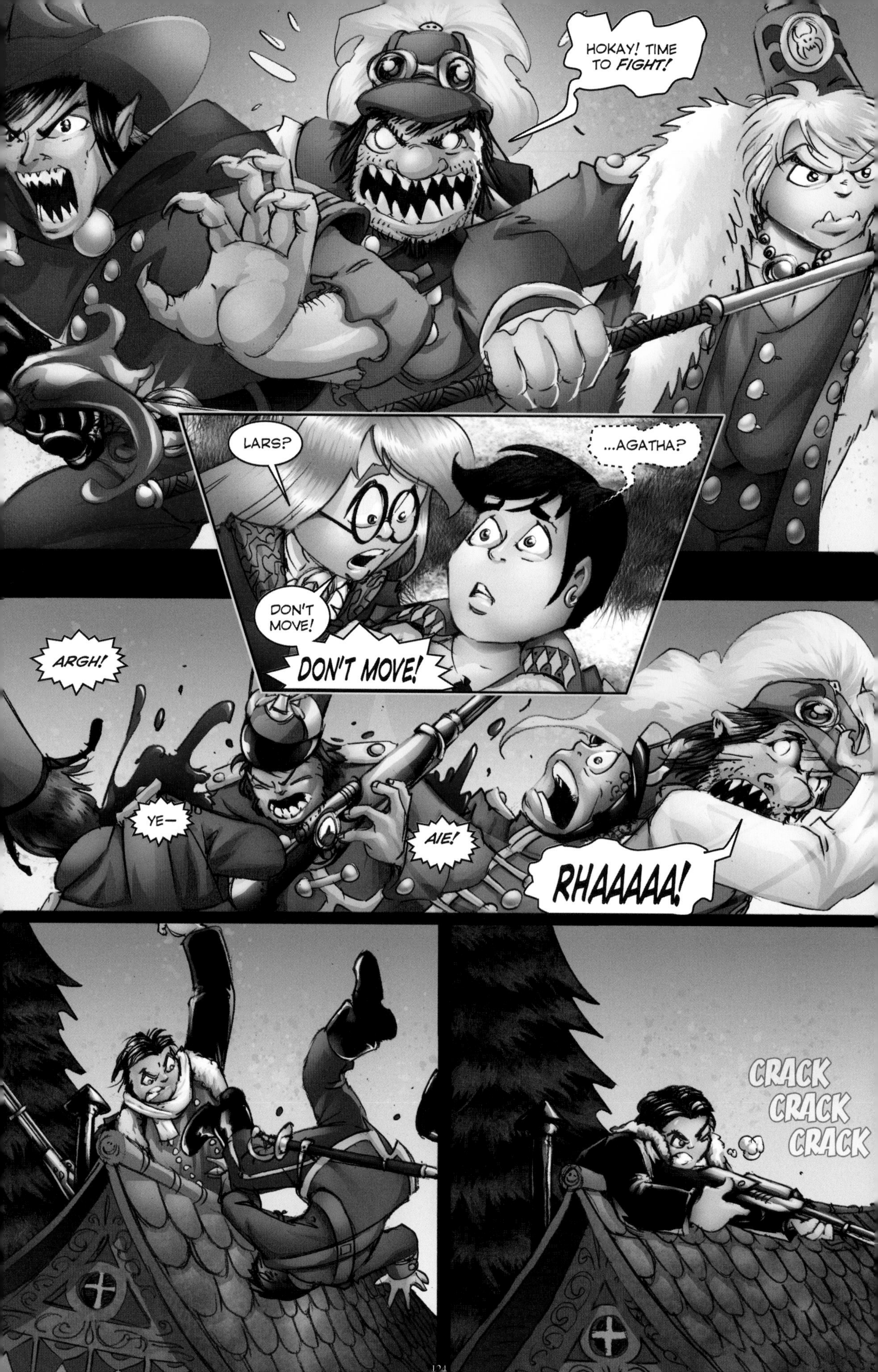
HOKAY! TIME TO FIGHT!
LARS?
...AGATHA?
DON'T MOVE!
DON'T MOVE!
ARGH!
YE—
AIE!
RHAAAAA!
CRACK
CRACK
CRACK

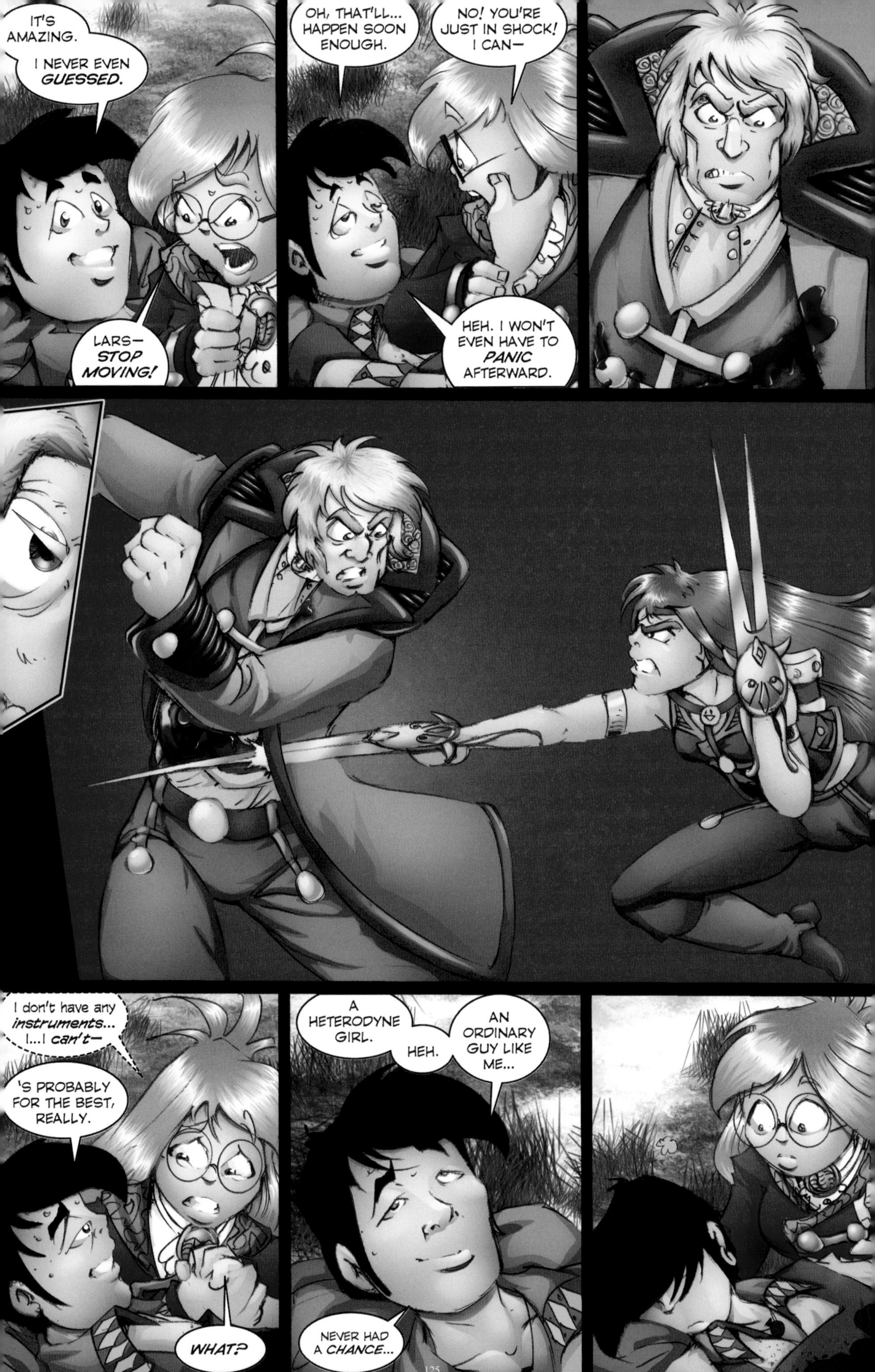

IT'S AMAZING.
I NEVER EVEN *GUESSED*.
LARS— *STOP MOVING!*
OH, THAT'LL... HAPPEN SOON ENOUGH.
NO! YOU'RE JUST IN SHOCK! I CAN—
HEH. I WON'T EVEN HAVE TO *PANIC* AFTERWARD.
I don't have any *instruments*... I...I *can't*—
'S PROBABLY FOR THE BEST, REALLY.
WHAT?
A HETERODYNE GIRL.
HEH.
AN ORDINARY GUY LIKE ME...
NEVER HAD A *CHANCE*...

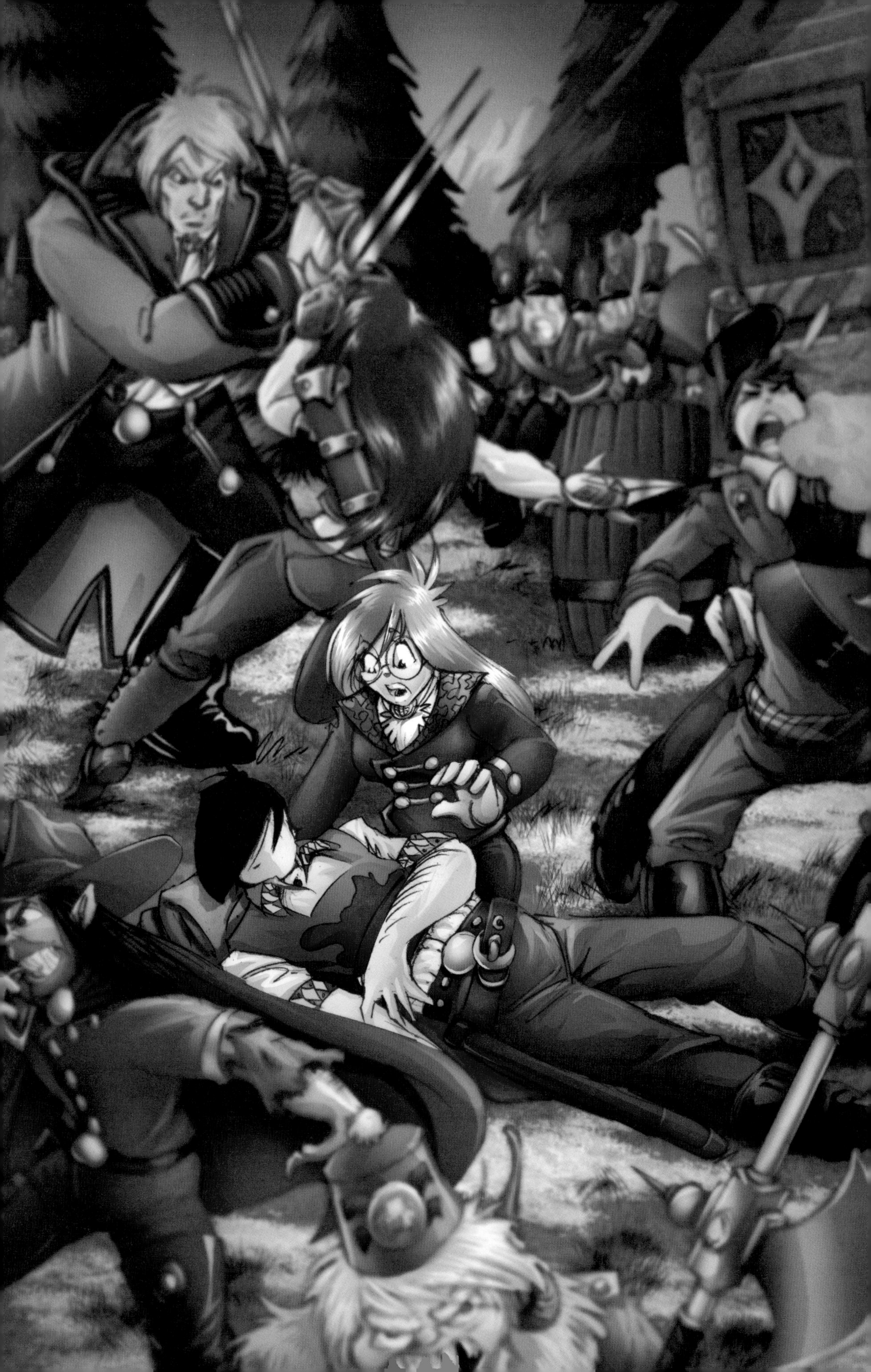

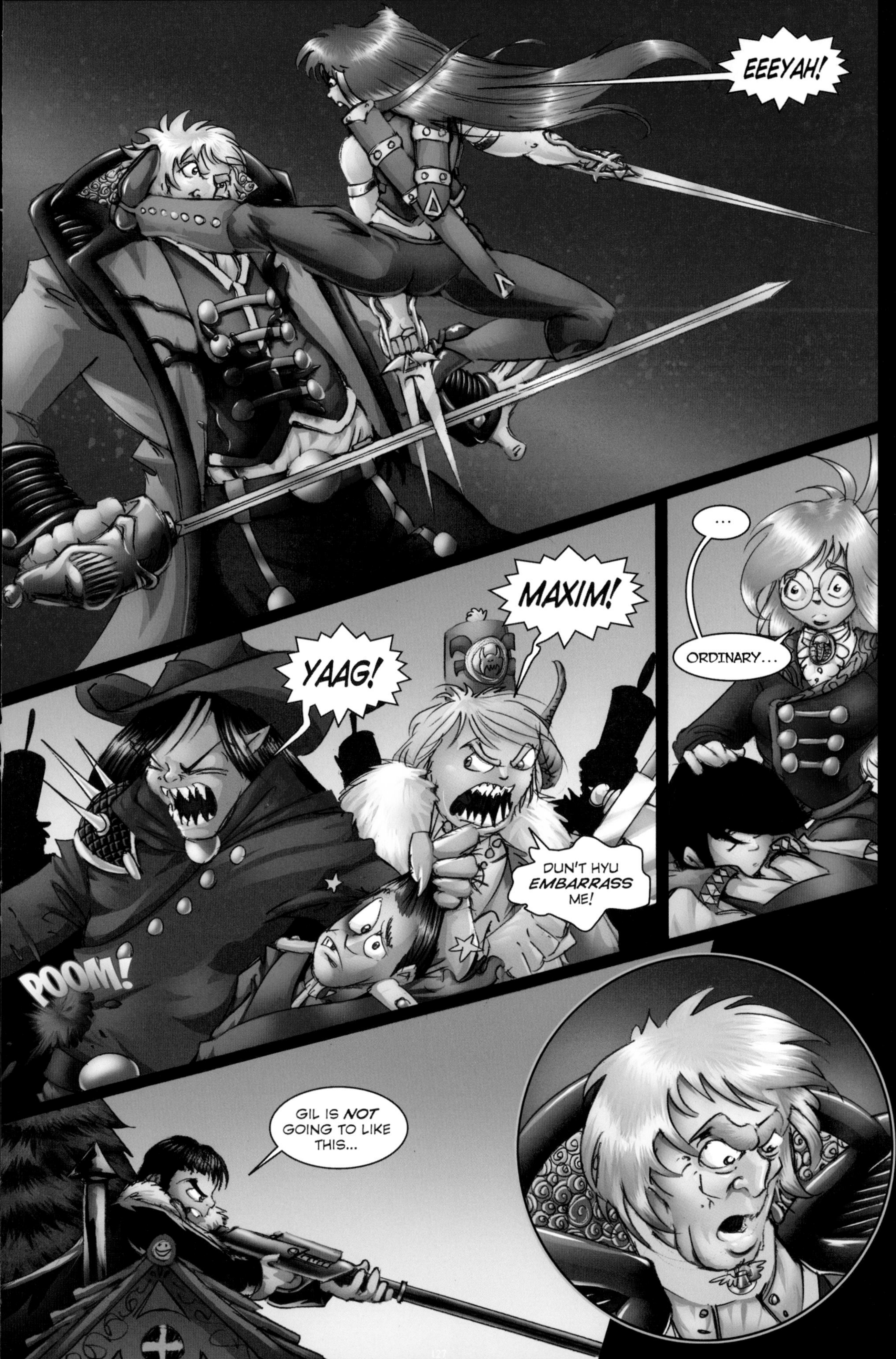
EEEYAH!
MAXIM!
YAAG!
DUN'T HYU EMBARRASS ME!
POOM!
...
ORDINARY...
GIL IS NOT GOING TO LIKE THIS...

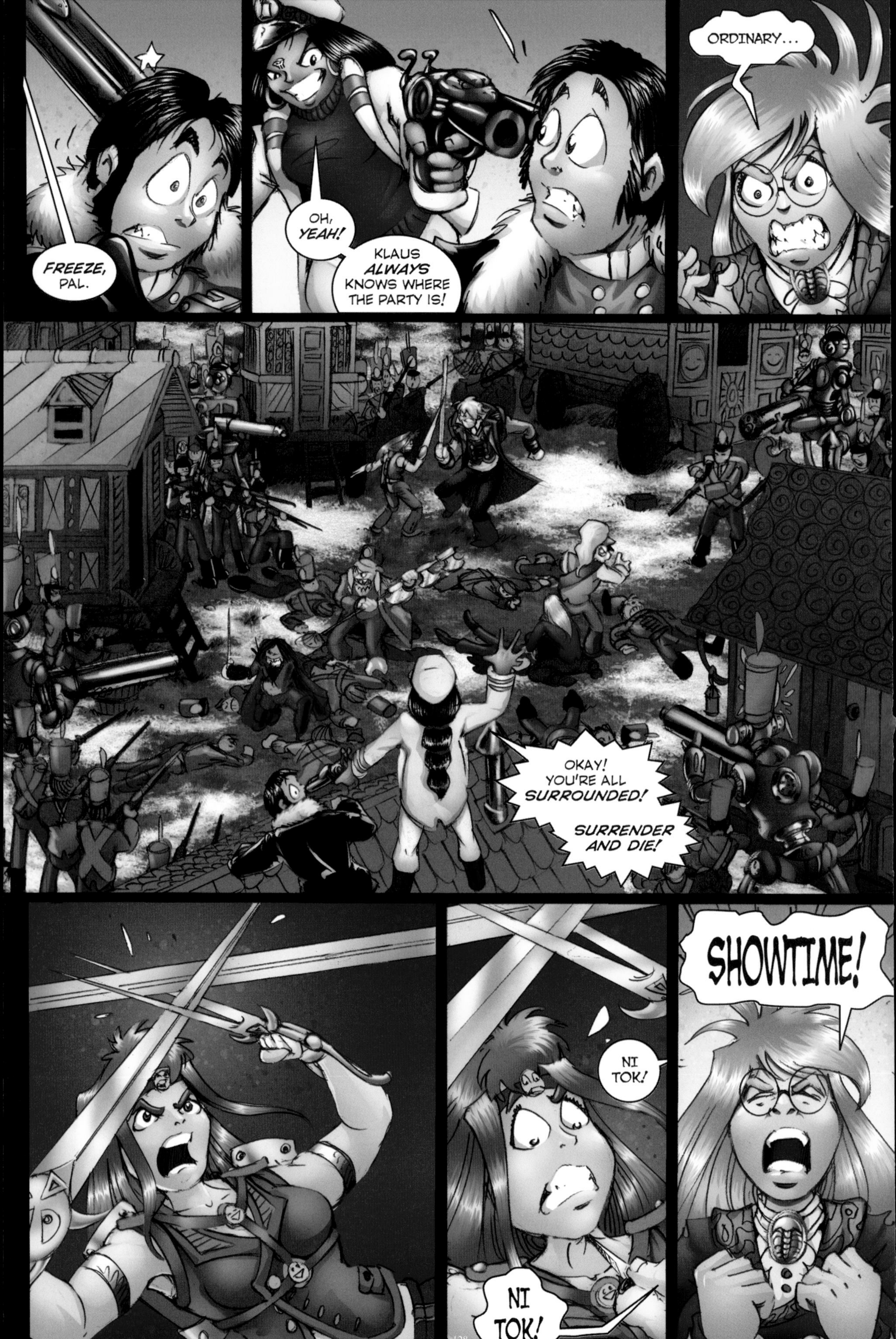
FREEZE, PAL.
OH, YEAH!
KLAUS ALWAYS KNOWS WHERE THE PARTY IS!
ORDINARY...
OKAY! YOU'RE ALL SURROUNDED!
SURRENDER AND DIE!
NI TOK!
NI TOK!
SHOWTIME!

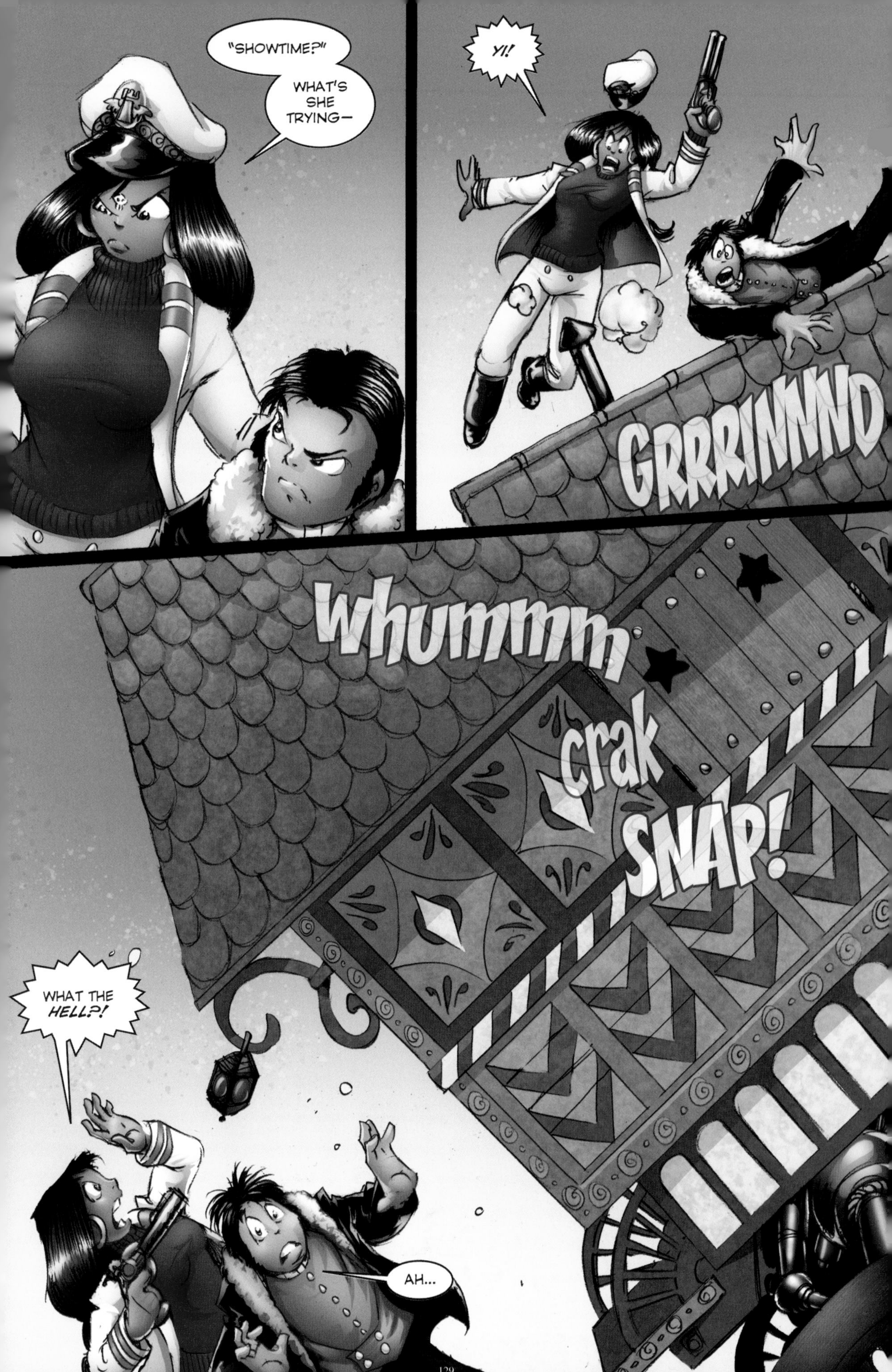
"SHOWTIME?"
WHAT'S SHE TRYING—
YI!
GRRRINNND
whummm
crak
SNAP!
WHAT THE *HELL?!*
AH...

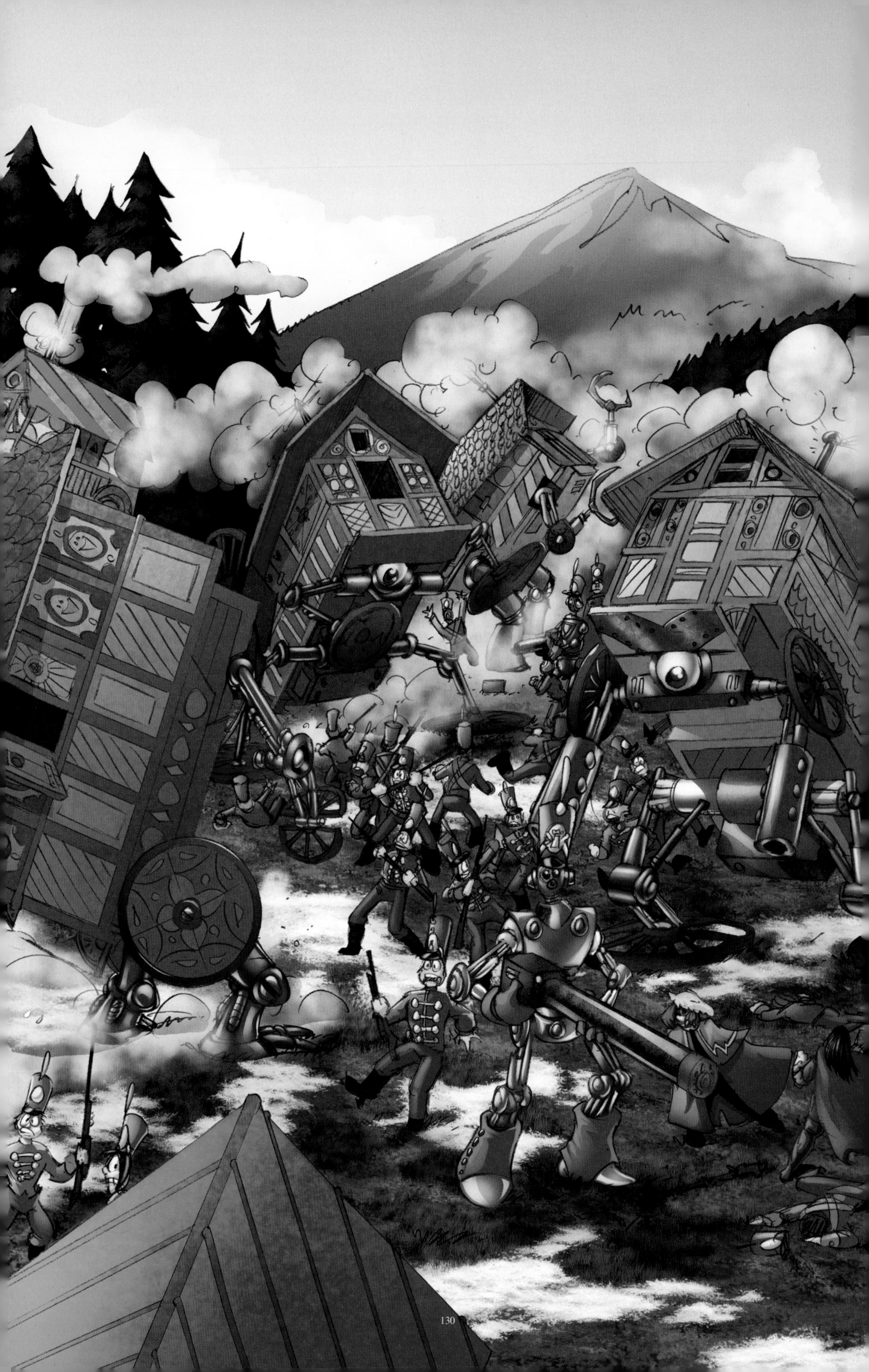

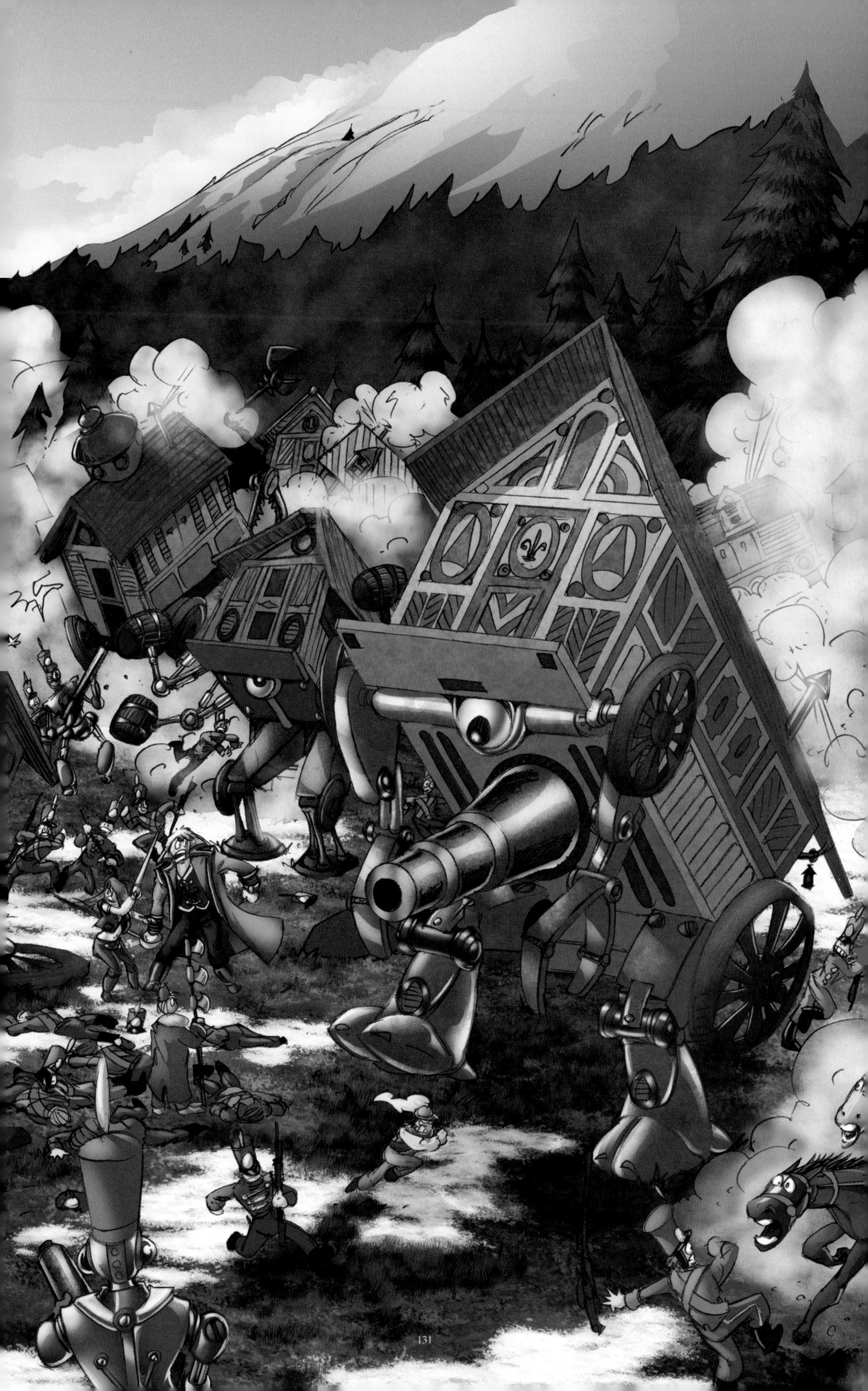

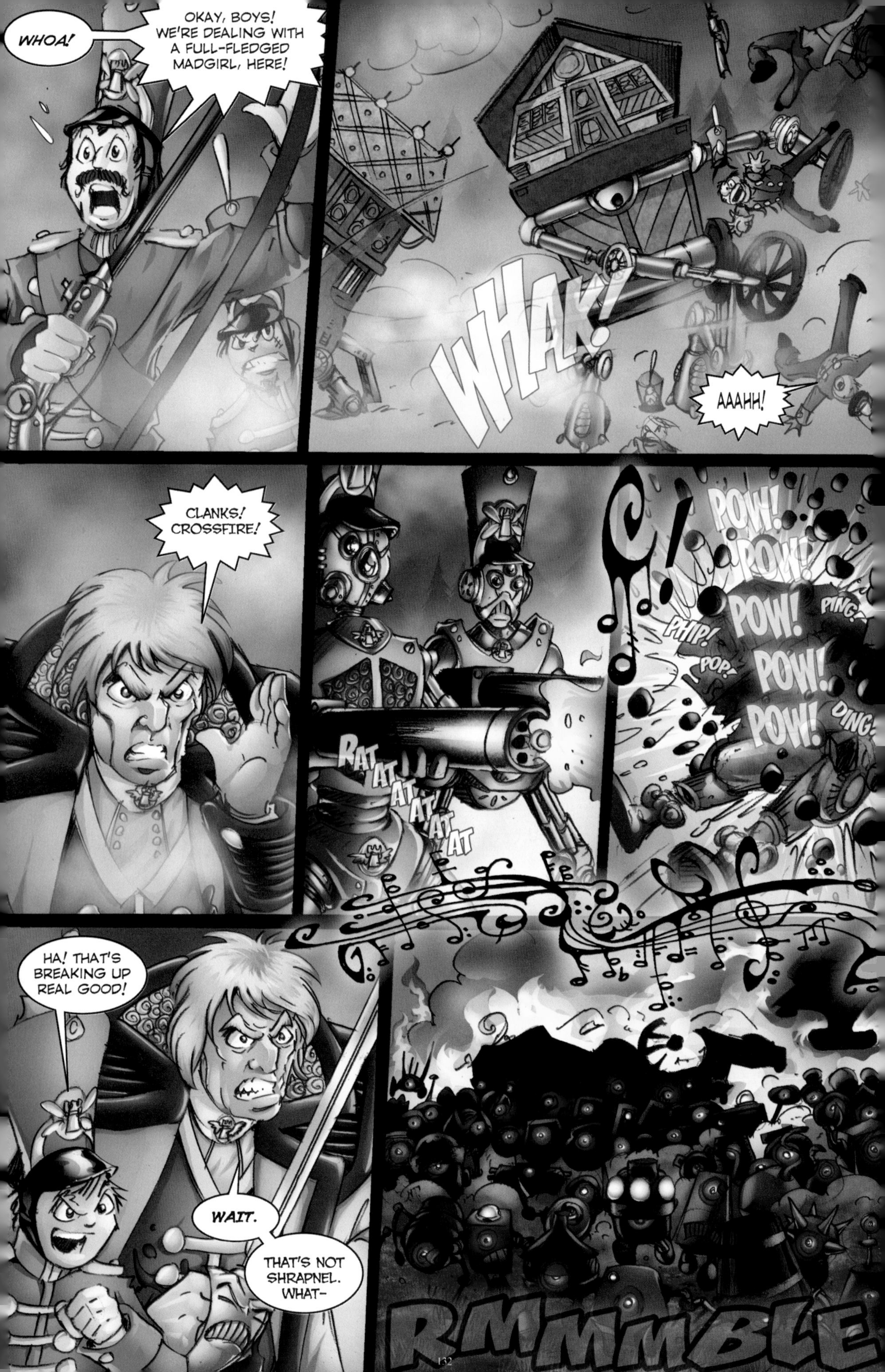

WHOA!
OKAY, BOYS! WE'RE DEALING WITH A FULL-FLEDGED MADGIRL, HERE!
WHAK!
AAAHH!
CLANKS! CROSSFIRE!
RATATATATATAT
POW! POW! POW! PING! PHIP! POP! POW! POW! DING!
HA! THAT'S BREAKING UP REAL GOOD!
WAIT.
THAT'S NOT SHRAPNEL. WHAT-
RMMMBLE

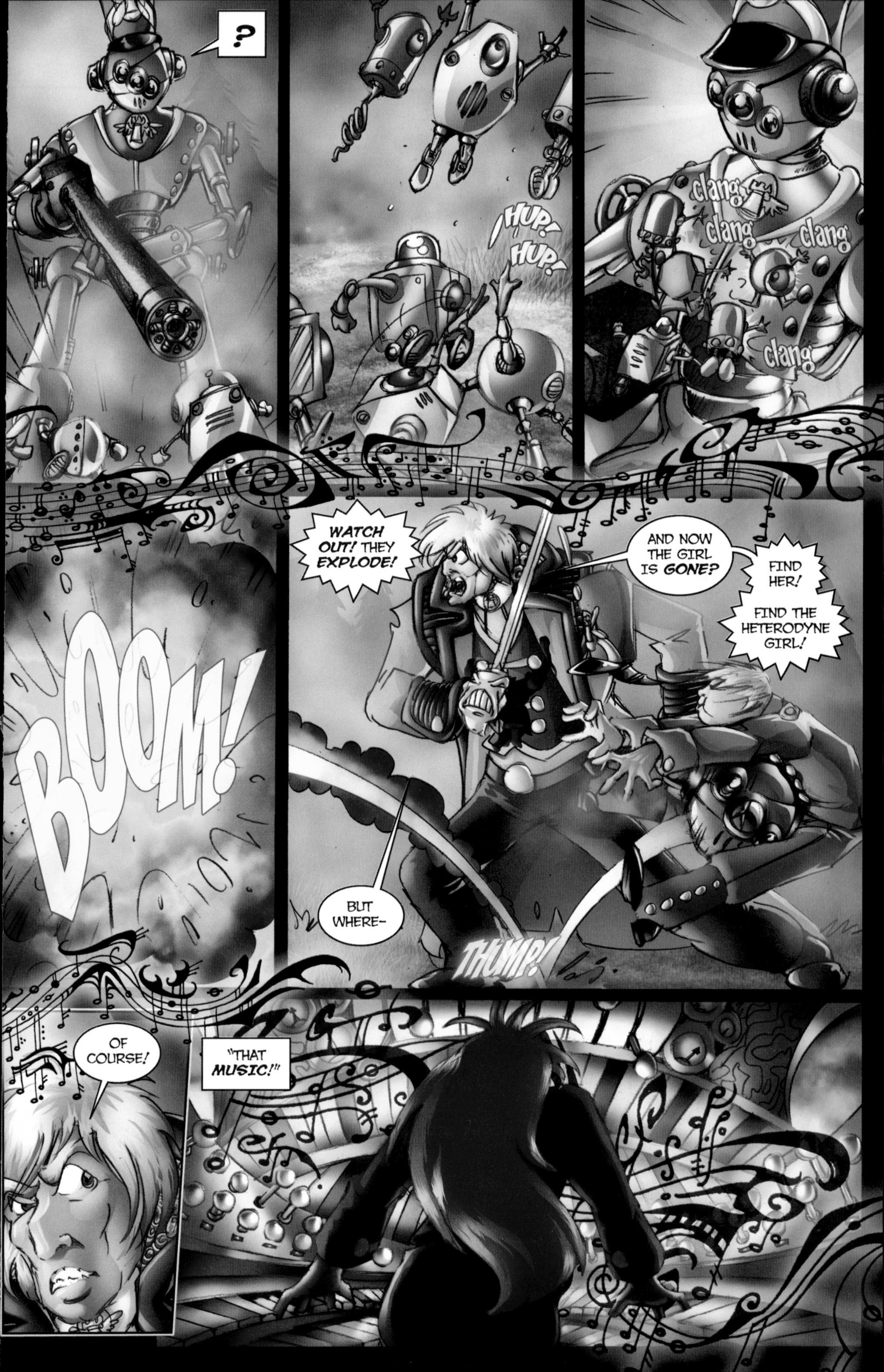
?
HUP!
HUP!
clang
clang
clang
clang
BOOM!
WATCH OUT! THEY EXPLODE!
AND NOW THE GIRL IS GONE?
FIND HER!
FIND THE HETERODYNE GIRL!
BUT WHERE-
THUMP!
OF COURSE!
"THAT MUSIC!"

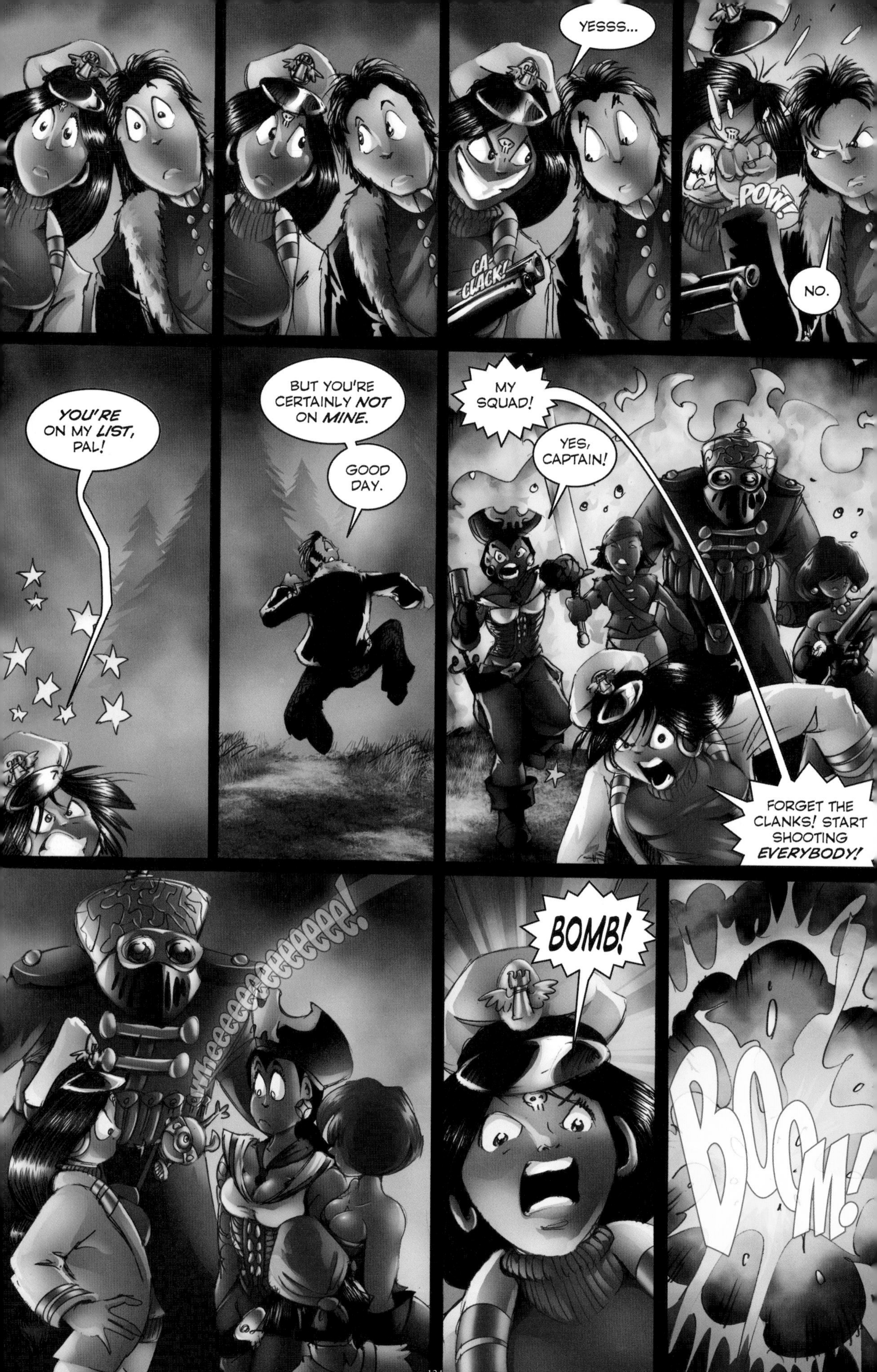
YESSS...
CA-CLACK!
POW!
NO.
YOU'RE ON MY LIST, PAL!
BUT YOU'RE CERTAINLY NOT ON MINE.
GOOD DAY.
MY SQUAD!
YES, CAPTAIN!
FORGET THE CLANKS! START SHOOTING EVERYBODY!
BOMB!
BOOM!

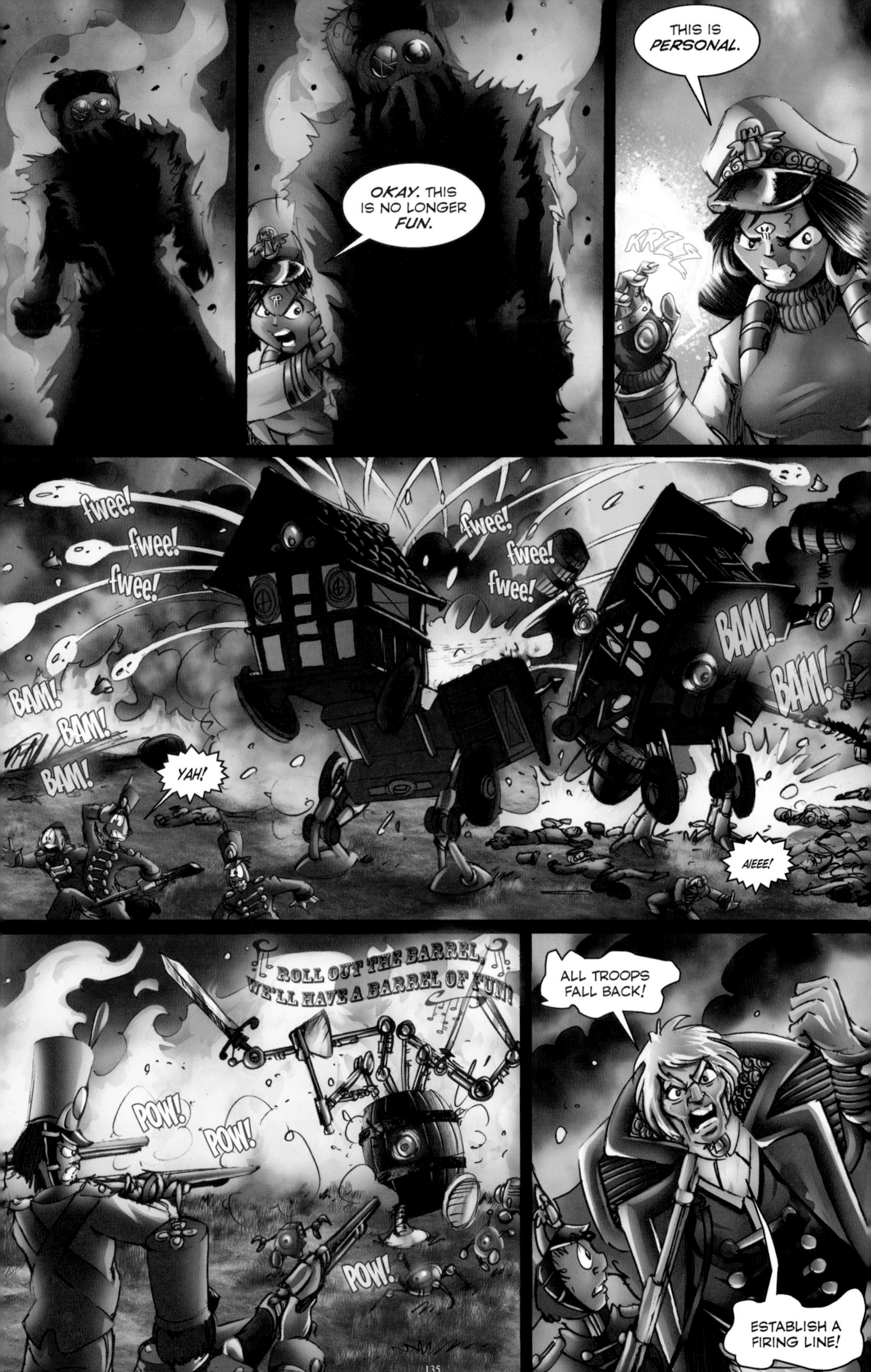
OKAY. THIS IS NO LONGER FUN.
THIS IS PERSONAL.
fwee!
fwee!
fwee!
fwee!
fwee!
fwee!
BAM!
BAM!
BAM!
YAH!
BAM!
BAM!
AIEEE!
ROLL OUT THE BARREL, WE'LL HAVE A BARREL OF FUN!
POW!
POW!
POW!
ALL TROOPS FALL BACK!
ESTABLISH A FIRING LINE!

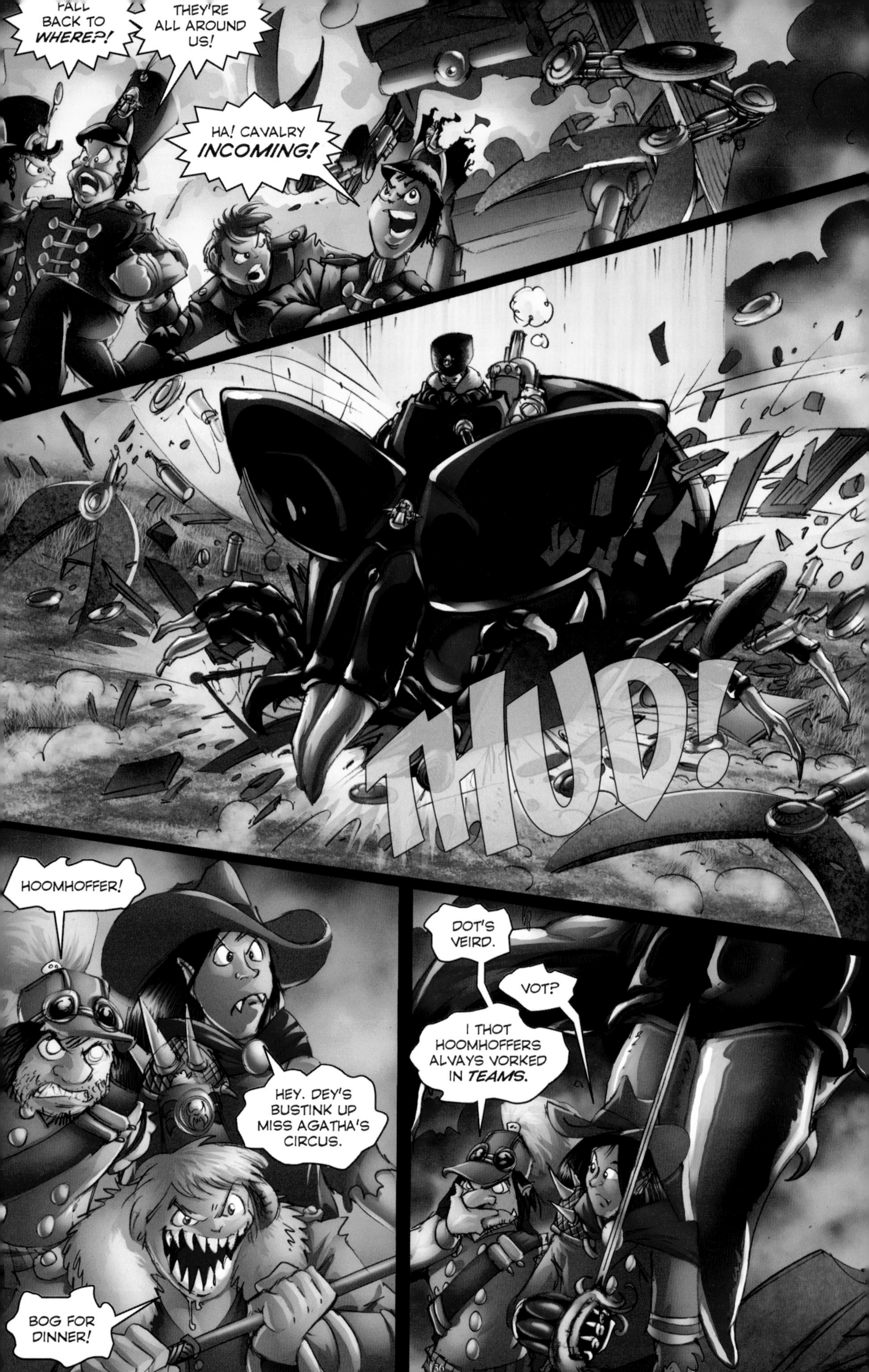
FALL BACK TO WHERE?!
THEY'RE ALL AROUND US!
HA! CAVALRY INCOMING!
THUD!
HOOMHOFFER!
HEY. DEY'S BUSTINK UP MISS AGATHA'S CIRCUS.
BOG FOR DINNER!
DOT'S VEIRD.
VOT?
I THOT HOOMHOFFERS ALWAYS VORKED IN TEAMS.

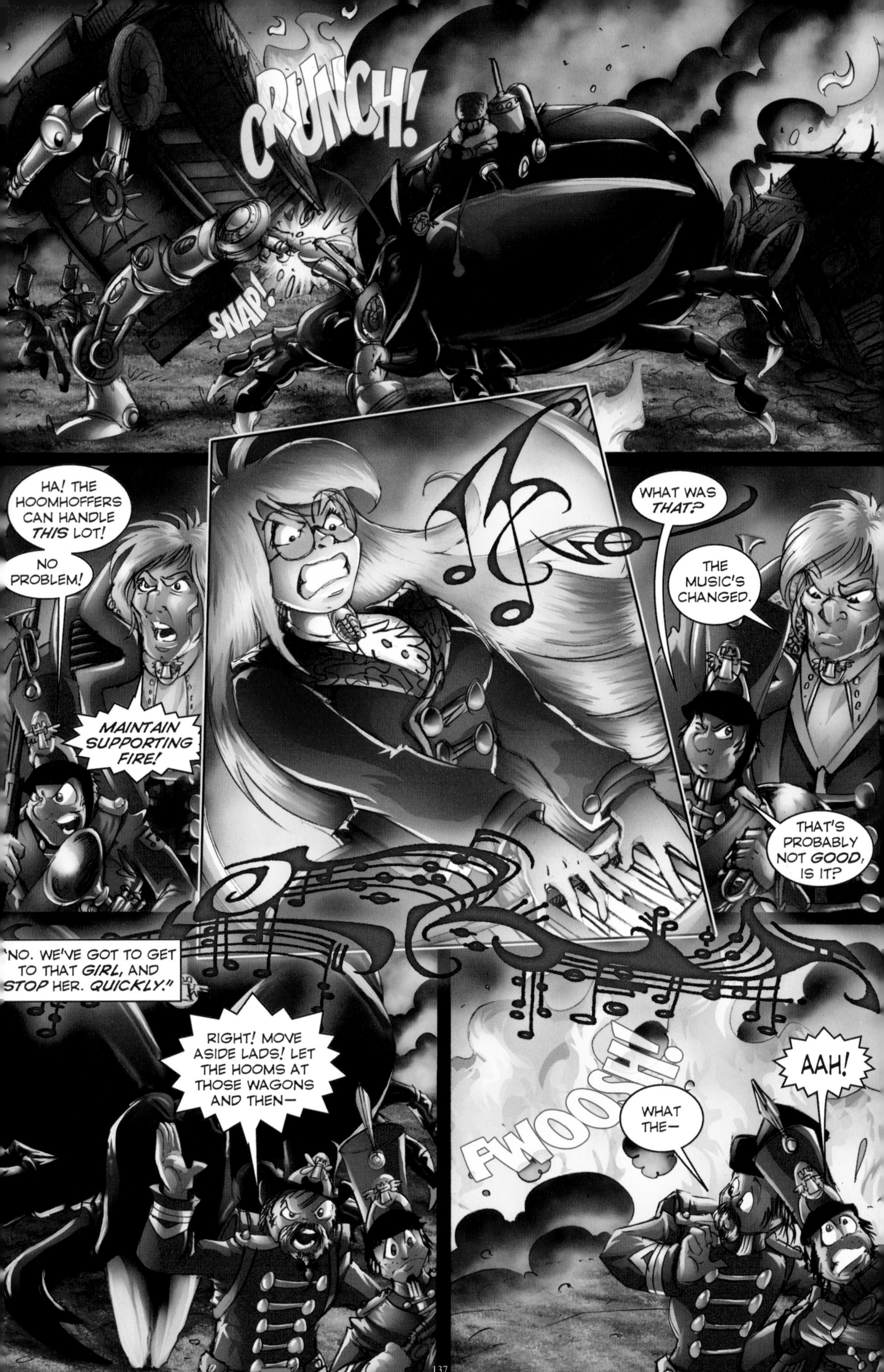
CRUNCH!
SNAP!
HA! THE HOOMHOFFERS CAN HANDLE THIS LOT!
NO PROBLEM!
MAINTAIN SUPPORTING FIRE!
WHAT WAS THAT?
THE MUSIC'S CHANGED.
THAT'S PROBABLY NOT GOOD, IS IT?
"NO. WE'VE GOT TO GET TO THAT GIRL, AND STOP HER. QUICKLY."
RIGHT! MOVE ASIDE LADS! LET THE HOOMS AT THOSE WAGONS AND THEN—
FWOOSH!
WHAT THE—
AAH!

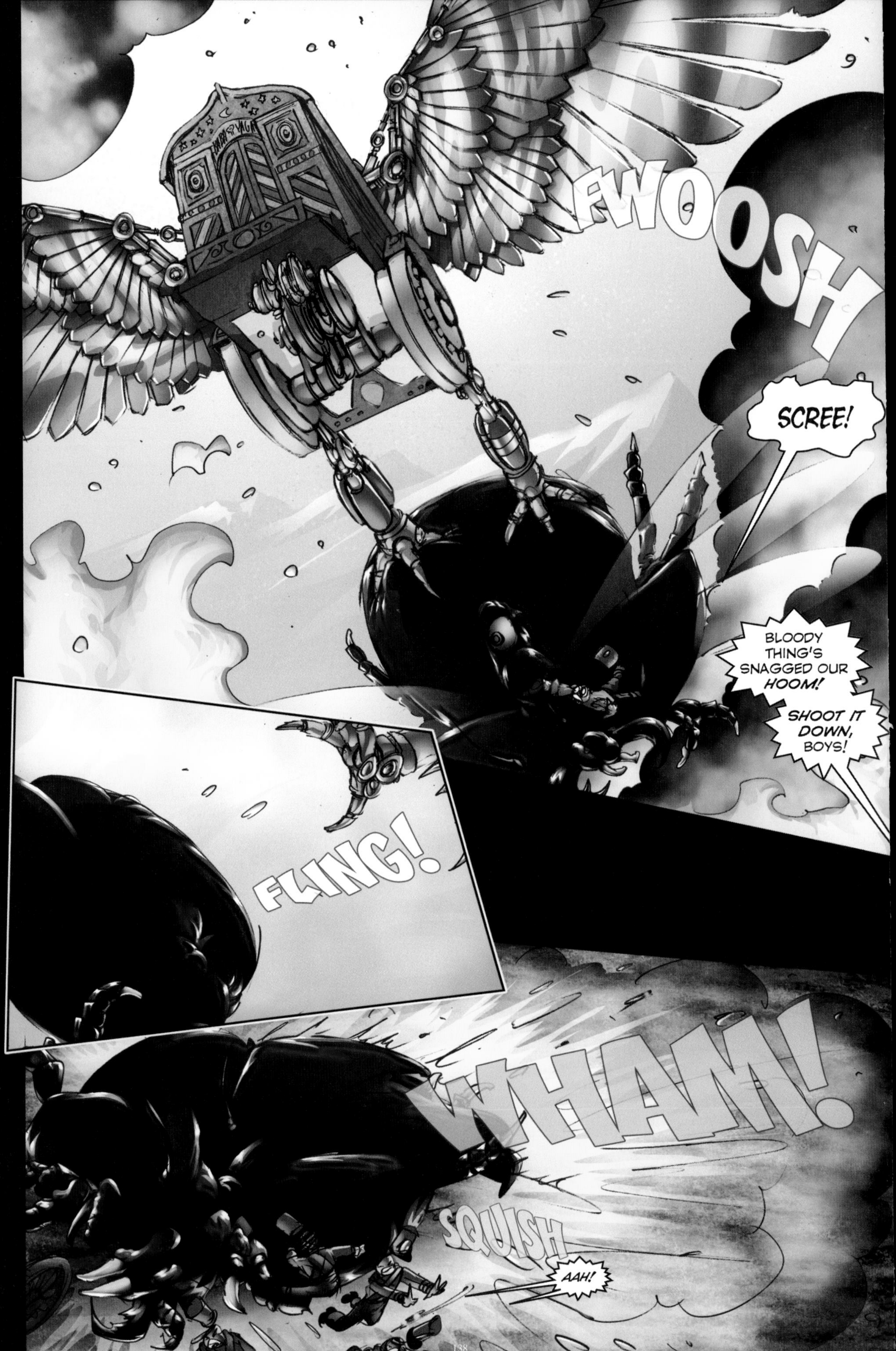
FWOOSH
SCREE!
BLOODY THING'S SNAGGED OUR HOOM!
SHOOT IT DOWN, BOYS!
FLING!
WHAM!
SQUISH
AAH!

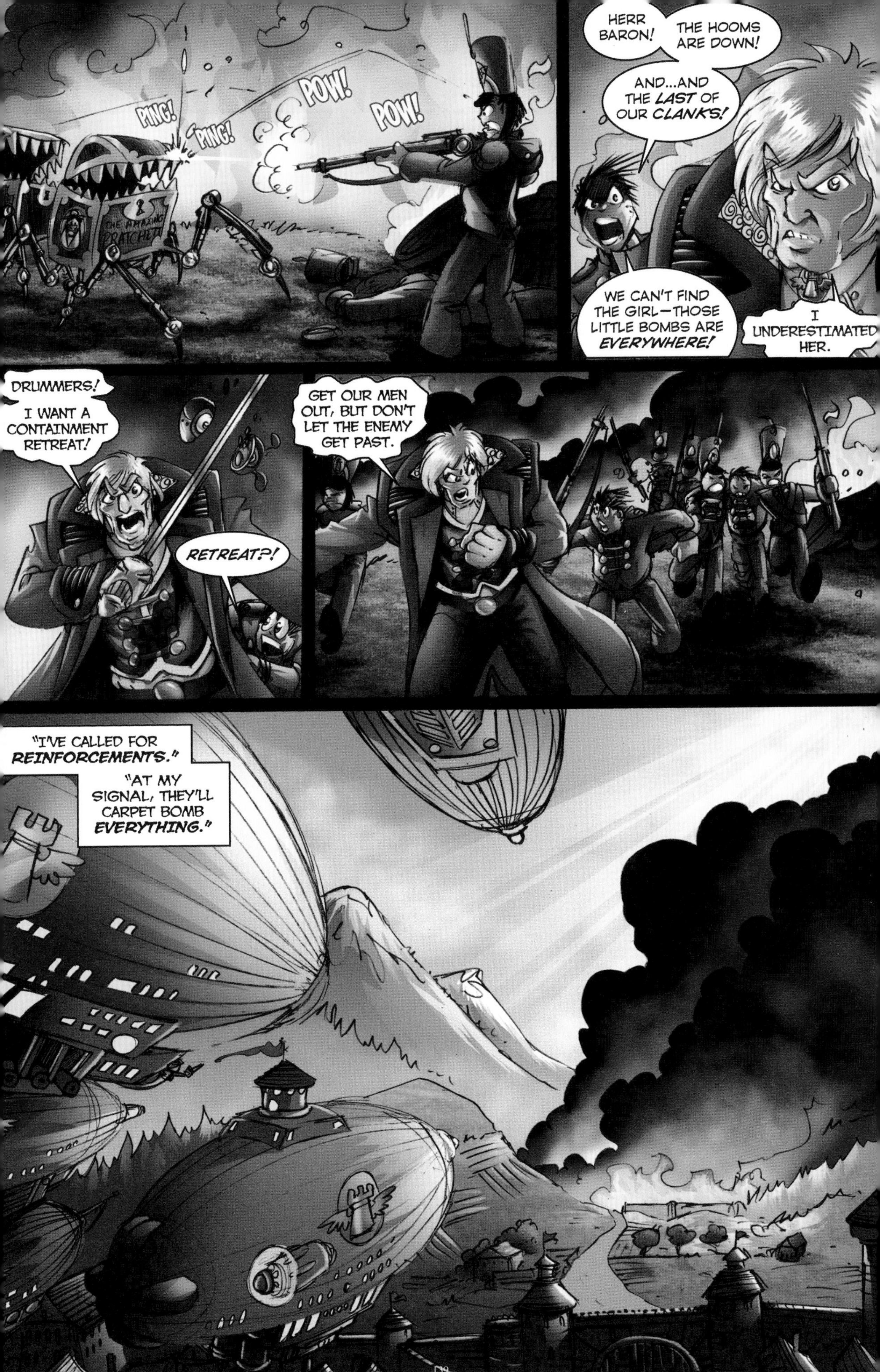
PING!
PING!
POW!
POW!
THE AMAZING PRATCHETT
HERR BARON!
THE HOOMS ARE DOWN!
AND...AND THE LAST OF OUR CLANKS!
WE CAN'T FIND THE GIRL—THOSE LITTLE BOMBS ARE EVERYWHERE!
I UNDERESTIMATED HER.
DRUMMERS!
I WANT A CONTAINMENT RETREAT!
RETREAT?!
GET OUR MEN OUT, BUT DON'T LET THE ENEMY GET PAST.
"I'VE CALLED FOR REINFORCEMENTS."
"AT MY SIGNAL, THEY'LL CARPET BOMB EVERYTHING."

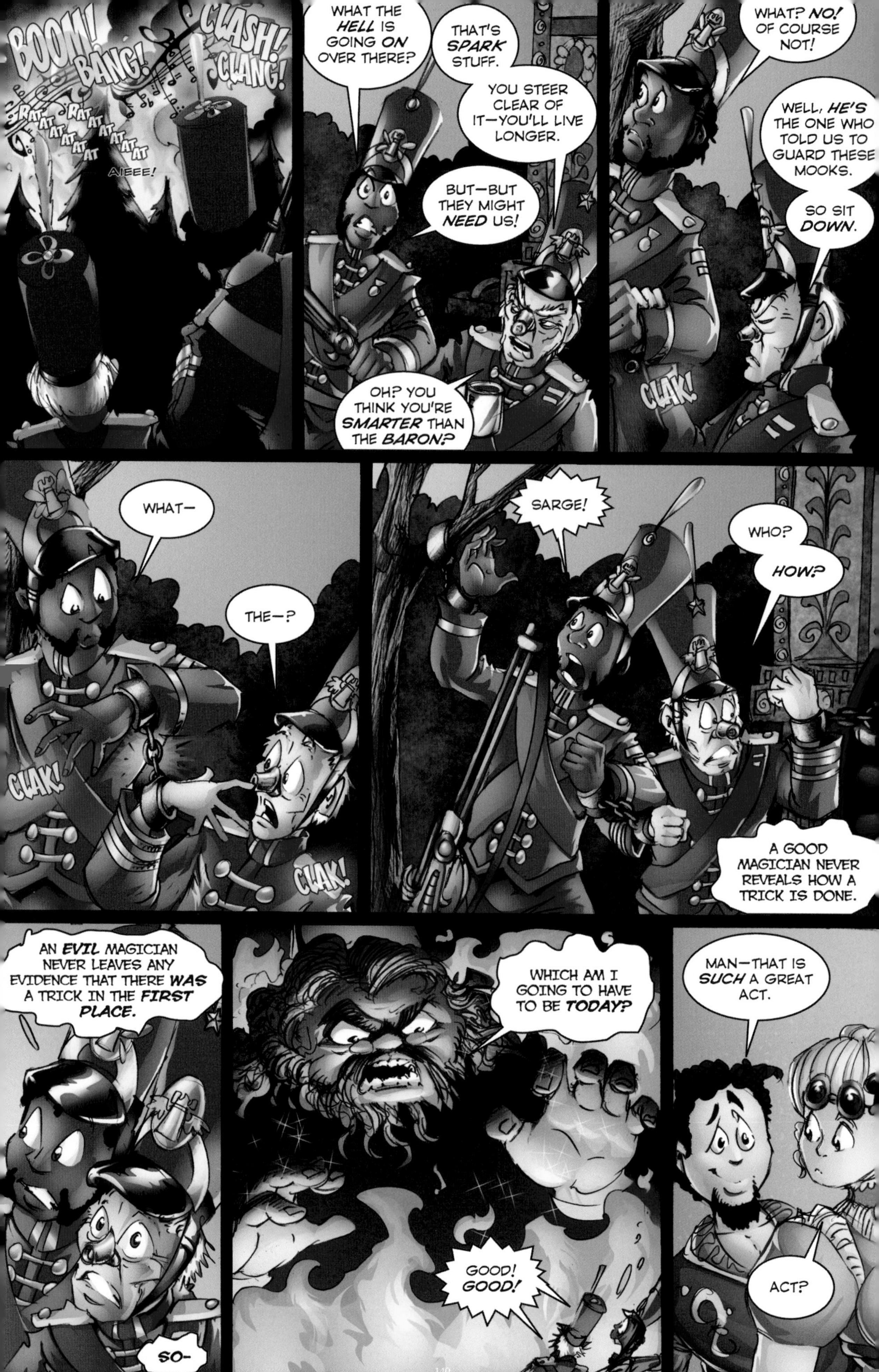

BOOM! BANG!
CLASH! CLANG!
RATATATATAT RATATATATAT
AIEEE!
WHAT THE HELL IS GOING ON OVER THERE?
THAT'S SPARK STUFF.
YOU STEER CLEAR OF IT—YOU'LL LIVE LONGER.
BUT—BUT THEY MIGHT NEED US!
OH? YOU THINK YOU'RE SMARTER THAN THE BARON?
WHAT? NO! OF COURSE NOT!
WELL, HE'S THE ONE WHO TOLD US TO GUARD THESE MOOKS.
SO SIT DOWN.
CLAK!
WHAT-
THE—?
CLAK!
CLAK!
SARGE!
WHO?
HOW?
A GOOD MAGICIAN NEVER REVEALS HOW A TRICK IS DONE.
AN EVIL MAGICIAN NEVER LEAVES ANY EVIDENCE THAT THERE WAS A TRICK IN THE FIRST PLACE.
SO-
WHICH AM I GOING TO HAVE TO BE TODAY?
GOOD! GOOD!
MAN—THAT IS SUCH A GREAT ACT.
ACT?

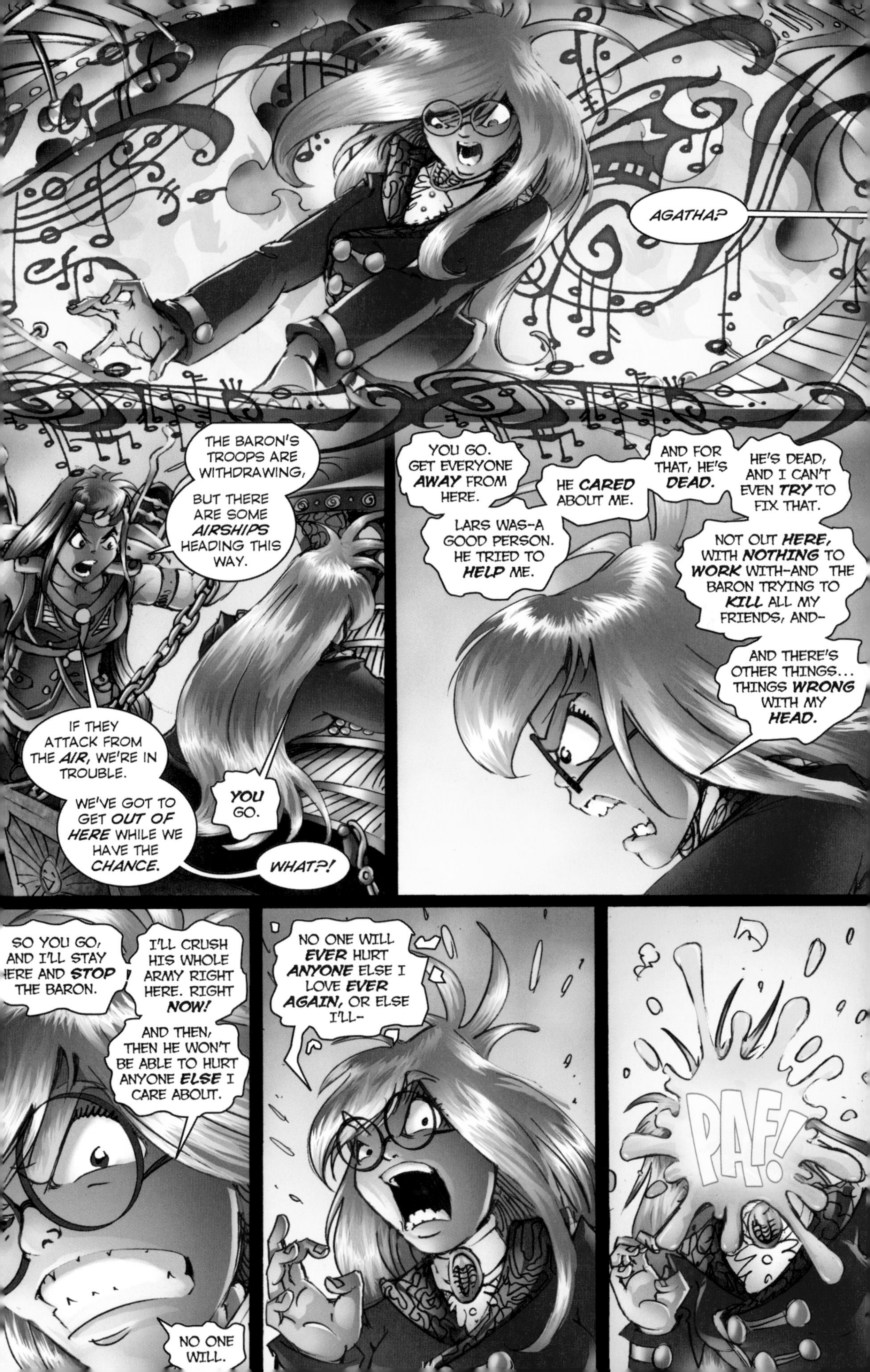

AGATHA?
THE BARON'S TROOPS ARE WITHDRAWING,
BUT THERE ARE SOME AIRSHIPS HEADING THIS WAY.
IF THEY ATTACK FROM THE AIR, WE'RE IN TROUBLE.
WE'VE GOT TO GET OUT OF HERE WHILE WE HAVE THE CHANCE.
YOU GO.
WHAT?!
YOU GO. GET EVERYONE AWAY FROM HERE.
LARS WAS-A GOOD PERSON. HE TRIED TO HELP ME.
HE CARED ABOUT ME.
AND FOR THAT, HE'S DEAD.
HE'S DEAD, AND I CAN'T EVEN TRY TO FIX THAT.
NOT OUT HERE, WITH NOTHING TO WORK WITH-AND THE BARON TRYING TO KILL ALL MY FRIENDS, AND-
AND THERE'S OTHER THINGS... THINGS WRONG WITH MY HEAD.
SO YOU GO, AND I'LL STAY HERE AND STOP THE BARON.
I'LL CRUSH HIS WHOLE ARMY RIGHT HERE. RIGHT NOW!
AND THEN, THEN HE WON'T BE ABLE TO HURT ANYONE ELSE I CARE ABOUT.
NO ONE WILL.
NO ONE WILL EVER HURT ANYONE ELSE I LOVE EVER AGAIN, OR ELSE I'LL-
PAF!

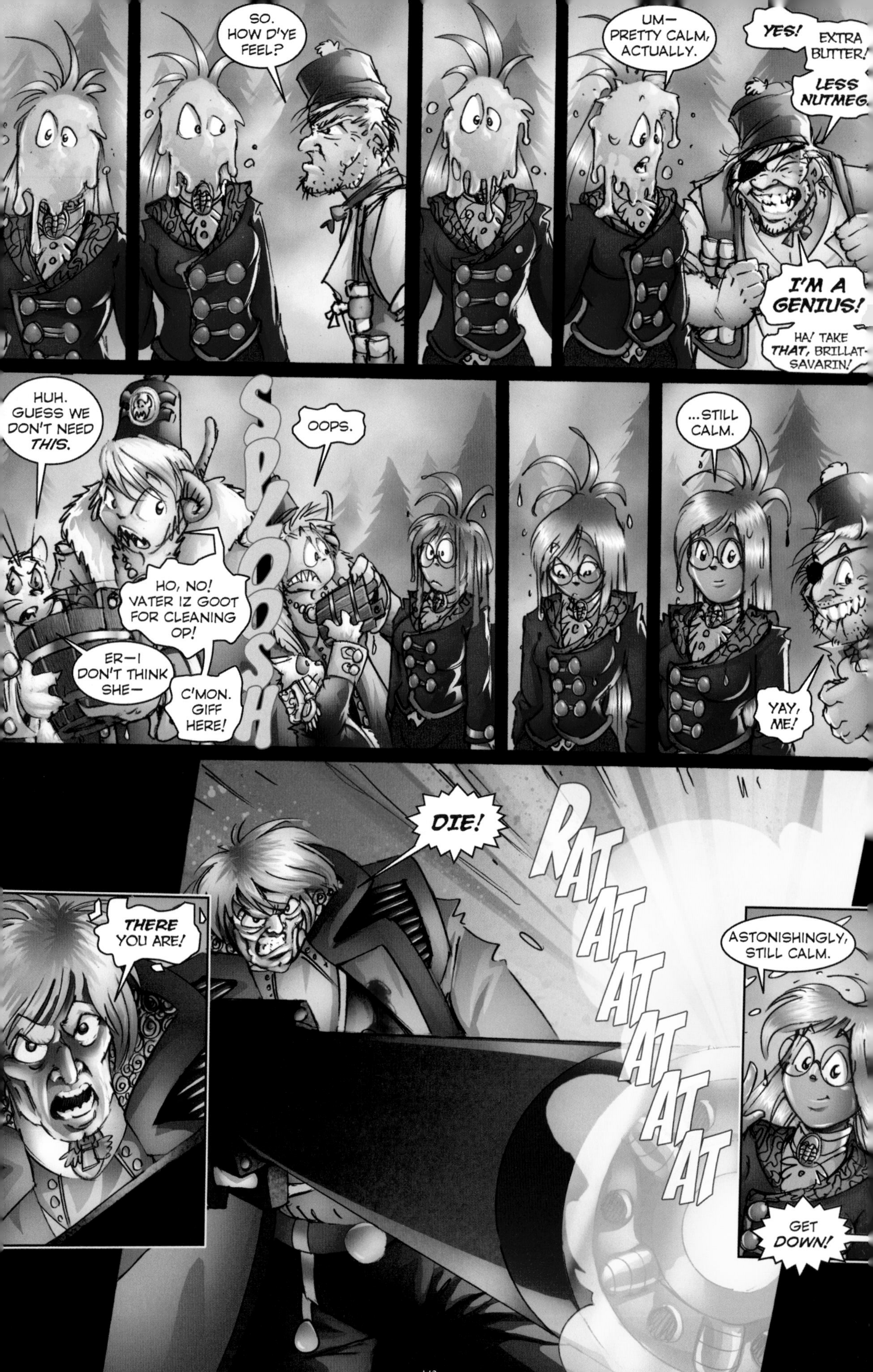
SO. HOW D'YE FEEL?
UM— PRETTY CALM, ACTUALLY.
YES! EXTRA BUTTER!
LESS NUTMEG.
I'M A GENIUS!
HA! TAKE THAT, BRILLAT-SAVARIN!
HUH. GUESS WE DON'T NEED THIS.
HO, NO! VATER IZ GOOT FOR CLEANING OP!
ER—I DON'T THINK SHE—
C'MON. GIFF HERE!
SPLOOSH
OOPS.
...STILL CALM.
YAY, ME!
DIE!
RATATATATATAT
THERE YOU ARE!
ASTONISHINGLY, STILL CALM.
GET DOWN!

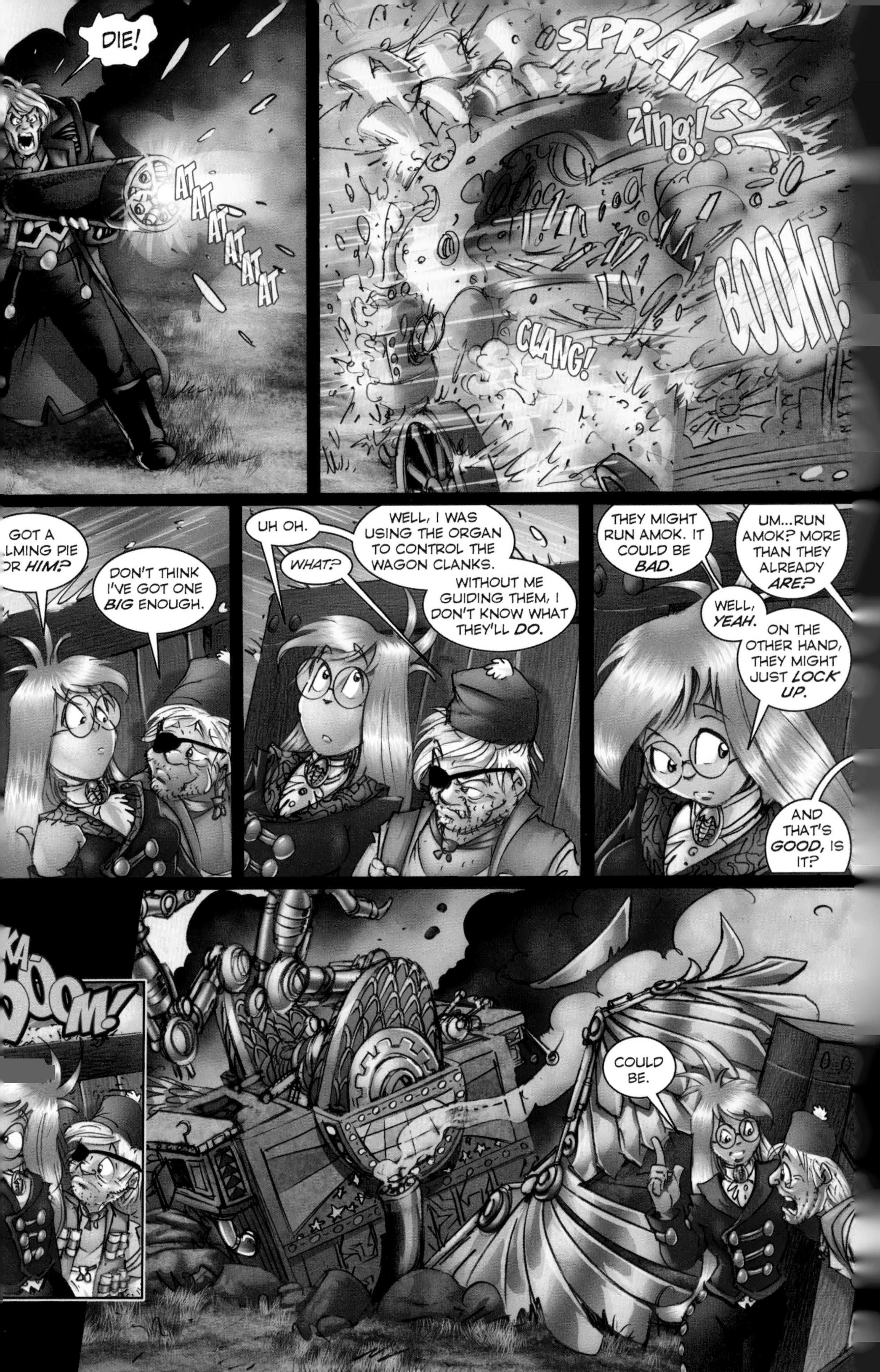
DIE!
AT AT AT AT AT AT AT
SPRANG!
zing!
BOOOM!
CLANG!
GOT A
LMING PIE
OR HIM?
DON'T THINK I'VE GOT ONE BIG ENOUGH.
UH OH.
WELL, I WAS USING THE ORGAN TO CONTROL THE WAGON CLANKS.
WHAT?
WITHOUT ME GUIDING THEM, I DON'T KNOW WHAT THEY'LL DO.
THEY MIGHT RUN AMOK. IT COULD BE BAD.
UM...RUN AMOK? MORE THAN THEY ALREADY ARE?
WELL, YEAH.
ON THE OTHER HAND, THEY MIGHT JUST LOCK UP.
AND THAT'S GOOD, IS IT?
KA-BOOM!
COULD BE.

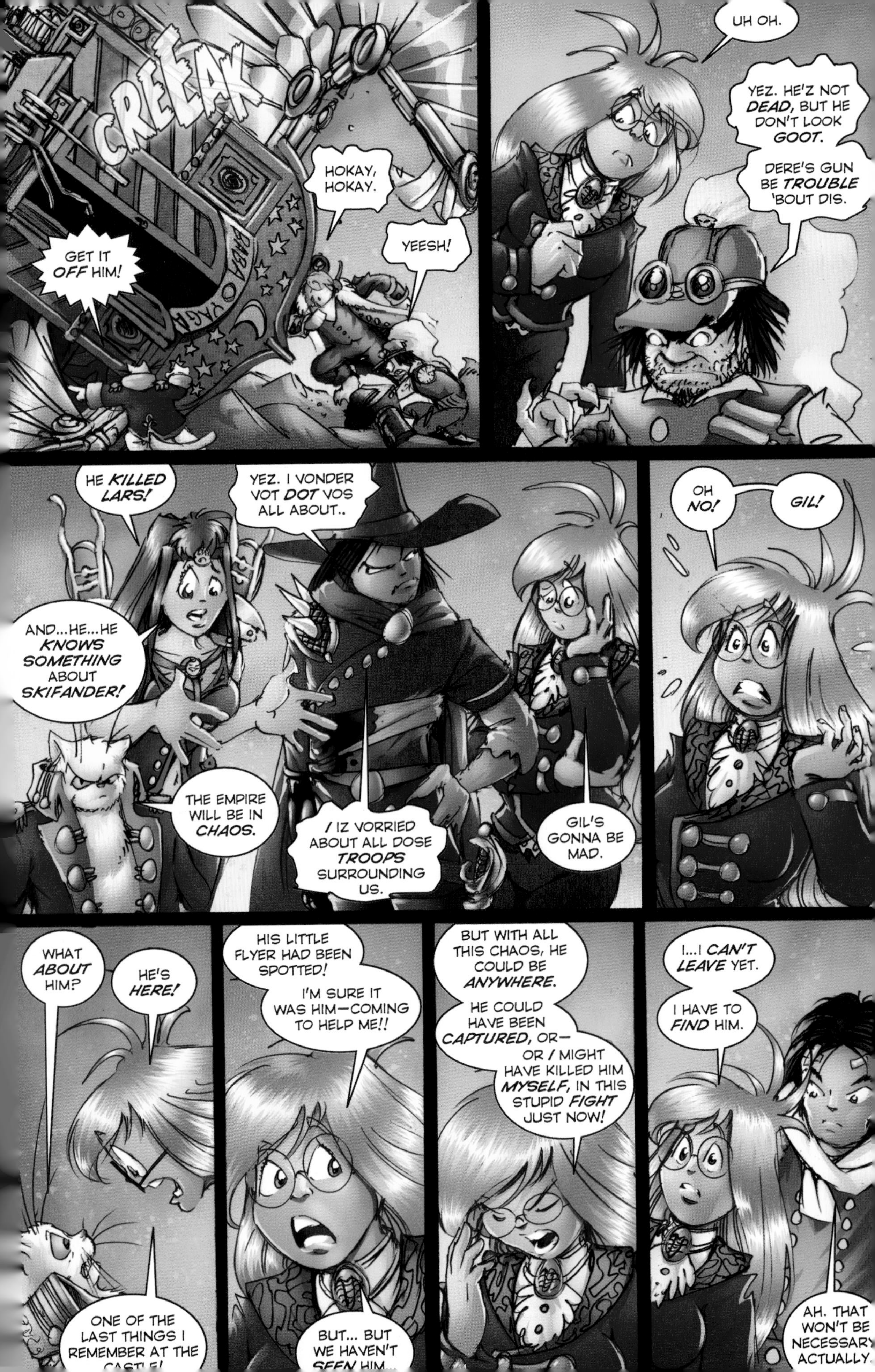
CREEAK
HOKAY, HOKAY.
GET IT OFF HIM!
YEESH!
UH OH.
YEZ. HE'Z NOT DEAD, BUT HE DON'T LOOK GOOT.
DERE'S GUN BE TROUBLE 'BOUT DIS.
HE KILLED LARS!
YEZ. I VONDER VOT DOT VOS ALL ABOUT..
AND...HE...HE KNOWS SOMETHING ABOUT SKIFANDER!
THE EMPIRE WILL BE IN CHAOS.
I IZ VORRIED ABOUT ALL DOSE TROOPS SURROUNDING US.
GIL'S GONNA BE MAD.
OH NO!
GIL!
WHAT ABOUT HIM?
HE'S HERE!
ONE OF THE LAST THINGS I REMEMBER AT THE
HIS LITTLE FLYER HAD BEEN SPOTTED!
I'M SURE IT WAS HIM—COMING TO HELP ME!!
BUT... BUT WE HAVEN'T
BUT WITH ALL THIS CHAOS, HE COULD BE ANYWHERE.
HE COULD HAVE BEEN CAPTURED, OR—
OR I MIGHT HAVE KILLED HIM MYSELF, IN THIS STUPID FIGHT JUST NOW!
I...I CAN'T LEAVE YET.
I HAVE TO FIND HIM.
AH. THAT WON'T BE NECESSARY, ACTUALLY.

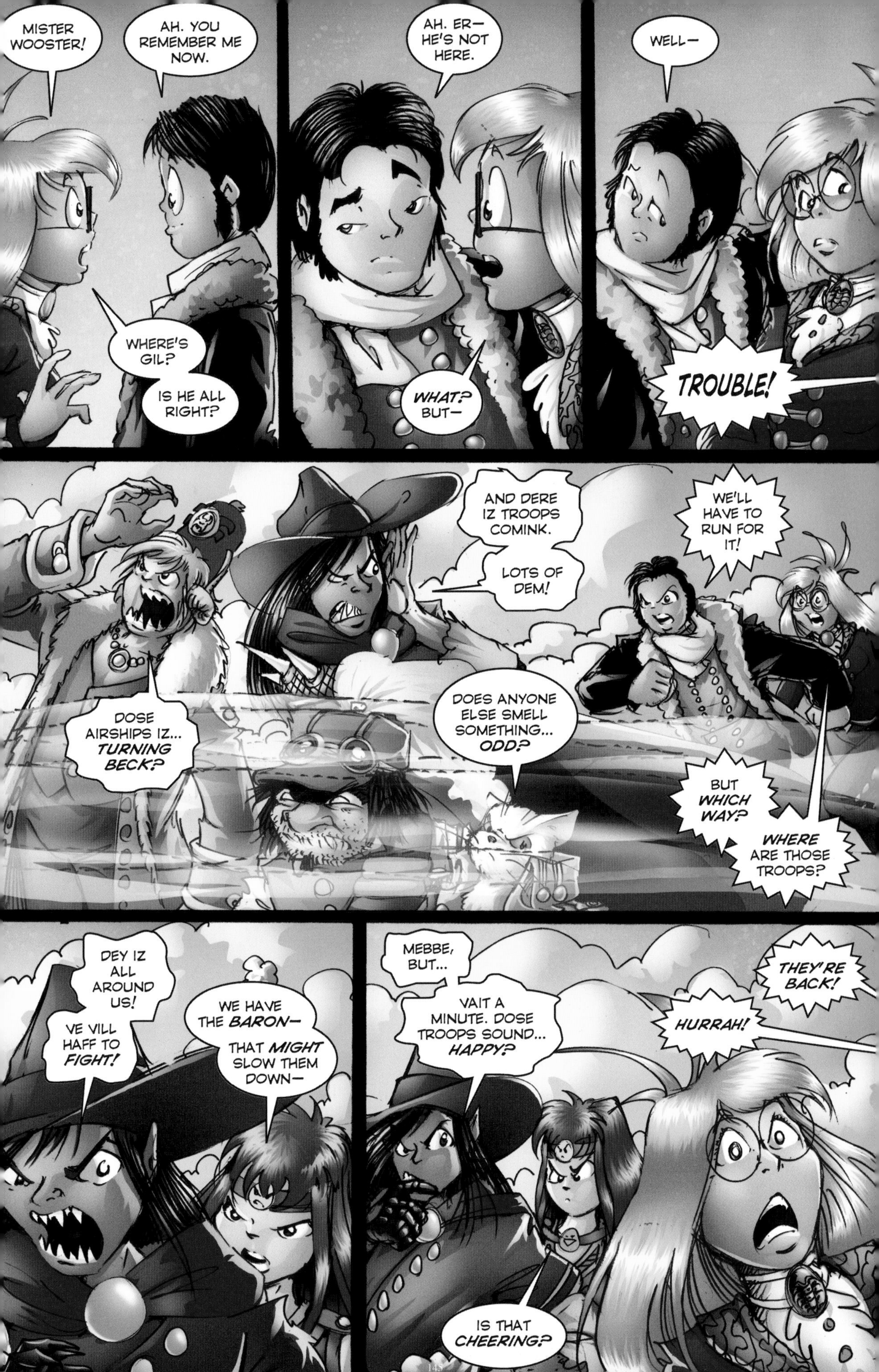
MISTER WOOSTER!
AH. YOU REMEMBER ME NOW.
WHERE'S GIL?
IS HE ALL RIGHT?
AH. ER— HE'S NOT HERE.
WHAT? BUT—
WELL—
TROUBLE!
AND DERE IZ TROOPS COMINK.
LOTS OF DEM!
WE'LL HAVE TO RUN FOR IT!
DOSE AIRSHIPS IZ... TURNING BECK?
DOES ANYONE ELSE SMELL SOMETHING... ODD?
BUT WHICH WAY?
WHERE ARE THOSE TROOPS?
DEY IZ ALL AROUND US!
VE VILL HAFF TO FIGHT!
WE HAVE THE BARON—
THAT MIGHT SLOW THEM DOWN—
MEBBE, BUT...
VAIT A MINUTE. DOSE TROOPS SOUND... HAPPY?
THEY'RE BACK!
HURRAH!
IS THAT CHEERING?

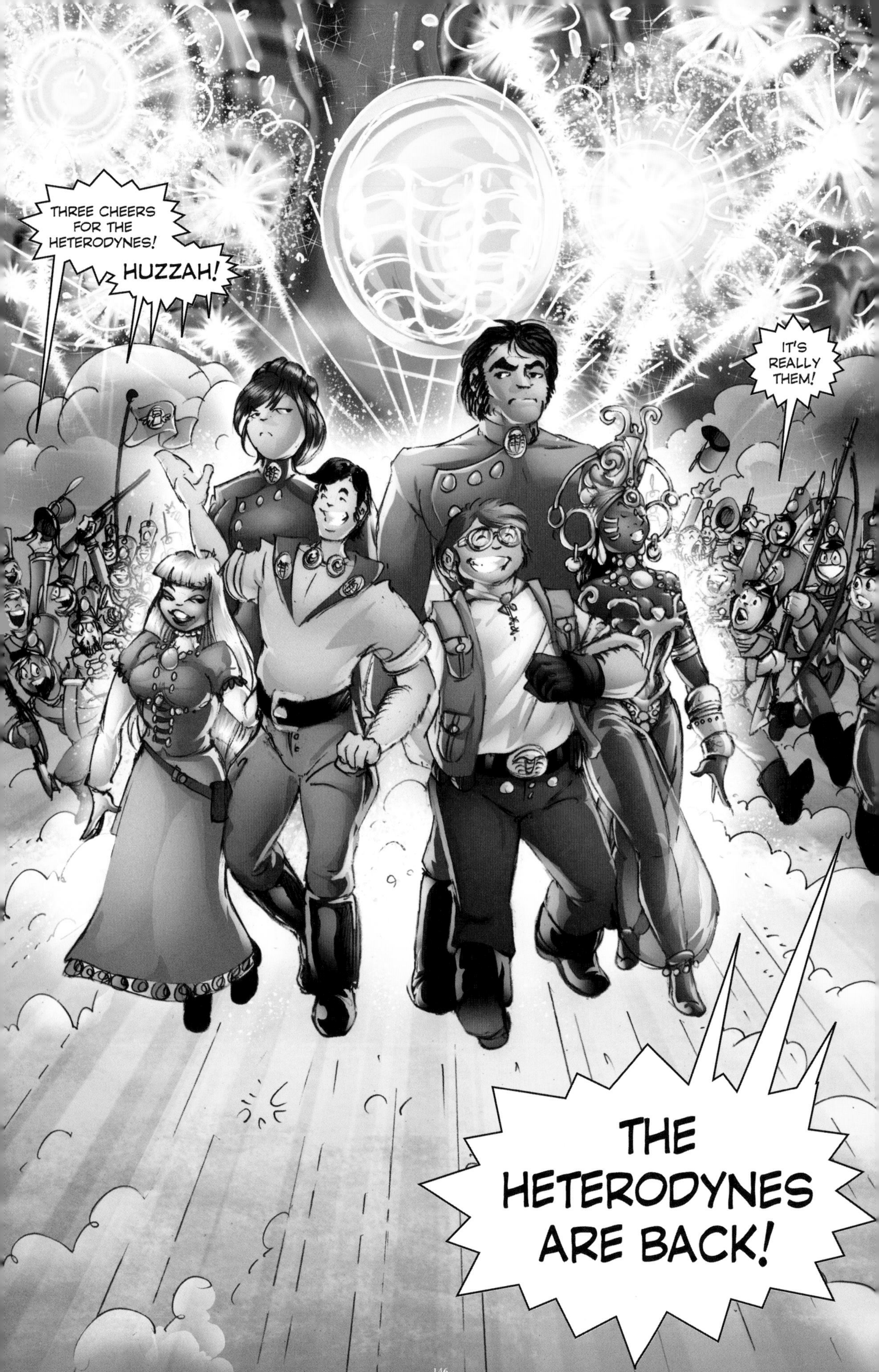
THREE CHEERS FOR THE HETERODYNES!
HUZZAH!
IT'S REALLY THEM!
THE HETERODYNES ARE BACK!

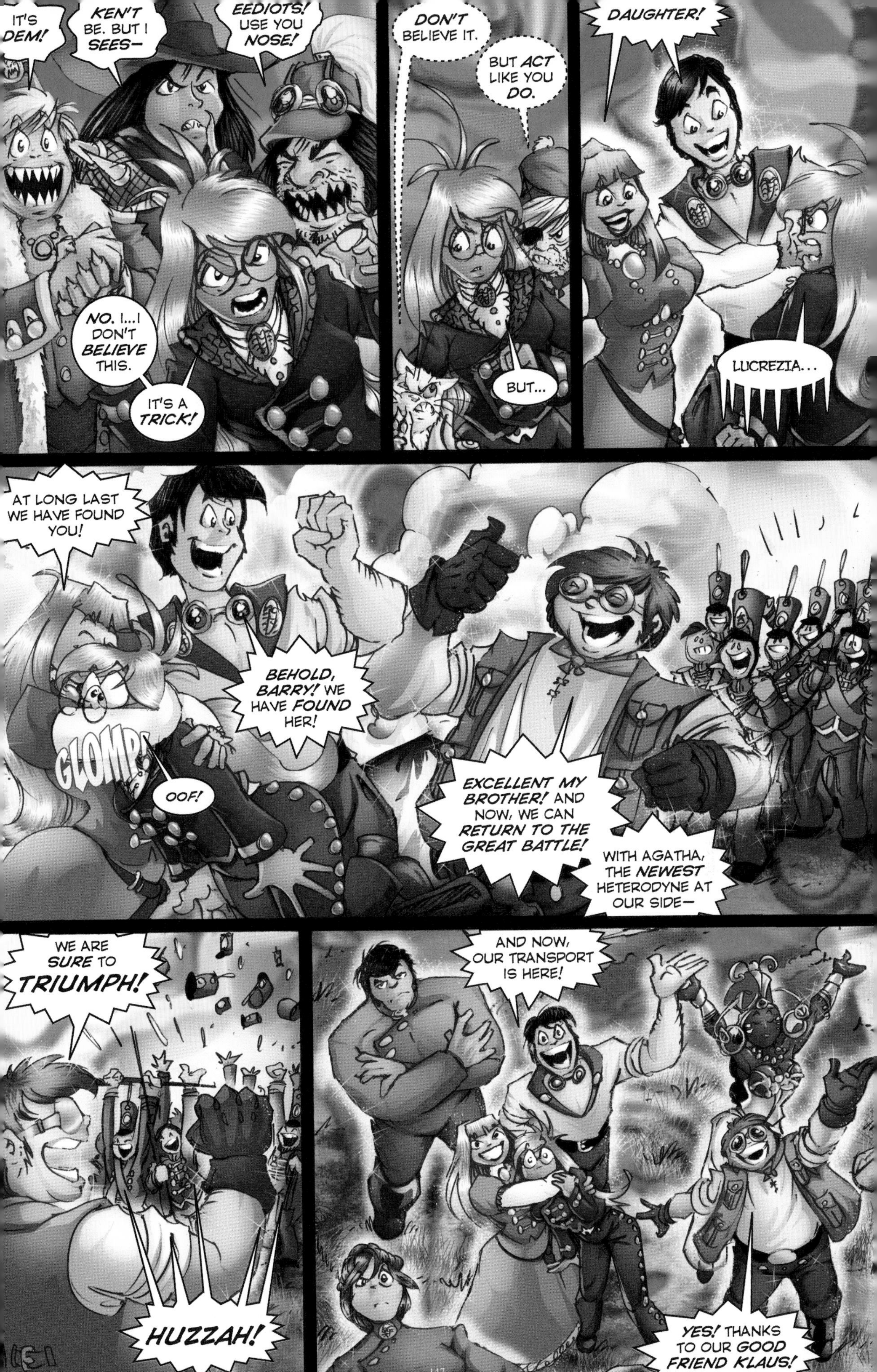
IT'S DEM!
KEN'T BE. BUT I SEES—
EEDIOTS! USE YOU NOSE!
NO. I...I DON'T BELIEVE THIS.
IT'S A TRICK!
DON'T BELIEVE IT.
BUT ACT LIKE YOU DO.
BUT...
DAUGHTER!
LUCREZIA...
AT LONG LAST WE HAVE FOUND YOU!
BEHOLD, BARRY! WE HAVE FOUND HER!
GLOMP!
OOF!
EXCELLENT MY BROTHER! AND NOW, WE CAN RETURN TO THE GREAT BATTLE!
WITH AGATHA, THE NEWEST HETERODYNE AT OUR SIDE—
WE ARE SURE TO TRIUMPH!
HUZZAH!
AND NOW, OUR TRANSPORT IS HERE!
YES! THANKS TO OUR GOOD FRIEND KLAUS!

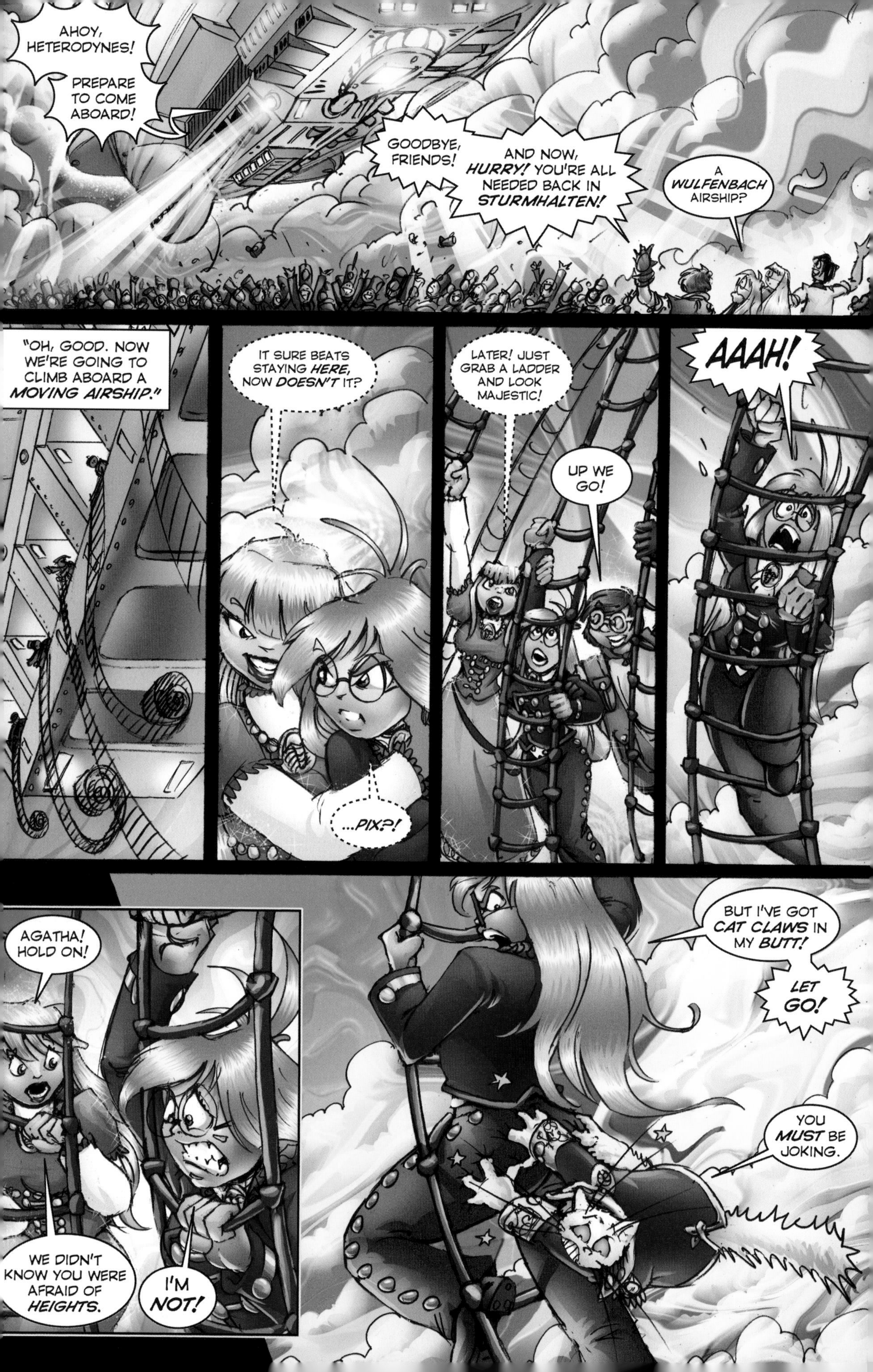
AHOY, HETERODYNES!
PREPARE TO COME ABOARD!
GOODBYE, FRIENDS!
AND NOW, HURRY! YOU'RE ALL NEEDED BACK IN STURMHALTEN!
A WULFENBACH AIRSHIP?
"OH, GOOD. NOW WE'RE GOING TO CLIMB ABOARD A MOVING AIRSHIP."
IT SURE BEATS STAYING HERE, NOW DOESN'T IT?
...PIX?!
LATER! JUST GRAB A LADDER AND LOOK MAJESTIC!
UP WE GO!
AAAH!
AGATHA! HOLD ON!
WE DIDN'T KNOW YOU WERE AFRAID OF HEIGHTS.
I'M NOT!
BUT I'VE GOT CAT CLAWS IN MY BUTT!
LET GO!
YOU MUST BE JOKING.

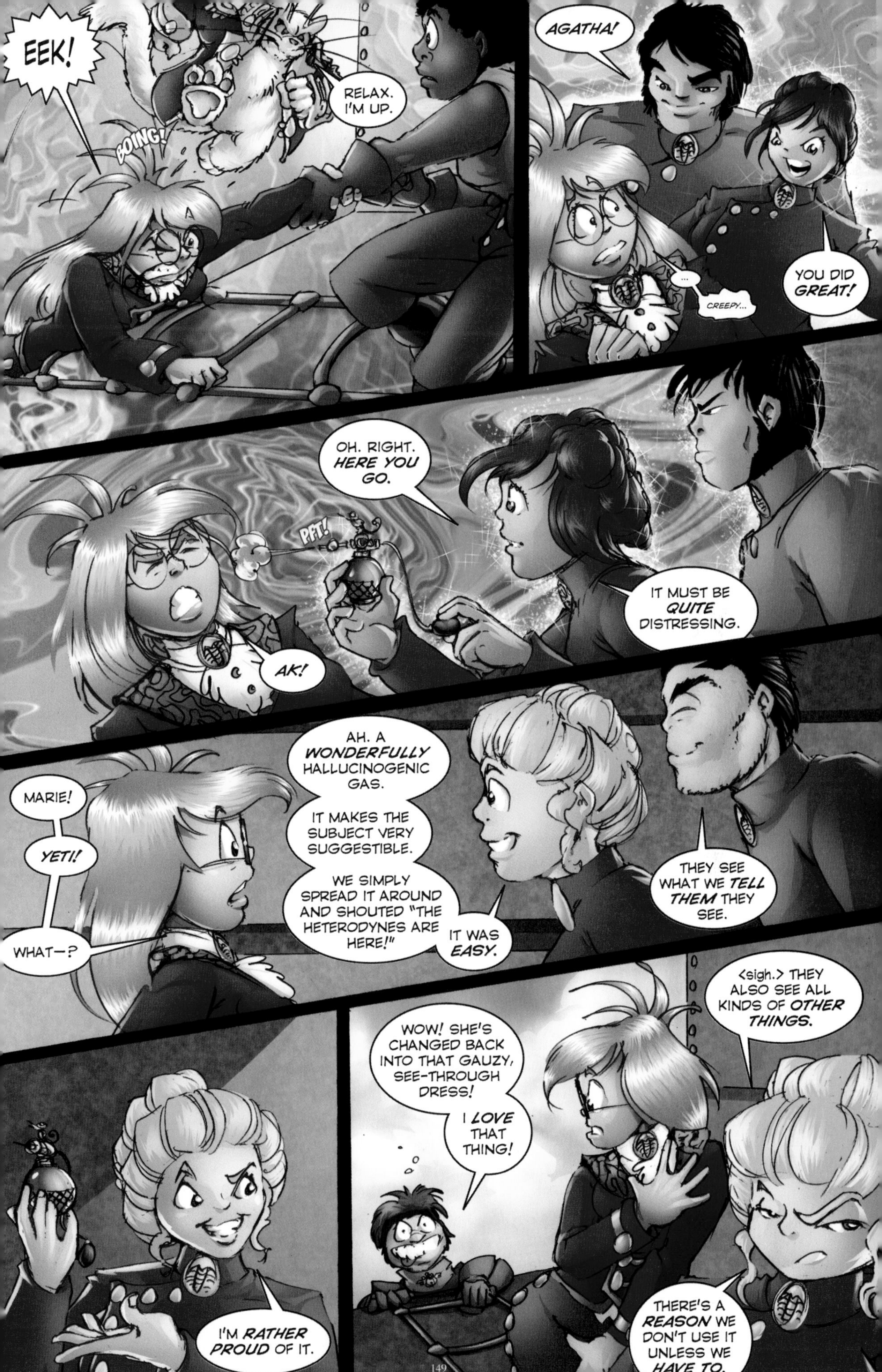
EEK!
BOING!
RELAX. I'M UP.
AGATHA!
...
CREEPY...
YOU DID GREAT!
OH. RIGHT. HERE YOU GO.
PFFT!
AK!
IT MUST BE QUITE DISTRESSING.
MARIE!
YETI!
WHAT—?
AH. A WONDERFULLY HALLUCINOGENIC GAS.
IT MAKES THE SUBJECT VERY SUGGESTIBLE.
WE SIMPLY SPREAD IT AROUND AND SHOUTED "THE HETERODYNES ARE HERE!"
IT WAS EASY.
THEY SEE WHAT WE TELL THEM THEY SEE.
I'M RATHER PROUD OF IT.
WOW! SHE'S CHANGED BACK INTO THAT GAUZY, SEE-THROUGH DRESS!
I LOVE THAT THING!
<sigh.> THEY ALSO SEE ALL KINDS OF OTHER THINGS.
THERE'S A REASON WE DON'T USE IT UNLESS WE HAVE TO.

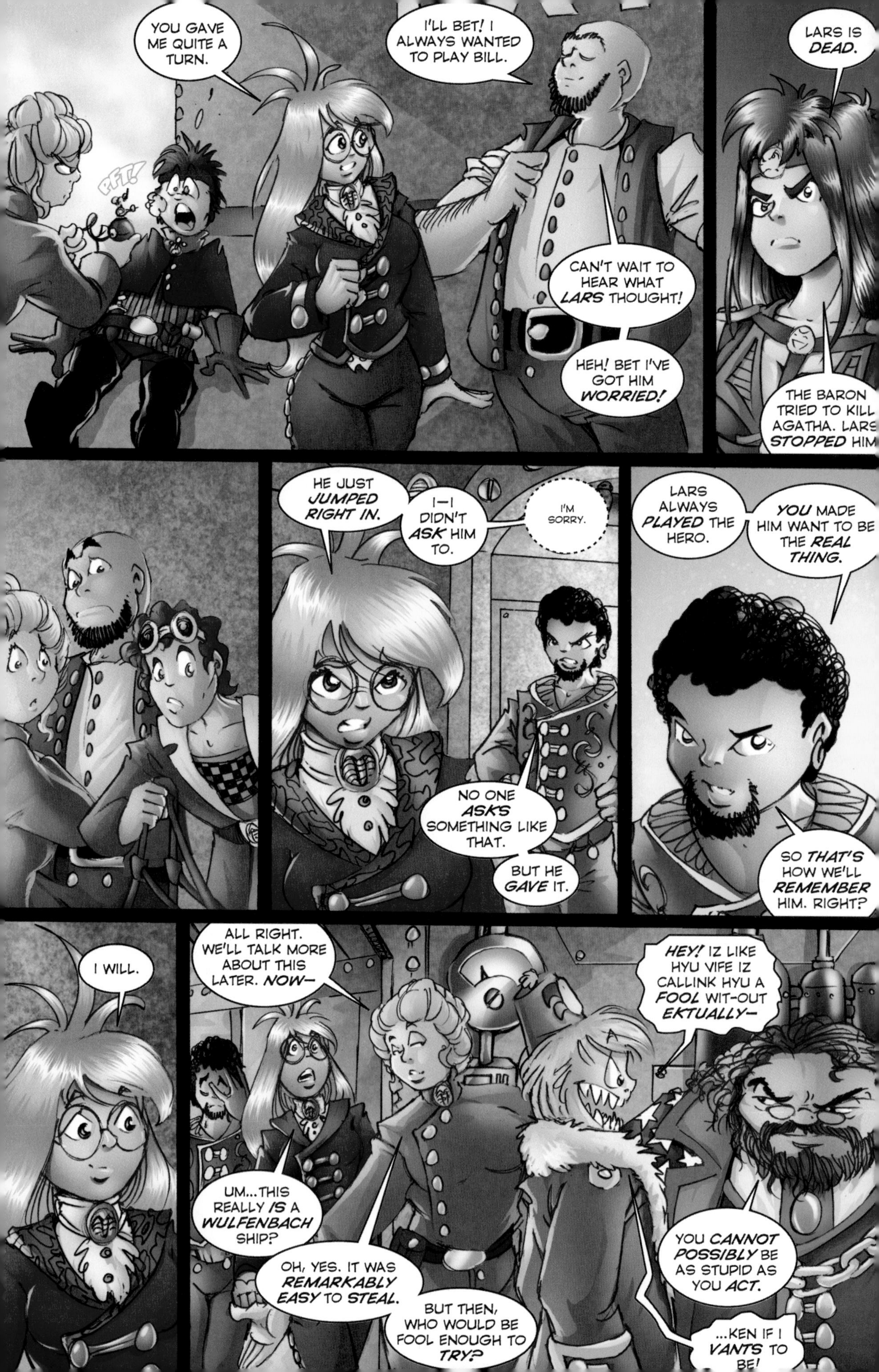
YOU GAVE ME QUITE A TURN.
I'LL BET! I ALWAYS WANTED TO PLAY BILL.
LARS IS DEAD.
PFT!
CAN'T WAIT TO HEAR WHAT LARS THOUGHT!
HEH! BET I'VE GOT HIM WORRIED!
THE BARON TRIED TO KILL AGATHA. LARS STOPPED HIM
HE JUST JUMPED RIGHT IN.
I—I DIDN'T ASK HIM TO.
I'M SORRY.
NO ONE ASKS SOMETHING LIKE THAT.
BUT HE GAVE IT.
LARS ALWAYS PLAYED THE HERO.
YOU MADE HIM WANT TO BE THE REAL THING.
SO THAT'S HOW WE'LL REMEMBER HIM. RIGHT?
I WILL.
ALL RIGHT. WE'LL TALK MORE ABOUT THIS LATER. NOW—
HEY! IZ LIKE HYU VIFE IZ CALLINK HYU A FOOL WIT-OUT EKTUALLY—
UM...THIS REALLY IS A WULFENBACH SHIP?
OH, YES. IT WAS REMARKABLY EASY TO STEAL.
BUT THEN, WHO WOULD BE FOOL ENOUGH TO TRY?
YOU CANNOT POSSIBLY BE AS STUPID AS YOU ACT.
...KEN IF I VANTS TO BE!

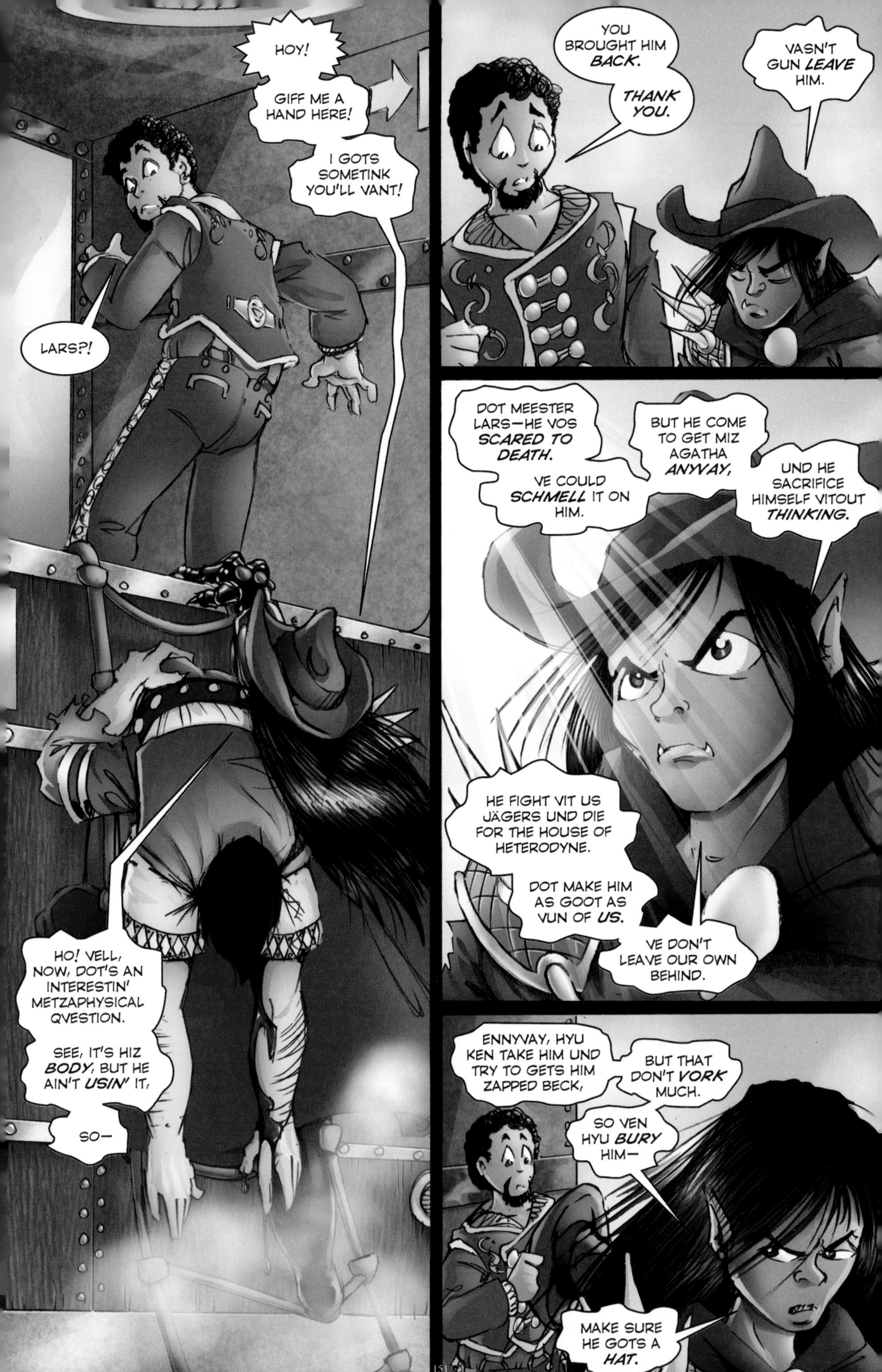
HOY!
GIFF ME A HAND HERE!
I GOTS SOMETINK YOU'LL VANT!
LARS?!
HO! VELL, NOW, DOT'S AN INTERESTIN' METZAPHYSICAL QVESTION.
SEE, IT'S HIZ BODY, BUT HE AIN'T USIN' IT,
SO—
YOU BROUGHT HIM BACK.
THANK YOU.
VASN'T GUN LEAVE HIM.
DOT MEESTER LARS—HE VOS SCARED TO DEATH.
VE COULD SCHMELL IT ON HIM.
BUT HE COME TO GET MIZ AGATHA ANYVAY,
UND HE SACRIFICE HIMSELF VITOUT THINKING.
HE FIGHT VIT US JÄGERS UND DIE FOR THE HOUSE OF HETERODYNE.
DOT MAKE HIM AS GOOT AS VUN OF US.
VE DON'T LEAVE OUR OWN BEHIND.
ENNYVAY, HYU KEN TAKE HIM UND TRY TO GETS HIM ZAPPED BECK,
BUT THAT DON'T VORK MUCH.
SO VEN HYU BURY HIM—
MAKE SURE HE GOTS A HAT.

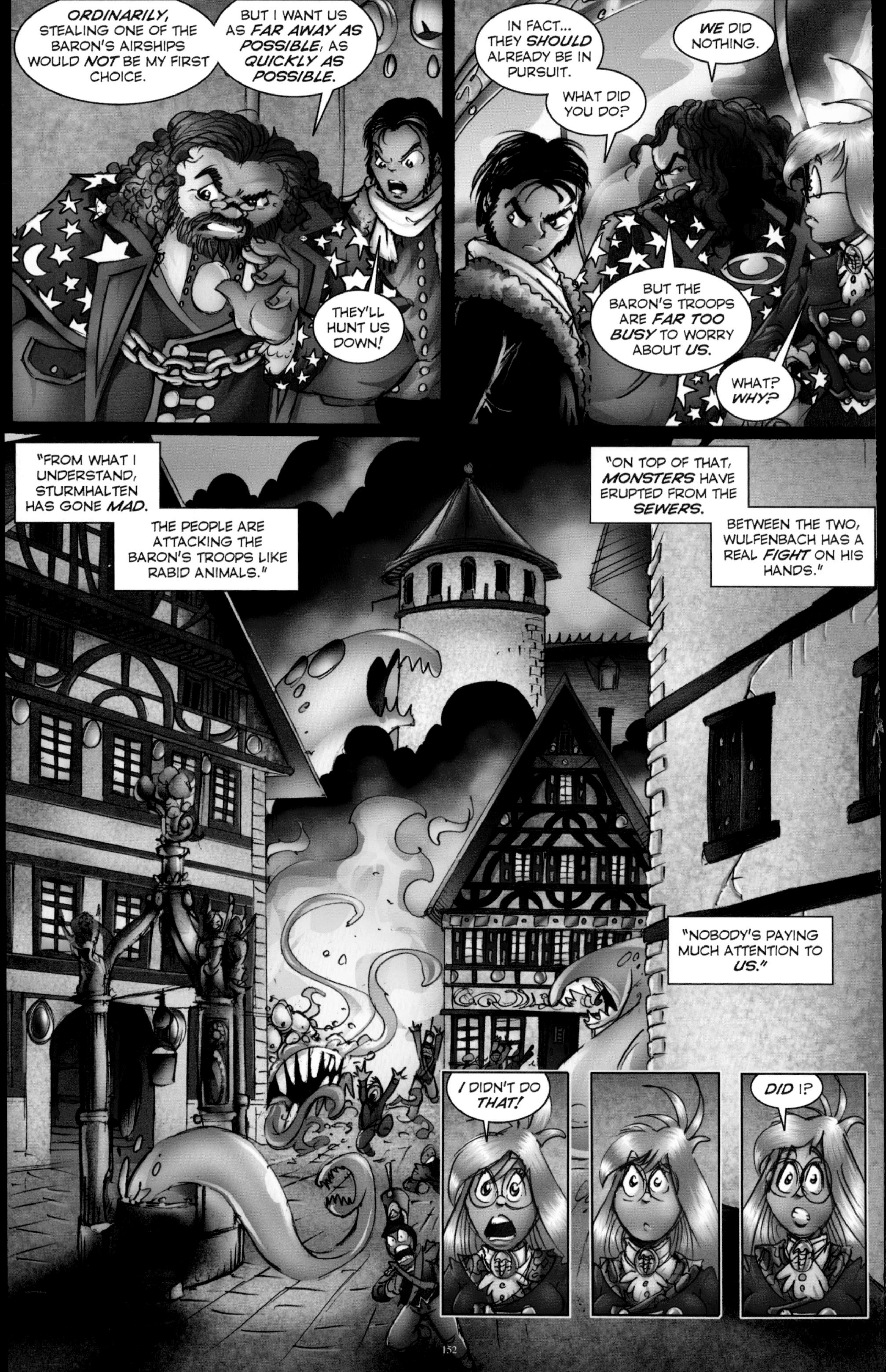
ORDINARILY, STEALING ONE OF THE BARON'S AIRSHIPS WOULD NOT BE MY FIRST CHOICE.
BUT I WANT US AS FAR AWAY AS POSSIBLE, AS QUICKLY AS POSSIBLE.
THEY'LL HUNT US DOWN!
IN FACT... THEY SHOULD ALREADY BE IN PURSUIT.
WHAT DID YOU DO?
WE DID NOTHING.
BUT THE BARON'S TROOPS ARE FAR TOO BUSY TO WORRY ABOUT US.
WHAT? WHY?
"FROM WHAT I UNDERSTAND, STURMHALTEN HAS GONE MAD.
THE PEOPLE ARE ATTACKING THE BARON'S TROOPS LIKE RABID ANIMALS."
"ON TOP OF THAT, MONSTERS HAVE ERUPTED FROM THE SEWERS.
BETWEEN THE TWO, WULFENBACH HAS A REAL FIGHT ON HIS HANDS."
"NOBODY'S PAYING MUCH ATTENTION TO US."
I DIDN'T DO THAT!
DID I?

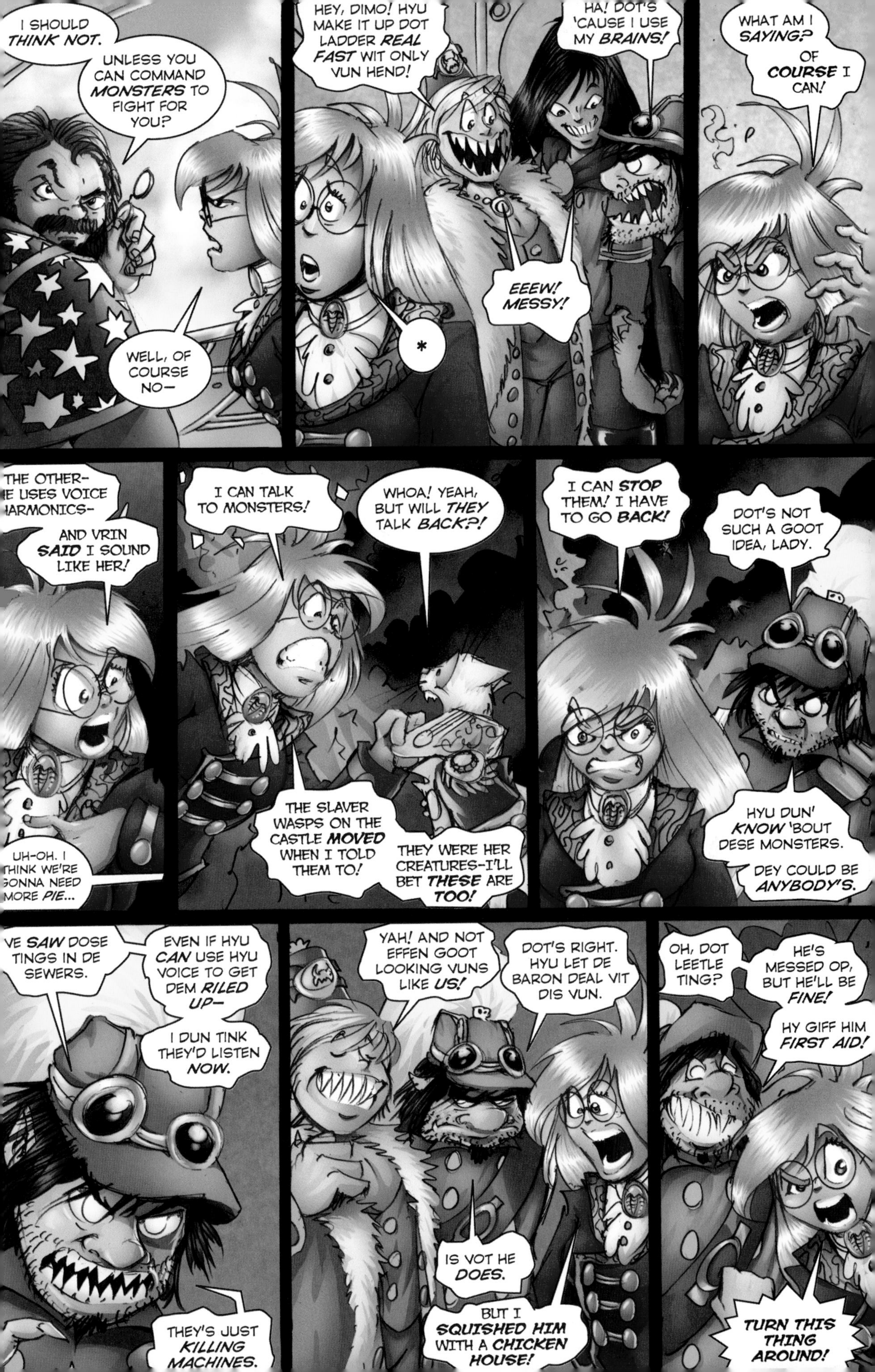

I SHOULD THINK NOT.
UNLESS YOU CAN COMMAND MONSTERS TO FIGHT FOR YOU?
WELL, OF COURSE NO—
HEY, DIMO! HYU MAKE IT UP DOT LADDER REAL FAST WIT ONLY VUN HEND!
HA! DOT'S 'CAUSE I USE MY BRAINS!
EEEW! MESSY!
*
WHAT AM I SAYING?
OF COURSE I CAN!
THE OTHER- E USES VOICE ARMONICS-
AND VRIN SAID I SOUND LIKE HER!
UH-OH. I THINK WE'RE GONNA NEED MORE PIE...
I CAN TALK TO MONSTERS!
WHOA! YEAH, BUT WILL THEY TALK BACK?!
THE SLAVER WASPS ON THE CASTLE MOVED WHEN I TOLD THEM TO!
THEY WERE HER CREATURES—I'LL BET THESE ARE TOO!
I CAN STOP THEM! I HAVE TO GO BACK!
DOT'S NOT SUCH A GOOT IDEA, LADY.
HYU DUN' KNOW 'BOUT DESE MONSTERS.
DEY COULD BE ANYBODY'S.
VE SAW DOSE TINGS IN DE SEWERS.
EVEN IF HYU CAN USE HYU VOICE TO GET DEM RILED UP—
I DUN TINK THEY'D LISTEN NOW.
THEY'S JUST KILLING MACHINES.
YAH! AND NOT EFFEN GOOT LOOKING VUNS LIKE US!
DOT'S RIGHT. HYU LET DE BARON DEAL VIT DIS VUN.
IS VOT HE DOES.
BUT I SQUISHED HIM WITH A CHICKEN HOUSE!
OH, DOT LEETLE TING?
HE'S MESSED OP, BUT HE'LL BE FINE!
HY GIFF HIM FIRST AID!
TURN THIS THING AROUND!

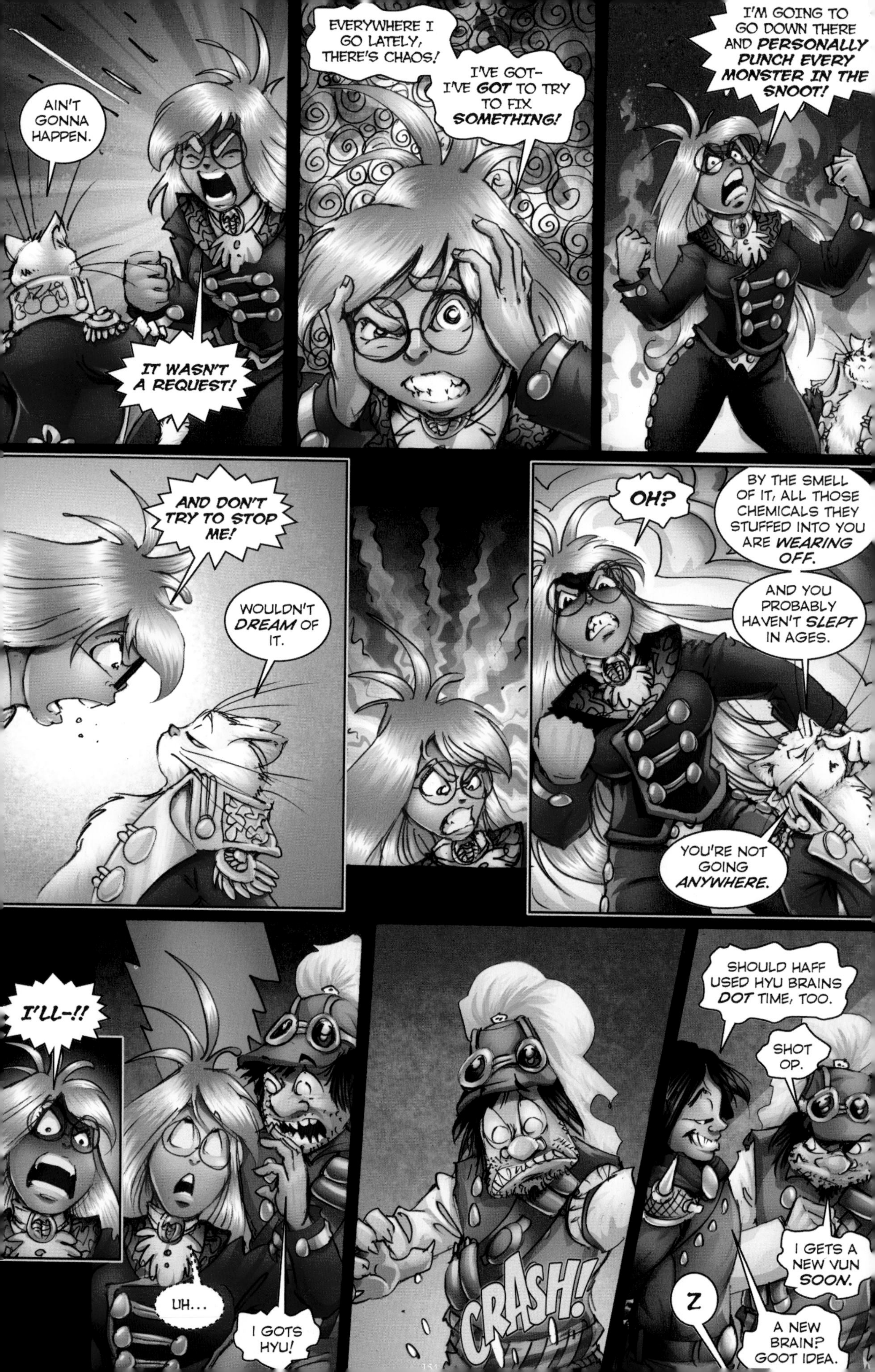
AIN'T GONNA HAPPEN.
IT WASN'T A REQUEST!
EVERYWHERE I GO LATELY, THERE'S CHAOS!
I'VE GOT- I'VE GOT TO TRY TO FIX SOMETHING!
I'M GOING TO GO DOWN THERE AND PERSONALLY PUNCH EVERY MONSTER IN THE SNOOT!
AND DON'T TRY TO STOP ME!
WOULDN'T DREAM OF IT.
OH?
BY THE SMELL OF IT, ALL THOSE CHEMICALS THEY STUFFED INTO YOU ARE WEARING OFF.
AND YOU PROBABLY HAVEN'T SLEPT IN AGES.
YOU'RE NOT GOING ANYWHERE.
I'LL-!!
UH...
I GOTS HYU!
CRASH!
SHOULD HAFF USED HYU BRAINS DOT TIME, TOO.
SHOT OP.
I GETS A NEW VUN SOON.
Z
A NEW BRAIN? GOOT IDEA.

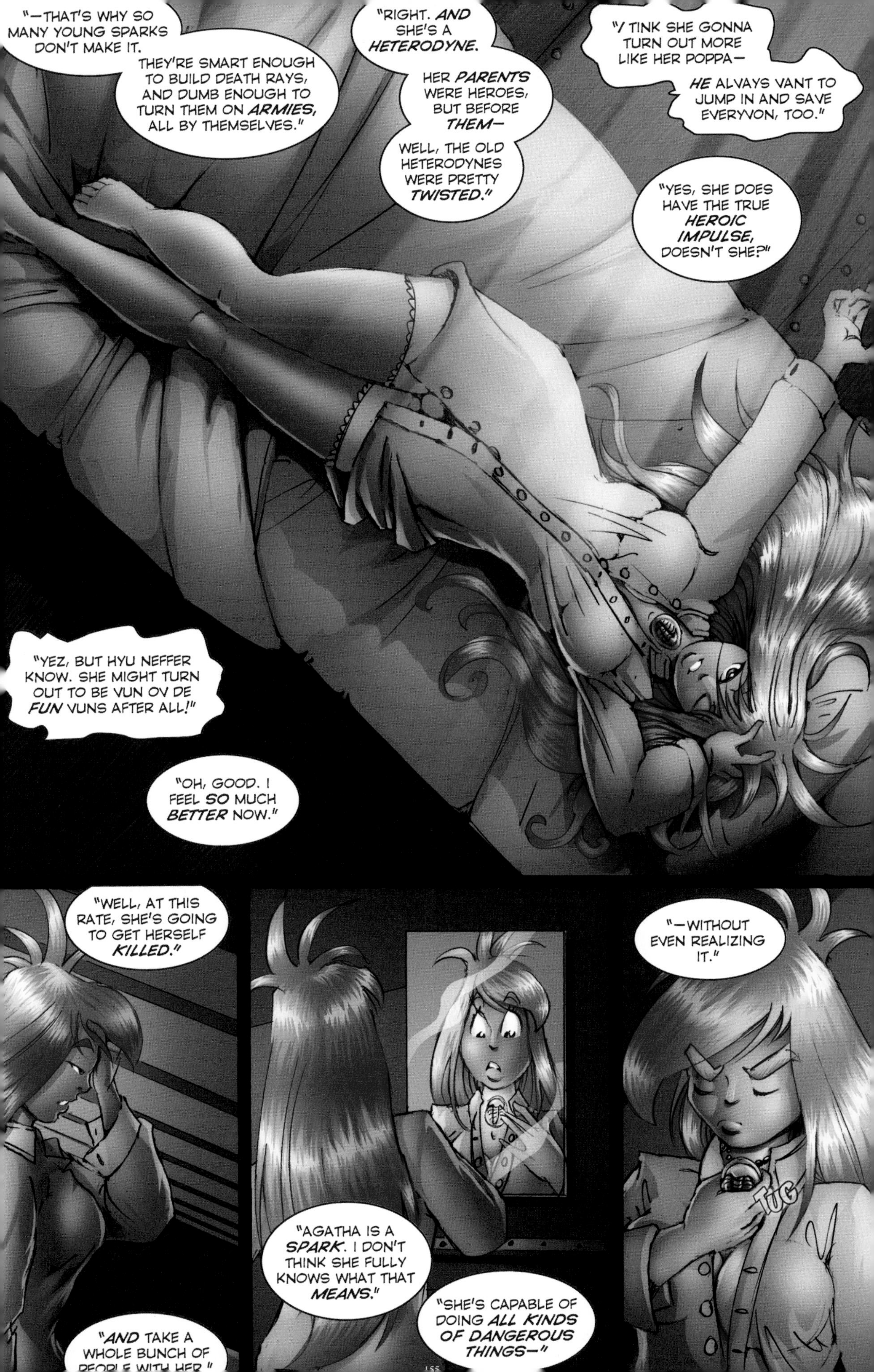
"—THAT'S WHY SO MANY YOUNG SPARKS DON'T MAKE IT.
THEY'RE SMART ENOUGH TO BUILD DEATH RAYS, AND DUMB ENOUGH TO TURN THEM ON ARMIES, ALL BY THEMSELVES."
"RIGHT. AND SHE'S A HETERODYNE.
HER PARENTS WERE HEROES, BUT BEFORE THEM—
WELL, THE OLD HETERODYNES WERE PRETTY TWISTED."
"I TINK SHE GONNA TURN OUT MORE LIKE HER POPPA—
HE ALVAYS VANT TO JUMP IN AND SAVE EVERYVON, TOO."
"YES, SHE DOES HAVE THE TRUE HEROIC IMPULSE, DOESN'T SHE?"
"YEZ, BUT HYU NEFFER KNOW. SHE MIGHT TURN OUT TO BE VUN OV DE FUN VUNS AFTER ALL!"
"OH, GOOD. I FEEL SO MUCH BETTER NOW."
"WELL, AT THIS RATE, SHE'S GOING TO GET HERSELF KILLED."
"AND TAKE A WHOLE BUNCH OF PEOPLE WITH HER."
"AGATHA IS A SPARK. I DON'T THINK SHE FULLY KNOWS WHAT THAT MEANS."
"SHE'S CAPABLE OF DOING ALL KINDS OF DANGEROUS THINGS—"
"—WITHOUT EVEN REALIZING IT."
TUG

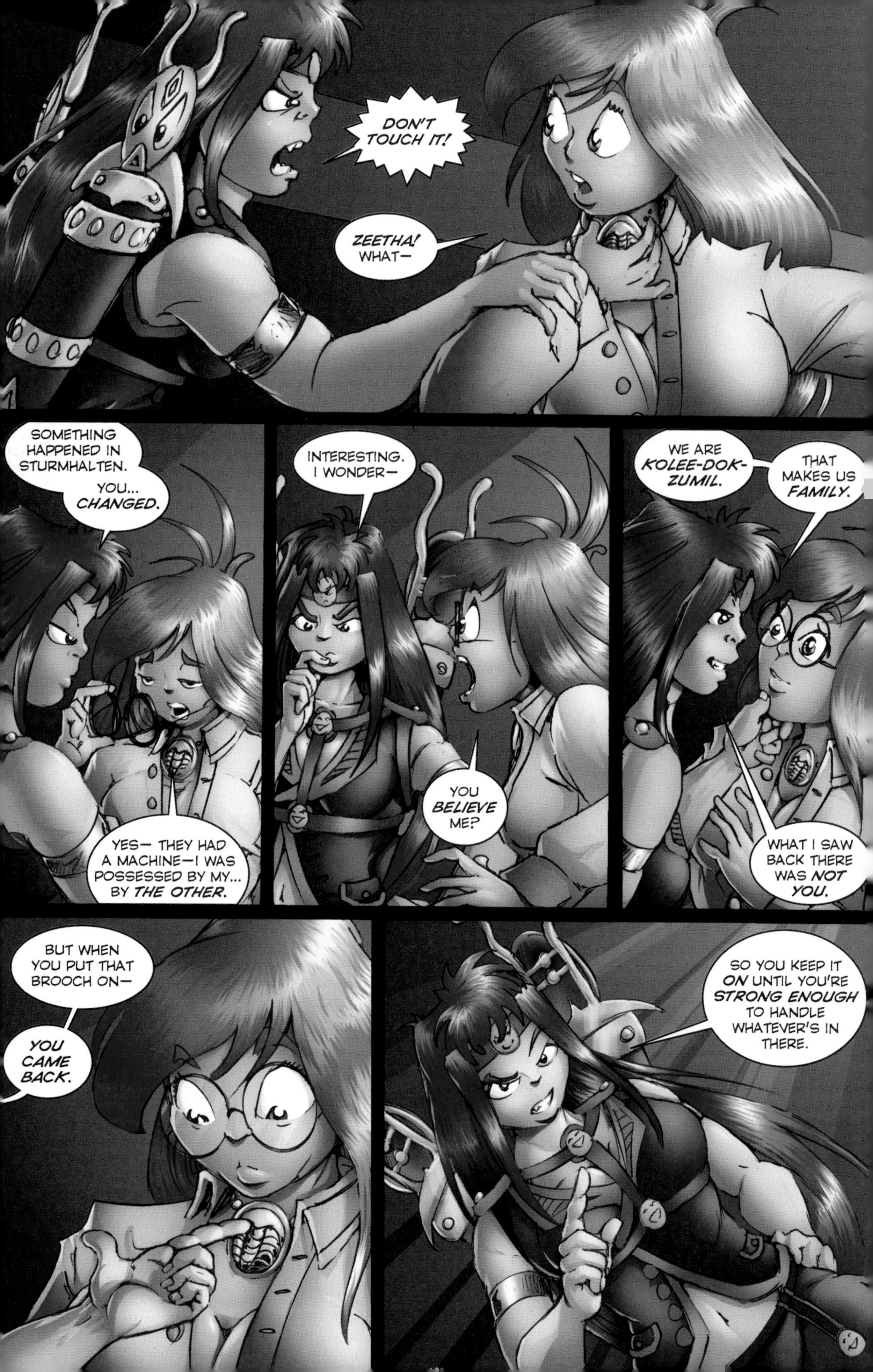
DON'T TOUCH IT!
ZEETHA! WHAT—
SOMETHING HAPPENED IN STURMHALTEN.
YOU... CHANGED.
YES— THEY HAD A MACHINE—I WAS POSSESSED BY MY... BY THE OTHER.
INTERESTING. I WONDER—
YOU BELIEVE ME?
WE ARE KOLEE-DOK-ZUMIL.
THAT MAKES US FAMILY.
WHAT I SAW BACK THERE WAS NOT YOU.
BUT WHEN YOU PUT THAT BROOCH ON—
YOU CAME BACK.
SO YOU KEEP IT ON UNTIL YOU'RE STRONG ENOUGH TO HANDLE WHATEVER'S IN THERE.

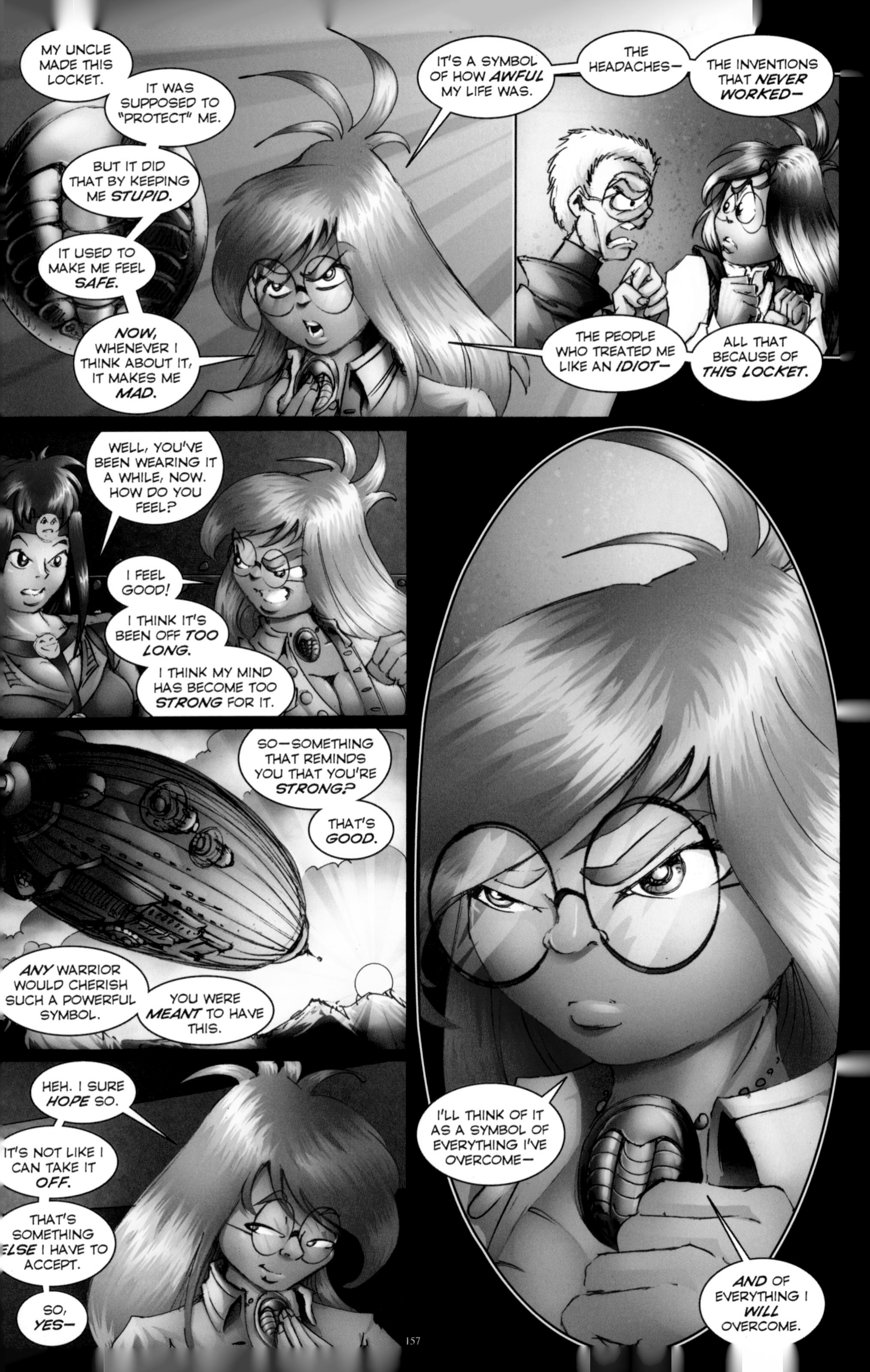
MY UNCLE MADE THIS LOCKET.
IT WAS SUPPOSED TO "PROTECT" ME.
BUT IT DID THAT BY KEEPING ME STUPID.
IT USED TO MAKE ME FEEL SAFE.
NOW, WHENEVER I THINK ABOUT IT, IT MAKES ME MAD.
IT'S A SYMBOL OF HOW AWFUL MY LIFE WAS.
THE HEADACHES—
THE INVENTIONS THAT NEVER WORKED—
THE PEOPLE WHO TREATED ME LIKE AN IDIOT—
ALL THAT BECAUSE OF THIS LOCKET.
WELL, YOU'VE BEEN WEARING IT A WHILE, NOW. HOW DO YOU FEEL?
I FEEL GOOD!
I THINK IT'S BEEN OFF TOO LONG.
I THINK MY MIND HAS BECOME TOO STRONG FOR IT.
SO—SOMETHING THAT REMINDS YOU THAT YOU'RE STRONG?
THAT'S GOOD.
ANY WARRIOR WOULD CHERISH SUCH A POWERFUL SYMBOL.
YOU WERE MEANT TO HAVE THIS.
HEH. I SURE HOPE SO.
IT'S NOT LIKE I CAN TAKE IT OFF.
THAT'S SOMETHING ELSE I HAVE TO ACCEPT.
SO, YES—
I'LL THINK OF IT AS A SYMBOL OF EVERYTHING I'VE OVERCOME—
AND OF EVERYTHING I WILL OVERCOME.

TO BE CONTINUED IN: **GIRL GENIUS® Book SEVEN**

AGATHA HETERODYNE & THE VOICE OF THE CASTLE

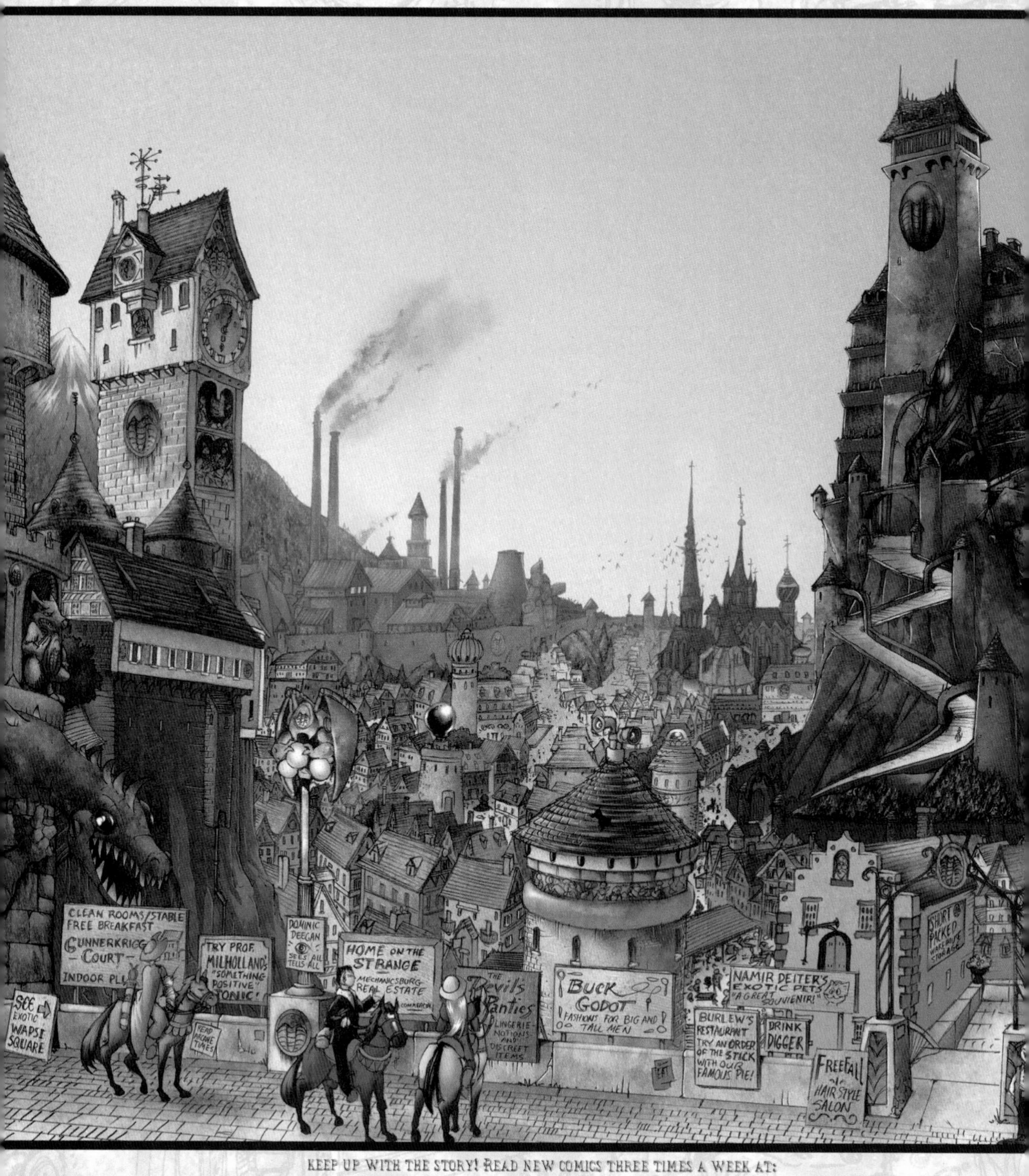
CLEAN ROOMS/STABLE
FREE BREAKFAST
GUNNERKRIGG
- COURT -
INDOOR PL
SEE → EXOTIC WAPSI SQUARE
TRY PROF. MILHOLLAND'S "SOMETHING POSITIVE" TONIC!
READ ARCANE TIMES
DOMINIC DEEGAN
SEES ALL TELLS ALL
HOME ON THE STRANGE
MECHANICSBURG REAL ESTATE
COMMERCIAL
THE Devil's Panties
LINGERIE - NOTIONS - AND DISCREET ITEMS
BUCK GODOT
FASHIONS FOR BIG AND TALL MEN
NAMIR DEITER'S EXOTIC PETS
"A GREAT SOUVIENIR!"
BURLEW'S RESTAURANT
TRY AN ORDER OF THE STICK WITH OUR FAMOUS PIE!
DRINK DIGGER
FREEFALL
HAIR STYLE SALON
SHORT PACKED
WAREHOUSE STORAGE

KEEP UP WITH THE STORY! READ NEW COMICS THREE TIMES A WEEK AT:

WWW.GIRLGENIUS.NET

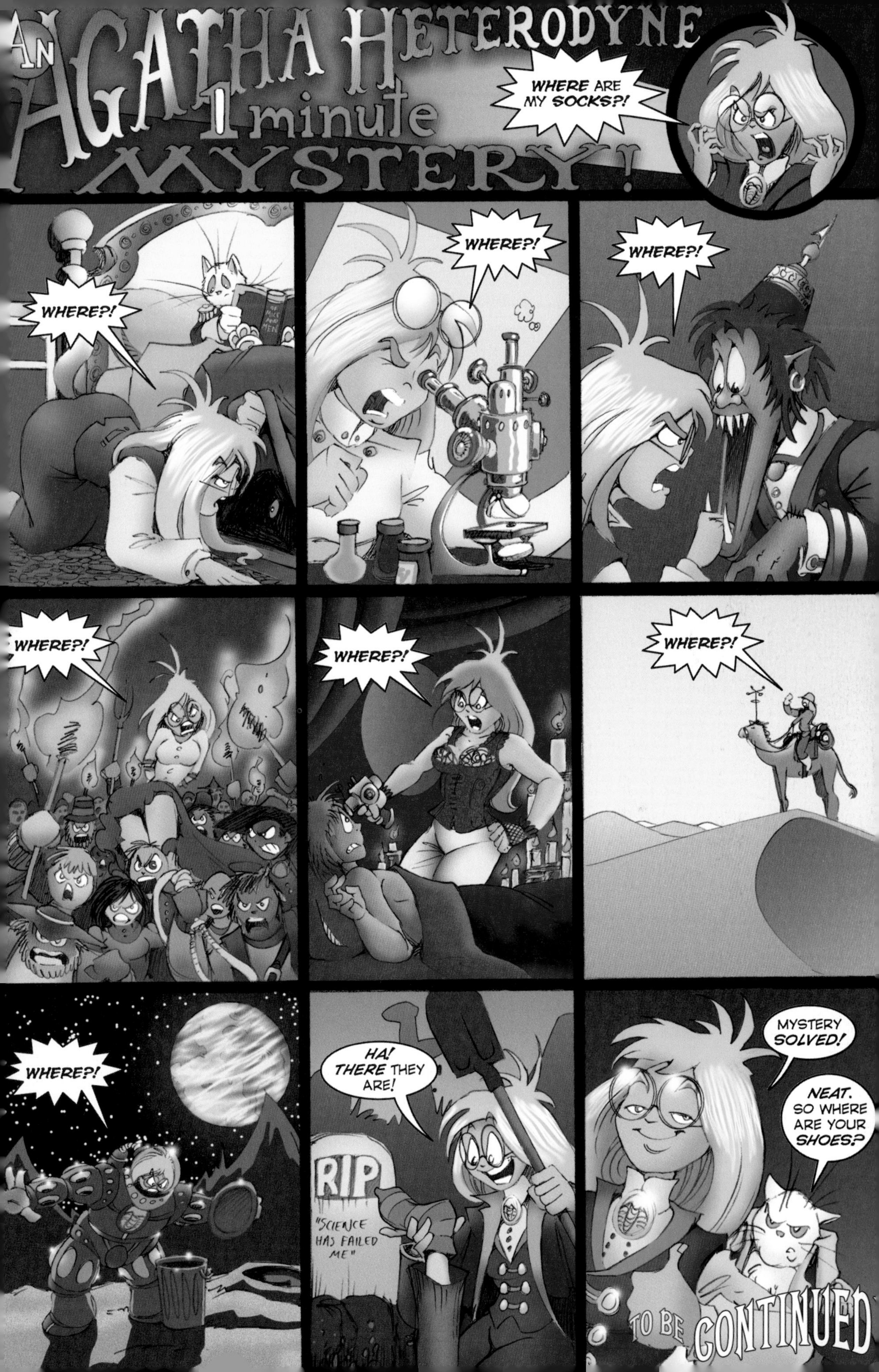

AN AGATHA HETERODYNE 1 minute MYSTERY!
WHERE ARE MY SOCKS?!
WHERE?!
OF MICE AND MEN
WHERE?!
WHERE?!
WHERE?!
WHERE?!
WHERE?!
WHERE?!
HA! THERE THEY ARE!
RIP
"SCIENCE HAS FAILED ME"
MYSTERY SOLVED!
NEAT. SO WHERE ARE YOUR SHOES?
TO BE CONTINUED

READ MORE COMICS ONLINE AT:

www.GirlGenius.net

MONDAY · WEDNESDAY · FRIDAY